BLOOD RED LINES

BLOOD RED LINES

How Nativism Fuels the Right

Brendan O'Connor

Haymarket Books
Chicago, Illinois

Published in 2021 by
Haymarket Books
P.O. Box 180165
Chicago, IL 60618
773-583-7884
www.haymarketbooks.org
info@haymarketbooks.org

ISBN: 978-1-64259-261-0

Distributed to the trade in the US through Consortium Book Sales and Distribution (www.cbsd.com) and internationally through Ingram Publisher Services International (www.ingram-content.com).

This book was published with the generous support of Lannan Foundation and Wallace Action Fund.

Special discounts are available for bulk purchases by organizations and institutions. Please call 773-583-7884 or email info@haymarketbooks.org for more information.

Cover design by Jamie Kerry.

Printed in Canada by union labor.

Library of Congress Cataloging-in-Publication data is available.

10 9 8 7 6 5 4 3 2 1

For my grandparents, Bob and Rita,
who left home to make a new life
in an unfamiliar place

CONTENTS

PREFACE

One must take history as it comes, whatever course it takes.
—Rosa Luxemburg

On February 28, 2020, as the novel coronavirus known as COVID-19 spread across the world, a group of congressional Republicans sent a letter to officials in the Departments of Defense, Health and Human Services, and Homeland Security articulating their concern that sufficient action was being taken to protect US citizens from the disease, which they worried would spread across the border with Mexico. "Given the porous nature of our border, and the continued lack of operational control," they wrote, "it is foreseeable, indeed predictable, that any outbreak in Central America or Mexico could cause a rush to our border." This, they warned, would "impose a new burden at our southern border that will threaten the safety and health of individuals in the United States and cause a humanitarian crisis of epic proportions along our border and at detention facilities."[1]

In fact, the virus was more likely to spread from the United States to Central America than the reverse—due in large part to the ongoing US policy of mass detention and deportation.[2] What is more, there already was a humanitarian crisis of epic proportions along the US-Mexico border and in immigration detention facilities. Health and sanitation conditions in the migrant camps outside border towns, swollen with asylum seekers forced to remain in Mexico while their applications were processed (thanks to policy changes made under President Donald Trump), were poor even before the global pandemic.[3] A doctor, himself an asylum seeker, predicted that a COVID-19 outbreak at the 2,500-person migrant and refugee encampment in Matamoros would be "catastrophic."[4] Another doctor, detained at the South Louisiana ICE Processing Center, warned that "many people will die if we are not released."[5]

Fearing arrest and detention by Immigration and Customs Enforcement (ICE) agents, undocumented immigrants working on the precarious fringes of the US labor market began to withdraw from what few social services were available to them.[6] Estimates vary, but of the approximately three million farmworkers employed in the United States, making on average between $17,500 and $20,000 a year, at least half are undocumented immigrants.[7] The pandemic hit just as peak harvesting seasons began for many crops that have to be picked by hand, often by workers living in cramped housing provided by their employers—ideal conditions for the virus to spread. In California, for example, strawberry growers were switching from paying an hourly rate to a piece rate, as they do every year. Such shifts are meant to incentivize working faster, but they also mean that time spent on precautions to wash one's hands or maintain six feet of distance was money lost.[8] "We won't stop working," Luis Jimenez, a dairy worker and organizer with the Alianza Agricola in New York State, said. "We're willing to risk the virus. But I didn't come here to die. I came so that my family in Mexico will live. We don't know what will happen to those who get sick. How will we pay our bills and send money to help our families survive?"[9] Just across the border with Mexico, the virus spread through US-owned factories, known as maquiladoras, killing workers as companies ignored federal orders to close.[10]

At the same time, ICE and Customs and Border Protection (CBP) escalated their surveillance efforts in so-called sanctuary cities—that is, cities that have made some token effort not to comply with federal deportation proceedings—deploying heavily armed tactical units to "flood the streets," as one official put it.[11] In New York City, immigration arrests doubled.[12] As panic over outbreaks spread through detention centers, many of the immigrants held within rebelled, rioting and organizing hunger strikes.[13] Guards at a detention center in New Jersey dismissed detainees' requests for more toilet paper and soap with disdain. "They don't do anything," Ronal Umaña, a thirty-year-old detainee from El Salvador said. "They only yell at us and tell us that if we complain—that 'unless we see you get really sick, or you really have a high fever, we can't do anything with you.' So we say, 'If we have a bad fever, and lots of us are sick, we can die here,' and they say, 'Well, you're going to have to die of something.'"[14]

Years before the coronavirus pandemic hit the United States, Trump, a notorious germaphobe, was using the language of national hygiene to agitate his supporters. In 2015, not long after declaring Mexican immigrants drug dealers and rapists, Trump warned that "tremendous infectious disease is pouring across the border" thanks to immigration.[15] In the fall and winter of 2018, as attention turned toward caravans of asylum seekers traveling en masse from Central America to the United States, a former ICE agent, David Ward, warned Fox News viewers that these migrants were carrying "diseases such as smallpox, leprosy, and [tuberculosis] that are going to infect our people," despite the fact that the last known case of smallpox occurred in 1977.[16] Just a few weeks later, Tomi Lahren, a far-right commentator and Fox Nation host, warned her viewers that asylum seekers would bring tuberculosis, HIV/AIDS, chickenpox, and hepatitis to their communities.[17] A framed photo of Lahren with US Border Patrol officials hangs in the agency's DC headquarters.[18]

I began reporting on the US far right at the beginning of 2016, my attention captured by the militia members who seized control of the Malheur National Wildlife Refuge. Learning about the history that led to that moment, I was fascinated by the celebrity of the Bundy family, the movement's simultaneously amateurish and sophisticated use of social media, and, above all, the proliferating political tendencies, shifting alliances and affiliations, and changing orientation toward state power. While antigovernment sentiment had defined the so-called Patriot movement under the Obama administration, far-right activists of various stripes, including the much younger cohort of the "alt-right," were recuperated into mainstream politics through Trump's insurgent campaign for president. I found myself repeatedly returning to the question of the relationship between the policy makers (elected and unelected), wealthy donors, and intellectuals of the ruling class and the reactionaries making their presence known both in tweets and in the street. This was, I came to believe, another way of articulating the question of the relationship between capitalism and white supremacy.

When I started down this path, I was writing for *Gawker*, a New York media gossip website that had transformed itself into one of the internet's most high-profile antagonists of the twenty-first-century power elite. For better or for worse, *Gawker* would pick a fight with anyone. This, among other things, had made it a target for the very kinds of people I was interested in: billionaires and fascists. Harassment and death threats were part of the job at Gawker Media, which included similarly acerbic websites like *Jezebel*, *Deadspin*, and *Gizmodo*. (*Jezebel's* overwhelmingly female staff still endure terrifying misogyny.) As the 2016 primary proceeded, however, the virulence escalated, driven in part by reactionary glee at *Gawker's* impending demise: a lawsuit brought by the professional wrestler Terry Bollea, a.k.a. Hulk Hogan—and secretly funded by Trump-supporting Silicon Valley billionaire Peter Thiel—bankrupted the company. Not long after Trump received the Republican Party's nomination, *Gawker* ceased publication.

Shortly thereafter, the hosts of an influential "alt-right" podcast invited me on their show to talk about Gawker shutting down. Unable to ignore my sense of morbid curiosity, I accepted. I did think there might be some journalistic value in it, too. At the time, many of us who were writing about the "alt-right" still were not sure quite what to make of it. I certainly wasn't. Perhaps that was naive. By the end of the conversation, however, it became clear to me that these people were fascists: not just edgy internet trolls trying to get a rise out of people, but deeply, terrifyingly sincere political actors trying to make their way toward a world where anyone who did not fit into their vision of strength, beauty, or worth was eliminated. Nothing would make them happier, I realized, than to see me and my friends dead. They could not be treated as interesting if reprehensible characters. This was something different, if not quite new.

In the years since that day, I have tried to understand the forces driving this country as it lurches from crisis to crisis. I investigated the dark money flowing from the wealthiest US families through academia, DC policy shops, and election campaigns, shaping politics and ideas. I covered fascist rallies from Portland, Oregon, to Washington, DC, watching police beat people who had gathered to defend their communities. In the Rio Grande Valley, I played with children while their mothers, organizers on the front line of the struggle against the deportation machine, trained in direct action tactics; later, I learned that we had been under surveillance by the US military.[19] In Arizona, I stood sweating before the gates of an ICE detention center in the middle of desert and felt a deep chill. In Burlington, Vermont, I marched with dairy workers, many of them undocumented, demanding dignity and fair pay. I became increasingly involved in my union and joined the rapidly growing Democratic Socialists of America—two experiences that would become fundamental to my understanding of what was happening around me and what was at stake. I watched as Bernie Sanders's second presidential campaign, which called for the decriminalization of border crossings and the dismantling of the immigration enforcement apparatus, shattered against the wall of "electability." I've listened to the stories of workers and migrants living under the most exploitative of conditions and have had countless conversations with working-class people of various political orientations—

communists and anarchists, leftists and liberals, revolutionaries and reformers—about what is to be done.

Despite my best efforts, much remains opaque to me. This, at least, is clear: immigration today is useful to capitalism not only as a source of cheap labor but as a source of division within the working class—a "problem" best left unresolved. "It is not hypocrisy for Donald Trump to both provoke anti-immigrant sentiment while also staffing undocumented immigrants in his business, it is good strategy," human rights scholar Suzy Lee argues. "It not only serves to silence his immigrant workers, many of whom are too afraid of detention and deportation to demand better wages or working conditions, it serves to undermine the labor movement as a whole, channeling native workers' frustration and anxiety away from class exploitation and inequality."[20]

But immigration is not only a source of division and profit. "Migration itself," the editors of the leftist journal *Viewpoint* wrote in an essay on the migrant caravans that made their way toward the US-Mexico border in 2018, "is a political challenge to the capitalist state and a refusal to accept the conditions of exploitation offered in the capitalist system."[21] Immigration offers a glimpse of what the French political philosopher Alain Badiou calls the communist hypothesis: that the world into which we are born need not necessarily be as we find it—that another world is possible.

In order to make our way toward that world, however, we must have a clear view of the obstacles in our way. As I write this, the Trump campaign's efforts to delegitimize democratic processes in battleground states like Pennsylvania, Arizona, and Georgia appear to be failing and Joe Biden looks likely to eke out a victory in the 2020 presidential election. Barring a truly unprecedented upheaval, the former vice president will be inaugurated in two months. But even as the Trump administration becomes a memory and not a present political fact, it would be a mistake to imagine that the forces that put him in the White House have receded. Even in the unlikely event that the Republican Party purges itself of his influence, Trump himself likely isn't going anywhere.

Already operatives are threatening that he will run for president again in 2024, although the safer bet is probably that he will return to the media.[22] What shape the far right will take remains to be seen; further street violence and stochastic terror seem all but guaranteed.

Meanwhile, Biden will assume office facing a split Congress (pending two Senate run-off elections in Georgia) and a reactionary judiciary. In the White House, he'll be met with "Congressional resistance on anything transformational, whether on the budgetary or regulatory front," a JPMorgan strategist told the *Financial Times* as the stock market boomed just two days after the election. "That is great news for those who think that government inaction is generally good for asset prices over the medium term."[23] Not that anyone who thought this way had much to worry about. "Nobody has to be punished," Biden told wealthy donors during the primary campaign. "No one's standard of living will change, nothing would fundamentally change."[24]

With this book, I have attempted to shed some light on the machinery of exploitation and oppression used by the ruling class. Built over the course of decades, it is a bureaucratic behemoth, no less brutal for its lumbering inefficiency, that carries the genocidal mania of the settler past into the present. As with all things, however, what has been made can be unmade. It begins when we imagine it so.

Chapter One

THE FEAR IS ALWAYS THERE

It is not the head of a civilization that begins to rot first. It is the heart.

—Aimé Césaire

We hadn't yet made it to our first waypoint when Dr. Sara Vazquez slowed the truck to a halt. Leaning forward into the dashboard, she peered up at the sky. "Vultures," she said, without looking away. "Better check it out." There were six of us crammed into the pickup, the bed of which was packed with gallon jugs of water, cans of beans, and bags of Fritos. I took a swig from my own bottle and opened the door. The heat hit first, and then the smell: rotting flesh.

Pulling apart the barbed wire of a cattle fence that lined the dirt road where we'd stopped, the crew spread out, heading in the direction of the circling vultures. The wind swirled and died, picking up the stench and carrying it away. Then, about fifty yards from the road, I saw a few of the birds huddled together around something, obscured by the saguaro cactus and cholla. Drenched in sweat, I took a few more steps until I had a clear line of sight. And then I could see—antlers. Not human. A deer carcass, partially decomposed.

1

I called out to Dr. Vazquez and the others, volunteers from Tucson doing desert aid work with the humanitarian group No More Deaths, to let them know.

We got back into the truck, heading farther into the desert toward our first stop, where we'd park and then hike into the hills. We did this half a dozen times over the course of the day, carrying water and food to leave at points along known migrant trails. Sometimes, we'd find backpacks that had been emptied and left behind, along with slippers that people buy in Mexico border towns before making the crossing. Designed to fit over other shoes, the slippers hide one's tracks. We left them, and the backpacks, where they were. Someone else might need them.

Since the early 1990s, thousands of people have died crossing the border into the United States from Mexico, though it is impossible to know exactly how many. In 2018, the US Border Patrol estimated that at least 7,209 migrants had died in the desert since the 1994 implementation of its "Prevention Through Deterrence" policy, which pushed border crossers from more densely populated areas into the hostile environment of the desert.[1] This number is understood to be a drastic undercount, however, as it did not include the number of bodies recovered by anyone other than the US Border Patrol, including local law enforcement—which have their own reporting difficulties—and aid groups.[2] Even if it were possible to reconcile all of these different counts and come up with a number of bodies recovered, this still would not offer a full accounting of the deaths on the border. This is because of what the desert does to dead bodies: it makes them disappear.

"If you have ever come across a carcass left out in the open that is in the early stages of rot, you know such bodies are miniature biological laboratories," Jason De León, an anthropologist, writes in *The Land of Open Graves: Living and Dying on the Migrant Trail*, a study of the effects of "prevention through deterrence."[3] Between 2012 and 2013, De León conducted a series of experiments in which he killed several pigs, dressing them in the clothes that a border crosser would wear, and brought their bodies into the desert to observe their decomposition. There, he found, death does not bring rest or stillness: with maggots and vultures feasting on them, the carcasses began to vanish in a matter of days. Clothing fell away, and with it any identifying object, carried off by insects, animals, and the wind. "With enough time, a person left to rot on the ground can disappear completely."[4] By one estimate, there are two additional deaths for every body recovered from the desert.[5]

Such is one potential fate that awaits those who leave their homes and head for the US-Mexico border, whether one is a Oaxacan farmer bankrupted by DC-backed trade policies, a Salvadoran teenager fleeing gang violence exported from Los Angeles, or simply a child who wants to be reunited with their mother, who may have left years before, looking for work. Those who make it across the border, either through the desert or by other routes, join millions of other undocumented people living in the United States, part of a layer of the US working class—that is, migrant labor—whose political marginalization is as necessary as its economic exploitation. Even as they pick berries and milk cows, work construction and service jobs, and care for the children of the middle class and tend to golf courses, the country's deportable workers exist in a state of rights-lessness unlike any other.

Maru

"The fear is always there," Maru Mora-Villalpando told me.[6] A forty-eight-year-old undocumented woman from Mexico City who has been living in the United States since 1992, Mora-Villalpando is an organizer with La Resistencia, a Washington State–based group that provides support to people detained at the Northwest Detention Center in Tacoma. She's also been outspoken about her own immigration status—she overstayed a tourist visa—for years: "Some people don't go public with their status because they think, 'Oh, they're going to come after me.' But I wanted to be ready. I want it to be on my terms." The fear of deportation changes the way that immigrants move through the world. It keeps students, whether themselves undocumented or the children of undocumented parents, out of school—especially in the wake of mass raids.[7] It leads to undocumented women dropping domestic abuse cases, or declining to report incidents of sexual assault and rape at all.[8] It keeps undocumented workers from organizing to fight for better wages and conditions.[9]

In December 2018, Mora-Villalpando received a letter from the federal government ordering her to appear before an immigration judge, making her just one of many undocumented activists who were targeted by ICE under President Donald Trump.[10] "I saw my name, and I kind of laughed about it, because I had thought they would be here at my door. Instead, they send me a letter," she recalled. But then she saw that her daughter, Josefina Alanis Mora, had tears in her eyes. "I really, really hate when anybody makes my daughter cry, so I got really angry. We just walked to the car. I told my daughter: 'Don't worry. Everything's going to be fine. You can cry as much as you need to, but I'm going to make these motherfuckers pay if they ever try to separate us.'"

Mora-Villalpando had started to prepare her daughter, who was born in the United States, for this possibility long before, when she was divorcing her husband. At the time, Josefina was about five years old. "I had to prepare her," Mora-Villalpando said. "Nobody should have to have this conversation with their children. Obviously, when somebody goes through a divorce, or somebody dies in the family, those sorts of things, you have conversations. But having to say, 'Hey, ICE might come and take me, and I might never see you ever again,'" she continued. "Nobody should have to say that."

It was also for her daughter's sake that Mora-Villalpando began organizing and thinking systematically about how people end up being detained by ICE at all—and how it could be otherwise. This was difficult enough before the Trump administration, but as many organizers and activists I have spoken to told me, the constant stream of crises—some national, but many more local— since January 2017 has left little time or energy to think about their nature and origin. "Personally, it took me years to understand how much damage the capitalist political system had created in our world," Mora-Villalpando said. "Coming from Mexico, from a place that was invaded by Europeans and colonized, I grew up with a colonized mind, in a colonized context."

"We are not only dealing with the monster of detention and deportation; we are also dealing with the monster of liberalism," she continued. "We all need to eat, but we also should have the right to eat wherever we're at. We should all be able to be able to cook ourselves food without having to kill ourselves in a job that is dangerous, without having to compete for wages—wages set by somebody else. All these rights that we should all have, we don't have them because it's so much easier to pit us against each other, to have us compete for the last things that are left for a few of us."

Claudia

Claudia Rueda was six years old when she came to the United States. "I knew I was different, because I didn't speak English," she told me.[11] "I thought my difference was something great. I was proud to be Mexican." She made good grades—good enough that, in high school, she qualified for a college prep program. Participation, however, required a social security number. "That's when it hit me: 'Like, wow, I can't do this, just because of a number. I've been working my ass off, and it doesn't really matter,'" she said. "I saw it in my sister also getting denied for a college program. I saw it in my parents not getting their wages, or my dad getting stopped by police for not having a driver's license."

Rueda's mother, Teresa Vidal-Jaime, was detained in April 2017, during a joint operation conducted by the US Border Patrol and the Los Angeles County Sheriff's Department ostensibly targeting a Boyle Heights drug ring. Vidal-Jaime wasn't arrested on drug charges but on suspicion of living in the United States without authorization.[12] "Even though she wasn't involved, they still took her," Rueda said. "They come into our communities, they use any excuse to take anyone who is around." Vidal-Jaime was only released, over ICE's objections, after several weeks of protests led by Rueda. Days later, the border patrol arrested Rueda.[13] Again, the pretense was a drug raid. Again, Rueda was not charged with any drug-related offenses, only with violating US immigration law. "It was retaliatory," Rueda told me. "They were mad that I was speaking up, that I was talking . . . on the news. They used that to punish me, to silence me."

The twenty-two-year-old was already in a state of shock when Customs and Border Protection agents showed up outside her aunt's house, also in Boyle Heights. "I couldn't believe it was happening," she said. "I was already traumatized that they took my mom. I thought my whole life was falling apart." They took her to a detention center downtown. "In that place, they try to keep everyone in a constant state of fear," she said. "To eat, you have to go through metal detectors, random searches—there are so many rules. If you don't make your bed, you can get a strike, and if you get three strikes you get sent to isolation, which people call 'the hole.' You're not treated like a human being."

"The first time I received some money [in detention], being able to buy some conditioner reminded me of my humanity. Everything is dry and deprived. You feel like no one," Rueda told me. "That place causes a lot of mental anguish and depression," she said. "There's a psychologist, but it's just for the look of it. They just say, 'Drink more water.'"

Still, Rueda kept organizing, even in detention. "I did my best trying to help people," she said. "I made friends, I helped with their asylum applications. A lot of people are coming from distant countries, and they make them do asylum applications in English and they don't know English. So I was helping with translation." After her release, Rueda applied for protections under the Deferred Action for Childhood Arrivals (DACA) program and was denied.[14] Legal filings described her as the "paradigmatic" DREAMer—that is, the kind of young immigrant who would be covered by the proposed Development, Relief, and Education for

Alien Minors Act—a model student who grew up in the United States and is civically engaged. But Rueda herself was ambivalent about this particular strategy. "We can't choose who we fight for in our community," she said. "Our humanity shouldn't be defined by whether we have a diploma or broke a law. Our humanity should always be put first, under all circumstances. Humanity shouldn't only be for DREAMers, it should be for every immigrant."

Even after she was released from detention, as she waited for a lawsuit over her DACA application to be litigated, Rueda's life was still shaped by her experience inside. "Before, I was more able to do more—to sit down and strategize, to be part of a space or a group," she said. After her release, her depression and anxiety became debilitating. "It was really hard to integrate back into society. I was really sad. I would isolate myself. It was so traumatizing—it affected me a lot mentally," she said. "I wasn't able to concentrate on daily tasks, even school or organizing. I actually did a campaign for one of my detention roomies, and raised bond for them to get out, but I noticed that I wasn't able to do much, because it was mentally too much, so I took a step back. It was too traumatizing, I would have anxiety and nightmares, I kept stuttering, would lose my train of thought, forget things a lot."

This was the intended effect, Rueda believed. "Even though I was free, mentally, I didn't feel free," she told me. "I think it's part of the agenda: keeping people in a state of fear. Trying to silence me and what I have to say about what I've been through. They want complacent people—they don't want people who are out there exposing what's going on, how they're dehumanizing people, how state violence creates this trauma in our communities to keep us under control."

Security Culture

Donald Trump is not the first modern president to fetishize "border security." Between them, the Clinton, George W. Bush, and Obama administrations conducted twenty-seven million deportations.[15]

Democrats and Republicans alike have allowed a "culture of cruelty" to flourish within the immigration enforcement agencies.[16] Both parties are complicit in the transformation of the Sonoran Desert into a death trap surveilled not only by the heavily militarized border patrol but by right-wing vigilantes and militias.[17] The massive expansion of the carceral state and its subsequent privatization was a bipartisan project, preceded by a set of shared ideological assumptions about immigration, the border, and national sovereignty that were the necessary preconditions for Trump's election: among them, that immigration, absent regulation and control, posed a threat to national sovereignty; that it was appropriate for the border to be militarized; that it was acceptable for there to be a criminalized underclass of people in this country subject to deportation. Under the Trump administration, the federal government's efforts to deport as many people as possible—part of a wider effort to rid the country of vast swathes of immigrants, whether or not their presence is authorized—escalated, radicalizing into something categorically different than what preceded it. But liberals and liberal institutions accepted, expressed, and embedded these nativist impulses, paving the way for a new kind of state violence.

Trump did not introduce ethnonationalism to US politics. Rather, it is endemic: the United States is an explicitly and foundationally white supremacist country. In the early twentieth century, institutional white supremacy in the United States was the envy of racists the world over—particularly in Germany, where Nazi policy makers looked to both Jim Crow laws in the South and federal immigration restrictions as models to pursue in the Reich, reserving special admiration for the 1882 Chinese Exclusion Act, the 1917 Asiatic Barred Zone, and the 1924 Immigration Act. "The United States stood at the forefront in the creation of forms of de jure and de facto second-class citizenship for blacks, Filipinos, Chinese, and others," James Q. Whitman writes in *Hitler's American Model*. "This," he argues, "was of great interest to the Nazis, engaged as they were in creating their own forms of second-class citizenship for German's Jews."[18]

As far as Hitler and other Nazis were concerned, in the 1920s, US immigration laws were the best (and only) example of *völkisch* citizenship legislation in the world—that is, legislation that would secure the racial character of the United States.[19] They weren't only interested in legislation, either. In 1938, Dr. Gerhard Peters wrote an article for *Anzeiger für Schädlinskunde,* a pest science journal, citing the US government's use of Zyklon-B in delousing chambers on the border with Mexico two decades earlier. Peters would go on to become the managing director of Degesh, the German company that had supplied Zyklon to both the US government and, later, the Nazi death camps.[20]

Those same laws, so admired by the Nazis, have also drawn praise from members of Trump's administration. In a 2015 interview with Steve Bannon (then executive chairman of *Breitbart News*) Senator Jeff Sessions said, "In seven years, we'll have the highest percentage of Americans, non-native born, since the founding of the Republic," Sessions would go on to become Trump's first attorney general, while Bannon helped run Trump's presidential campaign before serving as his "chief strategist" in the White House, leaving in August 2017 to organize right-wing movements internationally. "Some people think we've always had these numbers, and it's not so," Sessions continued, referring to immigration figures. "It's very unusual, it's a radical change. When the numbers reached about this high in 1924, the president and Congress changed the policy, and it slowed down immigration significantly." The 1924 quotas lasted until the passage of the Immigration and Nationality Act of 1965, which abolished the racist National Origins Formula.[21] The 1965 reforms "went far beyond what anybody realized," Sessions lamented. "We're on a path to surge far past what the situation was in 1924."[22]

Trump himself cited the 1965 law in a speech dealing with immigration ahead of the 2016 election. "We've admitted 59 million immigrants to the United States between 1965 and 2015," he told rally-goers in Phoenix, Arizona. "We take anybody. 'Come on in, anybody. Just come on in.' Not anymore." He continued, "We will break the cycle of amnesty and illegal immigration. We will break the cycle. There will be no amnesty. People will know that you can't just smuggle in, hunker down and wait to be legalized. It's not going to work that way. Those days are over."[23]

In fact, it never worked that way; those days never existed. But Trump's remarks, as they so often do, revealed a deep anxiety at the heart of the American experience, to which his long-promised border wall is a monument. This anxiety stems from a contradiction that has structured US politics since the beginning of the settler-colonial genocide of the Indigenous peoples of North America: the contradiction between capital's need for labor and the liberal state's need for citizens—in other words, between the economic imperatives of capital and the political imperatives of the nation-state.

In a racially homogenous nation, the immigration scholar Lisa Lowe argues, these imperatives are theoretically complementary. In the United States, however, this contradiction has produced differentiated (that is, racialized and gendered) labor—fractured and segmented and therefore more readily exploitable, both economically and politically.[24] In the late nineteenth century, the state, in service to capital, sought to mediate this conflict through the "exclusion and disenfranchisement" of Chinese immigrant workers. "Capital could increase profit and benefit from the presence of a racialized and tractable labor force up until the point at which the Chinese labor force grew large enough that it threatened capital accumulation by whites," Lowe writes. "At that point, by excluding and disenfranchising the Chinese in 1882, the state could constitute the 'whiteness' of the citizenry and granted political concessions to 'white' labor groups who were demanding immigration restrictions."[25] With the United States Supreme Court's ratification of Chinese exclusion, the state asserted its control over immigration as a matter of national sovereignty. Foreshadowing contemporary fears of demographic replacement and white genocide, immigration at the end of the nineteenth century was framed specifically as a potential form of "foreign aggression and encroachment."[26] As Mae Ngai points out in *Impossible Subjects*, "The association of immigration control with the state's ability to wage war reveals that sovereignty is not merely a claim to national rights but a theory of power." Specifically, the power to create and maintain a white-dominated republic.

Historically, the overwhelming majority of border crossers coming into the United States from Mexico were young men from Mexico, but that had already begun to change by the time Trump took office. Starting in 2011, CBP has apprehended a growing number of migrant families and children, largely from the Central American countries known as the Northern Triangle: El Salvador, Guatemala, and Honduras.[27] Thanks to more than a century of US imperialism, migrant flows between the Northern Triangle and the United States have long existed. Decades of acute political and economic instability, inaugurated by the Reagan administration's intervention in the region's civil wars of the 1980s—as well as accelerating climate crises—led to hundreds of thousands of Central Americans picking up and heading north.

In fiscal year 2019, the US Border Patrol reported making 851,508 apprehensions on the southwest border (including 76,020 unaccompanied children), up from 396,579 in 2018 and 303,916 in 2017.[28] The vast majority were what CBP refers to as OTMs— Other Than Mexicans—a stark reversal of the demographics just a decade earlier. Also in 2019, ICE arrested about 143,000 undocumented people—a drop of nearly 10 percent compared to the year before, which Acting Director Matthew T. Albence attributed to ICE agents being redeployed to support CBP at the border— and removed 267,258 people, a slight increase from the 256,085 that were removed a year before. Most people apprehended by the US Border Patrol ended up in an ICE detention center, where they would be held, on average, for 34.3 days. On any given day, ICE was holding somewhere around 50,000 people in its custody, though sometimes that number would spike to more than 56,000.[29]

Still, the impact that immigrants and refugees have had on the United States and Europe's political discourse is vastly disproportionate to the actual number of immigrants and refugees seeking new lives there—which itself pales in comparison to the number of people who will be displaced by climate change, financial crises, and war in the coming decades. According to the International Labour Organization, there were 164 million immigrant workers worldwide as of 2018, almost half of whom were concentrated in North America and Europe.[30] Globally, the United Nations recognizes about 65 million people who have been "forcibly displaced" from their homes—of those, about 25 million are living outside the countries where they were born. In 2016, according to the Internal Displacement Monitoring Centre, about 31.1 million people were forced to move within their own countries as a result of violence and natural disasters.[31] According to one Environmental Justice Foundation study, over a six-year period leading up to the Syrian civil war, between 2006 and 2011, successive droughts forced about 1.5 million people to migrate to that country's cities, where their access to food, water, and jobs remained precarious.[32] Likewise in Bangladesh, hundreds of thousands of people have been forced to seek shelter in the capital Dhaka's slums as a result of coastal flooding, while desertification in West Africa (and the proliferation of militias) has forced millions from their homes and into refugee camps in Cameroon, Chad, Niger, and Nigeria.[33]

Estimates of the coming number of environmental refugees vary: according to the UN International Organization for Migration, anywhere between twenty-five million and one billion people could be displaced as a result of climate change by 2050.[34] Tens of millions will be displaced as a result of climate change in the next decade alone, and most of those people will come from Sub-Saharan Africa, South Asia, and Latin America.[35] (Researchers at Columbia University estimate that there could be as many as 450,000 people seeking refuge in the European Union annually by 2100.)[36] A robust, healthy democracy with strong social programs and an appropriate sense of historic responsibility might be able to manage these changes. But the violent reactions to current immigration trends in the United States and Europe do not bode well for the future. Since 2017, even as it persecutes the undocumented, the Trump administration has been working to "effectively eliminate asylum," as one American Civil Liberties Union lawyer put it.[37]

The asylum program that Trump took control of when he was inaugurated was largely the product of a 1990 settlement agreement between the federal government and a number of human rights organizations and religious groups, including American Baptist Churches (ABC). While the United States had accepted asylum-seekers and refugees for decades, its policies were largely ad hoc, often guided more by US foreign policy interests than the conditions that people were fleeing. Hardly any Guatemalan or Salvadoran refugees were granted asylum under the Reagan administration, in large part because doing so would have meant acknowledging that the US-backed anticommunist death squads that the refugees were fleeing were a root cause. Meanwhile, the asylum claims of those fleeing Nicaragua and the left-wing Sandinistas were overwhelmingly granted.

After the ABC Settlement Agreement, as it came to be known, this changed. Thousands of Central Americans were permitted to apply for asylum, their claims adjudicated by a newly formed corps of asylum officers contained within the Immigration and Naturalization Service but exerting autonomy from the law enforcement apparatus.[38] The people hired to be asylum officers were largely aid workers and civil rights attorneys—that is to say, not people with a military or police background. "I remember coming on board with this group of bright-eyed do-gooders and facing real hostility from the INS career folks, partly because—well, we weren't viewed as real immigration officers," Michael Knowles, one of the first officers hired into the newly formed asylum corps, told me. "The typical career path of an immigration officer would be military, then they'd go to border patrol for a few years, and then a lot of them would move on to become port of entry inspectors or detention and removal officers. Eventually some of them would, as they got older and more experienced in the law, become what were called examiners: they'd be the people interviewing folks for visas, green cards, naturalization, or asylum." He continued: "And then all of a sudden in come all of us. We're going to be asylum officers and not come up through that system. We were viewed as suspect."

Decades later, Trump became president and Knowles was still an asylum officer. He was also president of his union, AFGE Local 1924, which represents 2,500 US Citizenship and Immigration Services workers, including more than 300 workers in the Asylum and Refugee Programs division. Thanks to union protections, Knowles and other activists in the union have been able to critique the Trump administration's policy changes from within, especially by submitting amicus briefs in lawsuits filed by outside organizations.[39]

"Some of us believe that they are determined to dismantle— or if not dismantle, radically transform—the asylum program," Knowles told me, referring to the Trump administration, "to wind back the clock to pre-ABC settlement, and put [the asylum corps] back where they think it ought to be: as an arm of law enforcement staffed and directed by law enforcement officers."

"We have always been sort of anathema to the rest of the law enforcement folks," he added. "The fact that a migrant can say, 'I want asylum,' and they must let them see an asylum officer who works by a different set of rules—in their mind, that's just something that they've never liked, and they're determined to get rid of that."

The Logic of Elimination

In the first years of the Trump administration, each day seemed to bring with it new reports of CBP and ICE's depravity in their pursuit of undocumented immigrants—a set of executive orders signed shortly after the president's inauguration was intended to "take the shackles off" enforcement agents, as then press secretary Sean Spicer put it, apparently without irony—or the horrors of the detention centers and CBP stations where tens of thousands of people were held every day. Conditions at one overcrowded border station, in El Paso, Texas, where there were only four showers for 756 immigrants, were so bad that agents armed themselves in preparation for a riot.[40] At another facility, many detainees hadn't showered in over a month.[41] In the detention centers, ICE agents threw migrants into solitary confinement at the slightest provocation, often establishing segregated areas for hunger strikers, as well as migrants with disabilities and those identifying as or perceived as LGBTQ. Detainees with mental illness were frequently held in isolation, where they suffered hallucinations and suicidal ideation, sometimes engaging in self-harm.[42] In four months spanning the end of 2019 into the beginning of 2020, three migrants in ICE custody died by suicide.[43]

In 2017–18, the Trump administration implemented a "zero tolerance" policy, wherein the Department of Homeland Security (DHS) separated migrant parents, apprehended at the border, from their children, who were transferred to the custody of the Department of Health and Human Services. As was later revealed, the policy, which began as a secret pilot program in El Paso, was launched without any plan to reunite the separated families.[44] Many children, already traumatized by the violence they'd fled or experienced during their journey to the United States, were further traumatized.[45] At one detention facility, as kids screamed for their mothers and fathers, a CBP agent joked: "Well, we have an orchestra here." He sneered, "What's missing is a conductor."[46]

The children, meanwhile, were forced to take care of each other.[47] "The guards are asking the younger children or the older children, 'Who wants to take care of this little boy? Who wants to take of this little girl?' and they'll bring in a two-year-old, a three-year-old, a four-year-old," an immigration attorney recalled in an interview with the *New Yorker*. "And then the littlest kids are expected to be taken care of by the older kids, but then some of the oldest children lose interest in it, and little children get handed off to other children. And sometimes we hear about the littlest children being alone by themselves on the floor."[48] After the December 2018 death of seven-year-old Jakelin Caal Maquin in CBP custody, a pair of government whistleblowers warned: "We fear that unless U.S. authorities stop detaining children, Jakelin will not be the last child to die in government custody."[49] Such atrocities, however, began long before Trump's election: between 2009 and 2014, at least 214 complaints were filed against CBP agents for abusing or mistreating migrant children in their care. Only one was ever disciplined.[50]

In June 2019, Representative Alexandria Ocasio-Cortez, one of a number of legislators elected with the help of a growing US socialist movement in the previous midterms, compared the detention centers to concentration camps, provoking an enormous backlash from both the Republican Party and the Jewish establishment. The young, Jewish left came to her defense. "How do we forget that the Third Reich had a very specific term for sending populations to its camps, and later, for sending them to the gas? That term was deportation," writer Jacob Bacharach noted.[51] "What," journalist Noah Kulwin asked, "is the meaning of a phrase like 'never again' when the institutions that proselytize it also argue that Holocaust memory cannot be sullied by the present tense?"[52]

Later that summer, Jewish leftists, in coalition with immigrant-led organizations like Movimiento Cosecha, began holding demonstrations outside ICE facilities around the country. Mobilizing masses of people to disrupt the agency's operations, they were building on the Occupy ICE campaign of a year before, when activists began blockading ICE facilities in response to the Trump administration's family separation policy. Operating under the aegis of Never Again Action, these organizers took Ocasio-Cortez's invocation of "concentration camps" seriously: "We have seen this before. We won't let it happen again. Never again is now," the group announced.[53] "We look at what is happening and what our government is doing to immigrant communities," a Never Again organizer told the *Daily Beast*.[54] "We see nothing less than a mass atrocity. While conditions might not exactly mirror the Holocaust, we shouldn't wait for them to mirror the Holocaust to take action. That's why we say 'never again' means never again for everyone, and never again means now." Appealing to the moral authority of their Jewishness, these activists condemned the immigration regime in uncompromising terms.[55] "It's been really powerful for Never Again Action to verbalize solidarity with communities being terrorized every day," Catalina Santiago, an organizer with Movimiento Cosecha, told *Vice News*. "They are popularizing the outrage on this issue and the demand for protection of immigrants."[56] Others were more blunt: "Fuck the semantics. Children are dying. That should be enough."[57]

Concentration camps, journalist and historian Andrea Pitzer writes in *One Long Night*, have been in continuous existence in various places around the world for more than a century. "Barracks and barbed wire remain their most familiar symbols, but a camp is defined more by its detainees than by any physical feature. A concentration camp exists wherever a government holds groups of civilians outside the normal legal process—sometimes to segregate people considered foreigners or outsiders, sometimes to punish."[58] They are a uniquely modern phenomenon comparable to the atomic bomb, she argues. "Just as other kinds of bombs existed before nuclear devices were developed, concentration camps also had precursors, but nonetheless represented a deliberate escalation and transformation of previous tactics."[59]

Immigrant detention centers clearly fit this description, but then the debate over whether to call the detention centers "concentration camps" was never really about how to categorize the treatment of migrants. To acknowledge the full reality of what was happening on the US-Mexico border to undocumented immigrants and their families in the interior, and to the communities in which they live and work necessitates a reckoning with the country's blood-soaked history, guided by what the Australian historian Patrick Wolfe calls "the logic of elimination." This is the foundational logic of settler-colonial societies like the United States (and Australia), which involves not only the "summary liquidation" of Indigenous people but also the creation of a new colonial society over and against that which has been expropriated.[60]

"Many have noted that had North America been an unpopulated wilderness, undeveloped, without roads, and uncultivated, it might still be so, for the European colonists could not have survived without forcibly appropriating the Indigenous peoples' developed lands and resources," the historian and activist Roxanne Dunbar-Ortiz has written. "They appropriated what had already been created by Indigenous civilizations. They stole already cultivated farmland and corn, vegetables, tobacco, cotton, and other crops domesticated centuries before the arrival of European invaders who took control of the deer parks that had been cleaned and maintained by Indigenous communities, used existing roads and water routes in order to move armies to conquer, and relied on captured Indigenous people to identify the locations of water, oyster beds, and medicinal herbs."[61]

The settler-colonial invasion is not a singular event isolated in the past, but an ongoing, adaptive phenomenon that continues to structure the United States and its politics.[62] One discursive dynamic that has proven particularly resilient is the representation of Natives as "unsettled, nomadic, rootless," Wolfe observes, regardless of their actual social practices or the fact that settlers themselves had come from elsewhere. Such depictions are a necessary precondition for the elimination of the Native and the expropriation of their land: "The reproach of nomadism renders the native removable."[63]

According to the logic of elimination, the condition of removability is tied to one's connection to the land—that is, to the ownership of private property. As exemplified in the 1887 Dawes Act, which permitted some Natives to become US citizens through the privatization of their land—which in turn undermined collective treaty lands—this was the only kind of connection that really mattered.[64] "Private ownership," Nick Estes writes in *Our History Is the Future*,

> is seen, under US law, as the highest possible form of ownership, while Indigenous occupancy is seen as temporary; thus, collective Indigenous occupancy is seen as temporary; thus,

collective Indigenous ownership and use could be dissolved for private ownership, but not the other way around. But because private property is exclusive, the two systems of land tenure fundamentally could not overlap. The confinement and removal of Indigenous peoples to reservations was racial segregation, and Indigenous peoples were the original "Red Scare."[65]

The maintenance of both the settler-colonial project and the bourgeois nation-state hinges on the occupation of space and the control of territory. Therefore, they also depend on the production and defense of boundaries, borders, and barriers, within which new social and property relations can be inscribed. Having displaced Indigenous peoples and rendered their lands a commodity to be controlled by individual members of a particular racialized class, settlers and colonizers came to see themselves not only as "native" but threatened with displacement in turn. Thus is immigration rendered a "problem." In a further cruel and ironic twist, immigrants, long settled in their communities—the majority of the undocumented population in the US have lived here for five years or more—are targeted by the roaming paramilitary bands of ICE, which descend from nowhere to disappear those they deem a threat.[66]

When a person crosses the US-Mexico border without authorization, they may reside within the geographical boundaries of the country but can never be a part of the nation. No matter how long they live here, what kinds of relationships they build, how assimilated they become, they always remain in an individualized state of exception—not only criminal but a noncitizen, and therefore subject to all manner of violence and terror from which others are nominally protected. This is supposed to happen out of sight—the mass grave of the Sonoran Desert attests to that—but it is nevertheless supposed to happen. They are rounded up and deposited into the walled-off torture chambers of prisons and detention facilities, themselves far removed from the institutions of civil society that might, under pressure, contest the existence of such places, or at least the conditions within them.

The displaced are the enemy by virtue of their very displacement, and when the repressed memories of genocide and violence return, they manifest as fear of retribution. "Mexican Aliens Seek to Retake 'Stolen' Land," read the headline of a story in the right-wing *Washington Times* covering the 2006 immigrant protest movements.[67] "The 'reconquista' movement is marked by the flying of the Mexican flag over the American flag and has all the elements of a violent nationalist movement with the terrorist implications," the reactionary blog *Patriot Post* commented around the same time. "If they do in fact resort to violence, all bets are off in regards to the status, guest worker or otherwise, of any illegal alien in this country from south of the border."[68] In Trump's now-infamous speech announcing his 2016 presidential campaign, much of the outrage focused on his description of immigrants as criminals and rapists. Less attention was paid to the way he described the phenomenon of immigration itself: Mexico is "sending" people.[69] "When Mexico sends its people, they're not sending their best," he said.

Trumpian bombast notwithstanding, the US-Mexico border has always been a selectively permeable one, regulating the movement of migrant labor while allowing for the unimpeded flow of capital. "Despite anti-migrant exclusionary rhetoric, it is not in the interests of the state or capital to close down the border to all migrants," Harsha Walia writes in *Undoing Border Imperialism*.[70] Both the state and capital want a "two-tier hierarchy of citizenship," in which noncitizen workers can make no claim on the state's obligations, are paid less than minimum wage, have no access to social services, and can be deported for organizing or simply because they are surplus labor. "For this underclass, their selective inclusion within the nation-state as well as legal (un)national identity as foreign or temporary normalizes the status of their unfree labor and exclusion from the state's regime of rights."[71]

Even before taking office, Trump himself knew he could only go so far. "We're going to do a wall," he said on the campaign trail in 2015. But, he added, "We're going to have a big, fat beautiful door on the wall."[72] In January 2019, speaking to the American Farm Bureau Association, Trump acknowledged the necessity of a mechanism allowing seasonal farmworkers from Mexico to cross the border, actually promising to loosen regulations on employers who rely on temporary migrant labor. "It's going to be easier for them to get in than what they have to go through now," he said.[73] Even as his enforcement regime spread terror through immigrant communities, the Trump administration consistently worked to make it easier for agricultural firms to bring in temporary workers.[74] As Daniel Denvir notes in *All-American Nativism*, "Business prefers legalization, but that doesn't rival priorities like tax cuts and deregulation; if it did, business would abandon the Republican Party."[75]

Immigrants in the United States, regardless of their legal status, are caught between two segments of the capitalist class, each of which seek their immiseration: the industrial agribusinesses, construction firms, and meatpacking plants that benefit from an underclass of unorganized and impoverished workers, on the one hand, and the defense and security firms that keep them in a state of constant criminality and deportability, on the other. Maintaining a distinction between citizen and noncitizen requires an ever-expanding security apparatus, which itself becomes a source of profit. The border constantly generates fresh crises on which the immigration-industrial complex feeds. There is not a crisis at the border; the border *is* the crisis. And it is a crisis of capitalism.

The true threat to Western democracies is not from without, but within—not mass immigration, but mass inequality. According to the Economic Policy Institute, in a reversal of historical trends, widening income inequality in the United States has accelerated since 2008: the incomes of the top 1 percent have grown faster than those of the bottom 99 percent in almost every state.[76] In 2015, the top 1 percent of families made 26.3 times as much income as the bottom 99 percent.[77] Wage growth is even more limited for women and people of color than white workers or men.[78]

The typical worker's wage has remained stagnant while CEO pay has increased from about 20 times to 278 times greater than the average wage from 1965 to 2018.[79] The top 1 percent now control 40 percent of wealth in the US—more than at any point since at least 1962.[80] However, income inequality is not simply a problem in itself, either on moral or material terms; it is a political problem. The rich do not merely accrue wealth for the sake of the luxurious lifestyles it allows. Wealth is power, and that power is to be wielded.

Reporting on the June 2018 International Border Summit, investigative journalist Todd Miller described the emergence of a "global border system" alongside (or perhaps running through) more traditional ideas about national sovereignty. "This apparatus in its totality included more than 77 border walls, billions upon billions of dollars' worth of surveillance technology—including biometrics—and tens of thousands of armed agents guarding the dividing lines between Global North and Global South. From the United States to Europe to Australia, the planet was filled with detention centers crammed with hundreds of thousands of people, families, groups, even full communities who had dared to cross lines, often because of hardship or persecution, evils established by colonial powers and enforced by their successors," Miller writes in *Empire of Borders: The Expansion of the US Border around the World*. "The border apparatus has to be looked at as a global regime, reconfiguring before our eyes, the arsenal of the Global North sorting, classifying, and repelling or incarcerating people from the Global South."[81]

Under the Trump administration, while the immigration enforcement apparatus of the state has been redirected toward an explicitly ethnonationalist agenda, fascists and white nationalists have sought to gain a foothold in the public sphere the way that many social movements do: occupying space with rallies and demonstrations, developing their own media and propaganda outlets, and running electoral candidates. Some among their ranks have carried out mass shootings. A paralyzing fear spreads in the wake of both state and stochastic terror, allowing the fascists and proto-fascists more room to maneuver. "Electoral success was not the most important precondition of fascist arrival in power," historian Robert Paxton notes in *The Anatomy of Fascism*. "The deadlock or collapse of an existing liberal state was more crucial."[82] In the 1920s and 1930s, he argues, the constitutional state in both Germany and Italy had ceased to function long before the fascists actually seized control. "The collapse of the liberal state is to some degree a separate issue from the rise of fascism. Fascism exploits the opening, but is not the sole cause of it."[83]

Likewise today, many people in the United States have abandoned the political process altogether, disillusioned with the ability of the state to protect them from the market and with apparently inept national parties even as the GOP continues its decades-long fight to disenfranchise as many voters of color as possible. Meanwhile, the labor movement is in disarray, and the Democrats are at their most effective when coopting and crushing left-wing challenges to the status quo. It feels as though the country has come to a precipice.

Fascism's appeal, as German communist Clara Zetkin noted in 1923, was that it "rouses and sweeps along broad social masses who have lost the earlier security of their existence and with it, often, their belief in social order."[84] In Italy, fascism did not begin as a theory of society and the state, Emilio Gentile argues. Rather, it started as a "charismatic movement produced by an extraordinary situation," wherein the fascists were united not by doctrine or ideology but by "an attitude, an experience of faith."[85]

Although it arises in periods of crisis—in Zetkin's words, as "an expression of the decay and disintegration of the capitalist economy and as a symptom of the bourgeois state's dissolution"— fascism is not simply the most violent form of class and race war, or the bourgeoisie's fury visited upon a rising proletariat. "Fascism is quite different from all that," Zetkin wrote. In fact, she argued, fascism arrives precisely because the workers' movement is weak and unable to preempt fascism's appeal.[86] "There is a blatant contradiction between what fascism promised and what it delivered to the masses," Zetkin noted. "All the talk about how the fascist state will place the interests of the nation above everything, once exposed to the wind of reality, burst like a soap bubble. The 'nation' revealed itself to be the bourgeoisie; the ideal fascist state revealed itself to be the vulgar, unscrupulous bourgeois class state."[87]

While it shares many characteristics with earlier forms, fascism today, in the United States and elsewhere, looks different than in its classical period in the twentieth century. Drawing upon existing myths and ideas about race and nationhood, the fascism of our era is a *border fascism*. Thanks to Trump and others, it now courses through the Republican Party and even finds Democratic sympathizers. It is transforming the way that conservatives and liberals alike conduct their politics, and presents the greatest obstacle to the victory of working and oppressed people around the world over the exploiting class. As Zetkin told the Reichstag in 1932, just before Hitler took power, socialism would only come by "forging an iron-like community of struggle of all working people in every sphere ruled by capitalism."[88] To forge such a community, we must understand what it is that we are struggling against.

Chapter Two

ONLY STRONG MEASURES WILL SUFFICE

The world, which is the private property of a few, suffers from amnesia. It is not an innocent amnesia. The owners prefer not to remember that the world was born yearning to be a home for everyone.

—**Eduardo Galeano**

In the early 1940s, Detroit was home to both the anti-Semitic radio broadcaster Father Charles Coughlin, a fascist sympathizer, and the progressive, integrationist United Auto Workers union. Racial tensions in the city had been escalating for years.[1] One sweltering summer afternoon in June 1943, a fight between Black and white Detroiters at a park turned into a brawl. For the two days that followed, police and white vigilantes swarmed through the city's Black neighborhoods. Twenty-five Black people were killed, including eighteen by police. Many were shot in the back.[2]

Two years later, a young white family, the Tantons, moved out of the city, prefiguring the waves of white flight in the decades to come. "My parents decided that they'd had enough of the city," John Tanton, who was eleven years old at the time, would later recall. "I guess my father was ahead of the curve that way. He got sick of the city long before it was a common thing to do." The next chapter for the family was owning and running a farm. It was not an easy life, but young John Tanton found himself drawn to nature. "I was very much taken with the land," he recounted. "I loved to garden and still do. I liked to take care of the chickens and the turkeys and that sort of thing." A popular student and gifted athlete, he won a scholarship to Michigan State University, where he intended to study agronomy, or soil science, before switching to chemistry. He went on to medical school at the University of Michigan and became an ophthalmologist, but throughout he maintained an interest in issues of environmentalism and conservation, which in turn led him to the question of population. "I began to wonder why all of these conservation problems were cropping up," Tanton recalled. "I became convinced, and I don't recall exactly how, that increasing numbers of people were part of the problem."[3]

Initially, Tanton, along with his wife, Mary Lou, looked to family planning organizations, setting up a Planned Parenthood clinic in northern Michigan, and talking to new mothers in the maternity ward of a local hospital about not having more children. "Women who have just had a child are usually highly motivated not to have any more for a while," he remarked.[4] Soon enough, though, Tanton would begin looking for other tools of population control, toying with an idea he called "passive eugenics" and finding like-minded allies in organizations like Planned Parenthood and the Sierra Club.

In 1970, Tanton's advocacy on issues of population control led him to a conference in Chicago, the Congress on Optimum Population and the Environment, where he met writers like Paul Ehrlich and Garrett Hardin (authors of *The Population Bomb* and "The Tragedy of the Commons," respectively), as well as Willard Wirtz, who served as labor secretary to John F. Kennedy and Lyndon B. Johnson, and Hubert Humphrey, the former vice president.[5] The connections he made to this part of the environmental movement would serve him well. Hardin would prove an enduring intellectual partner in the years to come, and Roger Conner, a liberal who Tanton met in the late 1960s while preparing for the first Earth Day, would become the first executive director of the Federation for American Immigration Reform, which Tanton would establish nearly a decade later.[6] He also soon connected with Cordelia Scaife May, a fellow amateur naturalist and avid conservationist.

A seminal moment in Tanton's political development came in 1974, when he happened upon an advertisement in *Science* magazine for an essay contest hosted by the Limits to Growth Conference, supported by Texas oilman George Mitchell.[7] While the essay he wrote would only come in third place, Tanton would identify it later as the first time he formalized his thoughts on the connections between conservation and immigration. The essay sounds many themes that would remain prominent throughout the rest of his life, including Tanton's belief that in advocating for greater limits on immigration to the United States, he was speaking truth to power, bravely giving voice to a controversial view that few would dare speak aloud. "As the principal countries currently receiving immigrants—the United States, Canada, Australia—reach or surpass the limits of population which they can support, they will likely move to curtail immigration," he wrote. "As with the coming material equilibrium we should ask whether this is a good or a bad thing. Is the end of significant international migration an evil to be deferred as long as possible, or could it be a benefit to be welcomed and encouraged with all deliberate speed?"[8]

Likewise, Tanton voiced his long-standing concerns over the "demographic implications" of immigration. "Migrants from the less developed countries bring their traditionally high fertility patterns with them," Tanton warned. "This is another move away from stability."[9] Tanton argued that an influx of migrants threatened the social consensus—the "unanimity of values and purposes," as he put it—necessary to meet "the emerging qualitative environmental goals" of developed countries. "These are unlikely to be shared by the bulk of illegal immigrants who migrate looking for personal economic growth," he wrote.[10] "Immigration may be good for the vast majority of the migrants themselves. They find new economic opportunities and in the special case of refugees, new freedoms. It emerges, however, that their migration in the main runs counter to the real interest of both the countries of origin and the recipient countries, and the world as a whole."[11]

By the 1970s, the population control movement had gone mainstream. Paul Ehrlich was a frequent guest on Johnny Carson's *Tonight Show*.[12] Chapters of Zero Population Growth (ZPG), the organization through which Tanton met Roger Conner, had sprung up around the country and were especially popular on college campuses.[13] In 1975, Tanton would try (and fail) to push ZPG to take a more hard-line anti-immigration position. The organization's leadership rejected Tanton's efforts, a former staffer said, because "they were uneasy about getting into ethnicity—they didn't want to be called racist." Tanton and his allies, they said, "talk in very legitimate terms, about protecting our border and saving the nation's resources and so on . . . but the trouble is, after you've heard them, you want to go home and take a shower."[14]

Tanton's frustration with environmentalists' queasy response to his ideas about immigration led him to start building his own movement. "I found virtually no one was willing to talk about this!" he said. "It was a forbidden topic. I tried to get some others to think about it and write about it, but I did not succeed. I finally concluded that if anything was going to happen, I would have to do it myself."[15] And so he did, although not entirely by himself. In the decades to come, Tanton cultivated a handful of wealthy benefactors, though none was more important to his work than Cordelia Scaife May, a lonely member of Pittsburgh's wealthy Mellon family.

By 1979, Tanton had formed the Federation for American Immigration Reform (FAIR). The board of directors included several advocates who'd come out of the population control milieu, including Sidney Swensrud, former president and chairman of Gulf

Oil, and William Paddock, an environmental activist who had introduced Tanton to May. In one 1983 memo, between anecdotes about him mocking Black women in labor and overweight people trying to fit into eye-exam chairs, an aide notes that Tanton wants to "get close enough to Cordy to become her advisor in a decade or so."[16] (Cordy was May's nickname.) The relationship was a long and productive one. Just two years after expressing his desire to become May's "advisor" in 1983, Tanton described her as FAIR's single biggest supporter, followed by board member Swensrud, the former Gulf Oil chairman. (The Mellon family held a controlling interest in Gulf Oil for decades.) "That relationship is pretty well under control," Tanton reported.[17] His notes show that he was already thinking about how the childless scion would distribute her estate. "John became the one who would carry her legacy forward the way a son or a daughter would," Roger Conner, FAIR's former executive director of FAIR, told the *New York Times*. "John assured her what she believed in her life would carry on."[18]

His letters to her are filled with groveling and obsequiousness, punctuated by encouragement of the reclusive millionaire's most outlandish fears. A long paragraph toward the end of a March 21, 1995, letter describes pleasant activities like bird watching—both Tanton and May were avid naturalists—and visiting with Immigration and Naturalization Service (INS) officers in Nogales, Arizona. "It's great fun to sit in the yard and watch the acorn woodpeckers, and the half dozen species of hummingbirds that inhabit the area," Tanton mused. "We will also want to visit the INS at Nogales, since the illegals are now coming through Arizona following the (more or less) crackdowns that have been instituted at El Paso and San Diego."[19]

With May's support, Tanton established a small network of think tanks and nonprofits that would, in the decades ahead, grow to become the most powerful mainstream advocates of immigration restriction since the early nineteenth century—a key component in the ruling class's ideological machinery of exploitation and oppression. "What will it take to finally turn the tide decisively in our favor?" Tanton wondered in a September 4, 1997, letter. "Is it just a question of money? What would we do if we had more money?"[20] Two decades later, he would have his answer

In 2005, facing a terminal pancreatic cancer diagnosis, May asphyxiated herself with a plastic bag, leaving behind an $825 million estate.[21] In the years following her suicide, filings show, the Colcom Foundation, which was May's primary funding vehicle toward the end of her life, received $441,886,012 from May's estate and the Cordelia S. May Family Trust—another, more opaque funding vehicle—as well as all of her personal property and more than 450 acres of real estate.[22] Between 2006 and 2017, a decade span that saw unprecedented mobilization of migrant workers, comprehensive immigration reform twice defeated in the US Congress, and the election of Donald Trump, May's Colcom Foundation poured approximately $138 million into the Tanton network, most of which would not have existed without her support in the first place.[23] The bulk of that money went to FAIR, the Center for Immigration Studies (CIS), and NumbersUSA, three of the biggest anti-immigration think tanks that Tanton either founded or nurtured.[24] In the Trump administration, political appointees in almost every federal department that touched immigration—as well as a (stalled) assistant secretary of state nominee—included Tanton network posts on their résumés.[25]

As it happens, taking donors and other interested parties on trips to the US-Mexico border like the one Tanton described to May is a fundraising tactic that the CIS still uses "to illustrate dramatically the illegal immigration situation," as Tanton once put it.

> The best place to see this is at San Diego. We developed a good relationship with the border patrol there. They would take us out late in the afternoon to see the general lay of the land. We looked over the area called the Soccer Field, right down on the border. We could see people collecting on the Mexican side, cooking their meals, getting ready for the dash into the United States when the sun finally went down. Then we would go back out with the border patrol at night and use their infrared night scopes to watch people cross and to see the mounted border

patrolmen apprehending them. Some of us went up in the helicopter and also got that view. It's a very dramatic and telling experience, so much so that we set up a regular system of border tours in order to give people this experience.[26]

CIS hosts similar tours to this day.[27] "The relentlessness of this illegal influx heading north can be defeating for those who have dedicated years of their life to securing the border," a CIS official reported after a tour of the US Border Patrol's Tucson sector in 2019. "Even young agents, who signed up for the excitement of being out in the field, get discouraged. Their frustration stems mostly from the persistent lack of political will to enforce the law."[28]

Mellon, Scaife, May

The Mellon family fortune was built on oil, steel, and war, as well as politicking and a willingness to protect the family's wealth by any means necessary. Cordelia Scaife May's great-grandfather, Judge Thomas Mellon, a banker and financier described in a Communist Party USA pamphlet from 1933 as a "studious old skinflint," once wrote that the spreading struggles of the late nineteenth century between the capitalists and the working class "indicates a demoralized condition of public sentiment, which may require blood to purify."[29] (He also thought that accused criminals should commit suicide—or, as he put it, "manfully rid the world of their presence, and society of the expense and trouble of their trial and punishment.")[30] Her great-uncle, Andrew Mellon, a banker, served as treasury secretary to Presidents Warren Harding, Calvin Coolidge, and Herbert Hoover, dedicating himself to rolling back (or working around) the gains of the early twentieth-century progressive movement, particularly the income tax. His policies in office encouraged the speculation of the 1920s, which ended in the Great Depression. "During the 11 years he held the office of Secretary of the Treasury, Andrew Mellon's private fortune and that of his family leaped from the hundreds of millions to over a billion," the CPUSA pamphlet reads. "Mellon served not merely himself but his class, and in serving his class served himself."[31]

The more the family's fortune grew, the more hideous their home life became. Cordelia and her brother, Richard, were raised by the family's staff in a home that was dominated by their mother's alcoholism and their father's resentment. The scion of a fallen Pittsburgh family, Alan Magee Scaife was not trusted with any part of the Mellon family business but for looking after his wife's inheritance, according to journalist Jane Mayer.[32] The family specialized in "making each other totally miserable," Cordelia once said. "I don't remember any laughter in that house."[33] (Designed by an architect who mostly worked on prisons, the house was referred to as Penguin Court—so-called for the ten penguins that lived on the grounds.[34] Richard had it demolished after his parents' deaths.) Both siblings would also grow up to be alcoholics, their lives defined by bullying, corruption, and violence. Sarah Mellon Scaife, their mother, was "just a gutter drunk," Cordelia told the *Washington Post*. "So was Dick," her brother. "So was I."[35] In fact, Richard's drinking would almost get him kicked out of his boarding school, Deerfield Academy, until his family donated money for a new dormitory. He made it to Yale, only to be expelled after rolling a keg of beer down a flight of stairs, breaking a classmate's legs. Yale gave him a chance to repeat his freshman year, but he flunked out.[36]

For many years, Cordelia's political spending and activity was overshadowed by that of her brother, who had made more than $600 millions' ($1.4 billion adjusted for inflation) worth of donations over the course of four decades, including at least $340 million (about $620 million in today's dollars) to explicitly conservative causes and institutions, the *Washington Post* found in an investigative series published in 1999.[37] "Together these groups constitute a conservative intellectual infrastructure that provided ideas and human talent that helped Ronald Reagan initiate a new Republican era in 1980, and helped Newt Gingrich initiate another one in 1994," journalists Robert G. Kaiser and Ira Chinoy wrote. Thanks to Scaife's contributions, "conservative ideas once dismissed as flaky or extreme moved into the mainstream." Scaife, who once called a reporter for the *Columbia Journalism Review* a "fucking communist cunt," would go on to make some $1 billion in political and philanthropic contributions over a fifty-year period, anticipating the billionaire industrialist Koch brothers' reign over and shaping of right-wing US politics for half a century.[38]

Richard Scaife's impact was most visible in the Reagan era, when his money helped establish and support the institutions that would formalize and continue that administration's political and ideological agenda like the Heritage Foundation, the Hoover Institution, the Center for Strategic and International Studies, and the American Enterprise Institute. Between 1974 and 1992, Richard Scaife made about $200 million in contributions to right-wing institutions.[39] Later, during Bill Clinton's presidency, Scaife poured some $2.4 million into the conservative magazine the *American Spectator* to pursue what would come to be called "the Arkansas Project." The project—the "vast right-wing conspiracy" identified by Hillary Clinton—led to the proliferation of many of the most egregious smears against the Clinton family, culminating in the theory that they had Vincent Foster, a deputy White House counsel, murdered.[40] As it happened, the *Spectator* was happy to take Scaife's money to pursue pretty much any lead that came its way—except for this one. The billionaire, who had given the magazine at least $3.3 million even before the Arkansas Project was launched, pulled his funding after it ran a critical review of a book by Christopher Ruddy asserting that Foster had not taken his own life, but had in fact been murdered.[41] Ruddy, now a close friend and confidante of President Trump, had been fired from the *New York Post* for his obsessive theories about Foster and was then hired by the *Pittsburgh Tribune-Review*, which Scaife owned.[42]

In multiple venues, Scaife referred to Foster's death as the "Rosetta Stone" of the Clinton administration. "Once you solve that one mystery, you'll know everything that's going on or went on—I think there's been a massive coverup about what Bill Clinton's administration has been doing, and what he was doing when he was governor of Arkansas," he once said. "Listen, [Clinton] can order people done away with at his will. He's got the entire federal government behind him." He added, "God, there must be 60 people" associated with Bill Clinton "who have died mysteriously."[43]

There may have been a bit of projection at work here, as Scaife had a mysterious death in his own past: Robert Duggan, the man who introduced him to conservative politics in the first place, and to whom Cordelia Scaife May was briefly married. According to the *Washington Post*, in 1956, Duggan, then Cordelia's boyfriend, helped Richard become a Republican committeeman in Allegheny County.[44] Duggan was later elected district attorney of Allegheny County in 1963, with Richard Scaife serving as his campaign treasurer. In 1964, Richard Scaife became very involved in Arizona senator Barry Goldwater's presidential campaign, meeting with the candidate, an early avatar of white backlash to the civil rights movement, repeatedly and contributing generously to his campaign. (Richard and Cordelia's mother, Sarah, once lent the Goldwater family her private airplane.) He donated generously to Richard Nixon's reelection bid in 1972, writing 330 separate checks to different front organizations for the campaign to skirt the campaign finance laws then in place. Following the Watergate scandal, Richard distanced himself from Nixon and electoral politics in general, focusing his attention on building institutions.

That same year, the Internal Revenue Service and the US attorney for Western Pennsylvania opened a corruption investigation into Duggan, who was in his third term as the Allegheny DA. Richard Scaife turned on his old friend, but Cordelia remained convinced that Duggan was being set up, and secretly married him.[45] "Why did I marry Bob? I married him because it was the most overt thing I could possibly do to affirm my faith in him just then," she told a family biographer. (She'd been married once before, in 1949, to Herbert A. May Jr., whose father, another Pittsburgh industrialist, was married to Marjorie Merriweather Post, one of the wealthiest women in the world.[46] Cordelia and Herbert divorced after just six months.) On the day that a six-count indictment charging him with tax fraud was filed, Duggan was found dead on his farm, a shotgun wound in his chest and the gun on the ground a few feet away. The official explanation was that he had died by accident or suicide, but Cordelia reportedly believed that her brother had had something to do with his death. She would not speak to him again until shortly before her death in 2005.[47]

It appears that decades earlier Judge Mellon had foreseen this breakdown while contemplating the consequences of his accumulated wealth for posterity. "The normal condition of man is hard work, self-denial, acquisition and accumulation," he wrote in 1885. "As soon as his descendants are freed from the necessity of such exertion they begin to degenerate sooner or later in both body and mind."[48] A self-deprecating recluse, Cordelia named her home outside Pittsburgh "Cold Comfort," a reference to the 1932 novel *Cold Comfort Farm*—also the inspiration for the Colcom Foundation's name—which features a female protagonist "of every art and grace save that of earning her own living."[49] While May would come to be Tanton's most generous donor, it was the oilman Swensrud whose financial contributions got FAIR started. He made his first contribution in 1979 through the Sidney A. Swensrud Foundation—$9,477 to help get the organization off the ground—and gave at least $2.7 million over the next two decades.[50]

A Malthusian Conclusion

In an oral history, Swensrud recalled coming home to Iowa on break from college to work on his uncle's farm, where he would argue and drink with the farmhands, many of whom were members of the Industrial Workers of the World (IWW). Prohibition was in force, but the Wobblies always knew how to get booze. "They were nice guys. One of them was a pretty good cartoonist. He could sit down and draw something and it was pretty good. I remember he presented me with a little drawing he made of me sitting reading a book. He said that was the thing he remembered about me. I was always reading a book," Swensrud said. "This cartoonist fellow was one of the officers of the IWW so he had the party line down pretty well. But nobody can argue as much as two guys interested in economic theory, so we had a lot of discussions—always friendly though."[51]

Like Tanton, Swensrud had been involved in population control efforts throughout the 1970s. In college, he had studied the English political economist Thomas Malthus and was deeply taken with his theories about economic development and over-population—that population, if allowed to increase without limits, would eventually overwhelm the resources needed to sustain it. "I thought his logic was convincing," Swensrud said.

> I still think the logic is exactly right. The consequence Malthus warned about has been frustrated by other developments and some forward passes, as it were, in economic development. We've had the Industrial Revolution, and we've had the American Frontier, and we've had birth control. All those things put off our facing of the consequences. But they're still there. Birth control was the big factor in this country and in Europe and Japan. But in the Third World and other countries excessive population growth marches irresistibly onward toward a Malthusian conclusion.[52]

Over the course of his career at Standard Oil and then Gulf Oil, Swensrud was invited to join the boards of Planned Parenthood Foundation of America and the International Planned Parenthood Foundation. "I found all this very rewarding, because I have had this strong concern about overpopulation," he said. "I guess somehow I am sort of an economist too. In fact, I had all the requirements for a doctor's degree in economics at Harvard. It seemed to me that it must be considered an uneconomical thing for a country to have more people than there's either need for, or for whom there is any possibility of achieving a good standard of living." He continued: "I guess I have always been against waste. It just seems to me, a waste of something very important to allow population to exceed the number which will preserve the most optimum per capita standard of living that can reasonably be attained and sustained in the country in question." Or, as he put it elsewhere: "In the Bible it says, 'Be fruitful and multiply.' Well, I don't know. . . . If you ever looked at the eggs that a frog lays or a female fish has in its roe, you would likely decide that nature didn't count on many of her offspring surviving."[53]

Swensrud also supported sterilization as a means of population control, serving as director of the Association of Voluntary Sterilization (previously known as the Human Betterment Association of America, later the Association for Voluntary Surgical Contraception, and today as EngenderHealth).[54] As the organization's name indicates, Swensrud believed that sterilization should be voluntary—for the most part. "The purpose of the government is to be of benefit to the people in the country of which it's the government. If that involves some coercion, well there are areas where I believe some constraints on population may be a duty of the government," he said. When it came to sterilization, "in a country that has had dictators for a long time [such as India or China], and the people are used to being coerced, then I think coercive measures might possibly be made to work."[55] For Swensrud, certain groups of people weren't fit to make their own decisions, by virtue of their race, history, and culture.

Like many in the population control milieu, Swensrud would insist that his concern was fundamentally about the number of people living in the world generally and in the United States specifically, relative to the resources available to them necessary to sustain a decent quality of living. However, this insistence obscures the conflation of "population" with "demographics" that lies at the base of much of this thinking. "These are life and death questions about the future of the globe," Colorado governor Richard Lamm wrote in the forward to the biography of John Tanton and his wife Mary Lou, written by John Rohe. "But does it require a question of 'life or death' before a nation considers population a threat and attempts to set limits? Does a nation or a region have to let its demographic situation deteriorate to intolerable limits before it acts?"[56]

This conflation covers up a deep anxiety not only about changes to the racial (or "cultural," to use another code word) composition of the United States but also about changes in the racialized distribution of resources. "My views about immigration are entirely based on my views as an American and what I think is best for our country, from the standpoint of numbers," Swensrud said.

> I don't see any reason why a country can't consider its own interest. I believe generosity is an admirable thing up to a point, but being careless and not having proper regard for your own future is not admirable in my view. When our ancestors came here it was good for them and good for the U.S.A. I would tend to be selfish when it came to sharing the advantages we have achieved in this country with everybody else in the whole world who wanted to come here. We cannot do that and still maintain any kind of decent standard of living for ourselves. Just imagine what would happen if we said, "Any people in the world that want to come here may do so, and they will have the same rights as every other person in this country as soon as they get here." Well, that to me would result in this country becoming poverty-stricken, and the advantage that we have really earned for ourselves by being more cautious in our policies and all that—we would just lose the whole thing. I am not in favor of that. I don't think we need to make any apologies about defending the things we've got; that's one of the rights of people, to defend the position they have achieved.[57]

Swensrud never comes out and declares himself an advocate for a white ethno-state, but his thinking contains within it clear echoes of both settler colonialism and lebensraum—the German concept of "living space" that became an ideological tenet of Nazism justifying the regime's expansion across Europe and the extermination of conquered non-Aryan peoples. These echoes lie in what is unsaid—who he means when referring to "our ancestors" and the "decent standard of living" that "we have really earned for ourselves." He is talking about the material benefits of being a white US citizen of European descent.

This obsession with defending the country's sovereign material wealth is ironic, given his history as the president and chairman of an international oil conglomerate with major holdings in countries like Kuwait and Venezuela.[58] Gulf Oil's wealth and power were built in a time of expansion and plunder. It is only after having gained and consolidated control over production and distribution that US capitalists like Swensrud begin talking about limits—never on himself or his class, but on others. He lamented:

> I think that the world has gone on a long time, and that present civilization has gone on a long time, so that the resources of any particular country, including the United States, are pretty well determined, and we've got only so much tillable land, we're already on a decline in a good many of our basic minerals. We don't have the iron ore we had at one time. We don't have the oil reserves that we had. And I think I'm not too clear about timber, but my belief is that timber is tending to diminish, too. And so it goes through a pretty long list of substances that we're going to need, so I don't believe that it's in our interest to keep adding to our population beyond the extent of our resources.[59]

Thus, the threat of immigration. "If, as a country, we want a good standard of living, then we have to make sure that we don't overpopulate our world," he argued. "Just think about it, in terms of Mexico and the United States: Mexico is having a heck of a time—they have too many births, they can't find jobs for the number of people they are spawning. That creates a problem for the U.S. as well as themselves, because they want to flood our country with their excess people." As for how this might suppress standards of living, Swensrud offered the following example: "Space itself is an important element in a standard of living. When you drive downtown and can't find a place to park, your standard of living has been diminished."[60]

Stage Theory

Swensrud said openly what others in the Tanton network were more careful to veil. As Tanton saw it, the political project being undertaken by FAIR—if successful—would invite three kinds of responses. "The First Stage is the knee-jerk reaction that the United States is a nation of immigrants, where people refuse to even consider or talk openly about immigration as a potential problem. They quote the Statue [of Liberty]'s poem, 'Bring me your tired, your poor,' and that's the end of the discussion," he explained to FAIR's newly hired development director in 1985. "The Second Stage is the Caveat Stage where people say, 'Now I want you to understand that I'm not racist, nativist, or mean, but I've been thinking about this, and what is the effect on the American Blacks that have to compete in Miami when they can't speak Spanish?' So, that's the pause where they say, 'I'm not a bad person, but I've been thinking about it, and it sounds like there is some substance here.'" He continued: "The Third Stage is when we can have free and open discussions about it. . . . One of FAIR's basic goals is to make immigration a legitimate topic."[61]

While this may sound like a relatively modest goal today, at the time it was transformative: immigration restriction was a fringe position in a country that had a mythology of itself as a "nation of immigrants," distancing itself from the deadly legacy of nativism and eugenics that had culminated in Nazism. In a 1981 memo to Senator Alan Simpson, Governor Richard Lamm, a Democrat from Colorado, expressed his (and FAIR's) interest in working with the Wyoming Republican to pass federal legislation reforming and restricting the US immigration system. "It is important to eventual passage of legislation that you assist sympathetic organizations and individuals," the governor advised. "The support of wealthy and important people is vital to the success of such an effort," he continued. "These people must be cultivated and stimulated to support and defend your legislation."[62]

According to Tanton biographer John Rohe, who later helped lead Cordelia Scaife May's Colcom Foundation, FAIR learned an important lesson in the course of its early fundraising efforts. "The areas most responsive to FAIR's appeals were those that felt the consequences of immigration most acutely: California, Texas, and Florida," Rohe writes. "FAIR soon learned that, surprisingly, the political system in these jurisdictions was unresponsive. Politicians in the areas most dislocated by rapid immigration found it difficult to withstand the pressure for expanded immigration. Thus, paradoxically, FAIR's most outspoken political allies in the immigration reform movement were from states least threatened by immigration."[63] (This remains true.)[64] The assumption here is that politicians in racially and ethnically diverse states, cowed by their immigrant constituents, were unable to serve the needs of aggrieved whites. FAIR was never a grassroots organization, but it was learning to appeal to whites by blaming their problems on immigrants.

Senator Simpson of Wyoming, then a state with few immigrants and little in the way of anti-immigrant politics, would prove a useful ally to the organization. "The pressures by many of the forces who have kept immigration unrestricted will grow as they perceive threats to their positions," Lamm predicted in his letter to the Wyoming senator. "A key to success is maintaining the appearance of a center or moderate position. FAIR is willing to provide counter-balancing pressure, both by itself, and by appropriate stimulation of other organizations."

And so it did. "When FAIR was started back in 1979, we tried to make it a 'full service' organization, doing under one roof all of the functions necessary to move a public policy question forward. It gradually became apparent that there were reasons for splitting some functions off," Tanton wrote in a 1988 memo. "First there was the question of bilingualism and assimilation, which the FAIR board declined to take on, setting the stage for the development of US English. Then for reasons of independence from the lobbying organization, the academic effort was split off in the form of the Center for Immigration Studies (CIS). Quite similarly, the Immigration Reform Law Institute (IRLI) was formed, in part because some donors did not wish to contribute to FAIR as long as it was active in the courts."[65]

Splitting some of these functions into different organizations came at least in part thanks to the suggestion of Greg Curtis, an adviser to May. "Greg has said that they would prefer to fund the same projects under different organizations rather than giving huge chunks of money to one group," Kathy Bricker, one of Tanton's assistants, reported in a 1985 memo. "So he is encouraging the incorporation of both the litigation effort and the Center for Immigration Studies."[66] The seeming independence of the organizations helped support their shared vision.

FAIR remained the flagship operation, sustained with money from, as Governor Lamm put it, "wealthy and important people" and partnering with legislators to pass bills like the Immigration Reform and Control Act of 1986, which paired an increase in border enforcement (that is, more agents and more surveillance technology) with the possibility of temporary legal status and green card eligibility for some undocumented immigrants already in the country.[67] "It was a great achievement," Swensrud recalled. "Our organization was very helpful in finally getting it passed. . . . But in the end, we thought we had to make compromise on the question of amnesty." This, in his view, set a "very dangerous . . . very bad" precedent—one of the few strategic mistakes that Swensrud believed FAIR had ever made.[68]

Swensrud also believed it was a strategic error to underemphasize FAIR's actual aim, which was to have almost no immigrants coming to the United States at all, whether legally or illegally. "I would like to have seen us stress much more our desire to see the number of immigrants, just as such, reduced on the grounds that immigration constitutes a very substantial part of the increase in population in this country," Swensrud said. "If we didn't have any immigration, or only as much immigration as we had emigration, then we wouldn't have any increase in population as a result of immigration."[69]

"Immigration wasn't thought, by most legislators or a great many people, to be a source of overpopulation, but it really is," he added, "especially when you consider not only the immigrants, but their progeny."[70] But it was FAIR's rhetorical focus on unauthorized immigrants, rather than legal immigration, that helped secure its legislative victories.

A Highly Undesirable Situation

Throughout his life, John Tanton denied that his work was racist, accusing critics like the Southern Poverty Law Center (SPLC), which has designated both FAIR and CIS as hate groups, of being "smear merchants."[71] In 2019, CIS filed a lawsuit against SPLC, alleging that its inclusion on the list of hate groups constituted wire fraud under the Racketeer Influenced and Corrupt Organizations (RICO) Act and caused CIS at least $10,000 in damages.[72] "CIS regularly opposes higher levels of immigration for sound public policy reasons, not because of any animus toward immigrants as human beings," the group said in a press release.[73] Within the year, however, a federal judge would throw out the lawsuit on the grounds that CIS's complaint did not actually demonstrate that SPLC had made a false statement. To be a racist, Tanton and his acolytes seem to have imagined, is to be crude and unsophisticated, which was impossible to reconcile with his self-conception as a man of science and letters. "I believe that ideas rule the world, and that the pen is mightier than the sword," Tanton said in one of his oral histories. "I have all along seen the immigration battle as really a skirmish in a wider war, a wider war of fundamental ideas."[74]

Thanks to Tanton's very own archives, however, we know that the ideas he wielded most masterfully were racist to the core. His correspondence with donors and political allies reveal a casual anti-Semite and eugenicist of varying vulgarity who expressed his racism in the evasively pseudo-intellectual language of white nationalism. As he put it in a 1995 letter to May, "We should foster diversity *between* nations, not *within* them."[75] In another letter, he wondered whether immigrants who practice "Santeria and voodoo" would "help things" in the United States. "How about a larger Muslim population, with all the conflict that applies for some of our values, and with our Jewish population? And what about the general proposition of just having a more highly variegated populace—where is the core that holds the whole thing together?" he asked.[76] The provisions of the Fourteenth Amendment that bestow citizenship to people born or naturalized in the United States also gave Tanton pause. "Looking to the future, this may become a highly undesirable situation," he suggested.[77]

In a pair of 1998 letters to the FAIR board and to May, Tanton cited Kevin MacDonald, an academic anti-Semite popular with the contemporary "alt-right," in explaining the nature of Jewish opposition to immigration reform.[78] A few years earlier, he wrote that antiracism laws in France and Switzerland "have generally been pushed by Jewish interests who are offended by those who have challenged the received version of the Holocaust."[79] In another letter to May, Tanton identified himself as "a devotee of the Austrian ethologist, Conrad Lorenz [sic]."[80] Although Tanton does not mention it in his letter, Lorenz was a member of the Nazi Party and its Office for Race Policy.[81]

Tanton corresponded regularly with prominent white supremacists of the 1990s, including Peter Brimelow, whose 1995 book *Alien Nation* was published to much fanfare on the nativist right. May paid for his research assistant and to promote the book, at Tanton's behest. In it, Brimelow warned that our "white nation" was under siege: "There is no precedent for a sovereign country undergoing such a rapid and radical transformation of its ethnic character in the entire history of the world." This resonated so much with Tanton that on three different occasions he offered Brimelow, who would go on to publish the influential white nationalist website VDARE.com—named for Virginia Dare, the first English child born in North America—a job as a spokesperson for English Language Advocates (ELA), one of Tanton's advocacy groups pushing to make English the only official language of the United States.[82] ELA is now known as ProEnglish and is designated by the SPLC as a hate group. Brimelow has received at least $325,000 from Colcom.[83]

Tanton offered Brimelow money to support him on his book tour and talking points for interviews as well as analysis of immigration issues. "It's rather like developing a cough," he wrote in one 1995 letter, drawing upon his medical training and the long history of racist fear mongering about the fragile health of the body politic.[84] "If one checks into it early, simple inexpensive measures may suffice and one's lung health may continue unimpaired. However, if you wait until you're coughing up blood, have lost 20 pounds, and have swollen lymph nodes in the neck, the treatment is likely to be severe, painful, expensive, and perhaps ineffective. Palliation may be the best that can be hoped for." Tanton continued, "With the immigration problem, we may have missed our chance to nip it in the bud and now only strong measures will suffice." Later, in a moment of further despair, Tanton would echo May's fears about white people's dropping birth rates. "All of Western Civilization is running at sub-replacement fertility, and will within a generation or two disappear into the history books," he confided in a 1997 letter to Brimelow. "It looks as if Western Civilization, as attractive as it is in certain respects, is simply unable to meet the evolutionary test of reproductive success."[85]

Over the years, as Tanton and Brimelow secured grants and financial backers for each other, Tanton was advising and supporting a young Jared Taylor as he launched his new magazine, *American Renaissance*. *AmRen* would become a refuge of white nationalist "intellectuals" in the decades to come, holding regular conferences for besuited racists like David Duke and Richard Spencer, who reportedly called for "peaceful ethnic cleansing" in the United States at one year's event.[86] Among the advice Tanton offered Taylor was how to deal with accusations of racism: "One of my favorite responses is to ask for a definition of the term," he wrote in a January 6, 1992, letter. "Few of the people who throw it around have thought about it enough to have one ready, and if they do, can often not define racism in such a way as does not include themselves." Wayne Lutton, the editor of Tanton's own Social Contract Press, sat with Taylor on the board of the New Century Foundation, which publishes *American Renaissance*, for many years. The press is funded by US Inc., one of Tanton's umbrella organizations; Tanton and Lutton shared an office in Petoskey, Michigan.[87]

One *American Renaissance* favorite was Sam Francis, a New Century Foundation board member and contributor to the magazine, with whom Tanton corresponded directly, mostly exchanging book recommendations.[88] "I'd like to read a bit of [Italian communist Antonio] Gramsci," Tanton wrote. "Could you perchance suggest a good first book of his, or perhaps an anthology if there is one?" A few years before, Francis had written an essay on Gramsci's theory of hegemony for *Chronicles*, a magazine published by the now-defunct paleoconservative Rockford Institute.[89] (Today, *Chronicles* is published by the Charlemagne Institute, which describes itself as being "rooted in the Judeo-Christian, Greco-Roman tradition" and working "to defend and advance Western Civilization.")[90] Francis also wrote the "Statement of Principles" for the white supremacist Council of Conservative Citizens and edited Pat Buchanan's book *The Death of the West*, which Buchanan wanted to call "The Death of Whitey."[91] In the March 1995 issue of *American Renaissance*, Francis suggested that white people ought to consider "imposing adequate fertility controls on nonwhites."[92] Francis also received direct financial support from May—her Colcom Foundation gave him more than $200,000 before his death in 2005.[93]

Western Values

One of the clearest examples of Tanton and May's convergence with the white supremacists and fascists of the far right is found in their shared enthusiasm for Jean Raspail's dystopian novel *The Camp of the Saints*. "A million poor wretches, armed only with their weakness and their numbers, overwhelmed by misery, encumbered with starving brown and black children, ready to disembark on our soil, the vanguard of the multitudes pressing hard against every part of the tired and overfed West," Raspail writes in the novel's preface. "I literally saw them, saw the major problem they presented, a problem absolutely insoluble by our present moral standards. To let them in would destroy us. To reject them would destroy them."[94]

Camp of the Saints narrativizes what another French thinker, Renaud Camus, would later articulate as *le grand remplacement* (the great replacement), or what "alt-right" vulgarians would dub "white genocide." That is, the idea that white people in Europe and the United States are being supplanted by people of color through a combination of falling birth rates and immigration. (In its most extreme form, this theory takes an anti-Semitic turn: Who is orchestrating this genocide? The Jews, of course.) As Enzo Traverso argues in *The New Faces of Fascism: Populism and the Far Right*, for Camus, the "invasion" depicted in *The Camp of the Saints* has already come to pass, resulting in the *décivilisation* or "deculturation" of France, experienced primarily as an "erasure of national feeling."[95]

"In his eyes, mass immigration puts into question 'our will to preserve our culture, our language and, of course, our art of living and our behavior, our religion or what remains of it, our landscape and what survives of it, our laws, our customs, our habits, our food, our freedom,'" Traverso writes of Camus's work. "By obsessively denouncing immigration, melting pots, and cultural hybridity as a lethal threat to culture and civilization, Camus's essays update the old fear of 'blood mixture' (*Blutvermischung*). He would like to rehabilitate the concept of 'race,' even if he defines it as a legacy of a 'largely shared history' rather than a 'biological filiation.'"[96] In a similar vein, in a letter to May on October 6, 1997, Tanton responded to her concerns about "sub-replacement fertility rates in many of the developed countries."[97] Tanton assured his benefactor that his advocacy of population control would not obscure his commitment to white supremacy: "The idea behind the population movement was not [that] those of us who thought population was a problem would adopt permanent sub-replacement fertility, and eventually disappear from the scene, handing our territory over to the more fertile, and thereby lose the battle."

This previously obscure (and intensely racist) text has been made famous in recent years by Trump adviser Steve Bannon's wholehearted and repeated endorsements. "Admiration, or at least cautious respect, for *The Camp of the Saints* seems to be where conservative commentators and politicians align with white nationalists," the journalist Sarah Jones argued in an essay on the book for the *New Republic*. "It offers insight into the true nature of the right's fear of immigration, and shows the extent to which that fear has been normalized."[98] William F. Buckley called it "a great novel," wondering about the questions it posed with respect to migrants and refugees. "What to do? Starve them? Shoot them? We don't do that kind of thing—but what do we do when we run out of airplanes in which to send them back home?"[99] In 2015, Julia Hahn, then a writer for *Breitbart News*, wrote, "All around the world, events seem to be lining up with the predictions of the book," that immigrants from "failed countries" would "remake the West in the image of those failed countries."[100] (Almost immediately upon Trump's taking office, Hahn's old boss Steven Bannon hired her into the White House. She remained even after he left the administration.)[101] Steve King, the white nationalist congressman from Iowa, who frequently boosts the book, told *Unzensuriert*, a far-right Austrian website, that the book "should be imprinted into everybody's brain."[102] Rod Dreher, a senior editor at the *American Conservative*, suggested that the book contained some "important truths."[103] Marine Le Pen, president of France's National Rally party (formerly the National Front) keeps a copy in her office.[104]

The book is not only popular in elite circles. "*The Camp of the Saints* is a veritable fixture on alt-right forums across the internet," Jones found. "It stars in Stormfront threads and appears on reading lists disseminated on 8chan's /pol/ board. At VDARE, white nationalist writer Chris Roberts compared it to George Orwell's *1984*. *The Camp of the Saints* appears frequently on Reddit, in r/Europe and r/New_Right and r/DarkEnlightenment and r/The_Donald, where eager Trump fans even launched a live reading series. Matthew Heimbach, founder of the Traditionalist Worker Party, recommends the novel to his followers; so does Jared Taylor, founder of *American Renaissance*, which bills itself as 'the internet's premier race-realist site.'"

The Camp of the Saints exists in English almost entirely thanks to May and Tanton. After a first English translation failed to gain traction in 1975, May funded a second print run in 1983, giving $5,000 through the Laurel Foundation to the Institute for Western Values for the purposes of distributing the book.[105] "Our concern is that huge masses of immigrants are not becoming acculturated and moving into the mainstream," the foundation's president told the *Pittsburgh Post-Gazette* in 1988. "They are not learning English, and we believe it is preventing them from assimilating."[106] A former staff member of one Tanton organization, US English, recalled seeing her coworkers carrying copies of the book around the office.[107]

In 1995, Tanton's Social Contract Press published a third English-language run, again with support from May. "While Raspail's theme seemed quixotic when the book was published in 1973 (to all but those who were able to read the demographic tea leaves), subsequent events have made it seem much more prophetic," Tanton wrote in a 1995 letter.[108] In January 1999, he would thank Donna Panazzi, a May aide, for the heir's money and support for an emerging *Camp of the Saints* movie project. "I want you to know that I consider my reputation on the line in this project, which I very much want to see succeed," Tanton insisted.[109] The film was never made, but *Camp of the Saints*'s influence endured.

The Pioneer Fund

Throughout his life, Tanton expressed an enthusiasm for eugenics—and frustration that more people could not see its utility, blinded as they were by the memory of the Third Reich. "Hitler's reign in Nazi Germany did little to advance the discussion of eugenics among sensitive persons," he wrote in a paper titled "The Case for Passive Eugenics." Contrasting "passive" eugenics with Nazi-style "active" eugenics, Tanton argued that some degree of social engineering would actually benefit the minority groups that would be subject to it. "Far from being racist or genocidal, it seeks to improve the potential of minority groups, which will do more for their prospects than any increase in numbers which might be foregone through larger family size and reproduction outside the years of reproductive efficiency."[110]

To this end, he sought out the support of the Pioneer Fund, which contributed $1.2 million to FAIR between 1982 and 1994.[111] Incorporated in New York in 1937, the Pioneer Fund was ostensibly started to support two charitable purposes: one, to provide "for the education of children of parents deemed to have such qualities and traits of character as to make such parents of unusual value as citizens"; the other, to support "study and research into the problem of heredity and eugenics in the human race ... and ... into the problems of race betterment with special reference to the people of the United States, and for the advancement of knowledge and the dissemination of information with respect to any studies so made or in general with respect to heredity and eugenics."[112] Only one project of the first description was ever funded. By the time he died in 1972, the money that its textile magnate founder, Colonel Wickliffe Draper, poured into the Pioneer Fund made it the most important source of funding in the world "for scientists who still believed that white racial purity was essential for social progress," as the psychologist William H. Tucker puts it in *The Funding of Scientific Racism*. "The scientists' role in this alliance was to transform virulent racism into rational ideology by providing the authority to justify nativist beliefs in the innate superiority of 'Nordics' in both intellect and character and the threat to their greatness posed by any interbreeding with their racial inferiors."[113]

Long after explicitly eugenicist projects had fallen out of public favor, the Pioneer Fund kept eugenicist inquiry alive. In the latter half of the twentieth century, the fund increasingly contributed to organizations seeking to limit, restrict, or stop immigration to the United States—organizations like FAIR.[114] "We were all delighted to receive the recent contribution to our efforts from the Pioneer Fund," Tanton wrote in a 1984 letter to John B. Trevor Jr., then the fund's director, thanking him for his "steadfast support through the years."[115] In 1995, Tanton would even suggest that Trevor leave part of his estate to him. "If you are interested in funding a continuation of the work that you and your father have pursued; and if you're looking for some individual and/or institution through whom to work, I would be glad to talk with you about the possibility of the individual being me, and the institution being US Inc., the foundation I run," he suggested. "The haunting question: Where would we be today if it were not for Col. Draper's foresight and financial arrangements? I hope you'll want to be the next Col. Draper!"[116] Trevor's father, John Trevor Sr., was an influential nativist who was instrumental in shaping the Immigration Act of 1924, which introduced a national origins quota system to US immigration law.[117] Tanton was fond of sharing copies of Trevor's unpublished autobiography, writing to FAIR board member Donald Collins in 2001 that FAIR should look to the work of a man who warned of "diabolical Jewish control" of the United States as "a guidepost to what we must follow again this time."[118]

Tanton had no qualms about any of this. "The Fund has five or six million dollars of capital, which was given to be used on population and eugenic problems," he wrote in a letter to Garrett Hardin, the nativist ecologist who wrote "The Tragedy of the Commons" and another beneficiary of the Pioneer Fund.[119] Hardin's essay had an insidious and enduring influence on the way even liberal-minded Americans thought about the world, becoming a kind of shorthand or received wisdom that could be readily deployed to wave away anything beyond the most individualized response to social questions.[120] The nativist underpinnings of his worldview were made explicit in his later piece on "Lifeboat Ethics," in which he compared rich countries to comfortably appointed vessels carrying wealthy people, while the world's poor are packed into overcrowded lifeboats. "Continuously, so to speak, the poor fall out of their lifeboats and swim for a while in the water outside, hoping to be admitted to a rich lifeboat, or in some other way to benefit from the 'goodies' on board," Hardin wrote. "What should the passengers on a rich lifeboat do?" The answer: let them drown.[121]

Desperately, Tanton searched for ways to recuperate eugenicist ideas without having to deal with their stigma, suggesting once that the writings of the prominent eugenicist—and avid conservationist—Madison Grant were in need of a "reassessment."[122] In his 1916 book, *The Passing of the Great Race*, which would prove hugely influential on nativists of his day as well as contemporary far-right activists like Richard Spencer, Grant wrote that Mexicans "should be deported as fast as they can be located and funds made available," notwithstanding the "storm of protest [that] will arise from the radicals and half-breeds claiming to be Americans, who will all rush to the defense of their kind."[123] In a 2009 review of a biography of Grant for Tanton's journal the *Social Contract*, F. Roger Devlin, books editor for *Occidental Quarterly*, a white nationalist website, and self-identified member of the "alt-right," wrote of Grant: "Having worked to save buffaloes, antelopes, eagles and bears, it seemed only natural to him to turn to the preservation of his own kind, viz., Americans threatened by the flood of foreign immigration of the early twentieth century."[124]

In a 1988 memo on the "status of the U.S. population movement," Tanton again expressed his frustration that eugenics were not getting a fair hearing. "Concerning the improvement of our 'nature,' i.e., our genetic backgrounds, few would object to getting rid of genes that produce physical diseases, though the means of doing so would provoke discussion. But we live here with the legacy of the Nazi era. Any efforts towards improving the human genetic stock, particularly as it applies to mental ability, are automatically seen as 'racist,' that catchall phrase for anything one doesn't like," he wrote.[125] In a 1995 letter to Robert K. Graham, the inventor of shatter-proof eyeglass lenses, Tanton promised that he and Lutton, the Social Contract Press editor who also worked on the white nationalist *Occidental Quarterly* for many years, would have "some serious conversations about what might be done to breath [*sic*] some life back into the eugenics movement, whether through restarting the American Eugenics Society, or some other means."[126] But first, they would have to deal with the branding issue: "One of the big questions is whether we need to try a new name—some euphemism—or whether we should go ahead with the present one and fight the battle for respectability," Tanton allowed. "I hope you will think about it as well." The inventor presided over a $70 million fortune, with which he founded a sperm bank for Nobel Prize winners—a barricade against those he called "retrograde humans" and the threat of communism.[127] "I should try to find some project that he would like to finance," Tanton noted in a memo.[128]

Even as he worked to preempt or blunt accusations of racism, Tanton's enthusiasm for the eugenicist project, "passive" or otherwise, revealed an abiding affinity for hierarchy and authoritarianism. "Modern medicine and social programs are eroding the human gene pool," he wrote in one letter.[129] "Within a population, which elements should be encouraged to reproduce?" Tanton wrote in another, to one of Cordelia Scaife May's advisers.[130] "This is a fascinating topic, once the subject of much public discussion. With the fall from favor of eugenics, it has disappeared from view." Motivated by the fear of unchecked population growth in the United States—driven by the arrival of new immigrants, who, according to Tanton, would consume resources and degrade the environment—his goal was to cultivate eugenicist, nativist, and restrictionist ideas in the public consciousness without them being recognized as such. "Somewhere in between this Scylla and Charybdis," he wrote, "society will be forced to decide who will live and who will die, and what the criteria of worth are."[131]

Making Immigration Policy Great Again

In 2007, with majorities in both chambers of Congress ahead of the presidential election, Democrats, with the support of President George W. Bush, sought to pass comprehensive immigration reform, intending to override a filibuster from the likes of Jeff Sessions with more moderate Republicans' help. Their efforts failed, both because many labor unions and immigration justice groups were ambivalent about the legislation—it would have paired a pathway to citizenship for unauthorized immigrants with more draconian border enforcement and a guest-worker program—and also thanks to an astroturf opposition campaign organized by FAIR and CIS as well as NumbersUSA, which had benefited greatly from May's death two years earlier.[132] From 2002 to 2004, the "immigration-reduction organization," as it describes itself, received $255,000 from the Colcom Foundation; from 2005 to 2007, following May's death, it received $6.4 million.[133] The money was well spent: the Tanton network, and NumbersUSA in particular, "lit up the switchboard for weeks," Mitch McConnell later told the *New York Times*. "And to every one of them, I say today: 'Your voice was heard.'"[134]

Colcom continued funding the network, and by the time Democrats brought comprehensive immigration reform back onto the agenda in 2013, the Republican Party had shifted such that people like Sessions were no longer an embarrassment but exemplary. In C-SPAN footage from committee hearings on the "Gang of Eight" legislation, a CIS staffer, Janice Kephart, temporarily serving as counsel to the Senate Judiciary Committee, can be seen providing notes and whispering in Sessions's ear. When House Majority Leader Eric Cantor lost a shock primary challenge that many (including CIS) saw as a referendum on immigration, what tepid Republican support there had been for reform evaporated.[135]

At the time, it seemed as though this would be the extent of the Tanton network's influence: impeding reform efforts through the careful cultivation of influence with select members of Congress and a relatively small but mobilized activist base. Then Donald Trump revealed just how deep the nativist current in American politics still runs.

It was clear from the outset, of course, that Trump's presidential campaign would be built around fear of immigrants and people of color; however, the May–Tanton network's influence lent an ideological coherence that might otherwise have been lacking. Representatives from NumbersUSA and CIS reportedly met with high-level Trump campaign officials throughout the presidential race, and Trump himself cited CIS research in speeches, campaign ads, and his now-deleted immigration plank.[136] "That's how you define success if you are a think tank," CIS director Mark Krikorian said.[137]

Personnel from the May–Tanton network (or those friendly to it) have been installed in key positions throughout the Trump administration; a number of policies the Trump campaign supported and that the administration has pursued appear to be drawn directly from proposals incubated within the Tanton network. Stephen Miller, who has spoken at CIS events and frequently refers to its work, joined the Trump campaign from Jeff Sessions's office in January 2016; he would soon be joined by Jon Feere, legal policy analyst at the CIS.[138] Both men went to work for the Trump administration: Miller, of course, in the White House, and Feere as a senior adviser at ICE. "It has been an honor to work as a policy advisor for the Donald J. Trump for President campaign and I hope to continue my service within the administration," a blurb at the top of Feere's résumé read. "An ideal position would allow me to help craft immigration policy while providing a defense against agenda items favored by the Washington establishment."[139] On the morning of Trump's inauguration, Feere tweeted, "It's time to make immigration policy great again."[140]

As a policy adviser, Feere could be appointed without Senate confirmation, where he would have been subject to public questioning about his background and views. Instead, he was able to operate with a broad mandate and without any real oversight, acting as Miller's man inside ICE. The two emailed regularly to coordinate on policy questions and shape the administration's response to critical media coverage. In July 2017, when right-wing media began speculating that Thomas Homan, the acting director of ICE, was being insufficiently supportive of Trump's immigration policies, Feere strategized with Miller. "I considered offering my own quote in defense of Homan," he wrote in an email released under the Freedom of Information Act (FOIA) to the watchdog organization American Oversight. "But that risks . . . creating a silly narrative putting me against you. All of this is preposterous. . . . Right now it would be very helpful for the White House, if not you, to provide a solid quote . . . to nip this narrative in the bud."[141] In another email, Feere offered Miller a detailed progress report on what he'd been working on that week, emphasizing his efforts in locating "potentially helpful storylines" about immigrants—irrespective of their legal or citizenship status—who'd committed crimes.[142]

Feere was not a newcomer to the nativist cause. In 2015, he testified before the House Judiciary Committee's Subcommittee on Immigration and Border Security on, as he put it, "the very interesting issue of birthright citizenship."[143] Like Tanton, Feere was against birthright citizenship—the provision of the Fourteenth Amendment that stipulates that anyone born in the United States is a US citizen. Birthright citizenship has long been a target of the far right, and in recent decades more mainstream conservatives have lent their support to efforts to restrict the Fourteenth Amendment: House Speaker Newt Gingrich's Congressional Task Force on Immigration Reform had called for the denial of citizenship to the children of undocumented immigrants in 1995, while more recently the Heritage Foundation's Hans von Spakovsky wrote about the "fundamental misunderstanding" of the Fourteenth Amendment that has led to the children of undocumented immigrants being treated as US citizens.[144]

"This whole debate is the result of a phenomenon that is sort of happening without anyone at the helm. No one is really clear exactly when the first illegal immigrant was entered into the country. No one is really clear as to when the first birth tourist came here," Feere told Congress in his testimony. "Some Administration decided to say, you know what, go ahead and give them a Social Security number, give them a U.S. passport. And it just sort of happened at some point. And no one really knows when."[145] As president, Trump repeatedly threatened to abolish birthright citizenship.[146] While it was always unlikely that he would ever be able to make good on it, it was a powerful message simply to make the threat.

While Feere remained ensconced at ICE, FAIR's former executive director, Julie Kirchner, held several different positions in the Trump administration. In January 2020, she was tasked with heading up the Office of the Immigration Detention Ombudsman, a new role created by Congress to oversee civil rights complaints stemming from abuses in detention centers.[147] Before that, she was ombudsman at US Citizenship and Immigration Services (USCIS) and an adviser at CBP. During her tenure there, she helped draft the RAISE Act, which drastically cut authorized immigration through a number of legislative and bureaucratic measures, including by halving the number of refugees the United States would accept—long a goal of the Tanton network and something with no real support in the Republican Party before Trump's ascendance.[148] After it received Trump's endorsement, Stephen Miller defended the bill by citing CIS.[149]

In November 2018, Miller invited CIS director Mark Krikorian, who once lamented that Haiti "wasn't colonized long enough" to benefit from slavery, to the Eisenhower Executive Office Building to discuss the administration's immigration policies.[150] Miller's old boss Jeff Sessions has also cited the group's specious research to defend political claims: when pressed for empirical data to back up the attorney general's claim that the Deferred Action for Childhood Arrivals (DACA) program "denied jobs to hundreds of thousands of Americans by allowing those same illegal aliens to take those jobs," the Department of Justice provided editorials written by CIS staffers. Ronald Mortensen, a CIS fellow, was nominated to run the State Department bureau that oversees aid for refugees and stateless people. (The Senate didn't take up Mortensen's nomination, so the administration had to re-nominate him.) Various Tanton groups have attended ICE stakeholder meetings, including CIS, FAIR, IRLI, and NumbersUSA.

In a 2001 letter, Tanton explained the network's lobbying strategy, later carried into the Trump administration and taken up by the right-wing media. "Our plan is to hire a lobbyist who will carry the following message to Republicans on Capitol Hill and to business leaders: *Continued massive immigration will soon cost you political control of the White House and Congress,* given the current, even division of the electorate, and the massive infusion of voters about to be made to the Democratic side," he wrote. (Emphasis in the original.) "We are about to replay the Democratic hegemony of 1933-53, fueled back then by the massive immigration of 1890-1924." In short: "The goal is to change Republicans' perception of immigration so that when they encounter the word 'immigrant,' their reaction is 'Democrat.'"

At least three former FAIR lobbyists held high-level positions in the Trump administration: Maya Noronha, who was part of FAIR's team lobbying against comprehensive immigration reform in 2013, became a special adviser at the Department of Health and Human Services; Elizabeth Jacobs, who has advocated for reducing refugee admissions, was hired as senior policy adviser at USCIS; so too was Robert Thomas Law, who is actually FAIR's former lobbying director. When his replacement, R. J. Hauman, emailed Law about a "DACA Replacement Chart" that FAIR was drafting, Law teased him: "I see you didn't waste time updating your signature line."[151]

Law maintained communications with his former employer, using his position in the administration to offer political advice. On November 28, 2017, he emailed Bob Dane of FAIR and Dale Wilcox of IRLI to let them know about an upcoming event with Kirchner that a professional association, the American Immigration Lawyers Association (AILA), had been pushing to its members. "Flagging for your attention next week's CIS Ombudsman's conference. It would be great to have a FAIR/IRLI presence since AILA has been heavily promoting," Law wrote. "The agenda is [*sic*] hits two major issues of interest: E-Verify and H-1B."[152] Popular with restrictionists, E-Verify is a program wherein employers can confirm that their employees are eligible to work in the United States. Less popular with restrictionists, H-1B is a category of temporary visa offered to immigrant workers.

Before joining USCIS, Law coauthored FAIR's "Immigration Priorities for the 2017 Presidential Transition," a special report on immigration that offered a litany of policy proposals, many of which the Trump administration would take up. "The American family is increasingly bearing the costs of urban sprawl, environmental degradation, traffic congestion, increased crime, overburdened health care, overwhelmed public schools and debt-ridden state and municipal governments—all results of uncontrolled immigration," the report claims, channeling both Tanton and Trump. "A nation without borders will rapidly lose its ability to protect its citizens and exercise its sovereignty."[153]

Documents released in the course of litigation brought by the ACLU of Southern California and the National Temporary Protected Status (TPS) Alliance, seeking to block the termination of temporary protected status for migrants from Sudan, Nicaragua, Haiti, and El Salvador, provide one example of how, once he was placed in government, Law was able to use his influence to advance FAIR's agenda. When a draft of a memorandum on whether to extend or terminate temporary protected status for Haitian migrants made its way to Law, he complained that it was "overwhelmingly weighted for extension which I do not think is the conclusion we are looking for." At the urging of Kathy Kovarik, another Trump appointee, who ran USCIS's Office of Policy and Strategy, Law edited the memo: "I made the document fully support termination and provided comment boxes where additional data should be provided to back up this decision," he reported.[154]

Many of the policies that have come to define the Trump immigration regime can be mapped onto wish lists produced by the Tanton network at various points in its history. One, prepared for members of Congress by FAIR in 2005, included demands for an end to family "chain migration," an end to the visa lottery, and an unprecedented investment in the border patrol.[155] Barely two months into Trump's presidency, his administration had discussed, proposed, or made policy out of more than a dozen items from a seventy-nine-point list published by CIS in April 2016.[156]

Following one of Trump's first executive orders on "Border Security and Immigration Enforcement Improvements," then Homeland Security secretary John Kelly issued a memo explaining, in part, how DHS would start detaining more undocumented immigrants, including people seeking asylum.[157] This echoed Item 29 on CIS's list, which demands that asylum seekers be held in DHS detention facilities.[158] "Doing so will restore integrity to an out-of-control system that encourages both border surges and asylum fraud," the CIS document alleges. Item 40 on CIS's list advocates that immigrant families who pay for their children to be smuggled out of countries like Honduras and El Salvador and into the United States be investigated and prosecuted for "child endangerment in cases where the minor is abused during the northward journey" (an argument which fails to recognize that some families deem the dangerous journey north preferable to the violence that awaits their children if they stay where they are.) A February 2017 DHS memo confirmed that the department would begin pursuing such cases: "Regardless of the desires for family reunification, or conditions in other countries, the smuggling or trafficking of alien children is intolerable."[159] Item 72 called for the formation of a "victims advocacy unit . . . providing services to those who have been victimized by illegal alien criminals." In April 2017, the Trump administration launched the Victims of Immigration Crime Engagement (VOICE) Office; people quickly began using the office's hotline to report family members, neighbors, and romantic partners they suspected of being undocumented immigrants to the federal government.[160]

Almost a year and a half into his administration, Trump's immigration policies have continued to reflect the Tanton network's proposals. Both the CIS document from April 2016 (Items 28–31) and FAIR's November 2016 recommendations to the Trump transition team recommend a more critical view of asylum claims; specifically, CIS maintains that asylum claims should not be granted to victims of domestic violence, a move that would block tens of thousands of people, mostly women, from finding refuge in the United States of America.[161] In June 2018, Jeff Sessions ordered immigration judges to stop granting just such claims, agreeing with a brief filed by IRLI, FAIR's legal arm, at Sessions's invitation.[162]

CIS has applied similar scrutiny to the idea of TPS, which items 32 and 33 of its April 2016 document assert should be "used sparingly and appropriately, if at all." The CIS document demands that the president "return 'temporary' to the spirit of the law, as was intended when the category was created to provide a humanitarian respite for aliens whose home country confronts a calamity such as a hurricane, earthquake, or other act of God." Late in 2017, Trump began doing just that, revoking TPS for 300,000 immigrants from Nicaragua, Haiti, El Salvador, Nepal, and Honduras.[163] "The disruption of living conditions in Honduras from Hurricane Mitch that served as the basis for its TPS designation has decreased to a degree that it should no longer be regarded as substantial," a DHS statement on the decision read.[164] State Department officials who criticized the administration's evisceration of TPS were ignored.[165]

Items 41–43 of the CIS document demand that the administration sharpen its enforcement practices at workplaces, expanding the use of the E-Verify program and ramping up ICE audits and raids. Trump's 2019 budget proposal included $23 million to make E-Verify mandatory for employers nationwide, and at a press conference in December, Thomas Homan, acting director of ICE, declared that he wanted to see a "400 percent increase" in worksite enforcement operations. "We're not just talking about arresting the aliens at these work sites," he said. "We are also talking about employers who knowingly hire people who are unauthorized to work."[166]

"If you're in this country illegally, and you committed a crime by entering this country, you should be uncomfortable," Homan told Congress in 2017. "You should look over your shoulder, and you need to be worried."[167]

The Man Who Would Be Czar

Other, more high-profile Trump allies have connections to the Tanton network as well: Kellyanne Conway worked as a pollster for FAIR, CIS, and NumbersUSA for decades before joining Trump's presidential campaign and then the White House; Kansas secretary of state Kris Kobach, who was leading the president's campaign to prove the existence of massive voter fraud only to find himself held in contempt of court, is counsel to IRLI, FAIR's legal arm.[168] In February, IRLI claimed in a press release to have filed a recent legal brief "at the request of Attorney General Jeff Sessions." The brief argued against the Obama-era practice of "administrative closure," which allowed immigration judges to temporarily remove cases from their already overburdened dockets. IRLI described this as "yet another unlawful de facto amnesty program," an analysis that Sessions shared.[169]

Kobach's name was floated for a number of positions in the Trump administration, including attorney general and "immigration czar," a role that the president sought to fill to coordinate immigration policy across all the federal agencies that interact with migrants. (According to the *New York Times*, Kobach reportedly had some conditions for taking that job: he would need an office in the West Wing and walk-in privileges with Trump, 24/7 access to a government jet, and a guarantee that he would eventually be nominated to DHS secretary.)[170] A Harvard- and Yale-educated attorney, he came to national prominence for his role in crafting a series of draconian immigration laws for state and local governments across the country, most notably Arizona's SB 1070.

Before joining the IRLI in 2003, however, Kobach served as an adviser on immigration law and border security to George W. Bush's Justice Department, where he helped create a database tracking visitors and immigrants from twenty-five countries, mostly Arab and largely Muslim.[171] (President Barack Obama dismantled the program just before Donald Trump took office.)[172] Kobach also used his position within the Department of Justice to push the unorthodox idea that state and local officials have the "inherent authority" to enforce federal immigration laws; in 2002, Attorney General John Ashcroft's Office of Legal Counsel issued a memo, reviewed by Kobach, supporting the "inherent authority" theory.[173]

In the years after he left the Bush administration, Kobach traveled around the country defending states and municipalities that sought to bring immigration enforcement under their own jurisdiction, approaching the courts as a venue to force policy changes. "To rigidly separate local government from federal government when we think about immigration enforcement is not only legally incorrect, it's also bad policy," Kobach said.[174] Since 2005, a joint investigation by ProPublica and the *Kansas City Star* found, Kobach has made at least $800,000 from his legal forays—most of which ended in defeat—including at least $150,000 during his time as Kansas secretary of state. This was on top of the compensation he was receiving from IRLI: a salary of $125,000 in 2005 and 2007, federal records show, and less than $50,000 in other years.

This activity culminated in 2010 with the passage of—and lawsuits against—Arizona's anti-immigrant law SB 1070, which effectively legalized racial profiling of the state's Latinx population. SB 1070 made it a misdemeanor crime for immigrants to not carry documentation with them at all times, and empowered police to detain "when practicable" anyone they suspected of being present in the United States without authorization.[175] The bill's primary sponsor, state senator Russell Pearce, contacted Kobach, who'd been involved in immigration politics in Arizona since 2006, to help draft the bill. "Slowly but surely, Arizona is showing that attrition through enforcement works," Kobach said, referring to an idea that bubbled up through the Tanton network in the mid-2000s.[176]

"Attrition through enforcement" is the nativist policy solution to the practical problem presented by the sheer number of undocumented immigrants in the United States. "Proponents of mass legalization of the illegal alien population, whether through amnesty or expanded guest worker programs, often justify this radical step by suggesting that the only alternative—a broad campaign to remove illegal aliens by force—is unworkable. One study put the cost of such a deportation strategy at $206 billion over the next five years," Jessica Vaughan, director of policy studies at CIS, wrote in 2006. "But mass forced removal is not the only alternative to mass legalization."[177]

"A strategy of attrition through enforcement, in combination with a stronger border security effort," she continued, "will significantly reduce the size of the illegal alien population at a reasonable cost. Reducing the size of the illegal population in turn will reduce the fiscal and social burdens that illegal immigration imposes on communities."[178] In other words, Vaughn was arguing that while there are too many undocumented people in the United States to deport every single one, to create a path to citizenship would be to reward ostensibly criminal behavior. The way around this impasse, according to people like Vaughn and Kobach, is to make life in the United States of America so intolerable for people whose families have fled murder, rape, and kidnapping that they return from whence they came: "self-deportation," as Mitt Romney, on whose 2012 presidential campaign Kobach was an adviser, put it.[179] As a matter of law, this policy vision was expressed most clearly in SB 1070, the very text of which read: "The intent of this act is to make attrition through enforcement the public policy of all state and local government agencies in Arizona."[180]

Pearce, the law's sponsor, didn't only turn to Kobach for help drafting and passing his legislation: he also sought support from the American Legislative Exchange Council (ALEC), the secretive "bill mill" that brings together lawmakers with corporations, industrial associations, and lobbying groups to shape model legislation for those elected officials to introduce in their states.[181] ALEC's sponsors have included ExxonMobil, the National Rifle Association, and Koch Industries—as well as CoreCivic and Geo Group, the country's two largest private prison companies, and Sodexho Marriott, the largest food service provider to private prisons.[182] In the 1990s, CoreCivic (then Corrections Corporation of America) cochaired ALEC's Criminal Justice Task Force, which was renamed the Public Safety & Elections Task Force in 2009 before being disbanded in 2012.[183] The task force was not only responsible for shaping and promoting the model legislation that would become SB 1070—Pearce brought a draft of the bill to a 2009 ALEC meeting in Washington, DC—but also the so-called Stand Your Ground law that was used in Florida to justify the death of Trayvon Martin, and a model "Voter ID" bill, the basis for some of the country's most restrictive voting laws.[184] In January 2010, when Pearce introduced his legislation in the Arizona statehouse, thirty-six cosponsors signed onto the bill almost immediately—two-thirds of whom had either been in attendance at the ALEC meeting in December or were members of the group.[185] Over the next six months, thirty of them received donations from prison lobbyists or prison companies. Four days after it hit her desk, Governor Jan Brewer, whose spokesman and campaign manager were both also prison lobbyists, signed the bill.[186]

Referred to by civil rights groups and migrant justice activists as the "Show Me Your Papers" law, SB 1070 codified and formalized discrimination against Latinx people and Hispanics—or anyone else who police might "reasonably suspect" was in the United States without authorization. In 2012, the Supreme Court struck down much of the law, but left in place the provision allowing (but not requiring) law enforcement officers to ask about suspects' immigration status.[187] "Kobach's long game may have had less to do with creating legal precedent than it did with sowing social discord," the *New Yorker's* Jonathan Blitzer suggested when the Kansan's name was being floated for a position in the Trump administration. As local anti-immigrant proposals have sprouted in cities, towns, and states across the country, conditions for immigrants in those places deteriorate, even if the laws themselves never come to pass, are overturned, or are basically unenforceable. "This was how self-deportation was supposed to become a reality—if you put immigrants in the center of a raging populist debate at every level of state and local government, life got ugly for them," Blitzer wrote.[188]

Over the years, Kobach's legal efforts brought him into contact with many local reactionaries. Among them was Lou Barletta, who as mayor of Hazleton, Pennsylvania, pushed legislation that would legalize discrimination against Latinx people, ostensibly motivated by the May 2006 shooting death of twenty-nine-year-old Derek Kichline.[189] (Charges against two undocumented men in the case were ultimately dropped.)[190] In 2007, Barletta brought in Kobach to write the ordinances, which not only suspended business licenses of employers who hired undocumented immigrants but criminalized the renting of apartments to the undocumented, and to defend those ordinances in court when civil rights organizations sued the city. A federal judge struck down the laws not long after they were passed, and in 2010 an appeals court upheld the ruling.[191] Nevertheless, Barletta went on to spend eight years in Congress as a member of the House of Representatives, becoming one of the first Republican lawmakers to endorse Donald Trump during his bid for the party's candidacy.[192] He was rewarded with a spot on the executive committee of Trump's presidential transition team, and the president himself stumped for Barletta during his failed Senate bid in 2019.[193]

While he is no longer in Congress, Barletta remains on FAIR's board of advisers. At least as much as its former employees and political allies working in the Trump administration, the people sitting on FAIR's board of advisers and its board of directors, as well as on the CIS board of directors, show how deeply integrated in the conservative establishment these institutions were even before Trump was elected president. While their particular political agenda may have been marginal—or selectively deployed by party leadership—the social composition of this group reveals not only the basis for why they believe what they do about immigration but also how they were so well positioned to pursue their collective agenda when the chance came.

FAIR's board of directors includes Duane Austin, a retired army colonel who worked in communications for the Federal Communications Commission and the Immigration and Naturalization Service; James Dorcy, a thirty-year veteran of the Department of Justice and INS, who spent fourteen years in the border patrol and was elected president of the National Border Patrol Union; Randy Pullen, a former chairman of the Arizona Republican Party; and Frank Morris Sr., former executive director of the Congressional Black Caucus Foundation. Morris is also a founding board member of CIS. He sits on that board with Harry Soyster, a retired Army general and former director of the Defense Intelligence Agency; Jan Ting, a former assistant commissioner at INS; Daniel Vara, who worked as a senior legal counsel at INS, DOJ, ICE, and DHS; and Kent Lundgren, cofounder and past chairman of the National Association of Former Border Patrol Officers.[194] Peter Nunez, chairman of the CIS board, is a former US attorney for California's southern district.

The co-chair of FAIR's board of advisers, Brian Bilbray, was at one time chairman of the House Immigration Reform Caucus. Between stints in Congress, he worked as a lobbyist for FAIR. Former Reagan administration official Bay Buchanan, a one-time CIS board member, is the sister of Pat Buchanan, and managed his three presidential campaigns. She was also a senior adviser on Mitt Romney's 2012 presidential campaign. Scott McConnell, who cofounded the *American Conservative* magazine with Pat Buchanan and Taki Theodoracopulos, also sits on the FAIR advisory board, while running the Neil A. McConnell Foundation, which has donated to CIS.[195] John Philip Sousa IV, John Philip Sousa's birtherism-promoting great-grandson, is also an advisory board member. Further intellectual heft is brought by Carol Iannone, a member of the CIS board of directors, who is the editor at large of *Academic Questions*, a journal published by the Richard Scaife–funded nonprofit National Association of Scholars (on whose board of advisers longtime Tanton associate Richard Lamm sits), and is a regular contributor to *American Greatness*, a blog run by the Center for American Greatness.

The Southern Poverty Law Center has traced several members of FAIR's network to have ties to hate groups (other than FAIR itself, that is). Paul Nachman, a member of FAIR's board of advisers, is a prolific contributor to Peter Brimelow's VDARE.com, a viciously white nationalist website.[196] He has also distinguished himself as the largest individual donor to the campaign against an Oregon referendum on making driver's licenses available to undocumented people.[197] Nachman, who lives in Montana, once wrote a letter to the editor of the *Billings Gazette* warning that "the flood of immigrants drives wages and living conditions in our central cities toward those of the Third World," and that "illegal aliens bring us fearsome diseases such as tuberculosis (new, drug-resistant strains)."[198] K. C. McAlpin, who sits on the board of directors of ProEnglish (formerly English Language Advocates), and Don Feder, communications director for the World Congress of Families (WCF), both sit on FAIR's board of advisers. ProEnglish and the WCF are both SPLC-designated hate groups.

Nachman is not the only VDARE contributor on the advisory board—so too is its cochair, Don Collins, who is also chairman of FAIR's board of directors.[199] His wife, Sarah Epstein, is on the board of directors as well. She also sits on the board of the International Services Assistance Fund (ISAF), which Collins founded. ISAF has received funding from the Weeden Foundation, endowed by Frank Weeden, to promote quinacrine—a controversial, non-surgical form of female sterilization.[200] Frank's son Alan sits on FAIR's board of advisers; Alan's son Don is executive director of the Weeden Foundation, as well as treasurer of NumbersUSA.[201]

Immigration Skeptics

Long a fixture on Fox News, CIS fellows and staff members were cited more and more frequently in establishment liberal media after Trump took office, providing pseudo-empirical, social scientific-sounding justifications for the administration's latest anti-immigration moves. In an analysis of immigration coverage in the *Washington Post*, the *New York Times*, the *Los Angeles Times*, and *USA Today* between 2014 and 2018, researchers at Define American and the MIT Center for Civic Media found that "over 90 percent of the time that CIS was mentioned, it was without contextual information as to the nature of the group or its ties to the Trump administration."[202] The *nature of the group*, of course, was that it was an influential (and well-funded) node in a national network of nativist think tanks and nonprofits, with former staffers placed throughout various federal agencies and, in Stephen

Miller, a powerful ally in the White House.

In November 2019, the SPLC published a series of investigative reports based on a tranche of nine hundred emails shared with reporter Michael Edison Hayden by Katie McHugh, a former editor at *Breitbart News* who renounced the so-called alt-right after her sojourn through it.[203] The emails revealed just how fluent Miller, senior adviser for policy to Trump, is in white nationalist discourse—dropping casual *Camp of the Saints* references and links to VDARE.com and *American Renaissance* while using CIS's pseudo-scientific research to back up his ideology. Above all, they showed where someone like Miller got his ideas, how his thinking was shaped and how he tried to shape that of others, and how far he was willing to go to make his political vision a reality.

At the time the leaked emails were sent, Miller was working for Jeff Sessions, then a senator from Alabama. They revealed that Miller pushed Breitbart to cover various CIS "studies" and promoted the work of specific CIS authors. Among them was Jason Richwine, an immigration restrictionist who was forced out of the Heritage Foundation in 2013 after the discovery that his dissertation argued "the prediction that new Hispanic immigrants will have low-IQ children and grandchildren is difficult to argue against."[204] Since then, CIS saw fit to publish dozens of reports and blog posts by Richwine, who also remained a contributing writer at the *National Review*. Miller, the emails show, was a big fan of both Richwine and his dissertation adviser, George Borjas—himself a former CIS board member. Miller cited their research as he worked to shape the way the publication wrote about immigrants and immigration. His entreaties to McHugh were sprinkled with tactical flattery. "Elites can't allow the people to see that their condition is not the product of events beyond their control, but the product of policy they foisted onto them," Miller wrote. "They want people to feel helpless, retreat into their enclaves, and detach. Our job is to show people they can still control their destiny. Knowledge is the first step." Later that day, he added: "Btw—Bannon was praising your work on this to me again."[205]

This trove of emails presented a problem for CIS because its function within the wider network of nativist organizations in the United States was to present itself as non-ideological, rigorous, and studied. CIS "avoids making harsh, dispositional attributions about the immigrants themselves, placing the focus instead on protecting popular American institutions, public services, and national goals," sociologists Joshua Woods, Jason Manning, and Jacob Matz wrote in a 2015 paper on the organization's "impression management" tactics. Rather than engaging in populist demagoguery, CIS "depersonalizes its claims against immigrants by attributing them not to people or even analysts, but rather to scientific facts," they argue, suggesting "that 'data' lead inevitably to conclusions about the negative effects of immigration."[206]

When someone took those conclusions to their logical, violent endpoint, CIS executive director Mark Krikorian could only shrug. "If you have a guy who is going to be angry about immigration, have a killer offering reasons for shooting up immigrants, how could he not use reasons that have already been articulated by legitimate sources?" he said after the massacre in El Paso. "There's only so many concerns about immigration," he said. "Of course he's going to articulate reasons that already have been spelled out in great detail by immigration skeptics. I don't know how you avoid that."[207] What's more, Woods, Manning, and Matz found, CIS made no mention of Tanton—without whom it would not exist—in any public-facing documents until a 2009 SPLC report revealed the extent of Tanton's ties to white nationalists, eugenicists, and anti-Semites. At first, Krikorian and his associates attempted to deflect, accusing the SPLC of waging a smear campaign and infringing upon the think tank's right to free speech. Before long, however, Jerry Kammer, a fellow at CIS, would publish a lengthy and contemplative piece about the controversy, admitting that Tanton was "one of several individuals who were instrumental in starting the Center for Immigration Studies."[208]

While left-wing Democrats like Alexandria Ocasio-Cortez and Ilhan Omar responded to the SPLC investigation with calls for Miller to resign, the White House replied by calling the SPLC "an utterly discredited, long-debunked far-left smear organization . . . beneath public discussion."[209] Even more insidiously, Trump administration staffers began telling reporters on background that criticism of Miller, who is Jewish, was anti-Semitic.[210] One fascinating deatil was that a statement from *Breitbart News* to the SPLC regarding the report on Stephen Miller's emails to its staff specifically addressed his admiration for *The Camp of the Saints* in language that echoes Kammer's deflections of nearly ten years prior. "No one in our senior management has read the book, 'Camp of the Saints,' but we take *The New York Times* at their word that it is a 'cautionary tale,' and the *National Review* at theirs that 'the central issue of the novel is not race but culture and political principles,'" the Breitbart spokesperson said. In 2009, Kammer had contrasted the SPLC's condemnation of the book with the praise found in outlets like the *Daily Telegraph* and the *Atlantic*.[211]

The point here is not to dwell on the influence of this particular book, but to draw out the significance of the response from organizations like Breitbart and CIS under pressure: *How can a book that the* Atlantic *wrote about be racist? Also, we haven't read it.* When the far right sidesteps criticism by pointing out that the liberal establishment shares their views—or at least finds them worthy of serious, "objective" analysis—they are not making things up; on the contrary, they are offering us a way to see American politics much more clearly. After all, long before it published David Frum's concentration camp apologia "If Liberals Won't Enforce Borders, Fascists Will," the *Atlantic* published Robert Kaplan's 1994 essay "The Coming Anarchy," about how global inequality, a despoiled environment, and mass migration would remake the world.[212]

The Kaplan essay triggered a wave of fear and anxiety among lawmakers and bureaucrats, which, as Todd Miller has noted, the Clinton administration would channel into further securitization of both US climate and immigration policy. "Shortly after it was published, the undersecretary of state, Tim Wirth, faxed a copy of the article to every US embassy across the globe. President Bill

Clinton lauded Kaplan and Thomas Homer-Dixon, the environmental conflict scholar whom Kaplan featured in the article, as 'the
beacons for a new sensitivity to environmental security,'" Miller
writes in *Storming the Wall: Climate Change, Migration, and Homeland Security*. "The U.S. government created a senior post for Global Environmental Affairs and an environmental program, because
'it was critical to its defense mission.' In 1994, Secretary of State
Madeleine Albright said, 'We believe that environmental degradation is not simply an irritation but a real threat to our national
security.'"[213] As it turns out, Tanton was also a fan of Kaplan's work.
"Those who hope for a dissolution of national borders should draw
us a picture of how such a world might look. My view closely par-
allels that of Robert Kaplan who sees a breakdown of civil society,"
he wrote in *Social Contract*, the white nationalist journal he funded,
shortly after "The Coming Anarchy" was published. "Without a
nation-state to look after their interests, will people transfer their
loyalty up to some form of world government or down toward their
own racial, ethnic, religious, linguistic, tribal, or other group? This
latter seems the more likely as we look around the world today."[214]

All We Lack Is a King to Advise

Throughout the 1980s, Tanton organized several meetings that
would bring together members of the Republican Party establishment and some Democrats with representatives of the nativist
far right—politicians, writers, activists, and academics. The first of
these meetings were held at Governor Richard Lamm's mansion in
Colorado. "In an attempt to move the immigration issue, it seems
worthwhile to assemble some of the sages of the realm, to get their
advice on how to proceed," Tanton wrote in a memo.[215] "We hope
the Laurel Foundation can underwrite these useful sessions." (The
Laurel Foundation, which Cordelia Scaife May established in 1951,
is now a division of the Colcom Foundation.)[216] Tanton referred
to the participants in these sessions collectively as the "WITAN,"
based on the Old English word *Witenagemot*: "Garrett Hardin

suggested the nickname of WITAN for the group, an abbreviation for Witenagemot, an ancient Anglo-Saxon council called to advise the English King on administrative and judicial matters. All we lack is a king to advise!"[217]

The sessions were held at least once a year, sometimes twice. Between them, Tanton would solicit thoughts, feedback, and commentary from attendees, seeking out a consensus position among a group that included participants as varied as labor economist Vernon Briggs, who organized with César Chávez, and Jared Taylor. "There's a real leadership quality in a man who can bring together so many different points of view to work together towards a common goal," Taylor said.[218] In 1988, as several states were about to take up ballot initiatives on making English their official language, one of Tanton's memos was leaked to the *Arizona Republic*.[219] In it, he posed a number of questions that he would later try to frame as thought experiments, rather than evidence of his own beliefs. In any case, they revealed an intense anxiety among the WITAN about the effect of mass migration across the US-Mexico border, lightly coded as cultural but self-evidently racial. "Will Latin American migrants bring with them the tradition of the *mordida* (bribe), the lack of involvement in public affairs, etc.? What in fact are the characteristics of Latin American culture, versus that of the United States?" Tanton asked.

Tanton would later elaborate on this in one of his oral self-histories. "I think there is such a thing as an American culture, however difficult it may be to define," he mused. "For instance, the United States is the most philanthropic society on the face of the earth, and most of the work that FAIR and our opponents do is supported by philanthropy. Few, if any, other cultures have developed the idea of public philanthropy as strongly as we have here." It is not so surprising that Tanton would identify the beneficence of US capitalists as the country's defining characteristic, given how reliant he was upon them. "I have an average mind, but as I look back in on myself, and try to be objective, one thing I have been is very, very persistent," he reflected in the same oral history. "If one hangs in there over a long period of time, it's amazing what can be achieved, especially if the opposition is not as persistent." Tanton's individual persistence was at its root made possible by the greater persistence of wealth across generations in the United States, coming to fruition in the hundreds of millions of dollars that Cordelia May left to the Colcom Foundation when she died. What endures is not any individual or personality but capital and institutions. Tanton's best political skill was not his analysis or his rhetoric but his ability to flatter wealthy racists. He was not a great theoretician, leader, or organizer but an adroit servant of capitalists' self-interest. This is how the capitalist class exerts power—not by engaging in democratic politics but by creating a bulwark against it.

Even if Tanton recognized this dynamic, what he failed to appreciate (or chose to ignore) is that the very idea of public philanthropy as it is practiced in the United States is wholly the creation of the wealthy industrialists and corporate scions seeking ways to consolidate and protect their money over time. While the practice of establishing private family trusts and foundations, and of spending copious amounts of money on ostensibly philanthropic (though in fact political) causes, is now commonplace among the capitalist class, it was not always so. The first of these institutions, the Rockefeller Foundation, was formed in 1913. A century later, there were over 100,000 private foundations in the United States, controlling over $800 billion.[220] "The tax code turned many extraordinarily wealthy families, intent upon preserving their fortunes, into major forces in America's civic sector," Jane Mayer writes in *Dark Money*. "In order to shelter themselves from taxes, they were required to invent a public philanthropic role."[221] Upon their father's death, May and her brother, Richard Mellon Scaife, were the beneficiaries of two charitable trusts of $50 million each, structured such that, after twenty years of donating all net income from the trusts to nonprofit charities, the siblings would receive their $50 million principals. Their mother did the same in 1961, setting up a pair of $25 million trusts, and again in 1963, setting up another $100 million in trusts for her grandchildren. In a secret memoir, obtained by Mayer, Mellon Scaife gloated, "Isn't it grand how tax law gets written?"[222]

It was the most reactionary, most chauvinistic elements of the ruling class that Tanton served, whose fears and anxieties were articulated in the WITAN. Their concerns were not limited to the number of migrants making the journey to the United States but also the long-term consequences, across the generations. "Can *homo contraceptivus* compete with *homo progenitiva* if borders aren't controlled? Or is advice to limit ones [*sic*] family simply advice to move over and let someone else with greater reproductive powers occupy the space?" Tanton wrote in the leaked memo. "Perhaps this is the first instance in which those with their pants up are going to get caught by those with their pants down!" And then, perhaps most forebodingly, Tanton asked: "As Whites see their power and control over their lives declining, will they simply go quietly into the night? Or will there be an explosion?"[223]

Following the leak of the "*mordida*" memo to the *Arizona Republic*, Tanton's liberal and moderate allies fled. Respected news anchor Walter Cronkite, who'd sat on the advisory board of U.S. English, the Tanton group pushing the English-only referenda, resigned.[224] Linda Chavez, a former official in the Reagan administration who'd been hired to lead US English, also resigned. Warren Buffett, who'd provided FAIR with financial support, withdrew his funding.[225] Tanton distanced himself publicly from the campaign, resigning as chairman of US English.[226] In the end, however, the proposal to ban the Arizona state government from offering Spanish-language services passed by 12,000 votes out of 1.1 million.[227]

Subsequently, Tanton sought to repair the damage, addressing high-ranking members of his network. "Part of my job as board member or chairman of these groups was looking ahead, hopefully far enough to see over the horizon. To help myself and others in this task, I instituted in 1984 a set of biannual 'think tank' meetings," he wrote. "The WITAN meets informally and off the record, to enable free-ranging discussions in which people can take such provocative, ridiculous or absurd positions as would best stimulate discussion and thinking." Ultimately, he remained defiant: "Despite objections to the casual language of the first draft of my memo, the issues it addresses still remain. They are central to our nation's future, as indeed they are to many other nations around the globe which face similar problems across tribal, racial, ethnic, linguistic, and religious lines. Shall we bury our heads in the sand, or try to deal with them?"

To that end, a few months later, in January 1989, Tanton would write another memo, addressed to members of the "WITAN Defense Committee," outlining his fundamental political principles—and, by extension, the network's. Some of these are platitudes: "I hold to the metaphor of the melting pot, not of the salad bowl." Some are more insidious: "A common language is an important part of an infrastructure of a modern society, just as is a common set of weights and measures, or a common currency," and "Americans, as well as immigrants, have their own distinctive culture, however difficult of definition it may be." Some veer into the realm of racist conspiracy theory: "The loss of lands by Mexico to the United States in 1836 and 1848 is still intensely felt by a small but important group of activists. These feelings are largely confined to persons of Mexican origin, as it was Mexico that suffered the loss," he wrote. "Such memories can last for generations, as innumerable situations around the world will attest. Without ever expecting to put these feelings completely behind us, we must focus on our current problems and present situation and try to move forward from here. There is good reason for the concept of a statute of limitations in the law. At some point, one must move on."[228]

This last is an allusion to the *reconquista*—the view, held by some Chicanx nationalists that Mexicans and Mexican Americans should seize territory annexed by or ceded to the United States in the nineteenth century. The prevalence of this view is frequently overstated by nativists and white nationalists—and is sometimes even adopted by them—as part of what Leo Chavez calls the "Latino Threat Narrative." In a 2004 article on "The Hispanic Challenge" for *Foreign Affairs* magazine, Samuel Huntington, the political scientist famous for his theory of the "clash of civilizations," wrote, "Demographically, socially, and culturally, the *reconquista* (re-conquest) of the Southwest United States by Mexican immigrants is well underway."[229] In 2006, Jim Gilchrist, the founder of the Minuteman Project, a media-savvy border militia, dedicated two chapters in his book *Minutemen: The Battle to Secure America's Borders* to "The Trojan Horse Invasion" and "The *Reconquista* Movement: Mexico's Plan for the American Southwest."[230] Gilchrist cowrote his book with Jerome R. Corsi, who would go on to spread the conspiracy theory, popularized by Donald Trump, that President Barack Obama was not a citizen of the United States. In 2017, Corsi was hired by the website InfoWars as its DC bureau chief, and was later subpoenaed as part of the Mueller Special Counsel investigation.[231]

According to Chavez, all these fears are linked. "In the Latino Threat Narrative, Latina fertility is represented as a threat to the nation, and Latinas and their children are a key component of the reconquest hypothesis," he writes in *The Latino Threat: Constructing Immigrants, Citizens, and the Nation.* "Issues range from population explosions to birthright citizenship, but at the core of the politics of reproduction are representations of the 'hot' Latina and her 'out-of-control' fertility. Latinas are represented as locked into a cultural tradition and Catholic religious doctrine that renders them slaves to childbearing. Through such representations, Latinas are integrated into a stratified system in which their reproduction is feared rather than valued. Their very bodies symbolize key aspects of the Latino Threat Narrative. Not surprisingly, the politics of reproduction does not stop at Latinas' bodies but also focuses on their children."[232]

As it happens, Tanton was a fan of Huntington's, and corresponded with him in 1997 about precisely this issue. "The people who have been the carriers of Western Civilization are well on the way toward resigning their commission to carry the culture into the future. When this decline in numbers is coupled with an aging of the core population, which means fewer bellicose young males willing to defend the home territory, and with an ideology that such defense is somehow morally illegitimate, it begins to look as if the chances of Western Civilization passing into the history books are very good indeed. The core peoples are being replaced by more reproductively vigorous stock from abroad," Tanton wrote in a letter to the political scientist. "Put otherwise: Can the West hold its territory, given the population decline foreordained by subreplacement fertility (a decline in both absolute numbers and proportionally), and given the aging of its populace, combined with the migration pressure of burgeoning third world populations, whose relocation is now encouraged by mass communications and facilitated by modern transportation? Frankly, I doubt it, especially if we consider all the other forms of lassitude with which we are beset."[233]

While for the most part couched in figurative or metaphorical language, Tanton would occasionally indulge directly in the discourse of "invasion." In a 1995 letter to the historian William H. McNeill, using his "just asking questions" rhetorical mode, Tanton wrote: "With a historian's perspective spanning several centuries, rather than the businessman's focus on just the next quarter, might current net immigration of about 900,000 legals and 300,000 illegals a year be construed as an invasion? Does it make a difference if those coming duplicate (as under the 1924 immigration laws) or differ from (as under the 1965 Act) the characteristics of the host society?"[234] Or, as he put it in a 1994 essay on "The End of the Migration Epoch" for the *Social Contract*, "If the developed countries cannot or will not control their borders, they will quickly be swamped in the remaining years of this century or the opening ones of the next." Mass migration of the poor from the Global South "would be viewed everywhere as an invasion."[235]

Cordelia May was even less circumspect: "When we hear of immigrants, we instinctively think of Mexicans because they are the most numerous and given the greatest press coverage," she wrote in a letter to her cousin.[236] "In truth, we are being invaded on all fronts. Filipinos are pouring into Hawaii. Almost anyone from the Caribbean countries and Eastern South America who can make it to the Virgin Islands or Puerto Rico can eventually make it to the U.S. mainland. Orientals and Indians come across the long stretches of unmanned border we share with Canada." The greatest threat that these immigrants pose, May argued, was not in bringing with them "criminal habits, radical political thought, exotic diseases, neighborhood disruption, etc." Rather, she wrote, "They breed like hamsters."

Tanton and May were far from the first to use such language. Nor was such language limited to private correspondence. As noted by Justin Akers Chacón and Mike Davis in *No One Is Illegal*, in the 1970s, Leonard Chapman, then the INS commissioner, was warning of "a vast and silent invasion of illegal aliens," while former CIA director William Colby spoke of "the most obvious threat" facing the United States: "There are going to be 120 million Mexicans by the turn of the century. . . . [The border patrol] will not have enough bullets to stop them."[237]

Tanton focused his anxiety on borders, barriers, and boundaries. "I believe we live in a world of limits and boundaries, however difficult it may be to exactly pinpoint these. I am not a cornucopian," he wrote in his WITAN Defense Committee memo. "I believe that the concepts of national borders and national sovereignty are both legitimate and essential, and that to hold this position is neither nationalistic nor xenophobic."[238] In the introduction to a book of essays on "The Ethics of Immigration Policy," published by Social Contract Press, Tanton offered a succinct account of what, in his view, borders are for. "Borders are a fixed line of geography and sovereignty. Borders also connote ethical values," he wrote.[239] "Borders uphold the living wage" and "connote stewardship," he continued. They also "connote freedom" and "facilitate self-determination." Without borders, Tanton argues, we will have more people; more people means more laws, as well as a greater array of conflicting and contradictory experiences and perspectives, which he believed would threaten the stability of civic institutions.

Taken on their own, such statements are commensurate with the long-standing tradition of liberal discourse on the nation-state. However, Tanton goes further, figuring the body politic as a literal body and immigration as a disease or poison. "My physician's perspective tells me that prevention is better than cure, and that early diagnosis, with concomitant mild treatment, is better than late diagnosis, when more drastic measures will be required, if indeed a cure can be effected at all. Diagnosis is more difficult and tenuous in the early stages of any malady, when the clues are less certain. Indeed, diagnosis is often more intuitive than strictly scientific. We should aim to 'diagnose and treat' any language (or social) problem in its early stages when there will, however, be differences among astute people of good will as to whether there are sufficient signs and symptoms to warrant diagnosis," he wrote in the 1989 memo. "If a diagnosis is agreed upon, the next question is whether outside treatment is needed, or whether the natural healing powers of the body politic can be relied upon! If treatment is needed, how mild, moderate, or drastic should the measures be?"[240]

Using the language of medicine, Tanton is able to discuss immigration as a political problem without addressing the implications of the political solutions he appears to suggest. In another 1995 letter to McNeill, Tanton wrote that "membranes, boundaries, and borders" are "fundamental" to understanding life. "An organism can die from two different forms of border defect: when the borders break down altogether, as when Jimmy Jones had his followers take cyanide some years ago. That poisoned their enzyme systems and destroyed the electrical potentials between the inside and outside of the cell, and caused death," he wrote. "The other form is sclerosis of a boundary, such as we see in diseases like scleroderma. There, very few things can get either into or out of the cell. The individual either dies from a lack of nutrition, or from the accumulation of waste."

Tanton continued, "So, biologically at least, what is needed is semipermeable membranes, ones that let in the good and useful, and keep out or discharge the bad. Perhaps that's the mental model that can be used in thinking about immigration policy."[241] Two years later, Tanton followed up with McNeill: "What we need is a courageous depiction of what the world might be like if we fail in the enterprise of maintaining borders, whether biological (medflies; hoof and mouth disease; malaria; etc.) or political. A future without national borders looks chaotic to me. There would be great damage to the natural world, to the wilderness and natural areas that are so important to me personally. Preservation, difficult as it is, is one of the motivating forces in my life."[242]

Under Siege

In 1988, Tanton suggested to his friend Leon Bouvier, a professor of sociology, consultant to the Select Commission on Immigration and Refugee Policy, and author of *Peaceful Invasions: Immigration and Changing America*, that white politicians should form a caucus to advance the interests of white people.[243] "I've been thinking a bit about the coming 'majority of minorities' in California, and elsewhere," he wrote. "By the year 2020, when everyone has become a minority, presumably the formation of a White political caucus, along with all the others, will be reasonable and justified. The fascinating question is at what points between now and 2020, will this become reasonable?"[244]

Apparently, it was not long before such a formation seemed reasonable—to Tanton, in any case. In 1993, he shared a prospectus for a new organization, the League for European-American Defense, Education, and Research, with his friend and collaborator Otis Graham, who helped found both FAIR and CIS. "In the United States," Tanton wrote, "there is currently no socially acceptable umbrella organization to which persons of European ancestry can belong to defend and promote their common interests. Absent such an organization in a highly organized society, European-Americans will continue to see their history rewritten, their character and accomplishments denigrated, and their faults magnified."[245]

However, it was not only the "character and accomplishments" of European Americans that was being denigrated, but "Western civilization" itself. "Western traditions and culture are under siege, particularly in academe, but also by some other interest groups which see running down Western Civilization as being to their advantage. In contrast, we see our heritage," he wrote, "as something to be proud of and worthy of support. We wish to reaffirm our attachment to Western Civilization."

And then, in as measured and succinct a formulation as one will find anywhere on the fascist and white supremacist far right, Tanton comes out and says what he really meant all along: "Demography is destiny. Projections by the U.S. Census Bureau show that midway into the next century, the current European-American majority will become a minority. In many areas of the country, this change will come sooner, or is already upon us. This is unacceptable; we decline to bequeath to our children minority status in their own land."

Chapter Three

THINK BOOTS, NOT BOOKS

But 'tis strange:
And oftentimes, to win us to our harm,
The instruments of darkness tell us truths,
Win us with honest trifles, to betray's
In deepest consequence.

—*Macbeth,* Act I, Scene 3

In March 2018, on a cold, gray Monday afternoon in East Lansing, Michigan, about five hundred militant antifascists gathered in a parking lot with the intention of stopping Richard Spencer, the high-profile white nationalist, from speaking at Michigan State University (MSU). Spencer had not been asked to come by any student group on campus, but had instead invited himself. After the university denied his initial request to speak, Spencer sued. As part of the settlement agreement, the white nationalist agreed to speak in the middle of spring break at the MSU Pavilion for Agriculture and Livestock Education, a venue more than a mile away from the main campus.

There in the parking lot, the antifascists kept each other warm, dancing to hardcore and hip-hop played over a wheeled-in guitar amplifier, sharing cigarettes and news from elsewhere. Some people talked about the leaked chat logs of the fascist gang Patriot Front, members of which were on their way to campus that very moment, while others discussed the arraignment of one of Spencer's followers the night before on weapons charges after he pulled a gun on protesters. About forty police officers in riot gear huddled at the far end of the parking lot. Bike cops on patrol swirled like gusts of wind.

Now and then, organizers affiliated with Stop Spencer at MSU, a coalition that included the MSU chapter of the Young Democratic Socialists of America, Redneck Revolt, and Solidarity and Defense (SnD), addressed the crowd. "Spencer is here because the MSU administration allows him to be here," Bob Day, a graying local anarchist and member of SnD's Detroit chapter, said. "Spencer is here because the state of Michigan pays all these fucking cops to come out and protect the fascists. The same MSU administration and the same government that's allowing Spencer to come in here and is allowing fascists to attack our communities and is protecting those fascists, that's the same administration and the same government that protected Larry Nassar for twenty years, and refused to listen when women said they'd been attacked," referring to the former USA Gymnastics national team doctor and osteopathic physician at the university who sexually abused hundreds of women and girls.[1]

The day wore on and the light grew harsher. Rumors surged that police planned to deploy a water cannon in the freezing weather. Armored trucks idled at the edge of our attention. A caravan of cars and trucks crawled up the road, stopping at a police barricade before inching back. Minutes later, a band of about fifty fascists came marching in a tight column led by Traditionalist Worker Party (TWP) chairman Matthew Heimbach—his tall, heavyset figure recognizable from a distance—and Spencer's right-hand man, Gregory Conte. They were here.

There was a brief pause as the column came up against the amassed antifascists, who swarmed past the barricades to meet it. Scuffles broke out, and then a brawl. Spencer was nowhere to be seen.

Just feet away from me, Conte was in handcuffs, screaming at the police. I asked him for a statement. Where was Spencer? Was this all going according to plan? "Their plan, maybe," he said with a glare. It was unclear whether he was talking about the antifascists or TWP.

Police intervened sporadically, mostly at the periphery, pulling combatants off those who fell. Intermittently, a line of bike cops cut across the melee, which would reconverge elsewhere. I don't know how many times this process repeated itself. In moments, I felt the whole affair take the shape of an absurd pantomime—a symptom of having watched this exact scene play out in person, on YouTube, and on Twitter so many times over the past few years. The sense of absurdity receded as soon as I looked into the fascists' eyes, dull with hatred and fear, or listened to the racial slurs and *Sieg heils* spat like poison, or when I saw, amid it all, Matthew Heimbach's delighted smile. You could read in it all the smug arrogance of a man who believes himself untouchable, his victory inevitable, and history his judge—only faltering once, at the sight of some brass knuckles heading his way.

Look White, Act White, Fight White

When I first met Heimbach, at the Republican National Convention in Cleveland in 2016, he told me he was there to meet with Trump delegates, though of course Heimbach declined to tell me which ones. He never fails to mention his connections to the European fascist parties, several of which have recently established themselves in parliamentary bodies. In *Everything You Love Will Burn*, journalist Vegas Tenold reveals that Heimbach was trained at the Leadership Institute, a think tank in Washington, DC, with alumni including Mitch McConnell, Grover Norquist, and James O'Keefe; that Heimbach is hugely influenced by Pat Buchanan; and that, on Inauguration Day 2017, Heimbach was introduced to a room full of GOP strategists and state legislators at the Capitol Hill Club, directly across from the Capitol building. "A few years ago the GOP wouldn't be able to even sit in the same room as you, but things have changed, and now we need each other," Heimbach's Republican contact told him, as quoted by Tenold. "This is a big day."[2]

Over the past several years, groups across the far-right spectrum, whether those growing out of the internet-based men's rights or Gamergate movements or the lingering remnants of the neo-Nazi movement of the 1980s and 1990s—the base of what would come to call itself the "alt-right"—began publicly and semi-publicly organizing under their own distinct banners. Political and ideological differences aside, groups like the Proud Boys, the TWP (now defunct), Identity Evropa (now called the American Identity Movement), and Patriot Front (a specific organization, not to be confused with the older, decentralized Patriot movement) aggressively and self-consciously sought to stake out their own aesthetics, uniforms, rituals, and identity markers. In the process of trying to build an autonomous political force, amid the factional jostling and the infighting, the "alt-right" has revealed its true nature. It is a constantly shifting network of personality cults, animated by misogyny, racism, and a libidinal desire for violence. Its politics are articulated by the reclusive but influential Andrew Anglin of the *Daily Stormer*: "The core concept of the movement, upon which all else is based, is that Whites are undergoing an extermination, via mass immigration into White countries which was enabled by a corrosive liberal ideology of White self-hatred, and that the Jews are at the center of this agenda."[3]

Attempts to bring the various feuding factions together have almost all failed, often thanks not only to antifascist resistance but also to the American investment in the mythology of individual heroes. Relatively cohesive fascist groups are frequently undermined by the actions of beefy Trump loyalists showing up in hockey pads and Greek warrior helms (echoing the neoclassical imagery Identity Evropa uses in allusion to the shared glorious past of Western civilization) to fight black-clad demonstrators. Or they're undermined by their own putative members.[4] "The key to understanding people who have become drawn into the Alt-American universe is the role that the hero myth plays in framing their worldview," journalist David Neiwert writes in *Alt-America*. "Dedicated Patriots and white nationalists, just like the hate criminals they inspire, genuinely envision themselves as heroes. They are saving the country, or perhaps the white race, or perhaps just their local community. And so anything, anything they do in that act of defense is excusable, even laudable."[5]

The most high-profile attempt to build a durable coalition of the street-fighting far right, staged on the streets of Charlottesville, Virginia, in August 2017, ended in death and disaster. Ostensibly, the occasion was to rally in defense of a monument to the Confederate general Robert E. Lee, the removal of which left-wing activists in the city had long demanded. In reality, the occasion was to organize a show of force: to descend upon a diverse, broadly liberal city and intimidate or fight anyone who dared oppose their presence. Hundreds came to what was actually the third of a series of escalating rallies that had begun earlier in the year, representing the spectrum of the insurgent far right: from the disciplined members of the TWP to the hard-drinking Proud Boys, from the grizzled neo-Confederates of the League of the South and the graying militia members of the Patriot movement to young, button-down-wearing members of Identity Evropa and screen-addled *Daily Stormer* readers. Together, on the night of August 11, led by Spencer, an alumnus of the University of Virginia, they marched onto the school's campus, bearing torches and chanting "Blood and soil!" and "Jews will not replace us!"[6] The next day, thousands of antifascists met them in the city's streets. For hours, local and state police allowed rolling brawls.[7] Dozens were injured, some critically. After the governor declared a state of emergency and riot police forced the two sides apart, the bulk of the far right's forces retreated from the city's downtown area. Bloodied and exhausted, the leftists who'd repelled them cheered, celebrating in the streets where just moments before they'd been fighting for their lives.[8] It was at this point that James Alex Fields Jr., who'd marched with a group called Vanguard America, rammed his silver Dodge Challenger into the crowd, injuring dozens and killing thirty-two-year-old Heather Heyer.[9]

In the months that followed, the spheres of influence on the "alt-right" cohered as much as they were ever going to, coalescing around a handful of relatively high-profile individuals: Heimbach, Spencer, and Anglin. For as long as he has been an open white supremacist, Heimbach has worked to bring into alignment the various sects, cults, cells, vanity think tanks, and independent publishers that compose the far right. In *Everything You Love Will Burn*, Vegas Tenold describes Heimbach's thinking: "Particular ideological quirks and doctrines were detrimental to building a movement. Rather than focus on what separated them—skinheads and KKK would never agree on most things, nor could the alt-right have played a part in the election of Donald Trump if they were specifically neo-Nazi or specifically anything else—they highlighted their common struggles and upcoming battles."[10]

Heimbach is himself both erudite and vicious, a street-fighting racist and anti-Semite who grounds his bloodthirsty vision for the world in the global history and scholarship of fascism. In mid-2016, he and Jeff Schoep of the National Socialist Movement (NSM) formed the Nationalist Front, a coalition of white supremacist political organizations that included older groups like the neo-Confederate League of the South and newer, internet-inflected formations like the fascist Vanguard America, united in the singular purpose of creating a white ethno-state.

"When I got involved with the white nationalist movement," Heimbach told me, "everything was constitutions, American flags, and bald eagles. It was about who could be the most American and what are states' rights. George Wallace tried this in '68 and '72. This has been tried and it doesn't work. It always unravels, because it's insincere."[11]

"If someone is willing to put down the American flag, put down the Constitution, put aside democracy and republican forms of government, and instead work towards the creation of an independent nation that's built for us and by us, I don't think they're going to be sidelined too much by an odal rune," he said, referring to the NSM's use of a symbol adopted from a proto-Germanic runic alphabet and imbued with mystical meaning as its insignia. It was inspired by the insignia of the SS Race and Settlement Main Office, which policed the brutal paramilitary Nazi organization to ensure its racial purity.

The TWP blended racial and ethnic resentment with an economic appeal—the promise of a white, national socialist utopia, cut from the decaying fabric of the United States. "We don't want to save America," Heimbach said. "We simply want to opt out." In other words, TWP wanted to secede and create an apartheid state with strong social welfare programs for white people.

Jews, for example, would not be permitted to participate in his white utopia. ("They have their own country.") Gay people or transgender people would not be welcome either, incompatible as they would be with traditional gender roles and sexual identities. ("We could provide compassionate care for them to be able to overcome this antisocial behavior.") People of color would be denied citizenship, obviously, as would some white people. ("Those that are engaged in antisocial behaviors or are diametrically opposed to our nation-state would not be welcomed within that. Following traditional European norms for behavior and fitting in as part of the people's community is necessary.") Heimbach offered a motto for his envisioned ethno-state: "Look white, act white, fight white," alluding to an essay by David Lane, most famous for coining the white supremacist slogan known as the Fourteen Words: "We must secure the existence of our people and a future for white children."[12]

The march onto Michigan State's campus and Spencer's speech there was supposed to bring the rival factions together after the recriminations that inevitably followed Unite the Right and the lawsuits filed in its wake. For a short time, it seemed as though it might have—or at least, it seemed as though they might have been able to tell themselves that it had. Spencer was able to give his speech, though only after having slunk into the livestock pavilion where the university administration had stuck him, through a back door, escorted by police. In the week that followed, both leftists and the "alt-right" claimed the day as a victory. Members of the Stop Spencer at MSU coalition pointed to the fact that they turned away the bulk of the "alt-right" fighting force, while the fascists gleefully shared photographs of themselves beating on leftists. An AltRight.com contributor who writes under the pseudonym "Ahab" celebrated the day's events, wherein the mannered bigotry of the National Policy Institute (NPI) was united with the street-fighting bloodlust of the TWP, as a momentous occasion in the development of American fascism—a tentative alliance between the "boots" and "suits," as the journalist Tenold puts it. "It is that moment of class unity, for the sake of our common race and identity as white Americans, and our determination to exist and not be wiped out from the pages of history, which is the deepest mission and purpose of the Alt-Right," Ahab wrote in a disquisition on an image of a tattooed TWP organizer, Johan Carollo, pulling NPI's clean-cut director of operations, Greg Conte, away from a police line and out of harm's way. "Not class conflict, which is organized and inflamed by the neoliberal enemy, but class reconciliation based on kindred blood and kindred destiny."[13]

A week after the battle of East Lansing, however, Heimbach foreclosed the possibility of any further reconciliation, and indeed any future the TWP might have had: He was arrested on domestic violence charges after allegedly assaulting his wife, Brooke Heimbach, and her step-father, Matt Parrott, who until this incident served as a party spokesman and strategist.[14] According to the police report, Matt Heimbach, and Parrott's wife, Jessica, who is not Brooke's mother, had been carrying on a three-month-long affair, which Parrott and his step-daughter, Heimbach's wife Brooke, had recently discovered. Within days, Parrott would withdraw from organizing. "I'm done. I'm out," he told a researcher from the Southern Poverty Law Center. "Matt Parrott is out of the game. Y'all have a nice life."[15]

Heimbach's arrest not only threatened the future of his own party but the movement as a whole. Anglin, having built a significant platform in the *Daily Stormer* and a following among its readership, had failed to make good use of both, shrinking away from confrontation or even significant material gain. "We are in no way ready to 'take to the streets,'" he wrote after Heimbach's arrest. "We have absolutely zero infrastructure. We do not have a huge pool of reliable, competent people. We do not have any stable organizations. . . . We do not really have much of anything at all." Even before Heimbach's arrest, Spencer himself balked at the prospect of more violent confrontations between the "alt-right" and an increasingly militant left. In a video statement he recorded bleary-eyed, he whined that law enforcement was not sufficiently clamping down on antifascist protesters—an absurd claim, given that nine undercover police officers were sent to surveil the protesters in East Lansing, thirteen of whom would face felony charges.[16]

"Antifa is winning to the extent that they are willing to go further than anyone else, they will do things—violence, intimidation, general nastiness—that no one else is willing to do," Spencer said, worrying that he won't be able to do any more public events. He may have been able to give his speech, but was run out of town the next day after walking into a coffee shop full of militant leftists. "The fact is that until this situation changes we're up a creek without a paddle," Spencer concluded.[17]

No Mere Echo

While the tendency of the "alt-right" to descend into infighting is partly attributable to the personalities that have strived for influence and leadership over the movement, it is also the result of several historical shifts the US far right has gone through in its orientation since the war in Vietnam. The most significant of these is the development—and, for a time, dominance—of a revolutionary tendency in the white power movement, creating a division between what antifascist researcher Matthew N. Lyons describes as "oppositional and system-loyal rightists." The "oppositional rightists" have made "a sharp break with the right's traditional role as defender of the established order, as one of the forces helping economic and political elites to maintain control."[18] In other words, between the war in Vietnam and the election of Donald Trump, factions within the US far right that sought out direct confrontation with the federal government exerted far more influence than they ever had before. According to the historian Kathleen Belew, this change was brought about in large part by the war in Vietnam itself, which provided white supremacist activists with a narrative of violence and betrayal they could use to mobilize traumatized veterans. "The white power movement that emerged from the Vietnam era shared some common attributes with earlier racist movements in the United States, but it was no mere echo," she argues. "Unlike previous iterations of the Ku Klux Klan and white supremacist vigilantism, the white power movement did not claim to serve the state. Instead, white power made the state its target, declaring war against the federal government in 1983."[19]

The war was one of attrition, shaped by white nationalist and Vietnam veteran Louis Beam's ideology of "leaderless resistance," which encouraged decentralized organizational structures and autonomous action. "Even if federal agents and a few journalists were aware of the white power movement, the mainstream public continued to see most white power violence as the work of errant madmen," Belew writes. "The phrase 'lone wolf,' previously used to describe criminals acting alone, was employed increasingly in the 1980s and 1990s to describe white power activists. This played into the movement's aim to prevent anyone from putting together a cohesive account of the group's actions. The white power movement's cell structure stymied the kind of public understanding that had worked to limit the civil rights–era Klan, as well as the political will that could have brought about real change in how the judicial system responded to violent white power activism."[20]

While individual acts of "white power activism" appeared to the wider public to occur in a vacuum, Belew argues that the use of violence against Vietnamese refugees in Texas, labor organizers in North Carolina, and migrants on the US-Mexico border worked as a mechanism to reconcile disputes between tendencies on the far right: "As violence came to the fore of the movement, distinctions among white power factions melted away. Klansman and neo-Nazis set aside their differences, which had been articulated largely by World War II veterans with strong anti-Nazi feelings, as the Vietnam War became their dominant shared frame. White men prepared for a war against communists, blacks, and other enemies."[21]

Crucially, this "revolutionary turn" paralleled a similar one in mainstream conservatism: the corporate antistatism of Ronald Reagan's administration and the triumph of neoliberalism. Conflict over immigration in California, where Reagan was governor from 1967 to 1975, shaped the future president's understanding of border politics. Vigilante violence against migrants exploded during his administration, as San Diego's growing suburbs encroached upon the surrounding farmland. A young David Duke organized Ku Klux Klan (KKK) members into a "border watch" at the San Ysidro port of entry; Vietnam veterans set traps, imitating those designed by the Viet Cong, throughout the Tijuana estuary, which they referred to as "Little 'Nam."[22] In his 1980 presidential campaign, Reagan, "as the standard bearer of an ascendant New Right," played upon the same resentment and radicalization of these veterans that white supremacist groups did, according to the historian Greg Grandin. "Once he was in office, Reagan's re-escalation of the Cold War allowed him to contain the radicalization, preventing it from spilling over (too much) into domestic politics," Grandin writes in *The End of the Myth: From the Frontier to the Border Wall in the Mind of America*. But even as Reagan directed militancy into the anticommunist campaigns in Central America, which he called "our southern frontier," support for the Contras in Nicaragua and the death squads of El Salvador, Guatemala, and Honduras created millions of new refugees, many of whom made their way to the United States. "As they came over the border," Grandin notes, "they inflamed the same constituencies that Reagan had mobilized to wage the wars that had turned them into refugees in the first place."[23]

The white power movement flourished under the material and political conditions wrought by the Reagan, George H. W. Bush, and Clinton presidencies. "The [Patriot] movement's anti-globalism is in large part a reaction to the growing power of multinational corporations and financial institutions, expansion of international free trade agreements, and movement of industry from the U.S. to the Global South and of workers from the Global South to the United States," Lyons writes of the '90s militia movement.[24] "While old-style supremacist views played a significant role within the [Patriot] movement, its driving force was a vision of unregulated property rights, an ideology of capitalist individualism. This is a doctrine of social inequality based not on biology or God, but on market competition. Ironically, this ideology is closely related to the free trade neoliberalism of the global corporate elites who the Patriot movement sees as its main enemy."[25]

Thus, the far right found itself in a contradictory position: ostensibly antistatist, even as it won control of the federal government. "From the 1970s forward, ideas of individualism and freedom broke loose from their Cold War counterbalances of social responsibility, morality, and justice," Belew suggests. "As Reagan said in his inaugural address about the nation's ongoing economic problems, 'In this present crisis, government is not the solution to our problem; government is the problem.'"[26] Such contradictions are pervasive throughout far right politics in general, and are especially acute in fascist politics in particular.

At the beginning of the twenty-first century, however, the "oppositional" politics that had come to dominate the militias of the Patriot movement began to shift once again. The terror attacks of September 11, 2001, reconfigured the relationship of the far right to the state by introducing a new enemy: political Islam. As the United States embarked on wars in Afghanistan and Iraq as part of the global "war on terror," the far right began to reconsolidate its support for the state. During the Bush years, militias prowled the borderlands, drawing upon the tradition of "organized private violence, usually in tandem with local law enforcement" that "shaped the racial caste-system of California agriculture, defeated radical labor movements like the IWW, and kept the New Deal out of the state's farm counties," as Justin Akers Chacón and Mike

Davis observe in *No One Is Illegal*. Writing amid the upsurge of migrant organizing that culminated in the May Day mobilizations of 2006, when nearly a million people participated in the "Day Without an Immigrant" strike, Chacón and Davis argued that the nativist vigilante was not a thing of the past, "but a pathological type currently undergoing dramatic post-millennial revival as many Anglo-Californians panic in the face of demographic decline and the perceived erosion of their racial privileges."[27]

Between 2004 and 2009, Jim Gilchrist's Minuteman Project grew to be an influential force, with approximately twelve thousand members at its peak, amid a burgeoning anti-immigrant movement, ostensibly motivated by a desire to "secure" the US-Mexico border through a combination of direct action and media pressure.[28] Indeed, Gilchrist and Minuteman Project cofounder Chris Simcox, who was arrested in 2013 for sexually abusing three girls, including his daughter, would prove adroit manipulators of the mass media. "Gilchrist's emphasis on nationwide awareness underscored the public-spectacle nature of the Minuteman Project and its goal of disciplining the federal government," Leo Chavez argues in *The Latino Threat*.[29]

According to its website, the purpose of the Minuteman Project was not only "to bring national awareness to the decades-long disregard of effective U.S. immigration law enforcement," but also "to protest the refusal of the Congress and the President to protect our borders from illegal immigrants who have not had their criminal background checks by, and through, the U.S. embassy in their home country, thereby creating an imminent danger to all Americans, and creating the dilution of U.S. citizens' voting rights by foreign nationals." Chavez observes that in focusing on the rights and privileges of citizenship, which they understood to be threatened by immigration, the Minutemen were articulating a much broader political vision than simply "protecting" the border.[30]

Still, the border militias was riven with splits and rifts. In 2009, Shawna Forde and two other members of the group she founded, Minuteman American Defense, were charged with the murder of Raul "Junior" Flores and his nine-year-old daughter Brisenia. Flores was rumored to have had a stash of money and drugs hidden in the house, and Forde recruited a group of men to help her steal it. Among them was Jason Bush, who claimed ties to the white supremacist Aryan Nations and would later be charged in the murder of another Latino man twelve years prior.[31] Together, they broke into Flores's home, posing as federal agents before shooting him and his daughter in the head. They shot Gina Gonzalez, Flores's wife, too, but she survived, playing dead on the floor and watching her daughter be executed. "He's all out of bullets by then because he used them on me and Junior," Gonzalez testified of Bush, who'd killed Flores before turning to Brisenia. "He stands here and he loads the gun right in front of her."

"I just hear her telling him, 'Please don't shoot me, please don't shoot me,'" Gonzalez testified. But he did, shooting the nine-year-old girl in the head, killing her instantly.

Thus did the vigilante ethos shift from the farms and valleys of the Southwest to the suburbs, the terror of "illegal" immigrants supplanting that of international communism.[32] Dwindling enthusiasm for the militias and the Patriot movement in the later Bush years would be transformed by the election of Barack Obama and the development of the Tea Party, which according to Neiwert became "a wholesale conduit for a revival of the Patriot movement and its militias."[33] This convergence proved fertile ideological ground: the radical libertarianism of the astroturfed Tea Partiers intermingling with the chauvinism of the militias and their white nationalist allies, bonded together with Alex Jones conspiracy theories, Fox News propaganda, and, as Grandin puts it, "an almost psychotropic hatred of Barack Obama."[34] Many members of these groups would become staunch Donald Trump supporters, and while the GOP has traditionally sought to maintain a certain plausible deniability in its relationship to the fringe right, the Trump campaign threw open Pandora's box, welcoming the avowed white supremacists, anti-Semites, and fascists who stalked the ideological fringes of US politics.

"We Want to Foster Civil Discussion"

In the early years of the Trump administration, the more hard-core elements of the so-called alt-right—the neo-Nazis, the neo-Confederate KKK affiliates, the esoteric fascists and white separatists—sneered at the Proud Boys, led by *Vice* cofounder Gavin McInnes, as insufficiently radical: a drinking club for libertarian nationalists who liked to get into fights. For all their differences, white nationalist leaders like Anglin, Heimbach, and Spencer could agree on one thing (other than the necessity of a white ethno-state), which was that the Proud Boys, with their silly initiation rituals and campy aesthetic, were ridiculous. But as Anglin drowned under lawsuits, Heimbach discredited himself as a movement leader, and Spencer's star in the media began to fade, the Proud Boys began to grow into something very few—either in the movement or outside it—had expected: a hegemonic force on the far right able to appeal to mainstream conservatives while also making space for white nationalists and fascists.

Anglin, Heimbach, and Spencer built their movements hoping to not just influence the Republican Party but wield political power in their own right. Heimbach strove to build an explicitly revolutionary organization in his TWP, flirting with insurrectionists like Atomwaffen Division.[35] The more genteel Spencer's Continental-style "identitarianism" provided a kind of intellectual framework, drawing from thinkers such as Julius Evola and Alain de Benoist to advocate for a white ethno-state.[36] But after anti-fascist activist Heather Heyer's murder in Charlottesville and the mobilizations across the country that followed, the influence of this revolutionary tendency (while still active) began to wane.[37] Less vigorously ideological groups like the Proud Boys observed Spencer and Heimbach's mistakes. Their more moderate strategies have, in turn, won them greater appeal by foregrounding ultranationalism and a vicious opposition to left-wing politics.

Insofar as the Proud Boys were closer to the mainstream of American conservatism than Anglin, Heimbach, and Spencer, this also made them even more dangerous. Anglin and Spencer weren't getting invited to speak at GOP events, but McInnes was; members of the openly terroristic Atomwaffen Division weren't running security for Republican candidates for Senate, but the Proud Boys were. They received sympathetic media coverage from Fox News, while actively recruiting new members not only from the "alt-right" but from racist skinhead groupings across the country. A violently reactionary subculture that had in recent years remained relatively self-contained, racist skinheads ("boneheads" to leftist skinheads), under the leadership of charismatic demagogues like McInnes on the East Coast and Joey Gibson of Patriot Prayer on the West Coast, was spilling into the streets of America's most liberal urban centers. It's no accident that the Proud Boys chosen uniform features black and yellow Fred Perry shirts—a favored skinhead brand.

The Proud Boys had been courting members of New York City's skinhead scene for a long time; McInnes himself has a white power tattoo associated with the neo-Nazi punk band Skrewdriver, whose merch he has been photographed wearing.[38] At least three of those who participated in a 2018 gang assault in New York were affiliated with racist skinhead crews long known to local antifascist and antiracist organizers, like the 211 Bootboys, a far-right skinhead gang based mostly in New York City, and Battalion 49, a predominantly Latino neo-Nazi skinhead gang.[39] Early in 2017, McInnes had defended the 211 Bootboys after some of its members attacked two brothers on the Lower East Side when they noticed an antifascist sticker on one of their phones.[40]

Pragmatically sidestepping the question of race, the Proud Boys make their proto-fascist appeal in the language of patriotic individualism: pro-America, pro-capitalism, and pro-Trump. Around the country, the group has replicated this approach, appealing primarily to people's class interests—as small business owners, for example, or as the children of families who fled socialist revolutions—as well as traditionalist gender politics, temporarily deferring the white nationalist project in the interest of swelling their ranks. When a white nationalist podcaster tried to get McInnes to say the Fourteen Words, a totemic phrase on the far right, he did not refuse outright but replaced "white" with "Western."[41]

This strategy has allowed the Proud Boys to gain entry into the Republican mainstream, as when McInnes was invited to speak at the Metropolitan Republican Club in upper Manhattan, the state GOP's home base in New York City, in October 2018. McInnes, Metropolitan Republican Club executive committee chair Ian Reilly told *Gothamist*, "is part of the right," comparing him to previous guests Tucker Carlson and Ann Coulter. "We promote people and ideas of all kinds from the right." Reilly continued. "We would never invite anyone who would incite violence."[42] Except this is exactly what they had done. McInnes had come to the Metropolitan Club to celebrate the fifty-eighth anniversary of the assassination of Inejiro Asanuma, leader of the Japan Socialist Party, by the ultranationalist Otoya Yamaguchi, on live television in 1960—an "inspiring moment," McInnes wrote on Instagram, which he reenacted with his employee (and fellow Proud Boy) Ryan Katsu Rivera. "Never let evil take root," McInnes later told his audience, referencing a meme involving Yamaguchi popular with fascists online.[43]

Outside, antifascist and antiracist demonstrators gathered to protest McInnes's appearance. As guests began to leave, a score of Proud Boys hung back and prepared for the coming brawl. "One Proud Boy cracked his knuckles behind me," reporter Carol Schaeffer wrote. "'I'm ready to swing right,' he said. 'Nobody better fuck with us tonight.'"[44] Scuffles and beatings followed, as they seemed to wherever the Proud Boys went. A dozen members of the proto-fascist gang stomped demonstrators who'd been caught in the open. "Do you feel brave now, faggot?" one yelled, according to documentary filmmaker Sandi Bachom and photojournalist Shay Horse, who witnessed the attack. Bachom's footage shows one assailant screaming "Faggot!" as he kicks someone curled up on the ground.[45] Other video includes a Proud Boy bragging, "Dude, I had one of their fucking heads, and I was just fucking smashing it in the pavement!" "That son of a bitch!" he continues. "He was a fucking foreigner." One of his friends yells the Proud Boys slogan: "Fuck around, find out!"[46]

Later, in an email to journalist Christopher Mathias, McInnes celebrated his compatriots, writing that one of their victims "stole a Proud Boys MAGA hat and was immediately tuned up," referring to the red "Make America Great Again" hats sold by the Trump campaign.[47] Throughout all of this, the NYPD declined to arrest a single one of the violent reactionaries roaming the city's streets. They did find time, however, to arrest three antiracist protesters.[48] "I have a lot of support in the NYPD and I very much appreciate that, the boys in blue," McInnes claimed in a podcast released soon after.[49]

At a press conference a few days later, New York City councilman Donovan Richards, chair of the Public Safety Committee, described the NYPD's response—and specifically that of the Strategic Response Group tasked with keeping the peace—as "inept, incompetent, and derelict in their duties." The police subsequently released photographs of three persons of interest—all of whom were immediately identified as Proud Boy affiliates by antifascists, their addresses and contact information posted online—and announced that they intended to arrest twelve people altogether, including nine Proud Boys.[50] New York Republicans, meanwhile, doubled down on their decision to welcome McInnes into the fold. "We want to foster civil discussion, but never endorse violence," Metropolitan Club officials said in a statement. "Gavin's talk on Friday night, while at times was politically incorrect and a bit edgy, was certainly not inciting violence."[51]

Little wonder that after the beatings, the Proud Boys unveiled a new war cry, celebrating Supreme Court Justice Brett Kavanaugh, another man who dominated his victims with impunity before retreating to the warm embrace of the GOP: "I like beer!"[52]

"There Are No White Supremacists Here"

This dynamic has played out time and again in liberal cities across the country, though nowhere more frequently or more violently than in Portland, Oregon, where every few months hundreds of ultranationalists, white supremacists, Trump supporters, and other reactionaries come looking for a fight under the guise of protecting free speech, protesting domestic terrorism, or, as was the case in the summer of 2018, campaigning for Joey Gibson, a notorious provocateur running for US Senate in Washington on a platform of Trump-inflected libertarianism backed by the street-fighting Proud Boys.

As riot cops fired flash-bang grenades at protesters, injuring at least two people and arresting four, Gibson led his supporters back and forth along the banks of the Willamette River, escorted by another contingent of armored police.[53] I asked him how his Senate campaign was going. "You're looking at it," Gibson replied. His crew was visibly frustrated: the sheer size of the counterprotest on this day had foiled their plans to march through the city, so cheering on the police would have to suffice. "USA! USA!" they chanted. A bagpipe on the antifascist side droned, accompanied by a snare drum and the intermittent booms of police ordnance.

For all the digital chaos wrought by the "alt-right," open-air political violence remains the most immediate way for figures like Gibson to radicalize and recruit young men into his burgeoning movement. Videos and GIFs of Proud Boys beating up antifa, in turn, become digital propaganda. And, to broaden their appeal, groups sympathetic or adjacent to the "alt-right" are ditching racist rhetoric for more mainstream political language. This allows them to appeal to a bigger group of middle-class Americans who wouldn't dream of joining the KKK but harbor deep resentment toward immigrants and approve of other parts of Trump's agenda.

They're also shifting from ethnically defined nationalism to a version that purports to target outsiders on the basis of their legal status, not the color of their skin. Significantly, the presence of people of color in this coalition allows Gibson and the Proud Boys to "prove" that they aren't racists at all. Gibson, for starters, identifies as Japanese American.[54] His deputy, Tusitala "Tiny" Toese, is American Samoan.[55] Both vehemently deny that either Patriot Prayer or the Proud Boys are white-supremacist organizations, though local antifascist and antiracist organizers have identified neo-Nazis and other organized white supremacists in their midst.[56]

This vexing situation is the product of a broader contradiction, expounded upon by Daniel Martinez HoSang and Joseph E. Lowndes in *Producers, Parasites, Patriots: Race and the New Right-Wing Politics of Precarity*. "While racial subordination is an enduring feature of U.S. political history, it continually changes in response to shifting social and political conditions, interests, and structures," HoSang and Lowndes write. "In this moment, racial disparities along many indices are at historically high levels even as racial inequality is everywhere denounced. At the same time, elite powers and interests from across the political spectrum have become invested in a symbolic form of multiculturalism and racial pluralism that was unimaginable a half century ago." By way of example, they point to Kay Coles James, the Black woman who is president of the influential conservative Heritage Foundation, or a book recently published by the libertarian Cato Institute that describes Frederick Douglass, the radical abolitionist, as a "self-made man" who eschewed "the interests of the collective." As HoSang and Lowndes put it, "These new modes of incorporation have done nothing to redistribute resources and power more equitably, but they have permitted elites to deploy narratives of racial uplift and difference in ways that legitimate their own authority."[57]

Outside the world of the Heritage Foundation and Cato Institute, this contradiction is even more stark. One masked Proud Boy I met at a rally in Portland, ostensibly there to support Gibson's Senate bid, told me that anyone in their crew who expressed racist views would be stomped out—but "not literally," the Proud Boy, who said his name was John, quickly added. But for every masked John, there's a "General Graybeard"—an older man who led members of the "Freedom Crew" and "Hiwaymen," two patriot groups from Arkansas, wearing tactical gear and bearing shields emblazoned with the Confederate battle flag. He explained that the imagery was about honoring the South's history. "We fly it so people know it's not racist," the self-proclaimed general explained. "It's about heritage. It's about the Constitution." When I asked masked John whether he accepted this explanation, he shrugged. "I gotta take that at face value," he said.

"We're here to support the Constitution of the United States of America, which is all about free speech and being able to assemble peaceably and talking about the things that we support," a Patriot Prayer supporter also named John told me. What exactly those things are proved more difficult to articulate: "It's a call to action. We believe this is a time to act in our country." The second John kept gesturing at Lionel, a recent immigrant from Cameroon, to prove his point. "I believe in peace, freedom, and everything else," Lionel concurred. "Me, I'm Black. We are also human. We have our voice too." While the majority of uniformed and armored Proud Boys and Patriot Prayer affiliates that day were white, a half dozen people of color (including Lionel) were happy to explain what brought them to the Freedom March. One forty-year-old Black man named James had been supporting Joey Gibson for about a year. "I admire people like Martin Luther King when they fought for civil rights and stuff like that," he said. "These guys, they look like they're taking a stand, and I want to take a stand with them."

"There are no white supremacists here," James, who is a scrap-metal worker, told me. "I get nothing but love. White supremacists don't let minorities into their ranks." And about those Confederate battle flags? "All it represents is the Southern states. It's just a flag." The left, he continued, was being paid by George Soros to spread disinformation. "I'm not getting paid for this. I'm here of my own accord. We're a diverse group," he continued. "We're all Trump supporters."

Leonor Ferris, a seventy-five-year-old immigrant from Colombia, laughed when I asked about the accusations of white supremacists in Patriot Prayer's midst. "I'm a Latina! How could they be white supremacists?" she asked. "Look at my skin! I'm not a white supremacist. I love people. I love every color." Ferris was not the only one to treat my questions as preposterous. "Do I look like a white supremacist to you?" Will Johnson, the Black owner of a small vid-

eography business, asked me. "I got dreadlocks!" Johnson went on
to claim that Hillary Clinton is so pro-abortion that she supports
killing newborn children. "The liberal media—which is against this
country, which is the enemy of the American people—they covered
it up, because they don't want people to know," he said.

Enrique Tarrio, president of the Proud Boys' Miami chapter,
told me that he has visited with members in Portland, Austin, New
York, North Carolina, and Georgia. "Not once have I dealt with
race," he said. "We have a diversity problem in our Proud Boys
Miami chapter—which is that we don't have enough white people." His Instagram account, which includes group photos of the
chapter's mostly white members, suggested otherwise.[58] "I've got
my 'Made in Mexico' tattoo. I go out with these people. There's no
white supremacists here. They just want to protect their country,"
Fernando, a thirty-six-year-old Mexican immigrant who works in
a warehouse, told me. "Every country should have people like that.
If you fight for your country, no matter which country it is, the
world will be strong. There will be no suppression, no corruption."

Patriot Prayer's ultranationalism comes out most vigorously
when its supporters talk about immigration. "We do need a wall,"
Johnson, the Black videographer, said. "We have walls in our homes.
The elitists have walls around their neighborhoods—gated communities. But they don't want to do one for those of us who don't
have that." James echoed this sentiment: "You came here illegally,
you break the law, you gonna be punished." Several months later, an
ICE contractor working for Geo Group, the private prison and immigration detention company, posted bail for a Proud Boy charged
with felony and misdemeanor assault.[59]

Nearly everyone at Saturday's Freedom March seemed as worried about the threat of the rising left as they were about immigrants. "We don't want communists," Ferris told me. "I came here
legally and I don't want to see what happened to Venezuela." She
continued, "The only thing communism brings is poverty. They can't
even eat over there. They don't have nothing in Venezuela. I used to
go to Venezuela to go shopping—beautiful stores." Toese, Gibson's

deputy, and several others sported T-shirts reading "Pinochet Did Nothing Wrong," referring to the Chilean dictator under whose rule tens of thousands of socialists and other dissidents were murdered and tortured.[60] "Make Communists Afraid of Rotary Aircraft Again," read the back of the shirt. Pinochet's soldiers were notorious for throwing enemies of the regime out of helicopters. On one of the sleeves, in red, capital letters, was the acronym: RWDS, or Right Wing Death Squads. The Proud Boys sold these shirts to raise money through 1776.shop, their online store.[61]

According to the Cuban-American Tarrio, small-business values were what drew him to the Proud Boys in the first place. Most of the Miami chapter's members run their own companies, he told me, and one of the fraternity's primary tenets is Glorifying the Entrepreneur. "My family came from a communist country," Tarrio said. "The only way to true freedom is entrepreneurship." Then he invited me to follow him on Instagram, which featured a link to his company's website—and posts about killing communists.

In the end, there wasn't much violence that Saturday. A handful of skirmishes flared as groups of Patriot Prayer supporters and counterprotesters each made their way home; Gibson's followers politely thanked the police for their service while antifascists jeered as Proud Boys piled into the repurposed school buses that shuttled them back to their cars. "I run this city," Tarrio sneered at a heckling local. "We'll be back." He would later be named Florida state director of Latinos for Trump. The organization's events are promoted on the Trump reelection campaign's official website. As one Republican operative later said, "The Trump campaign is well aware of the organized participation of Proud Boys rallies merging into Trump events. They don't care. Staff are to treat it like a coalition they can't talk about."[62]

What is confounding about groups like the Proud Boys is also what gives them their potency: using extrajudicial means—brawling with antifascists, beating up passersby, harassing nonviolent civilians, and calling for undocumented people's heads to be smashed on concrete—toward manifestly counterrevolutionary ends.[63] "We even obey traffic laws!" I heard one Proud Boy joke as he and his crew waited to cross the road after a Portland rally.

From one perspective, an organization like the Proud Boys is dangerous because it functions as a "pipeline" to even more violent ideologies. In a survey conducted by the Southern Poverty Law Center of users on the Right Stuff forums, long a haven for online fascists and white nationalists, 15 percent of respondents mentioned Gavin McInnes as either an important influence on their political development or as useful in converting others. While the top two sources of far-right radicalization were the chaotic and anonymous /pol/ forum on 4chan and *American Renaissance*'s Jared Taylor, McInnes ranked fifth out of twenty-four—ahead even of Richard Spencer.[64]

But treating membership in the Proud Boys as a transitional phase to something worse risks ignoring the threat that the Proud Boys themselves pose, especially given that on certain issues, like gender and immigration, there is little to no daylight between the "alt-right" (or "racial nationalists") and the "alt-lite" (or "civic nationalists"). As historian Alexandra Minna Stern argues, "An Escherian stairwell built on the ideological affinities of anti-feminism, xenophobia, and racial othering connects the Proud Boys to the alt-right."[65] Likewise for HoSang and Lowndes, the "alt-lite" is not simply a "gateway drug," but "the liminal space in which white supremacy and multiculturalism interact."[66]

"U.S. politics has always simultaneously toggled back and forth between deep fantasies of racial hierarchy and stated commitments to universal ideals in a mutually supporting dynamic," they write. "Movement between these positions has always given cultural meaning and material benefits to whites even as it allows for hegemonic legitimacy in a multiracial society. On the contemporary far right, the potency of white supremacy fuels authoritarian, masculinist notions of national identity for a broader group."[67]

On an episode of the explicitly white nationalist *Daily Shoah*, a podcast in the Right Stuff network, for example, the hosts and Proud Boy guests agreed "every single person should be vetted to the most extreme standard" and that "mass immigration of any group" should never be allowed.[68] "These prejudices are anchored to a rigid dogma of innate biological differences and natural hierarchies, and a corollary belief that the sacrosanct order of Western society is being dismantled at a vertiginous pace, rushing toward several possible endpoints, all of them tragic for white men and European peoples," Stern writes. "From this vantage point, the future of 'white well-being' hinges on the (re)imposition of natural hierarchies and biological differences."[69]

Digital *Squadrismo*

The so-called "alt-right" was just one way that the shifting, protean white nationalist movement articulated itself—a temporarily useful branding mechanism, basically, to be discarded once it had served its purpose. As the influence of particular leaders waned, others took their place, bringing with them different organizational and strategic ideas. Likewise, participants in the movement responded to external factors differently at different times. While there are certain shared assumptions and values, the far right is not a monolith—disputes and disagreements are hashed out over time, revisited, reconsidered, doubled back on, repeated, explored. This is not to say that the emerging fascist movement is a democratic one, simply that it is contradictory and creative. With the collapse of the white nationalist street presence—in other words, its effort to establish itself as a mass formation somewhat autonomous from the Republican Party—the movement beat a retreat to the safe spaces where it might rebuild its strength: conservative institutions and the internet.

White power activists have been organizing in digital spaces since such forums were created. For example, Louis Beam, a KKK leader in Texas, created "Aryan Liberty Net" for the Aryan Nations, which the *New York Times* reported in 1985 described itself as "a pro-American, pro-White, anti-Communist network of true believers who serve the one and only God—Jesus, the Christ."[70] "In the late 1990s, the movement largely relocated into the online spaces it had begun to build more than a decade earlier. Continued movement activity unfolded mostly out of public view," historian Kathleen Belew writes in *Bring the War Home*. Dylann Roof, the white supremacist who in 2015 executed nine Black people—Clementa Pinckney, Cynthia Marie Graham Hurd, Susie Jackson, Ethel Lee Lance, Depayne Middleton-Doctor, Tywanza Sanders, Daniel Simmons, Sharonda Coleman-Singleton, and Myra Thompson—at the Emanuel African Methodist Episcopal Church in Charleston did so without ever being a member of an organized group or spending very much time offline with other militant racists. "Because of the Internet," Belew argues, "Roof never had to meet another activist to be radicalized by the white power movement, nor to count himself among its foot soldiers."[71]

Antifascist activists, journalists, and scholars have begun tracing the social networks that proliferate across Facebook, Twitter, YouTube, and other sites, showing just how closely intertwined the "mainstream" and the "extreme" really are. One group of researchers found that YouTube users who began commenting on videos produced by those associated with the so-called Intellectual Dark Web (IDW)—a group of reactionary academics, activists, and writers seeking to reinvigorate mainstream conservatism without explicitly appealing to ethnonationalism—often ended up engaging with "alt-light" and "alt-right" YouTubers. "We find that the commenting user bases for the three communities are increasingly similar, and, considering Alt-right channels as a proxy for extreme content, that a significant amount of commenting users systematically migrates from commenting exclusively on milder content to commenting on more extreme content," they wrote. "We argue that this finding comprises significant evidence that there has been, and there continues to be, user radicalization on YouTube, and our analyses of the activity of these communities is consistent with the theory that more extreme content 'piggybacked' on the surge in popularity of I.D.W. and Alt-lite content."[72]

Few researchers have done more to illuminate these connections than Rebecca Lewis, whose theory of the "Alternative Influence Network" (AIN) triggered something of a meltdown across the far-right internet, which she described as "a coherent discursive system," the apparent ideological variety of its members notwithstanding. "Increasingly, understanding the circulation of extremist political content does not just involve [looking at] fringe communities and anonymous actors," Lewis wrote in "Alternative Influence: Broadcasting the Reactionary Right on YouTube," a report on her work published by the nonprofit organization Data & Society. "Instead, it requires us to scrutinize polished, well-lit microcelebrities and the captivating videos that are easily available on the pages of the internet's most popular video platform."[73]

Just as the dawn of the internet was accompanied by a set of techno-utopian fantasies about what kinds of changes it might bring, social media, with its emphasis on distributed, decentralized user participation and the concurrent, somewhat contradictory emphasis on micro-celebrity, has also been accompanied by its own set of myths. Early on, it was easy to believe that social media might facilitate the spread of egalitarianism and provide a platform for otherwise marginalized voices. In fact, social media has reified racial and gender divides and encouraged the proliferation of what media historian Fred Turner refers to as "authoritarian individualism."[74] By building a participatory culture around themselves, popular personalities on YouTube are able to distinguish themselves from mainstream, corporate news, Lewis argues.

> These distinctions highlight the "authenticity" of YouTube culture and pit it against the presumed formality, inauthenticity, and distance of legacy news media in a way that reflects the broader hostility of influencer culture to mainstream media. These qualities take on a fundamentally political meaning when juxtaposed against the influencers' politicized critiques of the mainstream news media. In this context, authenticity cultivated through transparency moves beyond a stylistic choice and becomes an alternative to the presumed opacity and silencing mechanisms of a politicized news media. When influencers describe their broadcasting choices in detail, they are also implicitly (and at times explicitly) claiming to provide a calmer and more rational alternative to sensationalized and hyperbolic

news media. Through this juxtaposition, the style of micro-celebrity presentation becomes fundamentally aligned with the anti-progressive, reactionary politics the influencers promote.[75]

Lewis found extensive cross-promotion between libertarians, conservatives, and white nationalists, united by opposition to leftist or even left-liberal politics condensed in the figure of the "Social Justice Warrior" (or "SJW"), a caricature of progressive concerns.[76] "By connecting to and interacting with one another through YouTube videos, influencers with mainstream audiences lend their credibility to openly white nationalist and other extremist content creators. This is both driven by, and results in, a shared set of ideas, which in turn helps create the potential for radicalization," Lewis argues.[77] What is more, she writes, it creates the potential for a collective social identity, which "helps them build influence and attract audiences. Specifically, they signify an identity of both social underdogs and a hip counterculture—courting young audiences looking for a community with a level of rebellion."[78] She concludes, "While many in the AIN criticize and mock progressive social movements for what they see as a 'victim mentality,' they also simultaneously position themselves as the genuine victims in society."[79]

From the outside, it's hard to reconcile such contradictions. How can a community of white men organized around support for what they perceive to be traditional social values—a rigid racial and gender hierarchy founded on private property—understand themselves to be victims? In *Alt-America*, David Neiwert suggests that the structure of the community itself might offer some idea:

> Increasingly, many people, especially those employed in technology-driven fields, are employed in corporate bubbles, consigned to cubicles and disconnected work partnerships, or they work from home and network with other people through the Web. For their social lives, they turn increasingly to chat rooms, email listservs, and political and special-interest forums. As social media platforms such as Facebook and Twitter took off toward the latter part of the new century's first decade, this phenomenon

became not only widespread but profoundly consequential, because what happened in people's online lives began affecting them in the material world—even though that digitized version of reality was only, at best, a simulacrum of real human interaction. . . . This is part of why conversations on the Internet so frequently dissolve into misunderstanding and readily traded insults: the other person is only there as an abstraction. There is no exchange of body or facial language, none of the nuance of vocal expression, none of the physical presence to enforce the reality that this is a living, breathing person with whom you are conversing. Without these things, what's left, really, is a digitized, relatively crude version of conversation and human company: a pure exchange of information and little more. We can't read a person's intentions online the way we can in real life, and so obscure motives and agendas can become a breeding ground for anger and paranoia.[80]

What this produces, in the end, are phenomena like Gamergate (a controversy surrounding a campaign waged by racist and misogynist videogame consumers that *Deadspin*'s Kyle Wagner in 2014 had presciently identified as "the future of the culture wars"), men's rights activists (sexually frustrated young men who have convinced themselves that feminism has upended the natural order of things), and the "alt-right."[81] Pursued by hordes of disaffected white men who spend their lives consuming media that assure them that the world is still theirs (or, more precisely, that it will be again), we are witnessing the development of a kind of digital *squadrismo*—a twenty-first-century version of the semi-autonomous fascist bands that roamed the Italian countryside in the late 1910s and early 1920s, not directly under Mussolini's control but united in their identification with him. "This aggression and viciousness is fed by neoliberal valorization of libertarian freedom, by wounded, angry white maleness, and by nihilism's radical depression of conscience and social obligation," the political theorist Wendy Brown argues. "It is discursively organized by neoliberal assaults on the social and the political and by neoliberal legitimation of indifference to the predicament or fate of other humans, other species, or the planet." There is pleasure in causing others pain, Brown writes, in humiliating those one perceives to have usurped one's rightful place: "This is humanity without a project other than revenge."[82] Thus, the digital *squadristi* descending upon feminists, Black Lives Matter organizers, and left-wing journalists to ruin their lives, harassing them off the internet and out of their homes, trying to get them fired, overwhelming them with threats to their families—in some cases, doing so with physical violence.

Nice, Respectable People

If micro-celebrities on YouTube and reactionary media outlets like *Breitbart News* served as important nodes connecting the far right to the wider conservative movement, part of what made these digital networks so potent is that they overlapped with the institutions of conservatism. While Beltway institutions like the Institute for Humane Studies and the Leadership Institute, or even FAIR and CIS, disavowed white nationalism, the frequency with which such disavowals had to be made limited how seriously they should be taken.

Leaked chat logs from far right groups proved particularly useful in revealing where white nationalists and fascists align with the conservatism of the GOP and where they diverge. In spring 2019, for example, antifascists identified two young men active in the Koch network as members of Identity Evropa: Derek Magill, a former president of the University of Michigan chapter of Young Americans for Liberty (YAL) who spoke at an event hosted by the Institute for Humane Studies in 2017, and Alex Witoslawski, former Illinois state chair of YAL and a former regional field coordinator for the Leadership Institute.[83] According to the independent media collective Unicorn Riot, Witoslawski applied what he learned at the Leadership Institute to his organizing with Identity Evropa, for example hosting media training sessions for other members.[84] It was not long before antifascists identified another YAL officer, Richard Golgart Jr., as a member of Identity Evropa.[85]

Working with both undercover antifascist activists and disgruntled former white nationalists, Unicorn Riot was able to compile a huge, searchable database of chat logs from various alt-right, white nationalist, and fascist organizations, the members of which frequently communicated on a platform called Discord.[86] Reviewing these conversations, I found evidence of the affinity and respect some in the movement have for the institutions of the Tanton network. In June 2018, for example, FAIR asked its followers to call their representatives in Congress to tell them to vote against Speaker Ryan's so-called amnesty bill. "It contains an amnesty for more than 1.8 million illegal aliens!" FAIR wrote on Twitter. Identity Evropa member "Conway–OK" dropped a link to the tweet in the "Nice Respectable People Group" server. "Time to flood the Congressional phone lines again," he wrote.

Within minutes, half a dozen white nationalists had called their congresspeople. "Mine asked for my contact info and zip code to store with my call log information (summary of conversation I assume), so I left my information (name/callback number) in order to add legitimacy to my call and show that people are't [sic] afraid to stand by their opinions/beliefs on the issue," one user, who claimed to be a student at Vanderbilt University, wrote under a pseudonym, "Sam Southern–TN." As Unicorn Riot discovered, Sam Southern–TN's messages in other, less PR-conscious servers, include anti-Semitic bigotry like "I fucking despise jews in America . . ." and racist griping about witnessing a "young white guy out w his [n****r] wife and their mulatto child."[87]

In chat logs from another leaked server—this one associated with a YouTube channel run by the right-wing journalist Tim Pool—users fixated on comments that FAIR spokesman Ira Mehlman provided to Fox News for a story on migrant caravans. "Probably there are multiple parties involved, who have an interest in challenging the sovereign right of the United States to determine who can enter the country and under what circumstances," Mehlman said.[88]

"Underline this . . . 'who have an interesting [sic] in challenging the sovereign right of the United States,'" a user named

"Dusty Morgan" wrote. "Trump is justified to use the Military to build that border barrier. This is a direct challenge to United States Sovereignty."[89]

In October 2018, a user going by "Jacob" on the "Nice Respectable People Group," asked his fellow white nationalists whether any of them could put him up for the summer as he applied for jobs and internships in Washington, DC. "How hard do you guys think it would be to get an internship at FAIR?" Jacob asked. "I wonder if they're kind of like the Republican Party and love it when young people sign up."[90]

"FAIR? That doesn't sound like something a white male is getting into," another user, Asatru Artist, replied.

"Federation for American Immigration Reform," Jacob explained. "Anti-immigration organization."

"Sounds perfect for white men then!" the other user quipped.

Jacob seemed particularly interested in becoming a professional white nationalist. "How crazy of a pipe dream do you guys think it is to work full time in this movement? I'm still planning to finish my college degree but I'd way rather work in this than computer science," he asked in October 2018. "To clarify, it doesn't have to be explicit identitarianism. It could be working for Numbers USA or something."[91]

"It's not crazy but it's far from a wise career choice. It depends on what your skillset is," Patrick Casey, one of Identity Evropa's earliest core organizers, replied, using the alias "Reinhard Wolff."[92] "Trying to make a living doing content creation is pretty hard given the financial hurdles we face. But offering web design skills, for example, is something that will likely always be needed."

"You can work for Trump or a PAC," another user, "Logan," chimed in, using the acronym for a political action committee. "I think it's a better move for our guys. It isn't as hard as you may think."[93]

"Would it be unwise to try to get a NumbersUSA/FAIR/CIS tier job?" Jacob asked Casey.

"I'm not too familiar with those organizations, but I can tell you that they're better funded than we are! So there's definitely a chance," Casey advised.

The conversation came up again two months later. "Are there any think tanks/nonprofit orgs that would be a good place for people with our views? There aren't any identitarian think tanks, of course—we know what happened with NPI—but places where one could develop oneself," user "Alex Kolchak–NY" asked two months later.[94]

"Ya dude FAIR, NumbersUSA, CIS are the best options," Jacob replied. "I personally would go for FAIR. Seems to be most in line with our immediate goals. Some people might not like them since they're not wignats though." ("Wignat" is short for "wigger nationalism," far-right slang for white nationalism.) "The final boss battle would be securing an Open Society Foundation grant and just burning through all that dough publishing our stuff," the user "Kolchak" joked. Open Society Foundations was founded by George Soros, the billionaire philanthropist who features prominently in anti-Semitic conspiracy theories around the world. "Kolchak" would later be identified by New York City–based antifascists as Christopher Hodgman, a student at the University of Rochester, US Army Reserve signal support systems specialist, and US Army ROTC cadet.[95]

Across factions and servers, white nationalists and fascists expressed appreciation for the work done by the organizations composing the Tanton network. Special praise was reserved for how easy NumbersUSA made getting involved in anti-immigrant activism. "I'm not sure if everyone is aware of a great site. www.numbersusa.com," the user "RighteousIndignation" wrote in the Iron March forums. "Then you go to the action board where you can send faxes to your congressmen."[96] Founded in 2011 by a Russian nationalist, Iron March was a popular community among fascists and neo-Nazis—several violent groups emerged from connections made on the site, including Atomwaffen Division and Vanguard America.[97] It was shut down without explanation in November 2017. Two years later, antifascists obtained and posted the forum's underlying database, including users' email and IP addresses.[98] "If you are not a Numbers usa activist sign up to get notifications on bills, it allows us to fax and email with the click of a button," user Trumpster1899 wrote in another server that was associated with right-wing YouTube personality Nick Fuentes. "NumbersUSA has stopped so many amnesties in the past with this activism."[99]

"Can we have an environment channel? Immigration is destroying land and the massive sprawl," one Identity Evropa member wrote in another server. "A lot of good groups doing positive work and I feel this is a great way to work towards getting environmentalist back into no population growth." Another responded: "Avoid the Sierra club. The Nature Conservancy is great. In each State there are other groups geared to local issues etc. Numbersusa.com pushes the environment issue regarding immigration as well."[100]

It wasn't just FAIR and NumbersUSA, either—work produced by CIS proved useful for budding white nationalists looking to take a more rigorous approach to their nativism. "I tried using the Center for Immigration Studies on my sjw sister," Identity Evropa member "Isabella Locke-MT" wrote in December 2018, using the acronym for "social justice warrior." "She said it doesn't count because it's a right-wing think tank and biased."[101]

Reading recommendations began pouring in. "For immigration's economics, read George Borjas," the user "MPI–VA" wrote. "For immigration's cultural impacts, read Robert Putnam. For immigration's history, read Peter Brimelow. For current immigration politics, read Daniel Horowitz. For left-wing criticism of immigration, read Jefferson Cowie and Angela Nagle."[102] A month earlier, the ostensibly leftist Nagle had written an essay arguing "The Left Case against Open Borders," published in the Trumpist journal *American Affairs*.[103]

And of course, there was always Charles Murray's *Bell Curve*, which used evidence like the racial gap in IQ scores to argue for essentially eugenicist welfare reforms.[104] "Cringe and Broke: spray painting NS symbols in public," MPI–VA joked. ("NS" stands for "national socialist.") "Based and woke: spray painting the black white bell curve graph in public."[105] About twenty of the authors cited in Murray's book received funding from the

Pioneer Fund.[106]

Fascists who aspired to serve in government would have been well advised to seek out John Elliott, the longtime director of the Institute for Humane Studies journalism program. Elliott helped get Katie McHugh, the former *Breitbart News* editor who would ultimately renounce the far right, a job at the *Daily Caller*. "John essentially selected me to come to DC as part of the libertarian–alt-right pipeline," McHugh told *BuzzFeed News* reporter Rosie Gray, a characterization that Elliott denied. "I chose Katie to mentor as a libertarian, not as a member of the 'alt-right,'" he wrote in an email. "The 'alt-right' didn't exist in 2011, and I've had no connection with the 'alt-right' since it was invented. I tried to be a mentor and a friend to Katie for a decade, even as she went down some of the dark paths of those fringe groups. But her decision to go down those paths had nothing to do with me. I truly feel bad for her."[107]

In fact, as Hannah Gais would report for *Splinter*, Elliott was deeply embedded in Washington, DC's white nationalist underground, talking politics and organizing social events over an email list called the "Morning Hate." "The group began coalescing on October 13, 2015, when Elliott drew together a few former mentees via email to organize so-called 'hateups,' or in-person meetings to discuss racism," Gais reported. "That's when Elliott also rattled off the code words the thread used in its chats: 'Hawaiians' was a stand-in for 'Hebes,' an anti-Semitic slur referring to Jews; 'Alaskans' for 'N's' (the n-word); 'our good friend' for 'AH' (Adolf Hitler); and 'our good friend's son' for Trump."[108] An example: during the 2016 presidential campaign, Elliott wrote that Trump reminded him of "our friend" who made "no mistakes" from 1932 to 1934.

Somebody Else's Babies

In *Making Sense of the Alt-Right*, political scientist George Hawley traces how contemporary white nationalism both draws upon and reacts against tendencies within the American conservative movement, like the paleoconservatism of Pat Buchanan and the John Birch Society and the radical libertarianism of the Koch network, all of which are united in their opposition to social programs and state-sponsored efforts to ameliorate racial or gender inequality. Paleoconservatives, Hawley writes, were "more comfortable talking about issues like immigration in explicitly ethnic terms" than their neoconservative rivals; thus, nativism had an intellectual home in the movement. The reactionary populism embodied by Trump, with the "alt-right" as its digital vanguard, not only recuperated this tradition but radicalized it.

I witnessed this firsthand at an airport hotel in St. Louis, Missouri, where Republican white supremacists, conspiracy theorists, and European neofascists came together for a three-day-long conference—the forty-seventh iteration of the Phyllis Schlafly Gateway Eagle Council, co-organized by the Eagle Forum Education & Defense Fund and the *Gateway Pundit*, a far-right blog that peddled so many anti-Clinton hoaxes during the 2016 election that it obtained a White House credential.[109] The September 2018 conference drew together many strains of right-wing extremism that have taken root in the conservative movement, and in so doing illustrated how the Trump presidency had managed to consolidate them into a semi-coherent whole. And while it billed itself as something like an "ideas festival" for conservatives, there was only one idea that mattered, articulated a dozen which ways: that white America is under threat and its defenders must do everything they can to preserve it.

While no one from the Tanton network appeared to be in attendance, the ideas Tanton pushed for most of his life were very much so. In fact, a section on the Eagle Forum's website listing "Other Organizations concerned with protecting America's borders" includes CIS, FAIR, NumbersUSA, and VDARE.[110] Congressman Steve King, who had come to Phyllis Schlafly's attention years before when he helped pass a bill making English the official language of government in his home state of Iowa, was to be honored with the "Phyllis Schlafly Award for Excellence in Leadership." Campaign finance records show that King received $16,187 from the US Immigration Reform PAC, a political action committee run by Tanton associates and allies, between 2002 and the beginning of 2020. Donors to the PAC in that time included both Tanton and his wife Mary Lou, Cordelia Scaife May, John Rohe, and FAIR board members K. C. McAlpin and Paul Nachman.[111] According to an archived version of the committee's now-defunct website, Mary Lou Tanton served as the PAC's president, while IRLI's Ian Smith, who would resign from his position in Trump's DHS after his ties to white nationalists were exposed, served on the committee's board. The page also includes a note of praise from King: "Over the years, the U.S. Immigration Reform PAC has compiled an enviable record of success electing strong candidates to office. . . . George Soros and his special interest allies are eager to roll back the progress we've made and keep the welcome mat down for mass immigration. We cannot let that happen."[112]

A month before his appearance at the Gateway Eagle Council, King had visited Austria and given an interview to Caroline Sommerfeld, a prominent theorist of the European far right, about what King described as Western civilization's "slow-motion cultural suicide," and what Sommerfeld identified as "the great replacement."[113] In St. Louis, one of the Schlafly clan introduced King by referring to a tweet of his that stated, "We can't restore our civilization with somebody else's babies." This was met with thunderous applause. When King took the stage, he repeated those words, and the crowd cheered again. He elaborated on his original statement, lamenting low birth rates, annual abortion numbers, and immigration from Mexico: "We have lack of conception; we have abortions in any number—nine hundred fifty thousand or more that we'll see this year; then on top of that, we're watching what's happening in this country and across Europe: the immigration question."

"Whenever you import a person from another country or another culture—even one person—you're importing the culture as well," King continued. "You transfer the culture, and you transfer also the crime rate." The crowd ate this up. "When you import young men from a country like [Mexico], that are 13, 14, 16, 17, 19 [years old], you're importing the most violent demographic from any civilization," he added. "No matter how peaceful they are, and you're transferring that into the United States."[114]

Conspiratorial and paranoid thinking structured much of the weekend's conversation. All those present—almost entirely white, mostly male, and, barring a small cohort of interns, extremely old—seemed to perceive themselves to be engaged in a Manichean, civilizational conflict of the individual versus the collective, good versus evil, Christianity versus Islam, or the West against . . . everyone else. For example, Tony Shaffer, a Trump 2020 campaign adviser employed by an obscure think tank housed within the evangelical Kings' College in Manhattan, described contemporary politics as "a clash of civilizations."[115] In a presentation to the Gateway Eagle Council titled "Trump Is Winning on Immigration and Europe Agrees," Shaffer expounded on his idea of "invasion by immigration," warning that "this migration, this sublimation of culture, is not a good idea, and it's part of a wider effort to destabilize Western culture."

Two European politicians, Dominik Tarczynski of Poland's ruling Law and Justice party and Petr Bystron, a member of parliament with Alternative für Deutschland (AfD), or Alternative for Germany, were there to confirm their support for the council. "We are a global movement. We are a strong movement. This is important to know," Bystron said, referring to other "right-wing, conservative, freedom-loving parties" like the Freiheitliche Partei Österreichs (FPÖ), or Freedom Party of Austria, and Lega Nord, in Italy. "We are serious supporters of the Trump movement," he continued. "We are for anti-establishment movements. It's not so much about right, left—we are against the establishment." He gave a few explanations of what he meant by "the establishment," variously "very leftist," "undemocratic," "the NGOs," and, simply, "Soros." Tarczynski also referred to Soros's influence: "Everyone knows it, but we have to say it out loud."

The so-called identitarian movement, organized principally

around the group Generation Identity, is "a front for the AfD," Bystron told me. "We have two different types of opposition: We are a political party; we have to be parliamentarian, keep it clear and separation from all the pre-parliamentarian opposition." Citing groups like the Identitarians and Pegida (a far-right anti-immigrant, anti-Muslim street movement in Germany), Bystron acknowledged that "there are many" such fronts. "We need them. Those are our people," he continued. "They are bringing important impulses for conversations in our society, they are demonstrating in the street, making actions. It's a kind of cooperation."

This cooperation is central to what Liz Fekete, director of the UK's Institute of Race Relations, describes in *Europe's Fault Lines: Racism and the Rise of the Right* as a "pre-fascist movement." As "a far-right *völkisch* party," Fekete argues (using the German word for a kind of mystical ethnonationalism), AfD is at the forefront of this movement, "the aim of which is to reform the political process and transform it into an authoritarian, *völkisch* system."[116] To that end, Bystron's "pre-parliamentarian opposition" has led thousands of Germans through the streets of cities like Chemnitz, hunting down people they thought might be Muslims or immigrants and reportedly attacking a Jewish restaurant.[117] (Bystron dismissed these accounts as "fake news.") But as Fekete notes, the AfD wrote into its 2016 manifesto that Islam was not welcome in Germany. "It has also called," she writes, "for Swiss-style plebiscites on asylum-seekers, mosques and minarets, attacked the burden that single-mothers and the 'mentally handicapped' place on the economy, argued that asylum shelters should be shut down and the money put into teachers' salaries, as well as challenging adoption rights for homosexuals and suggesting that police should have the power to shoot refugees at the border."[118]

As it happens, Bystron is not opposed to the immigration reforms brought by the European Union.[119] He supports freedom of movement for European citizens, for example. "There's no problem with Austrians, Czechs, Dutch people traveling around," he told me. "This is fine. But you can do it only if you protect our outer borders." Like King, Bystron and AfD claim not to be opposed to immigration in general; rather, they are for immigration under certain circumstances. "Yes, we want immigration, but under certain rules," Bystron said. "We want educated people, speaking German, with qualifications, and it's clear that they can integrate." He added, "Live with us, do your thing, but live according to our rules."

"The leftists are saying, 'Hey, open borders for everybody. Come in! No walls, no fences on the borders,'" he continued. However, "If you don't have the fences there, you have them at home." The implication is that migrants to Germany, primarily from North Africa and the Middle East—riven with wars fought and funded by the Global North—inevitably bring with them violence and crime. According to Bystron and the AfD, this threat can only be guarded against one of two ways: either collectively, at Europe's borders, or individually, with advanced home security systems.

"We need a 'Fortress Europe,'" Bystron told me, using an AfD talking point derived from World War II–era Nazi propaganda, which has also been adopted by the identitarian movement in a further display of the parties' close ideological and rhetorical alignment.[120] "We have acquired two million illegals—we have to send them all back," he added. "Restore the law again. Restore the security for our own people."

Chapter Four

IT'S THE BIRTHRATES

The duality of the worlds of rich and poor can only be sustained by force.

—Alain Badiou

The contemporary far right in the United States and Europe has come to be defined by a vexing mixture of basement-dwelling social ineptitude and legitimate murderousness. To understand this apparent contradiction, we must move past surface-level phenomena and consider the fundamental contradictions between democracy, with its ostensible commitment to formal equality, and capitalism in the United States. The paranoid fear of "white genocide" underlies both the proliferation of fascist bands and legalistic tactics like racist gerrymandering and mass incarceration; the former offer their extralegal assistance to resolve the contradiction posed by the latter to democratic norms.

Contrary to both fascist and liberal talking points, demographics are not destiny. While the reactionaries and nativists agitate over fears that hordes of immigrants will secure the inevitability of a minority-majority population, subjugating white people to their will, liberals rest easy in the knowledge that such demographic shifts will ensure the victory of progressive reforms. Both are wrong, if for different reasons. The fascist view is ludicrous on its face, but the liberal view is all the more dangerous to those who actually care about making a better world: it is both cynical, to the extent that it erases the suffering of those in the here and now, trapped under the boot heel of the Trump administration and its street-fighting supporters, and idealistic, to the extent that it misapprehends the political commitments of the forces of reaction, who will gladly eschew democracy for authoritarianism should the choice be necessary. Successful fascist movements have historically taken power not in coups d'état, but in coalitions—namely, historian Robert Paxton has shown, in coalition with center-right liberals whose influence is waning and conservatives seeking allies against the left.

The emerging reaction of the twenty-first century, whether it is upheld by elites or in the street, is best understood as preemptively counterrevolutionary—that is to say, anticipating the political instability of the coming decades and laying the groundwork to maintain existing property relations, power dynamics, and systems of social control. For all their objections to Trump's crassness and vulgarity, there is little resistance from liberal centrists and moderates to these fundamental processes. Polling shows wide support among this cohort in both the US and Europe for authoritarian rule, deep skepticism of democracy, and a lack of commitment to civil rights.[1] Leftist speech is disproportionately punished on college campuses, not right-wing ideas as is popularly imagined. In the last few decades, as part of its campaign to roll back the gains made by working people, the ruling class has sought to pull together a political coalition binding nationalism to neoliberalism and austerity to anti-immigrant sentiment. "Under cover of austerity, the right has deepened its aggressive raid on post-war egalitarian and inclusive social policies," the antiracist scholar Liz Fekete argues. "If order and authority are to be maintained in the face of the erosion of the social safety net—and without even the dream of social mobility to mitigate the hardships—then the state must become more coercive, the exercise of state power more brutal."[2]

The fascist threat is not an incursion upon polite society from its fringes. It is not something foreign and unknown, born on the outskirts of civilization, threatening now and again to rip down the gates. To the contrary: the door was already open.

Even as many of the most militant factions of the "alt-right" have retreated from street politics and movement building, fascistic rhetoric and ideas have continued to spread through mass media, both online and on television. "Various strata and segments of the public are designing fascism on their own terms out of the diverse materials, old and new, circulating in their and our midst. They are all activists; their agency is decisive in impelling a self-radicalizing mind set," anthropologist Douglas R. Holmes argues. "Rather than extravagant public spectacles exalting atavistic forms of leadership, what has emerged is a recursive, screen-mediated fascism that orchestrates—with the aid of bots and trolls—the ways of thinking, feeling, and experiencing of shadow publics networked in cyberspace."[3] In the end, violence is the ultimate expression of the fascist way of thinking, feeling, and experiencing. While in some instances, as Clara Zetkin, the German Marxist, noted of the "alt-right's" forebearers, "the fascist program is exhausted by the phrase 'Beat up the Jews,'" in other cases it is full of "pseudo-revolutionary phrases though without concrete measures for their implementation and all of it cloaked in the steel armor of the national ethos."[4] "If you are going to legally, socially, and through other means interrupt the formation of white nationalist communities, you can expect vigilante outbursts to increase," Mike Peinovich, a.k.a. Mike Enoch, an ally of Heimbach and Spencer, said on an episode of his podcast, the *Daily Shoah*, while mocking a report on extremism in the United States. "If you deny people the ability to form communities, what do you expect them to do?"[5]

Long a paradigmatic political question, the formation of communities—who is included and excluded, and how those choices are made—promises to move into the foreground as the existential crisis of climate change unfolds over the course of the coming decades. Border fascists have their answer at the ready. According to the Intergovernmental Panel on Climate Change's landmark report on the impact of 1.5°C global warming, climate change will be a "poverty multiplier" by 2030, making poor people poorer and increasing the number of poor people overall. "Climate change alone could force more than 3 million and 16 million people into extreme poverty, mostly through impacts on agriculture and food prices."[6] Urban areas in sub-Saharan Africa and Southeast Asia will bear the brunt of this. These regions, heavily dependent on agriculture, will likely see mass emigration. Crop yields will plummet in rural areas, and nutrition will erode globally, especially for children. Mortality will skyrocket. More than 350 million people in "megacities" around the world will be exposed to "deadly heat," leading to "greater risks of injuries, disease and death [. . .] increased risks of undernutrition; and consequences of reduced labor productivity."[7] Even if the Republican Party maintains a facade of climate skepticism, denialism, or feigned ignorance, the US national security apparatus has acknowledged the scale of the coming changes. The Department of Defense stated in its 2014 Quadrennial Defense Review that the consequences of climate change act as "threat multipliers that will aggravate stressors abroad such as poverty, environmental degradation, political instability, and social tensions."[8]

Untold millions, understandably enough, will leave their homes, either for cities within their own countries or cross borders to seek new lives elsewhere. They already are. Yet rather than being welcomed, they are met with gruesome and bloodthirsty hostility. Capitalism in crisis invites the reaction that racism readily provides: criminalization of the exploited and the oppressed, subject to heavily militarized control and containment, as well as scapegoating by the corporate media. The institutions shaped by John Tanton and animated by Cordelia Scaife May's brutal largesse are but one component in this ideology.

Capitalism needs borders, even if capital itself does not adhere to them. "The age of globalization is also an age of unprecedented transnational migration," sociologist William I. Robinson has written. "The corollary to an integrated global economy is the rise of a truly global—although highly segmented—labor market. It is a global labor market because, despite formal nation-state restrictions on the free worldwide movement of labor, surplus labor in any part of the world is now recruited and redeployed through numerous mechanisms to where capital is in need of it and because workers themselves undertake worldwide migration, even in the face of the adverse migratory conditions."[9]

The borders that separate one country from another are an artifact of politics and history. They were born of violence, and their maintenance demands violence. As the cycles of capitalism driving both mass migration and repression converge with the climate crisis, a new ideology of reaction is emerging that I call "border fascism."

The Great Replacement

Before he walked into the Tree of Life Congregation in Pittsburgh, armed with a Colt AR-15 and three Glock .357 handguns, Robert Bowers announced his intentions on Gab, a social media platform popular with white nationalists, fascists, and other reactionaries who have been kicked off more mainstream sites like Twitter. He targeted this particular synagogue because the congregation there had worked with HIAS, formerly known as the Hebrew Immigrant Aid Society, to resettle refugees in the Pittsburgh area. HIAS, Bowers wrote, "likes to bring invaders in that kill our people. I can't sit by and watch my people get slaughtered." Referring to the ongoing debate over strategy and aesthetics in the movement, he added: "Screw your optics, I'm going in."[10]

In the weeks prior, Bowers had fixated on a caravan of migrants from Central America moving through Mexico toward the US border. Trump had been agitating his base over this, but Bowers went even further, blaming Jews for the caravan's organization. "Jews are waging a propaganda war against Western civilization and it is so effective that we are heading towards certain extinction within the next 200 years and we're not even aware of it. You are living in a critical time in history where the internet has given us a small window of opportunity to snap our people out of their brainwash," read one post Bowers shared. "I have noticed a change in people saying 'illegals' that now say 'invaders,'" he wrote. "I like this."[11]

"I just want to kill Jews," Bowers told police while he was receiving medical treatment following a gun battle with Pittsburgh SWAT officers, according to the criminal complaint filed against him. "They're committing genocide to my people."[12] Federal prosecutors rejected an offer from Bowers, facing the death penalty, to enter a guilty plea in exchange for life in prison.[13]

In March 2019, less than six months after the shooting in Pittsburgh, another shooter took up Bowers's cause, livestreaming the execution of fifty-one people at two mosques in Christchurch, New Zealand. At the beginning of the stream, which spread quickly across Facebook and other social media sites, a man greeted the shooter, whose weapon was inscribed with white supremacist messages, to the mosque, in a manner that recalled the worshippers who welcomed Dylann Roof to the Emanuel African Methodist Episcopal Church in Charleston. "Hello, brother," he said.[14] The killer then shot him dead.

Brenton Tarrant, the accused, has pleaded not guilty to the massacre.[15] Apparently even more fluent than Bowers in the digital discourse of the fascist right, Tarrant was identified as the author of a manifesto titled "The Great Replacement," a direct reference to the book of the same name by French polemicist Renaud Camus. "It's the birthrates. It's the birthrates. It's the birthrates," the tract begins. "We are experiencing an invasion on a level never seen before in history. Millions of people pouring across our borders, legally. Invited by the state and corporate entities to replace the White people who have failed to reproduce, failed to create the cheap labour, new consumers and tax base that the corporations and states need to thrive," the manifesto continues. "This crisis of mass immigration and sub-replacement fertility is an assault on the European people that, if not combated, will ultimately result in the complete racial and cultural replacement of the European people." This, Tarrant concludes, is nothing less than "white genocide."[16]

Like Christopher Hasson, the Coast Guard officer and white nationalist who was accused in February 2019 of plotting "to murder innocent civilians on a scale rarely seen in this country," Tarrant was apparently inspired by Anders Breivik, the Norwegian fascist who killed seventy-seven people, mostly members of that country's Labour Party's youth wing.[17] Hasson had composed a list of targets, including journalists, politicians, and political organizations like the Democratic Socialists of America. In many respects, Breivik's attack—and the 1,516-page manifesto he published online just hours before he began his bloody work—set the paradigm for white nationalist terror in the years to come. He'd spent years interacting with other radicals online, reading and corresponding extensively with reactionaries of various stripes around the world, before taking action himself. "Breivik's form of mass murder requires long and systematic ideological preparation whereby the perpetrator manages to dehumanize the victims through words," anthropologist Sindre Bangstad writes in *Anders Breivik and the Rise of Islamophobia*.[18] "There can be little doubt that part of the radicalization process undergone by [Anders] Behring Breivik in the years leading up to 22/7 was his seeking alternative sources of information—'counter publics' structured by Islamophobia—on the Internet. Yet a thorough investigation demonstrates that many of Behring Breivik's sources were in fact quite mainstream and hardly unusual."[19]

While Breivik's manifesto is largely incoherent and contradictory, Bangstad's close reading reveals how readily Breivik was able to draw on mainstream Islamophobia to legitimize his more radical (and paranoid) views: the "hybrid, cut-and-paste" manifesto's "disturbed, delusional" final chapter, for example, is called "A Declaration of 'Pre-emptive War,'" which Bangstad argues he borrowed from the George W. Bush administration's neoconservative rhetoric justifying the 2003 invasion of Iraq. Likewise, Bangstad argues, Breivik appears to have internalized Samuel Huntington and Bernard

Lewis's "clash of civilizations" thesis—a kind of hyper-reactionary identity politics obsessed with the restoration of an imagined fallen order.[20] "As we all know, the root of Europe's problems is the lack of cultural self-confidence (nationalism)," Breivik wrote. "This irrational fear of nationalistic doctrines is preventing us from stopping our own national/cultural suicide as the Islamic colonization is increasing annually.... You cannot defeat Islamization or halt/reverse the Islamic colonization of Western Europe without first removing the political doctrines manifested through multiculturalism/cultural Marxism."[21] So-called cultural Marxism, Breivik and similarly conspiratorial right-wingers argue, is responsible for many cultural ills, from "Islamization" to feminism to political correctness.[22] This is an adaptation of the earlier, anti-Semitic conspiracy theory of "Judeo-Bolshevism," which imagined Marxism and communism to be a Jewish plot to take over the world.[23] In 2017, a high-ranking staffer on the National Security Committee sent Trump a memo that described opposition to his administration as being "centered on cultural Marxist narratives."[24]

In his "Great Replacement" manifesto, the Christchurch shooter cited both Breivik and Dylann Roof as inspiration, listing them among "those that take a stand against ethnic and cultural genocide," before adding that "I have read the writings of Dylan Roof and many others, but only really took true inspiration from Knight Justiciar Breivik."[25] (This honorific acknowledges Breivik's claim to membership in a secret organization of Knights Templar, descended from the Crusade-era order.)[26] While Tarrant, the alleged author, did not claim membership in any organization, he admitted to having made donations to nationalist groups around the world—including, it would later emerge, the Identitarian Movement of Austria. Tarrant gave 1,500 euros to the group, eliciting a thank-you note from its leader, Martin Sellner, and an invitation to have beer should he ever visit Austria.[27] Tarrant also donated 2,000 euros to Generation Identity, a related group in France.[28] Just weeks after the shootings in Christchurch, Austria's then vice chancellor Heinz-Christian Strache said that the fight against "population exchange" would remain a priority—and that the far-right FPÖ would continue to resist the purported replacement of European Christians with Muslims. Sellner claimed Strache's use of the term as a "political victory" and "a signal from the party to the base."[29] Strache's ruling coalition with the center-right Österreichische Volkspartei (ÖVP), or Austrian People's Party, fell apart shortly thereafter amid a corruption scandal.[30] A year later, ÖVP entered a coalition government with the Greens. "It is possible to protect border and the climate at the very same time," ÖVP leader Sebastian Kurz said.[31]

After the shootings in Christchurch, Renaud Camus said that he condemned the attacks, but told the *Washington Post* that he had no objection to the manifesto author's interpretation of his ideas. "To the fact that people take notice of the ethnic substitution that is in progress in my country?" he asked. "No. To the contrary." In fact, Camus said that he hoped the desire for a "counter-revolt" against "colonization in Europe today" would grow: "I hope it becomes stronger." Such "demographic colonization," as he put it, is "20 times more important than the colonization Europe did to Africa, for example."[32] After another massacre whose perpetrator was reportedly inspired by his work, in El Paso, Camus told the *New York Times* that, while he believed in the importance of nonviolence, he also was glad to see white supremacists embracing his idea that white Europeans are at risk of being replaced by immigrants, Muslims, and people of color. "Good for them," he said. "That is indeed my belief."[33]

For those tracing Camus's influence, this became a familiar dance. After fascists marched through Charlottesville, Virginia, in August 2017, leaving one protester dead and dozens injured, Camus was asked what he made of US fascists chanting "You will not replace us," an apparent allusion to the "great replacement" theory. "If the marchers are Nazis and/or anti-Semites, or if they make [violent] attacks—I am of course very much against all of that, and I cannot say they are inspired by me," Camus said. However, "I can very well understand why people in America would chant, 'We won't be replaced,' and I approve of that." He added, "Americans have every good reason to be worried about their country, one of the two main elements that make up Western civilization, being changed into just another poor, derelict, hyperviolent, and stupefied quarter of the 'global village.'"

"I pray for the conservation of all races, beginning with those which are the most under menace," Camus said. And which is the most under menace? "Probably the white one . . . the aristocracy of the world."[34]

Camus is part of a generation of French intellectuals that came to be known as the Nouvelle Droite, the New Right, which borrowed heavily from the Italian communist Antonio Gramsci and other leftists to articulate a kind of right-wing "metapolitics," or a new approach to the struggle over ideas and culture, from which political power, as they saw it, would flow. Led by Alain de Benoist and organized around the Group for Research and Study of European Civilization, or GRECE, which was formed in 1968, the intellectuals' signal achievement has been to shift the focus of racist discourse from biological to cultural markers of difference. This change came in response to the rise of civil rights and decolonial movements around the world, especially in the United States and Europe. In fact, the Nouvelle Droite thinkers would go so far as to co-opt much of the language of these movements, speaking in favor of representation, egalitarianism, and liberation.

The discursive shift, however, did not reflect a change in the Nouvelle Droite's underlying political project. "Alain de Benoist had been for years a white supremacist," historian David Renton argues in *The New Authoritarians: Convergence on the Right*. "One of the stories he tells in his memoir is of an occasion when he was in a restaurant and a nun asked if he would give to charities operating in the Third World, to which he replied that she 'look[ed] after monkeys.'"[35] Throughout the mid-1960s, according to Renton, de Benoist's writings are full of militant nationalism and dire warnings about the threat posed to Europe by mass immigration. "Yet in the 1970s de Benoist changed his approach and began to insist that all races were equal and that at the global level diversity should be supported," Renton writes. "This was not a move towards moderation but towards obfuscation. For by 'diversity' de Benoist meant something different from the term's normal use; that in each nation there should be complete nationality and racial homogeneity. Diversity meant, in other words, a series of multiple regional and national apartheid states."[36] Or, in the language of the New Right, "ethno-pluralism."[37] After the Front National broke through in France's 1984 elections, the Nouvelle Droite's discursive shift went mainstream, giving rise to what Bangstad, quoting Simon Weaver, calls a "liquid racism." This new form of racism, Bangstad argues, allowed Breivik to situate himself as carrying on a struggle for "indigenous rights": "as if 'white' native Europeans represented a 'tribe' in the Amazon forest on the verge of its very extinction, or a struggle for 'civil rights,' as if Behring Breivik were a latter-day Martin Luther King Jr. marching through Selma, Alabama, during the civil rights struggle of 1965."[38]

While Renaud Camus did not write his "great replacement" book until 2012, the discourse of the Nouvelle Droite prepared the ground for the theory's emergence and popularity and for alienated, paranoid white men around the world to imagine themselves not only as members of a marginalized and oppressed group, but, by taking up arms in defense of "their people," to be fighting on the side of revolution and liberation, rather than on behalf of the ruling class and the status quo. The "great replacement" theory offers adherents a way to resolve the contradictions in their beliefs, as well as an ideological justification for their brutal violence.

"The attack was not an attack on diversity, but an attack in the name of diversity," the New Zealand shooter, who declared himself an "ethno-nationalist," wrote in his manifesto. (Parts of the document are written in the manner of an interview transcript, conducted after the event; thus, Tarrant's use of past tense.) "In my mind a rainbow is only beautiful due to its variety of colours, mix the colours together and you destroy them all and they are gone forever and the end result is far from anything beautiful."

"I only wish I could have killed more invaders, and more traitors as well," the author wrote. "The only muslim I truly hate is
the convert, those from our own people that turn their backs on
their heritage, turn their backs on their cultures, turn their back
on their traditions and became blood traitors to their own race.
These I hate." Such slippage, conflating race and religion, puts
the lie to the whole New Right project. If to convert to Islam is
to become a "blood traitor," religion (and culture) is something
essential, inherent—to be found in the blood and the soil.

Catalysts

In April 2019, seventy-three minutes before John Earnest is accused of having opened fired at the Congregation Chabad synagogue in Poway, California, someone identifying themselves as
Earnest posted yet another white nationalist manifesto to 8chan's
/pol/, the anonymous online message board that Tarrant, the alleged Christchurch killer, also frequented. Tarrant "was a catalyst for me," the manifesto's author wrote. "He showed me that
it could be done. It needed to be done." Like Robert Bowers, the
alleged Pittsburgh shooter, whom he also cites, the manifesto's author wrote of a "meticulously planned genocide of the European
race"—planned, of course, by the Jews.[39] Four minutes after the
manifesto was posted to 8chan, a user responded: "Get the high
score."[40] That is, kill more people than prior mass shooters.

Since the Christchurch shooting, 8chan users, known to each
other as "anons," have become obsessed with beating that "high
score," demonstrating what journalist Robert Evans has called "the
gamification of terror."[41] Evans began monitoring 8chan shortly
after the mosque attacks in New Zealand: "Nazism is the constant
background noise on /pol/. The Poway synagogue shooter's manifesto was peppered with dumb jokes, but also included lengthy,
detailed and deadly serious anti-Semitic raving. Conversations on
/pol/ tend to go the same way," he wrote after Earnest allegedly attacked the Congregation Chabad synagogue. "In addition to talk

of inspiring and carrying out mass shootings, many anons engage in what is called 'siege-posting.' This is a reference to the book *Siege*, which is a collection of writings from American neo-Nazi James Mason. *Siege* was a major inspiration for the terrorist group Atomwaffen, among others. It urges autonomous terror attacks by individuals as a way to bring about the fragmentation and eventual destruction of American society. The goal is to spark a civil war that will allow for the violent realization of white nationalist/neo-Nazi goals."[42]

The fracturing and decentralization of the far right has meant that individual leaders like Andrew "Weev" Auernheimer, a writer for the *Daily Stormer*, are less able to exert influence and discipline on participants in the movement. However, this doesn't stop them from taking vicarious pleasure from the violence alleged killers like Bowers, Tarrant, and Earnest have wrought. "They're all getting statues," Auernheimer wrote after the Poway attack. "It's definitely the wrong thing, but they're all still heroes. Fools, but still heroes and martyrs."[43]

In August 2019, nineteen-year-old Santino Legan opened fire at the Gilroy Garlic Festival in California, killing three people—six-year-old Stephen Romero, thirteen-year-old Keyla Salazar, and twenty-five-year-old Trevor Irby—and wounding at least thirteen others before turning his gun on himself amid a firefight with police.[44] While the FBI opened a domestic terrorism investigation after discovering that Legan had compiled a "target list" of political organizations, religious institutions, and federal buildings, authorities were circumspect about his motivations, alluding to a "fractured ideology."[45]

Not long before the shooting, however, Legan posted a photograph of Smokey Bear, the fire safety icon, to his Instagram. "Read 'Might Is Right' by Ragnar Redbeard," Legan wrote in the caption. "Why overcrowd towns and pave more open space to make room for hordes of mestizos and Silicon Valley white twats?"[46] While less famous than other right-wing texts like *Camp of the Saints*, the 1896 *Might is Right* and its pseudonymous author have nevertheless achieved a position of influence in white supremacist circles for the book's nihilistic and fascistic celebration of social Darwinism. A review published by the anti-Semitic and white nationalist *Occidental Observer* concluded that the book contains a lesson for white people in the United States and Europe, who are "generally under threat" from immigration: "The lesson would be to gain power, economic as well as territorial, establish enclaves wherever convenient but eventually . . . re-conquer the whole of one's country."[47]

Six days after the Gilroy, California, shooting, twenty-one-year-old Patrick Crusius drove across Texas to a Walmart in El Paso, where he killed twenty-two people, including fifteen-year-old Javier Amir Rodriguez and Jordan and Andre Anchondo, both in their twenties, who died shielding their two-month-old baby from bullets.[48] Twenty-six people were injured. According to police in El Paso, Crusius has confessed to the shooting. He said that he was targeting "Mexicans."[49] Less than a half hour before the first 911 call came in, an unsigned manifesto titled "The Inconvenient Truth" was posted on 8chan, likely by Crusius. "In general, I support the Christchurch shooter and his manifesto. This attack is a response to the Hispanic invasion of Texas. They are the instigators, not me. I am simply defending my country from cultural and ethnic replacement brought on by an invasion," the manifesto claims, citing the same "great replacement" theory that has motivated white nationalist violence from Norway to New Zealand.[50]

Race mixing, the manifesto claims, "destroys genetic diversity and creates identity problems. . . . Cultural diversity diminishes as stronger and/or more appealing cultures overtake weaker and/or desirable ones." It continues: "I can no longer bear the shame of inaction knowing that our founding fathers have endowed me with the rights needed to save our country from the brink of destruction. Our European comrades don't have the gun rights needed to repel the millions of invaders that plaque [*sic*] their country. They have no choice but to sit by and watch their countries burn."[51]

"If we can get rid of enough people," the writer argues, "then our way of life can be more sustainable."

For all their evasions, jokes, and ironic rhetorical traps, the manifestos attributed to Tarrant and Crusius, the Christchurch and El Paso shooters, respectively, offer the clearest articulation of the emerging ideology of border fascism.

While the far right proliferates with labels—some self-given, some disavowed—nobody calls themselves a "border fascist." There are the white nationalists, racial nationalists, and the ethno-nationalists. Then there are the civic nationalists and the Western chauvinists. There's the "alt-right" and the "alt-light." There are fascists and ecofascists. There are neo-Nazis and identitarians and Western chauvinists. There are race realists and scientific racists. There are national socialists and national anarchists and national conservatives. To be able to differentiate between these groups and what they believe is a meaningful and necessary exercise for anyone who wants to understand their motivation, how they relate to each other and to establishment politics, and what might be done to stop them. But it is the shared principles and beliefs that hold all these formations together in a common project, and a wider movement, whether they are conscious of that or not, that deserves the most attention.

Some emphasize their revolutionary credentials and disdain their reformist brethren. Conversely, those who aspire to respectability and power—or simply want to be able to work for the *Daily Caller* or appear on *Tucker Carlson Tonight*—dismiss their more revolutionary compatriots as immature and undisciplined. But in the end, much of what appears to be ideological conflict between the radical and extreme right, the reformist and revolutionary right, or Matthew Lyons's "oppositional and system-loyal rightists" is nothing more or less than a divergence over strategy.

Like many fascists, the authors of the Christchurch and El Paso manifestos integrate pseudo-leftist (and revolutionary) rhetoric and ideas into their fundamentally reactionary worldview. "The American lifestyle affords our citizens an incredible quality of life," the alleged El Paso shooter appears to have written. "However, our lifestyle is destroying the environment of our country.

The decimation of the environment is creating a massive burden for future generations. Corporations are heading the destruction of our environment by shamelessly overharvesting resources."[52]

"Water sheds around the country, especially in agricultural areas, are being depleted. Fresh water is being polluted from farming and oil drilling operations. Consumer culture is creating thousands of tons of unnecessary plastic waste and electronic waste, and recycling to help slow this down is almost non-existent. Urban sprawl creates inefficient cities which unnecessarily destroys millions of acres of land," the writer continues. "The government is unwilling to tackle these issues beyond empty promises since they are owned by corporations. Corporations that also like immigration because more people means a bigger market for their products."[53]

Both Crusius and Tarrant, who explicitly identifies as an "eco-fascist," articulate a critique of capitalism—and corporations in particular—for despoiling the planet and being the main drivers of mass immigration and displacement. Crusius, however, is clear that his criticism is intended to discipline US capitalists, not overthrow them: "Corporate America doesn't need to be destroyed, but just shown that they are on the wrong side of history. That if they don't bend, they will break."[54] Likewise, as far as Crusius is concerned, individual consumers—or at least white consumers—aren't able to change. "Everything I have seen and heard in my short life has led me to believe that the average American isn't willing to change their lifestyle, even if the changes only cause a slight inconvenience," the El Paso shooter wrote. "I love the people of this country, but god damn most of y'all are just too stubborn to change your lifestyle. So the next logical step is to decrease the number of people in America using resources." That is, either by deportation—or massacre. Thus, when Crusius allegedly opened fire at the Walmart in El Paso, he allowed white and African American shoppers out of the building, targeting only those he identified as Latinx.[55]

"America can only be destroyed from the inside-out. If our country falls, it will be the fault of traitors. This is why I see my actions as faultless. Because this isn't an act of imperialism but an act of preservation," the manifesto reads. "My whole life I have been preparing for a future that currently doesn't exist. The job of my dreams will likely be automated. Hispanics will take control of the local and state government of my beloved Texas, changing policy to better suit their needs. They will turn Texas into an instrument of a political coup which will hasten the destruction of our country. The environment is getting worse by the year."[56]

Following the shooting, Kevin MacDonald, the anti-Semitic former academic whose work John Tanton recommended to Cordelia Scaife May, wrote on Twitter that he agreed with points made in the manifesto: "Agree with the shooter that the Dems see immigration as a path to permanent power and that pro-business elements in the GOP are cooperating. This won't be last bit of violence from people concerned about the Great Replacement. Political elites are playing a very dangerous game."[57] The *Daily Stormer*'s Auernheimer, who'd dubbed the Poway shooter a "hero," wrote that "random violence is not detrimental to our cause, because we need to convince Americans that violence against nonwhites is desirable or at least not something worth opposing anyways, because there's no way to remove a hundred million people without a massive element of violence."[58]

Tarrant, an "ethno-nationalist eco-fascist" who believes in "ethnic autonomy for all peoples with a focus on the preservation of nature, and the natural order," and looks to Donald Trump as "a symbol of renewed white identity and common purpose," is even more explicit in his critique of capitalists and the politicians that serve them:

> Make no mistake, the major impetus for the mass importation of non-Europeans into Europe is the call and want for cheap labour. Nothing drives the invasion more and nothing needs to be defeated more than the greed that demands cheap labour. Break it's [*sic*] back, anyway you can. Whether that is by encouraging and pushing increases to the minimum wage; furthering the unionization of workers; increasing the native birthrate and thereby reducing the need for the importation of labour; increasing the rights of workers; pushing for the increase in automation

or advancement of industrial labour replacement or any other tactic that is available. In the end human greed and the need for increasing profit margins of capital owners needs to be fought against and broken.

In a section of his manifesto that takes the form of question and answer, he put it even more bluntly: "Why do you blame immigrants and not the capitalists? I blame both, and plan to deal with both."[59]

Such critiques, however, are always issued in service of what the authors perceive to be white or European interests. "If an ethnocentric European future is to be achieved global free markets and the trade of goods is to be discouraged at all costs," Tarrant wrote. "Goods produced without care for the natural world, dignity of workers, lasting culture or or white civilizations [*sic*] future should never be allowed into the new morally focused and ethically focused European market."[60]

Likewise, the "ecofascist" emphasis on the environment—echoed in the Gilroy Garlic Festival shooter's Instagram posts—stems from the belief that white Europeans have a special claim to enjoy nature's beauty. "We were born from our lands and our own culture was molded by these same lands. The protection and preservation of these lands is of the same importance as the protection and preservation of our own ideals and beliefs," Tarrant apparently wrote. "The Europe of the future is not one of concrete and steel, smog and wires but a place of forests, lakes, mountains and meadows. . . . Each nation and each ethnicity was melded by their own environment and if they are to be protected so must their own environments."[61]

In a far-sighted analysis of this emerging trend, writer Matthew Phelan invoked Theodor Adorno's concern that "the survival of National Socialism *within* democracy" might be "potentially more menacing than the survival of fascist tendencies *against* democracy," applying this framework to the US environmental movement, with its roots in eugenics and population control.[62] "For most of our lives, we've lived with the persistent threat of extreme-right movements backed by capital invested in historical dead-ends such as fossil fuels and the freedom to pollute," Phelan warned. "But far-right movements backed by new sectors of the economy could threaten to be something far worse. They could be sustainable."[63] And while his influence had waned by the time of the Christchurch shooting, white nationalist Richard Spencer had years earlier recognized the appeal of a particular strain of ethno-environmentalism. "We have the potential to become nature's steward or its destroyer," Spencer wrote ahead of the deadly August 2017 "Unite the Right" rally in Charlottesville. "Putting aside contentious matters like global warming and resource depletion, European countries should invest in national parks, wilderness preserves, and wildlife refuges, as well as productive and sustainable farms and ranches. The natural world—and our experience of it—is an end in itself."[64]

In practice, this manifests as brutal, racist violence. "Why focus on immigration and birth rates when climate change is such a huge issue?" Tarrant asks himself in his manifesto. "Because they are the same issue, the environment is being destroyed by over population, we Europeans are one of the groups that are not over populating the world. The invaders are the ones over populating the world [*sic*]. Kill the invaders, kill the overpopulation and by doing so save the environment."[65]

The cumulative effect of all these attitudes has been devastating. "It's really hard to be alive as an immigrant right now and to not be sick and exhausted," Karla Cornejo Villavicencio, a DACA recipient, said after the El Paso shooting. "It feels like being hunted."[66]

Character and Composition

In July 2019, Laura Ingraham, a Fox News host, brought Texas lieutenant governor Dan Patrick onto her show to discuss the passage of a California bill that allowed low-income, undocumented adults under the age of twenty-five access to the state's Medicaid program.[67] Ingraham, whose show averages about 2.4 million viewers per night, described Texas as being "completely overrun by this illegal invasion."[68] She continued: "Calling it anything but an invasion at this point is just not being honest with people."[69]

Patrick has appeared on *The Ingraham Angle* multiple times to push talking points that sound an awful lot like the "great replacement" theory, telling Ingraham that Democrats and the "liberal media" want millions of immigrants "to continue to pour in to where they turn those into votes one day and they control the country," calling them "treasonous" for doing so.[70] "Here's a number that will startle your viewers. The Census projects that we will have about four million babies born in America next year. But this year, Laura, five million illegals will cross into this country illegally," Patrick said during one May 2019 appearance. "The one million we catch, and the four million we don't. So we have more people coming into this country illegally than we have babies born. The president is right to say that we have a right as a nation to select who comes to America."[71]

On August 2, 2019, a few weeks after California passed its Medicaid expansion for undocumented young people, Greg Abbott, the governor of Texas, sent a fundraising letter to supporters asking them to help him "defend" the state against unauthorized immigration. "The problems of illegal immigration never reach swanky limousine-liberal neighborhoods in New York and California!" he wrote. "Doing nothing will only lead to disaster for Texas, both economically and politically. Securing our border should be the federal government's job."

"If we're going to DEFEND Texas, we'll need to take matters into our own hands," the governor's letter read.[72] The next day, Patrick Crusius drove ten hours across the state, from Allen to a Walmart in El Paso, where he allegedly hunted down anyone with brown skin, killing twenty-two people.

There is nothing to indicate that Abbott's letter inspired the shooting directly. Given how explicit the El Paso manifesto's author was about his other influences, it would be hard to imagine him leaving Abbott out if his fundraising letter were a motivating factor; but the ideological alignment between these two actors is notable. As journalist Alex Press wrote after the Pittsburgh massacre, "No politician would endorse the actions of a Robert Bowers, but they know the impact their words and policies have on those like him who, eventually, will take them seriously and begin killing their neighbors. It's not a question of 'if' anymore—it's when and where."[73] Likewise, no politician or media personality would endorse the actions of a Patrick Crusius, and yet they will use the same language, the same ideas, the same tropes.

Ingraham has been pushing her watered-down version of the "great replacement" theory for some time. "Of this, my friends, you can be sure: your views on immigration will have zero impact and zero influence on a House dominated by Democrats who want to replace you, the American voters, with newly amnestied citizens and an ever increasing number of chain migrants," she told her audience ahead of the midterm elections, in October 2018.[74] Ingraham's podcast is a particularly rich vein of white nationalistic rhetoric. "The effort here is to replace kind of the old America with a new America who's not coming into the country legally. And the Democrats know that will tip the balance for them in every state where it's even close and that will just be an electoral lock forever," Ingraham said on a March 7, 2019, episode.[75] The next day, Pat Buchanan, the nativist paleoconservative whose political career in many ways anticipated the present moment, appeared on the podcast. "The whole character and composition of the nation is rapidly being changed," he said. "And we're becoming a different country without consulting the American people, who never voted for any of this."[76]

The next month, Ingraham returned to her theme that the country's "character and composition" are changing, thanks to Democrats and mass immigration. "Their goal is to change the country, any way they can. They can't win electorally, they want to change it demographically, or bring so many new people into the country that don't have an affinity for our history or our founding, that they'll be able to snooker them on socialism," Ingraham told her audience.[77] A week later, she rearticulated this idea, claiming that Democrats are "for replacing the current American population, or swamping the current American population, with a new population of people who are perhaps more hospitable to socialist ideals."[78]

"They can't risk a situation where a guy like Trump keeps getting elected," Ingraham said. As such, she claimed, Democrats were seeking immigrant voters that are "not in tune with the American founding, or even taught to love the American founding."

Ingraham is not the only member of the conservative establishment to deploy such ethnonationalist talking points. "It is a plot to remake America—to replace American citizens with illegals who will vote for the Democrats," Jeanine Piro, a Fox News host, said in an August 2019 appearance on the *Todd Starnes Show* on Fox Nation radio.[79] Earlier that month, the National Association of Hispanic Journalists (NAHJ) had announced that it was cutting ties with Fox News, specifically citing Starnes's rhetoric. "Starnes unapologetically states that America has 'suffered' from the 'invasion of a rampaging hoard of illegal aliens,' claiming that most 'illegal immigrants' are violent criminals, as well as casually using a reference for their immigration to the United States with the Nazis invading France and Western Europe in World War II," NAHJ president Hugo Balta, a senior producer at MSNBC, wrote in a letter to members.[80] During an appearance on Fox News after the Christchurch massacres, Walid Phares, an adviser to both Mitt Romney and Donald Trump's presidential campaigns, said, "It's very understandable what [the shooter] is trying to do on a political level." He added, "Obviously it's horrific and should be condemned completely on the action level."[81]

But no one at the network has done more to mainstream the "great replacement" conspiracy theory than Tucker Carlson. "The invasion of Europe intensified this weekend," he said during an April 2017 monologue, referring to migrants from North Africa who were rescued from drowning in the Mediterranean. Carlson continued:

> Last year, more than 350,000 migrants arrived in Europe from the third world, and many no doubt were good people, and their desperation is of course easy to understand given where they

came from. That does not alter the fact that they arrived without invitation illegally and at public expense, and that they will forever and profoundly change the demographics of the continent in ways that pretty much nobody who was born there ever asked for, or wanted, but that nobody is allowed to complain about for fear of being attacked as immoral. It's a huge deal, but hardly anyone ever mentions it. Does that sound familiar to you as an American? It ought to.[82]

He returned to the theme later that year. "Democrats know if they keep up the flood of illegals into the country, they can eventually turn it into a flood of voters for them," Carlson said in December 2017. "They don't have to foster economic growth, or be capable administrators, or provide good government. They just have to keep the pump flowing, and power will be theirs."[83] And again, in December 2018, he lamented that "nobody seems to pause and ask" why young Americans "can't afford to get married and have children, afford to buy homes and cars and their solution, the elite's solution, is we'll just bring in new people. . . . My concern is for my fellow Americans," Carlson continued. "And they can't afford to have children. But rather than fix their problems or even think about them we are like 'we'll just import new children.' . . . I'm not against the immigrants," he said. "I'm just, I'm for Americans. Nobody cares about them. It's like, 'shut up, you're dying, we're gonna replace you.'"[84]

Carlson's self-presentation has gone through several iterations during his time in the public eye, but a sensitivity to white grievance and anxiety has been consistent throughout. "His hostility to immigration and demographic change may be the closest thing to a sincere core belief running through his career," journalist and media critic Tom Scocca wrote.[85] Increasingly he would be called upon to deny the very existence of racism and white supremacy, as when, during the 2016 election, Carlson called then-candidate Hillary Clinton's remarks about implicit bias "absurd," demanding that people "be adults" rather than acting "like America is still in 1955."[86] After Trump was elected, Carlson dismissed charges that support for his candidacy was motivated by racial grievance on the basis that "the American Nazi Party and the KKK don't really exist in a meaningful [way]."[87] He argued that Jeff Sessions, then the senator from Alabama who'd advised the Trump campaign and would become attorney general, could not be racist because Alabama is such a diverse state.[88] Later, in response to criticism that compared the way that Fox News hosts talk about immigration with the rhetoric of the El Paso shooter, Carlson did not deny that the network was acting as a vehicle for white supremacy, but denied the very existence of white supremacy itself. "The whole thing is a lie," he said. It's "actually not a real problem in America."[89]

Leaked chat logs from white supremacist groups like Identity Evropa show how much members of such groups appreciated Carlson's coverage of the issues they cared about. "They include users praising the Fox host, claiming that he's the sole reason they tune in to cable, and calling him 'a lone voice of reason in the media,'" Cristina López of Media Matters for America and *Data & Society*, wrote. "The chats show many users praising Carlson for his subtlety in delivering extremist talking points as a strategic way of remaining on the airwaves, explicitly crediting Carlson with 'normalizing 80% of [Identity Evropa's] talking points,' and pointing out that figures like Carlson and Nazi sympathizer Ann Coulter 'know exactly what they're doing' to 'nudge people further to the right.' It is clear is that Carlson's fearmongering about changing demographics comes across to these extremists as an explicitly white supremacist talking point."[90] Likewise, the fascists of the *Daily Stormer* cheered when Carlson was tapped to take over serial sexual harasser Bill O'Reilly's time slot.[91] "The key to his success is that he destroys people everyone hates," one commentator for the website, Joseph Jordan (a.k.a. "Eric Striker"), wrote. "He mocks and berates an assembly line of Jewish liars, literally laughing at the absurdity of their canned talking points about everything from immigration to Russia to trannies."[92] Derek Black, the son of Stormfront founder Don Black and an ex–white nationalist, said that his family watches Carlson "once, and then watches it on the replay, because they feel that he is making the white nationalist talking points better than they have and they're trying to get some tips on how to advance it."[93]

As activists and media critics began drawing attention to the host's white nationalist rhetoric, businesses began to pull ads from his show, which was averaging about 2.8 million viewers per night. "Our country's economy is becoming more automated and tech-centered by the day, it's obvious that we need more scientists and skilled engineers," he said in the opening monologue of a December 2018 show. "But that's not what we're getting. Instead, we're getting waves of people with high school educations or less. Nice people, no one doubts that. But as an economic matter, this is insane."

"It's indefensible, so nobody even tries to defend it. Instead, our leaders demand that you shut up and accept this," he continued. "We have a moral obligation to admit the world's poor, they tell us, even if it makes our own country poor and dirtier and more divided. Immigration is a form of atonement."[94]

"My country actually is being invaded by other countries from the south," Carlson said in September 2019.[95] "Our leaders are decadent and narcissistic. They care only about themselves. They will never defend our nation. That's obvious and the rest of the world knows it," he had said earlier that year. "A new study from the Federation for Immigration Reform, FAIR, given exclusively to this show, shows the scale on which the United States is being plundered."[96]

Of course, fascists like Jordan and the *Right Stuff*'s Mike Peinovich delighted in Carlson's increasingly explicit white nationalism. "Tucker Carlson has been saying that immigration makes America dirty for years—like two years now, straight, and he hasn't had that much problems with the advertisers," Jordan said. "The trigger word there was 'dirty' and I think that first of all, [immigrants] are objectively dirty and like anything, theoretically you're not supposed to say that," Peinovich said. "When I saw that segment, I was like, 'Finally!' because this was doing, like, what we are talking about here, [but] for an audience of millions across the country—[the] most popular white talk show host in the country speaking to white people."[97]

Despite the growing advertiser boycott, Carlson was uncowed. "We plan to try to say what's true until the last day," he announced in his next monologue. "And the truth is, unregulated mass immigration has badly hurt this country's natural landscape."[98] It probably didn't hurt that he was getting supportive texts from Lachlan Murdoch—eldest son of Rupert, founder of Fox News.[99] But by the time he described Representative Ilhan Omar, a Democratic congresswoman from Minnesota and naturalized US citizen from Somalia, as "living proof that the way we practice immigration has become dangerous to this country," "a living fire alarm," and "a warning to the rest of us that we better change our immigration" policy, Carlson's primary audience was not his millions of viewers or even the Murdoch family, per se—it was President Trump.[100]

"For years, the conservative movement peddled one set of talking points to the rabble, while its elites consumed a more grounded and reality-based media," journalist Alex Pareene wrote in 2017.

> The rubes listened to talk radio, read right-wing blogs, watched Fox News. They were fed apocalyptic paranoia about threats to their liberty, racial hysteria about the generalized menace posed by various groups of brown people, and hysterical lies about the criminal misdeeds of various Democratic politicians. The people in charge, meanwhile, read the *Wall Street Journal* and the *Weekly Standard*, and they tended to have a better grasp of political reality, as when those sources deceived their readers, it was mostly unintentionally, with comforting fantasies about the efficacy of conservative policies. From the Reagan era through the Bush administration, the system seemed to be performing as designed.[101]

Then, the global economy imploded, Barack Obama was elected president, and the Tea Party happened. "Now, we have a president whose media diet defines his worldview, interests, and priorities. He is not one of the men, like most of those Tea Party members of Congress, whose existing worldview determined his media diet—who sealed himself off from disagreeable media sources," Pareene argued. "He is, in fact, something far more dangerous: a confused old man who believes what the TV tells him."

This was not figurative language: on any given day, if anyone wanted to know what was being discussed on Fox News at a given moment without turning on their television, they could check the president's Twitter feed. What this represented was a completely closed feedback loop among the president, the conservative propaganda apparatus, and the increasingly reactionary base, with each providing justification for the others' further radicalization.

"We don't have a country right now," Trump said in footage shown in one 2016 campaign ad. "We have people pouring in, they're pouring in, and they're doing tremendous damage."[102] The theme continued as he ramped up his 2020 campaign: between January and August 2019, the Trump campaign posted more than two thousand ads to Facebook that included the word "invasion," spending $1.25 million on Facebook ads about immigration beginning in late March.[103] (The campaign spent about $5.6 million on Facebook advertising in total during this period.) As the *New York Times* noted, the message was picked up by other Republican candidates, too. "Let's call this what it is—an invasion of our country," read one Facebook ad for a candidate for Senate in Alabama.[104] "I am running for governor of West Virginia," declared another candidate, the caption accompanied by an image of hundreds of brown faces walking along a road. "Sign up below to help me stop the invasion."[105] A Senate candidate in North Carolina echoed the theme: "We must defend our border from the invasion of illegal aliens into this country. We are literally being overrun."[106]

Obsessive, Paranoid, and Angry

On the morning of April 1, 2018, Trump tweeted, "Border Patrol Agents are not allowed to properly do their job at the Border because of ridiculous liberal (Democrat) laws like Catch & Release. Getting more dangerous. 'Caravans' coming. Republicans must go to Nuclear Option to pass tough laws NOW. NO MORE DACA DEAL!"

"These big flows of people are all trying to take advantage of DACA," he added. "They want in on the act!"[107]

It became clear that the president was likely reacting to a Fox News segment from earlier that day, in which border patrol union president Brandon Judd had offered his commentary on a group of about 1,200 migrants, mostly from Honduras, traveling together across Mexico toward the United States.[108] "Even if we're standing at the border with our hands out, saying, 'Don't enter, don't enter,' all they have to do is cross one foot into the border and we have to take them into custody," Judd complained. "If they ask for asylum, or they say, 'I fear to go back to my country,' then we have to process them under quote-unquote credible fear, which then allows them to be released into our country."[109] Between February 2019 and February 2020, more than a thousand asylum seekers waiting in Mexico for their applications to be processed reported suffering rapes, the murders of family and loved ones, kidnappings, and other abuses.[110] Deportees from the United States are frequently returned to their countries of origin only to be beaten, raped, and murdered.[111]

"They're going to create havoc and chaos. How many times do we have to hear stories of United States citizens being killed by people that are here illegally before we actually do something?" Judd asked, before suggesting that Republicans pursue the "nuclear option" of empowering CBP and ICE to detain migrants indefinitely.[112]

People from the Northern Triangle and southern Mexico had been making the journey to the United States in caravans for years, as moving in large groups proved safer and more effective than traveling in ones and twos. Numbers offered protection from both Mexican immigration enforcement agencies and the gangs and cartels known to assault and exploit migrants. "Going alone is risky. You're risking an accident, getting jumped by robbers, and even your life," twenty-nine-year-old Mateo Juan, who was making his third attempt to come to the United States, told *BuzzFeed News*. "All of that, and then you don't get to the United States. The caravan is slower but you know you're going to get there safely."[113]

But in 2018, right before the midterm elections, the caravans became a point of fixation for Trump and his nativist supporters. In October, as one particularly large group set off for the United States, the president deployed 5,200 active-duty military troops to join the CBP agents and national guardsmen already stationed at the southern border.[114] "Many Gang Members and some very bad people are mixed into the Caravan heading to our Southern Border," he wrote on Twitter, having already had to walk back claims that "criminals and unknown Middle Easterners are mixed in" with migrants from Central America.[115] "Please go back, you will not be admitted into the United States unless you go through the legal process. This is an invasion of our Country and our Military is waiting for you!"[116]

Immediately, the Center for Immigration Studies was available to provide pseudo-intellectual backup. Appearing before the House Oversight Committee's subcommittee on national security, in a hearing on "A Caravan of Illegal Immigrants: A Test of U.S. Borders," Andrew Arthur, a CIS fellow, testified that the caravan "calls the security of the border into question."[117] He continued, "The fact is most of the aliens in the caravan, should they come to the United States and claim credible fear, would likely be released to await an asylum hearing that may be years in the future, if they appear at all." On Fox News, Jessica Vaughan, the CIS's director of policy studies, said that the caravan and its organizers had a political purpose: to challenge US sovereignty. "They're not just going to sit back and be told 'no,' be told 'take a number,'" Vaughan said. "They want to make a scene at the border. They want to prove a point."[118]

Simultaneously, the president and his allies were promoting a conspiracy theory that the caravans were being funded by the Hungarian-born Jewish billionaire George Soros, a false narrative that had emerged in response to earlier caravans. According to an analysis by Jonathan Albright, director of the Digital Forensics Initia-

tive at the Tow Center for Digital Journalism, the rumor began circulating through private Facebook groups and pages in the spring.
"The claims of a *direct link* between intentional Soros funding and
the Latin/Central America Caravan appeared on March 30th. Of
course, this was a *different* caravan. But it is the origin of the larger
theme and keywords," Albright wrote. "You won't find . . . most of the
profiles where this type of rumor seeding begins through searches or
API calls, because it's happening in closed and semi-closed communities. The Caravan narrative has been pushed especially hard this
October by red hat fem-avatars within Facebook Groups."[119] ("Red
hat fem-avatars" refers to accounts whose default pictures feature
women wearing "Maka America Great Again" hats.)

In early April, Albright notes, the theory jumped from the
fringe to the mainstream when Lou Dobbs, a Fox Business host,
started alluding on air to the question of whether George Soros was
funding the caravans. As the 2018 midterm elections approached,
conservative rhetoric around the caravan escalated. "I want to talk a
little bit about who is funding the caravan," Laura Ingraham said in
October, noting that the Honduran "foreign ministry spokesman
cited political sectors as culpable—unidentified political influences. Somebody is funding these caravans."[120] The next day, Congressman Matt Gaetz, a young, Internet-savvy Republican from
Florida, tweeted a video of two people supposedly handing out
money to migrants to "join the caravan & storm the US border
@ election time," suggesting that the money came from Soros or
"US-backed NGOs."[121] Shortly thereafter, the president tweeted
the same video, with the caption: "Can you believe this, and what
Democrats are allowing to be done to our Country?" Gaetz wasn't
the only member of Congress to get in on the action: Representative Louie Gohmert, a Republican from Texas, told Fox News that
he "can't help but think the Democrats—perhaps Soros—may be
funding this, thinking it's going to help them."[122] While *Breitbart News* published a story that migrants traveling in the caravan
might bring "diseases that could pose a threat to public health,"
popular conservative radio host Michael Savage said that their ar-

rival would spell "the end of America as we know it."[123]

Conspiracy theories like these derive their power in part from the fact that they allow adherents to imagine themselves heroes in a hidden struggle, combatants in an epic war for the future of the nation. It is a tempting ideology under the best of circumstances; it is especially so when so little about the world makes sense and every day brings a new crisis. Conspiracy theories purport to answer questions while really making the world more mysterious; fascism likewise speaks to this desire, simultaneously infusing the world with mystery and providing the key to its unlocking. More than anything, adherents want to believe in themselves and the meaningfulness of their lives. Fascist conspiracism weaponizes the communities that coalesce around this desire. "Conspiracy theories are, in the end, not so much an explanation of events as they are an effort to assign blame," journalist Anna Merlan writes in her book *Republic of Lies: American Conspiracy Theorists and Their Surprising Rise to Power*. She goes on:

> More than questioning the official narrative, they are aimed at identifying the *real* perpetrators, the true power behind the throne, the hidden hand pulling beneath the surface. . . . The impulse is understandable, and it is an extension of our normal desire to hold power accountable. Often the motivations of ordinary conspiracy theorists are harmless: a desire to improve the world, to explain suffering—one's own and that of others—and to remedy injustice. People join the "truth community" to help expose the inner workings and also to be part of something, to be one of the select few who *know what's really going on.*[124]

As often happens, efforts to debunk the theory that George Soros was funding the migrant caravans may have simply amplified the theory—or, indeed, been taken by adherents as evidence of a wider effort to suppress it. "Truth and fact-checking travel along the same paths that conspiracies do. But the truth is often complicated, shaded, and demanding, and there's no denying that it often lacks the powerful, emotional, gut-level appeal of a conspiracy," Merlan argues. "Furthermore, by creating a legible, moral map of the universe, conspiracism can lead to a particular lack of empathy, a route so simple and straight and perilously narrow that it points, at times, directly to hatred. If you have found a genuine foe, you are free to loathe him or her as expansively as necessary."[125]

In his 1959 essay "The Meaning of Working through the Past," political theorist Theodor Adorno, citing his and others' research into the psychology of fascism, argues that authoritarian personalities are shaped not necessarily by ideology or political economy but by "a rigidity and an inability to react." Gripped by a contagious paranoia and seeking the safety of "collective delusions," they "identify themselves with real-existing power."[126] And so, around the time that Trump was telling reporters that he "wouldn't be surprised" if George Soros were funding the caravan ("I don't know who, but I wouldn't be surprised. A lot of people are saying yes"), one of his supporters, Cesar Sayoc, was sending pipe bombs to a series of targets—including George Soros.[127] Also just a few hours after Robert Bowers, motivated by the idea that Jews were facilitating the migration of nonwhite people to the United States, allegedly attacked the Tree of Life Synagogue in Pittsburgh, the president referred to the midterms, not for the first time, as "the election of the caravan."[128]

The commander-in-chief does not shy from encouraging such beliefs in his supporters, who feel themselves deputized to take action on his behalf. "In this darkness, Mr. Sayoc found light in Donald J. Trump," the thwarted terrorist's attorneys argued in a court filing. "He became obsessed with 'attacks' from those he perceived as Trump's enemies. He believed stories shared on Facebook that Trump supporters were being beaten in the streets. He came to believe that he was being personally targeted for supporting Trump." As the 2018 midterm elections approached, Sayoc's lawyers argued, he became "increasingly obsessive, paranoid, and angry," conflating "his personal situation with the perceived struggles of Trump supporters across the country, and even the President himself."[129]

While Sayoc's lawyers could reasonably argue that untreated

mental illness left him vulnerable and confused, there are echoes here of a deeper, more insidious dynamic. Since he announced his candidacy, Trump supporters have invoked the president's name while attacking or threatening women, minorities, and other political enemies.[130] At a July 2019 rally, Trump supporters chanted "Send her back! Send her back!" in response to the president's continued attacks on Representative Ilhan Omar. "It was an arresting scene: a predominantly white crowd of thousands, many in red 'Make America Great Again' hats, encouraging a receptive president to illegally deport one of his political opponents, who is a black, Muslim American woman," *HuffPost*'s Christopher Mathias reported.[131] Trump expanded his invective to include Representatives Alexandria Ocasio-Cortez, who is from New York, Rashida Tlaib, who is from Michigan, and Ayanna Pressley, who is from Ohio. The implicit point was to question the citizenship and rights of anyone not self-evidently of white European descent. Working in collaboration with ProPublica's Documenting Hate project, Mathias sifted through eight hundred examples over the course of four years of people being told—in some cases more violently than others—to "go back" to their countries.[132]

As ever, Trump's most radical supporters could be relied on to make the implicit explicit. In court filings, Matthew Heimbach, the white nationalist who was sued over his harassment of a young Black woman, Kashiya Nwanguma, during a Trump campaign event in 2015, argued that he had "acted pursuant to the directives and requests of Donald J Trump" and that "any liability must be shifted to one or both of them." In other words, when Trump responded to protesters by sneering, "Get 'em the hell out of here," Heimbach was simply following orders.[133]

WeBuildtheWall Inc.

Toward the end of 2019, as Trump prepared for reelection amid escalating impeachment proceedings, the spectacular wall that he had promised his supporters would be built on the US-Mexico border—which the Mexican government, he had assured them, would "pay for"—was nowhere to be found.[134] Bureaucratic barriers to immigration proliferated, and about seventy-six miles of existing fencing, which had gone up during the Bush and Obama administrations, were reinforced, but construction on a new border wall was blocked by funding questions, lawsuits, and a shifting political landscape.[135]

Even before formally announcing his candidacy in June 2015, Trump was offering the idea of the wall to potential voters. "We have to build a fence—and it's got to be a beauty," he said in a January 2015 speech at the Freedom Summit in Iowa. "Who can build better than Trump? I build. It's what I do. I build." He returned to the theme a few months later when visiting the Texas Patriots, a Tea Party spinoff group. Mexicans, he said, were pouring across the border like "vomit." "These are people—and some are very fine, I'm sure—but they're sending their killers, their rapists, their murderers, their drug lords. This is what we're getting," he said. "One thing I can tell you—I'm a great builder. I would build the greatest wall that anybody's ever seen. Believe me."[136] And they did.

During the 2016 campaign, Trump estimated that building the wall would cost $12 billion—paid for, again, by Mexico. Not long after he took office, an internal Department of Homeland Security analysis estimated that it would cost $21.6 billion, not including maintenance.[137] In April 2017, Senate Democrats issued a report projecting that the wall would cost nearly $70 billion to build and $150 million annually to maintain.[138] Even with Republican control of Congress, Trump wasn't able to find funding for the wall, which became a point of contention in every budget negotiation. Amid his very first budget fight, White House operatives signaled that they wouldn't allow funding for the wall to become a sticking point. "Building that wall and having it funded remains an important priority to him," White House adviser Kellyanne Conway said on *Fox & Friends* just months after Trump's inauguration. "But we also know that that can happen later this year and into next year.

And in the interim, you see other smart technology and other re-sources and tools being used toward border security."[139]

Democratic leadership made it clear from the outset of the Trump administration that they were willing to try to force a government shutdown over funding for a border wall (and would certainly do so without concessions), although they remained amenable to more technocratic "border security" options.[140] At one point, they were even willing to sign off on $25 billion in border wall funding if the president would agree to a pathway to citizenship for 1.8 million young undocumented immigrants—a proposal that Trump rejected.[141] He even went to so far as to argue that the wall would "pay for itself," citing the CIS in a tweet.[142] Ultimately, the omnibus spending bill for 2018 included a mere $1.6 billion for wall repairs. "I say to Congress: I will never sign another bill like this again. I'm not going to do it," he declared.[143]

In a meeting with Trump at the White House after Democrats had taken back the House of Representatives in the 2018 midterm elections, incoming speaker Nancy Pelosi and Senate minority leader Chuck Schumer effectively baited Trump into promising that he would shut down the government if he did not get funding for a wall. The longest shutdown in US government history ensued, brought to a close, in part, by growing pressure from overtired and cash-strapped workers, especially at the Transportation Security Administration, but also by Trump's decision to look elsewhere for funding for his border wall.[144] "We're going to confront the national security crisis on our southern border, and we're going to do it one way or the other," Trump said as he declared a national emergency, which would theoretically allow him to divert already appropriated funds. "It's an invasion."[145] But even this end run around the congressional budgeting process was soon tied up in the courts. And so, amid the constantly unspooling narrative of national degradation ("We don't have a country anymore," Trump was fond of saying), self-styled patriots began taking matters into their own hands.[146]

On December 16, 2018, less than a week before Trump would shut down the government, Brian Kolfage launched a $1 billion fundraising campaign on the crowdsourcing platform GoFundMe called "We the People Will Fund the Wall." In a matter of weeks, the campaign would raise more than $20 million from about 350,000 donors, which Kolfage had pledged to give to Congress to build the "big and beautiful" wall.[147] An air force veteran who'd had both his legs and his right forearm amputated as a result of injuries sustained during a rocket attack on his second tour in Iraq—the *Military Times* referred to him as the "most severely wounded airman to survive any war in U.S. history"—Kolfage had made a name for himself running vitriolic and conspiratorial online publications like *Trump Republic, Keep America First*, and *Right Wing News*. His family became minor conservative celebrities, documenting their vacations (paid for by charities) and VIP treatment at Trump rallies on social media. Kolfage's three-year-old son had his own Instagram account, with more than 62,000 followers.[148]

Late in December 2018, Kolfage incorporated WeBuildthe-Wall Inc. as a nonprofit organization in Florida, where he and his family lived. Two months later, he would appear at the Quail Creek Republican Club, just south of Tucson, Arizona, with an array of nativist reactionaries who had signed on to support the project, in one way or another. Kris Kobach, the former Kansas secretary of state and counsel to IRLI, FAIR's legal arm, was WeBuildtheWall's general counsel. Former White House chief strategist and *Breitbart News* executive chairman Steve Bannon, Breitbart Texas managing editor Brandon Darby, and former Colorado congressman Tom Tancredo joined the board of advisers. So, too, did Blackwater founder Erik Prince and former Milwaukee County sheriff David Clarke, as well as a number of veteran Tea Party operatives.[149]

After the new Congress was sworn in, with Democrats running the House of Representatives, Kolfage decided that he would pivot. Rather than donating the money to the federal government, WeBuildtheWall would build the wall (or part of it) themselves, "linking" the privately constructed portions to the federal government's wall "almost like a LEGO locks in," Kolfage said.

And while the Quail Creek Republicans responded enthusiastically, others were more indifferent. "As far as being worried about building the wall, one way or another, we don't really care," a local rancher, John Klump, told the *Phoenix New Times*. "We won't mind if they put the fence up better . . . just so we don't have to go get our cows always from the neighbors down in Mexico. Our neighbors have been—our neighbors in Mexico have been damn good. They always bring our cows back, and we always bring their cows back."[150]

Come the spring, WeBuildtheWall began construction on a half-mile stretch of wall in Sunland Park, New Mexico. "I have fought illegals on this property for six years," Jeff Allen, a caretaker on the land where they were building, said. "I love my country, and this is a step in protecting my country."[151] When local officials, including Sunland Park mayor Javier Perea, claimed that WeBuildtheWall was operating without the necessary permits, Kolfage responded in Trumpian fashion, accusing the Sunland Park government of having "a long history of corruption problems" and tweeting, "What cartel paid off the Sunland Park City officials to lie and shut down our wall project?!"[152] Perea, the mayor, started getting death threats. When a spokeswoman for the International Boundary and Water Commission, a federal agency on whose property WeBuildtheWall had constructed a gate, criticized the group, Kolfage called her "a thug probably getting kickbacks from Sinaloa."[153] Cease-and-desist letters be damned, he wrote, "We're not stopping until we're done."[154]

As Kolfage started looking for new locations in the borderlands to build sections of wall, he hosted another event that attracted even more high-profile conservative celebrities: Steve Bannon came to Sunland Park to see the half-mile wall Kolfage's group had built, as did former Trump campaign manager Corey Lewandowski and Citizens United president David Bossie. But the biggest catch of all was the president's son, Donald Trump Jr., and his girlfriend, Kimberly Guilfoyle. A laudatory quote from Don Jr. is displayed prominently on the organization's website, in a scroll of praise from political allies. "This is private enterprise at its finest," Trump Jr. said. "Doing it better, faster, cheaper than anything else and what you guys are doing is pretty amazing. It started from a grassroots effort and it's doing some wonderful things for an important issue." Lewandowski is quoted too ("People can't appreciate how beautiful this wall is until they come and see it for themselves") as are Texas Congressman Louie Gohmert ("They did this wall beautifully, it's just incredible") and National Border Patrol Council president Brandon Judd ("From Border Patrol agents' standpoints, those I represent, we have to have the support of the American public in order to secure the border, and that's why we're so grateful for 'We Build the Wall'").[155] The scroll sat above two glitchy livestreams of the Sunland Park construction site, which supporters were encouraged to monitor.

The permitting setback notwithstanding, Kobach lavished praise on WeBuildtheWall for how quickly it was able to complete the half-mile of steel wall in Sunland Park. "It shows how quickly a private organization can identify the problem, take the steps necessary to mobilize resources and get to the site, and then complete the project," he told reporters. "We do have agility and speed and determination, and that's what I hope you see on display when you look at this wall."[156] For his part, Kolfage claimed that the wall was already having a demonstrable impact. "We can patch one hole, it's gonna leak somewhere else," he said. "But it starts funneling people toward these other holes. Border Patrol agents no longer have to worry about this hole."[157]

But during a November 2019 trip to the border, as the organization began construction at a new location in south Texas, acting Homeland Security secretary Chad Wolf explicitly applauded Kolfage's efforts. "I welcome all that want to be part of the solution," Wolf said. "Obviously, when you're talking about a border wall system you have to do that in close connection with CBP [Customs and Border Protection], the Army Corps of Engineers and the like. The requirements that they have are pretty robust. . . . It has to meet certain requirements," he continued. "So if there are going to be private entities that do that, we want to make sure that we're talking to them." Gloria Chavez, the El Paso sector chief of the border patrol, echoed Wolf's encouragement. "The border wall structure is a critical tool for our enforcement strategy," she said. "Whether it's privately owned or government-owned, I welcome it because I know it's a proven concept."[158]

"It helps us manage the flow [of migrants] more effectively, not stop it," Chavez continued. "There is a misconception out there that the border wall is built to stop migration, and that's not the case. The border wall is built to help the Border Patrol, the agents manage the flow more effectively." The privately built wall in Sunland Park, Chavez said, "has been very effective."[159] The next day, Wolf traveled to the Rio Grande Valley, where the federal government was refurbishing part of the existing border wall and Kolfage's group was breaking ground on new construction, dismissing protests from locals with his characteristic flair. Father Roy Snipes, a local Catholic priest critical of any border wall, was "promoting human trafficking and abuse of women and children," Kolfage said. "Instead of driving around in expensive boats with media he should be helping . . . to combat the rampant pedophilia in the church." He also described local environmental activists, concerned about the impact that border wall construction would have on the nearby National Butterfly Center, as "left wing thugs with a sham butterfly agenda."[160] Wolf, meanwhile, reiterated his support for Kolfage, saying that he welcomed "all efforts to help secure the border as long as they're done in concert with the men and women at the Border Patrol."[161] Despite two federal restraining orders, stemming from lawsuits brought by the butterfly refuge and the International Boundary and Water Commission, WeBuildtheWall kept building.[162] That is, until August 2020, when federal prosecutors in New York indicted Kofage and Bannon on fraud and money laundering charges, alleging that the pair had taken more than $1,350,000 out of the funds raised for the project for their personal use and legal expenses.[163]

At one level, this was just another example of reactionary grifters finding ways to profit personally and politically from the virulent racism of the Trump era: Kobach used the group's mailing list to fundraise for his Senate bid (probably illegally), while the North Dakota construction company Kolfage hired to work on the wall appeared to leverage that publicity—and Trump's favor—into a $270 million federal contract.[164] This was more than petty corruption, however. It was a glimpse into the workings of post-crisis neoliberalism.

Chapter 5

EVERY STATE IS A BORDER STATE

So they sentenced Gregorio Cortez, but not for killing the sher-
iffs, as some fools will tell you even now, when they ought to
know better. No, not for killing the sheriffs but for stealing the
little sorrel mare. The judge sentenced him to ninety-nine years
and a day. And the enemies of Gregorio Cortez were happy
then, because they thought Cortez would be in prison for the
rest of his life.

—**Américo Paredes**

"Anyone who does not wish to discuss capitalism should also stay silent on the subject of fascism," political theorist Max Horkheimer wrote in 1939, reacting to the recent coining of "totalitarianism" as an ideology and mode of governance that could equally describe the regimes of Hitler and Stalin. "Strictly speaking, this is incorrect," Nicos Poulantzas responded several decades later. "It is he who does not wish to discuss *imperialism* who should stay silent on the subject of fascism."[1] Today, it is those who do not wish to discuss neoliberalism who should stay silent on the subject.

In 2008 and 2009, the world was gripped by recession. First the housing bubble burst, then small banks started to fail, and

163

then large investment banks. By the fall of 2008 it seemed that the entire financial system was on the verge of collapse, "something akin to a massive electrical power failure that threatened the entire economy," as historian Adam Tooze put it.[2] What looked to some like a transatlantic banking crisis, economist Grace Blakely has written, was something more colossal: "It was a structural crisis of financialized capitalism." Citing Marx's prediction that capitalism would eventually run out of space into which it could expand, Blakely argues that financialization allowed capitalism "to expand not just spatially, but temporally . . . [and] for profits to be extracted from the future through debt, ultimately leading to the financial crisis, but not before sustaining several decades of growth."[3] In other words, financialization—the economic practice of neoliberalism—is a kind of temporal imperialism.

The crisis is not over, Tooze argues, but has undergone "mutation and metastasis."[4] And contrary to leftist hopes, neoliberalism not only weathered the political and economic storm that it had unleashed but appeared to thrive in its aftermath. "It did more than survive: it *grew stronger by radicalizing itself*," the philosopher Pierre Dardot and sociologist Christian Laval argue. "The 2008 crisis, which for many should have ushered in a *post-neoliberal moderation*, facilitated a *neoliberal radicalization*."[5]

While aggressive state intervention was required to stabilize the global economy and allow the continued accumulation of capital, this is best understood not as evidence of the continued strength of state sovereignty but rather of state subordination to capital. Confronted with this changing reality, the states of the Global North have been gripped with panic, scrambling to reassert control in the most spectacular ways: by militarizing their borders and building walls. "Like all hyperbole," political theorist Wendy Brown suggests, these walls "reveal a tremulousness, vulnerability, dubiousness, or instability at the core of what they aim to express—qualities that are themselves antithetical to sovereignty and thus elements of its undoing."[6] Border walls have proliferated in recent decades. Border scholar Elisabeth Vallet has recorded an increase from fifteen at the time of the fall of the Berlin Wall to seventy-seven at the close of the second decade of the twenty-first century, two-thirds of which were constructed after September 11, 2001. And yet, these walls have failed to fulfill their intended purpose: rather than reinforce the sovereignty of the nation-state, they have memorialized its erosion.[7]

Even as it was increasingly subordinated to global capital, the nation-state continued to mediate crucial political questions and contradictions, some of which accrued new significance in the era of "neoliberal radicalization"—in particular, questions of political belonging and the contradiction between citizen and noncitizen. While the category of the "immigrant" was always socially constructed and historically contingent—as were the borders that the immigrant sought to cross—globalization moved the "crisis of citizenship" into a new context.[8] "Immigration restrictions in an era of mass global migration," Kelly Lytle Hernández writes, "triggered the creation of 'illegal immigration' as a new realm of social activity. As people from other countries stepped around US immigration restrictions, they stepped into the socio-political category of the illegal alien."[9] These categories—migrant labor, illegal alien, undocumented worker—exist in a distinct layer of the working class, whose presence and ambiguous legal status serves the purposes of capital. While US employers may make common cause with immigration restrictionists and nativists for political purposes, they do not actually want to stop immigration. In fact, the criminalization of immigration serves their bottom line: "It is the condition of deportability that [employers] wish to create or preserve," sociologist William I. Robinson argues, "since that condition assures the ability to super-exploit with impunity and to dispose of this labour without consequences should it become unruly or unnecessary."[10]

The unauthorized ("illegal") immigration that this produces is thus officially disavowed and yet unofficially necessary, Lisa Lowe argues, providing capitalists with a pool of low-wage, noncitizen labor with even fewer rights and protections than citizen workers.

The immiseration of such workers presents a political contradiction, however: "The liberal principles of American democracy are profoundly at odds with a tiered hierarchy of immigrant populations, enforced by the police functions that control and regulate immigrant and refugee flows," Lowe writes. "Again, as before, the state, and the law as its repressive apparatus, takes up the role of 'resolving' the contradictions of capitalism with political democracy."[11]

As capital moves ever more freely around the world, maintaining the division of the global working class into citizen/noncitizen labor—a division that intersects with gendered and racialized hierarchies—becomes ever more important to the capitalists' continued social control. The suffering of those fleeing the climate crisis, war zones, corrupt regimes, death squads, or simply looking for work underscores the fact that nation-states remain the ultimate arbiters of citizenship—and that citizenship offers protection.[12] To be a citizen of a country in the Global North is to enjoy particular (if limited) material benefits, especially compared to those of the Global South. In turn, this makes immigration legislation and policy a site of deep contradiction between the economic imperatives of global capitalism and the political imperatives of US national institutions. "Theoretically, in a racially homogenous nation, the needs of capital and the needs of the state complement each other. Yet in a racially differentiated nation such as the United States, capital and state imperatives may be contradictory," Lowe argues.[13] In the late nineteenth century, motivated by the need for cheap labor, US employers recruited immigrant workers to build the railroads and work the fields of the American West, even as those same workers—mostly Chinese at first, but from other countries in Asia as well—were excluded and disenfranchised. As the Trump administration made abundantly clear, the state's role in enforcing the racialized boundaries of citizenship has not abated, even if the political context has shifted.

"Whereas in the 1880s, nationalism meant asserting the sovereignty of young nations following the 1848 insurrections," Dardot and Laval argue, "contemporary nationalism is predominantly motivated by a desire to restore a lost sovereignty, fantasized in nostalgic, reactive fashion."[14] This nostalgia is motivated at least in part by the openness of the global economy, wherein capital enjoys nearly limitless mobility while labor is stuck in its place. What's more, in availing itself of that mobility, capital creates the conditions for nativist reaction. As political economist Margaret E. Peters has shown, technological advances and changes in trade policy have allowed low-skill, labor-intensive firms in the Global North to close up shop, moving to the Global South to exploit workers there directly without having to recruit them to migrate. Having done so, they are less likely to oppose immigration restrictions in their own country of origin. "Moving production overseas was all but impossible until the early twentieth century, as firms simply did not have the communications technology or managerial know-how to operate production far from headquarters. Even then, only a handful of the largest firms could operate in other countries," Peters writes in *Trading Barriers: Immigration and the Remaking of Globalization*. "The only choice most firms had was to bring labor to their capital."[15]

In the neoliberal era, this has changed: technological advances mean that firms can do ever more with ever fewer workers, and favorable trade policies allow them to do so in the cheaper—not to mention more dangerous—conditions of the Global South. "This allows anti-immigration groups, such as nativist organizations or organized labor, or the anti-immigration mass public to have more of a voice in deciding immigration policy, leading to restrictions," Peters argues. "The difference between earlier immigration and today is that the anti-immigration forces are winning because businesses have left the playing field."[16]

Into their place have stepped well-funded organizations like the CIS, FAIR, and NumbersUSA. Elsewhere, of course, there is the even more robust (and infamous) Koch network, which has supplanted the US Chamber of Commerce as a para-party organization on the Republican Party's right, aligned with it but exerting its own influence. In many respects, the agenda of the Koch network appears to be a typically conservative one: implementing lower taxes, rolling back government regulations, undermining unions, and shrinking the federal budget. "But the Koch vision of 'free markets' goes further, calling for pushing government out of almost every economically relevant sphere—even when already existing government subsidies, rules, agencies, or expenditures are 'business friendly' in the sense that they provide general infrastructure or work to the advantage of particular industries or firms," political scientists Alexander Hertel-Fernandez and Theda Skocpol argue.[17] "Ironically," Dan Denvir observes in *All-American Nativism*, "independent right-wing oligarchs who pursue idiosyncratic agendas now rival the Chamber of Commerce for influence thanks to the policy achievements of groups like the Chamber of Commerce, which helped those oligarchs make and keep their billions."[18]

While Trump—not exactly a big-business conservative—and the brothers clashed publicly, petty differences did not stop the Kochs from spending significant resources getting him elected in 2016, dropping $4.3 million on television ads solely in Wisconsin (long a front in their war against organized labor), compared with Hillary Clinton's $3 million state total.[19] Nor did it stop their operatives from staffing Trump's administration.[20] Even if the organized public has not become more nativist, as Margaret Peters's research indicates, left-leaning groups that have come to support more open immigration policies—including churches, unions, and civil rights groups—have not been powerful enough to counteract the influence of these nativist networks.[21]

Under these conditions, the old becomes new: extralegal violence against Black and brown poor people; vigilante terror in the borderlands; and a regime of gender brutality against women, queer and trans people, and sex workers. Above all, radicalized neoliberalism has ushered in a new era of white minority rule. "Throttling democracy was fundamental, not incidental, to the broader neoliberal program," Wendy Brown argues in *In the Ruins of Neoliberalism*.[22] In denying the very existence of society, as Margaret Thatcher notoriously did, the neoliberals remove the ground on which the struggle for social rights, social programs, and a social state can even exist.[23] That is to say, neoliberalism does not simply work to undermine civil rights, workers' rights, or women's rights, but denies those who would fight for such rights the conditions to engage in struggle on their behalf. Brown argues that this ideology, while most familiar to us when it is articulated in the language of personal responsibility and market competition, takes its most extreme form in the so-called alt-right. "Reducing freedom to unregulated personal license in the context of disavowing the social and dismantling society," she argues,

> anoints as free expression every historically and politically generated sentiment of (lost) entitlement based in whiteness, maleness, or nativism while denying these to be socially produced, releasing them from any connection to social conscience, compromise, or consequence. Lost entitlement to the privileges of whiteness, maleness, and nativism is then easily converted into righteous rage against the social inclusion and political equality of the historically excluded. This rage in turn becomes the consummate expression of freedom and Americanism, or freedom and Europeanness, or freedom and the West. With equality and social solidarity discredited and the existence of powers reproducing historical inequalities, abjections, and exclusions denied, white male supremacism thus gains a novel voice and legitimacy in the twenty-first century.[24]

Privatization—the commodification of what was once, to whatever limited extent, public and shared—necessitates the expansion of the security state to defend, control, and legitimate the new order, rendering "society as checkpoint," in the words of historian Greg Afinogenov. "When Trump was first elected, liberal commentators imagined that he would suspend elections and loosen constitutional restraints to create some radically new fascist order," Afinogenov wrote in an essay on immigration enforcement for *n+1* magazine. "With the connivance of congressional Democrats, this has turned out to be unnecessary; the resources of existing institutions were fully adequate. A permanent regime of racialized state terrorism has once again proved fully compatible with the cherished norms of the American republic."[25]

But as the mass shooters who take up arms against Jews at prayer or brown-skinned Walmart shoppers indicate, it is not just state terrorism that we are confronted with. Under this radicalized neoliberalism, the state's monopoly on violence is also being privatized, or at least removed from whatever limited democratic oversight was previously on offer. Vigilante groups—many of whose members are not from the borderlands at all—return to Texas, New Mexico, Arizona, and Southern California to stalk and harass migrants, surveilling asylum seekers as they wait in shelters for their applications to be processed and sometimes even apprehending border crossers in the desert before calling in CBP.[26] In October 2018, the National Border Patrol Council (NBPC) promoted a documentary called *Killing Free Speech*, in which CBP agents appeared with members of the Proud Boys and other far right groups. "The agents were tired of being called 'Nazis' or 'jack-booted thugs' or 'immoral,'" Terence Shigg, president of the San Diego chapter of the NBPC, told the *Intercept*. The film's director, Michael Hansen, a Danish propagandist, "was willing to let us speak freely," said Shigg. "And that's not something we generally get in the media."[27]

Militant white supremacists, white nationalists, and the "alt-right," from Dylann Roof to Brian Kolfage, draw legitimacy from the traditions of US nationalism and the Constitution, even as they reject the rule of law that ostensibly protects citizens and noncitizens alike from being gunned down in the street, their churches, their synagogues, or their homes. "Their words, rhetoric, and desired future differ little from those of the free market fundamentalists and constitutional originalists who actually control the federal institutions and many of the state governments," Roxanne Dunbar-Ortiz writes in *Loaded: A Disarming History of the Second Amendment*. "White nationalists are the irregular forces—the volunteer militias—of the actually existing political-economic order.

They are provided for in the Second Amendment."[28] As the crisis that began in 2008 deepens, these irregular forces will be called upon ever more frequently to defend the political-economic order that produced the crisis itself: to protect the border, to discipline revolting workers, and to maintain the rule of the white minority.

Technology, Partnership, and Innovation

By the time Donald Trump was elected president, many capitalists were well on their way to adjusting to the new realities of the twenty-first century, developing new ways to sustain accumulation even as the threat of overaccumulation loomed, most crucially through what sociologists William I. Robinson and Mario Barrera describe as "the militarization of global capitalism," which simultaneously allows the capitalist class to create new opportunities for capital accumulation around the world through wars and other violent incursions while also developing new means and methods of social control.[29] "The generation of conflicts and the repression of social movements and vulnerable populations around the world form accumulation strategies independent of any political objectives," Robinson and Barrera write. This logic renders immigrant labor doubly profitable. "First, it is labor that is highly vulnerable, forced to exist semi-underground and be *deportable* and, therefore, super-exploitable. Second, the criminalization of undocumented immigrants and the militarization of their control not only reproduce these conditions of vulnerability, but also in themselves generate vast new opportunities for accumulation."[30] In this way, one set of capitalists—those in the agriculture, construction, and service industries, for example—makes money directly exploiting the labor of undocumented workers, whose surveillance, detention, and deportation is profitable for a whole other set of capitalists—those in the defense, security, and technology industries.

Representatives of the latter gather at events like the Border Security Expo, which I attended in 2019. It was essentially a trade show for state violence, where law enforcement officers and weapons manufacturers convene to "identify and address new and emerging border challenges and opportunities through technology, partnership, and innovation," according to the expo's marketing materials.[31] I found many attendees in a defensive posture, acutely sensitive to the bad press they'd gotten since President Trump's inauguration.

Throughout the expo, in public events and in background roundtable conversations with reporters, officials from the various component parts of the Department of Homeland Security rolled out a series of carefully rehearsed talking points: ICE and CBP need more money, personnel, and technology. Taking migrants to hospitals distracts CBP officers from their real mission. The 1997 court settlement in the *Reno v. Flores* case, commonly known as the "Flores settlement," which prohibits immigration enforcement agencies from detaining migrant families with children for more than twenty days, is undermining the very sovereignty of the United States. "We want a secure border, we want an immigration system that has integrity," Ronald Vitiello, then acting head of ICE, told us in his keynote address. "We have a generous immigration system in this country, but it has to have integrity in order for us to continue to be so generous."

More of a technocrat than his thuggish predecessor, Thomas Homan, Vitiello also spoke at length about using the "dark web" to take down smugglers and the importance of having the most up-to-date data-management technology. But he spoke most adamantly about needing "a fix" for the *Flores* settlement. "If you prosecute crimes and you give people consequences, you get less of it," he said. "With *Flores*, there's no consequence, and everybody knows that," Vitiello told a small group of reporters during a briefing following his public remarks. "That's why you're seeing so many family units. We cannot apply a consequence to a family unit, because we have to release them."

As Vitiello was speaking, hundreds of migrants, including children and families, were being held by CBP under a bridge in El Paso, around 550 miles to the west. They were reportedly forced to sleep on the ground, with inadequate medical attention. "They treated us like we are animals," one Honduran man told *Texas Monthly*. "I felt what they were trying to do was to hurt us psychologically, so we would understand that this is a lesson we were being taught, that we shouldn't have crossed."[32] Less than a week after the holding pen beneath the bridge closed, Vitiello's nomination to run ICE was pulled amid a spate of firings across DHS. President Trump said he wanted to go "in a tougher direction."[33]

On the second day of the Border Security Expo, in a speech over catered lunch, Scott Luck, deputy chief of CBP and a career US Border Patrol agent, lamented that the influx of children and families at the border meant that resources were being diverted from traditional enforcement practices. "Every day, about 150 agents spend their shifts at hospitals and medical facilities with illegal aliens receiving treatment," he told the audience. Around us loomed movable cameras, fixed to the beds of pickup trucks. The newest models of surveillance drones hung from hooks. An armored truck bulged out into the walking path between booths. "The annual salary cost for agents on hospital watch is more than $11.5 million. Budget analysts estimate that 13 percent of our operational budget—the budget that we use to buy equipment, to buy vehicles for our men and women—is now used for transportation, medical expenses, diapers, food, and other necessities to care for illegal aliens in Border Patrol custody."

As far as Luck was concerned, every dollar spent on food and diapers is one not spent on drones and weapons, and every hour an agent spends guarding a migrant in a hospital is an hour they don't spend on the border. After his speech, he elaborated on this point in a private briefing with reporters covering the event. "It's not what they signed up for. The mission they signed up for is to protect the United States border, to protect the communities in which they live and serve," Luck said. "The influx, the volume, the clutter that this creates is frustrating." In his keynote, Vitiello had made a similar point, applying an Orwellian inversion: "We're not helping them as fast as we want to," he said of migrant families apprehended at the border.

Even when discussing the intimate needs of detained migrant families, the language border officials used throughout the expo to describe their remit was explicitly militaristic: achieving "operational control," Luck said, requires "impedance and denial" and "situational awareness." He referred to technology as a "vital force multiplier." (He at least stopped short of endorsing the president's framing that what is happening on the border constitutes an invasion, instead describing it as a "deluge.") Aging CBP stations, Luck told reporters, "are not luxurious in any way, and they were never intended to handle families and children." The solution, according to Vitiello, is "continued capital investment" in those facilities, as well as the cars and trucks necessary to patrol the border region and transport those apprehended from CBP custody to ICE detention centers; the IT necessary to sift through vast amounts of data accumulated through untold surveillance methods; and all of "the systems by which we do our work."

Unsurprisingly, caravans came up frequently at the Border Security Expo. During his own keynote speech, Vitiello described how ICE, and specifically its Homeland Security Investigations division, had deployed surveillance and intelligence-gathering techniques to monitor the progress of caravans toward the border. "When these caravans have come, we've had trained, vetted individuals on the ground in those countries, reporting in real time what they were seeing: who the organizers were, how they were being funded," he said, before going on an astonishing tangent:

> That's the kind of capability that also does amazing things to protecting brands, property rights, economic security. Think about it. If you start a company, introduce a product that's innovative, there are people in the world who can take that, deconstruct it, and create their own version of it and sell it as yours. All the sweat that went into whatever that product was, to build your brand, they'll take it away and slap it on some substandard product. It's not good for consumers, it's not good for public safety, and it's certainly an economic drain on the country. That's part of the mission.

In fact, brands and private industry had pride of place at the Border Security Expo. A memorial ceremony for men and women of the US Border Patrol who have been killed in the line of duty was sponsored by Sava Solutions, a tech firm that has been awarded almost half a billion dollars in federal contracts since 2008.[34] Sava, whose president spent twenty-four years with the Drug Enforcement Agency and whose director of business development spent twenty with the FBI, was just one of the scores of firms in attendance at the expo, each hoping to persuade the officials in charge of acquiring new gear for border security agencies that their drones, facial recognition technology, and "smart" fences were the best on the market. Corporate sponsors included familiar names like Verizon and Motorola, and other less well-known ones, such as Elbit Systems of America, a subsidiary of Israel's largest private defense contractor, as well as a handful of IT firms with aggressive slogans like "Ever Vigilant" (CACI), "Securing the Future" (Man-Tech), and "Securing Your Tomorrow" (Unisys).[35]

At one point during the expo, between speeches, I stopped by a booth for Network Integrity Systems, a security firm that had set up a demonstration of its Sentinel™ Perimeter Intrusion Detection System. A sales representative stuck out his hand and introduced himself, eager to explain how his employer's fiber optic motion sensors could be used at the border, or—he paused to correct himself—"any kind of perimeter." He invited me to step inside the space that his coworkers had built, starting to say "cage" but then correcting himself, again, to say "small enclosure." It was literally a cage. If I could get out, climbing over the fencing, without triggering the alarm, I would win a $500 Amazon gift card. I did not succeed.

Overwhelmingly, the vendors in attendance at the expo were there to promote this kind of technology: not concrete and steel, but motion sensors, high-powered cameras, and drones. CBP's chief operating officer John Sanders—whose biography on the CBP website describes him as a "seasoned entrepreneur and innovator" who has "served on the Board of Directors for several leading providers of contraband detection, geospatial intelligence, and data analytics solutions"—concluded his address by declaring the agency comparable "to any start-up." Rhetoric like Sanders's, ubiquitous at the expo, renders the border both bureaucratic and boring: a problem to be solved with some algorithmic mixture of brutality and Big Data.

The future of border security, as shaped by the material interests that benefit from border securitization, is not a wall of the sort imagined by President Trump but a "smart" wall. In 2019, CBP allowed the start-up Anduril to begin testing its artificial intelligence-powered surveillance towers and drones in Texas and California. Sam Ecker, an Anduril engineer, expounded on the benefits of such technology at the Expo. "A tower doesn't get tired. It doesn't care about being in the middle of the desert or a river around the clock," he told me. "We just let the computers do what they do best." Meanwhile, former DHS secretary John Kelly, who was Trump's chief of staff when the administration enacted its "zero tolerance" border policy, joined the board of Caliburn International—parent organization of the only for-profit company operating shelters for migrant children.[36] "Border enforcement and immigration policy," Caliburn reported in a 2018 SEC filing, "is driving significant growth."[37] In September 2019, Anduril was valued at more than $1 billion.[38]

Birthrates, Birthright

Nowhere is the ideological and strategic alignment between white nationalists and the mainstream Republican Party clearer than their stance on reproductive rights—John Tanton and Cordelia Scaife May's support for Planned Parenthood notwithstanding. The history of the US border and its role in the construction and defense of whiteness is also the history of the state's efforts to control women's labor, especially reproductive labor and sex work. Those efforts are implicit in the legislation and policing that surrounds the border. Occasionally, they become explicit, as in the case of Juan David Ortiz, the US Border Patrol agent alleged to have executed four sex workers: Melissa Ramirez, Claudine Luera, Griselda Cantu, and Janelle Ortiz.[39]

The federal government first gave itself the power to deport immigrants who were in the country legally in 1907, with the introduction of legislation that allowed it to police the sex trade. "Before that, to be deported an immigrant needed to be in violation of exclusions—for entering without approval," historian Torrie Hester writes. "Immigrants were criminally and civilly liable for what they did after entering the United States but were not deportable for it."[40] Congress followed up on the 1907 law ten years later, with the Immigration Act of 1917, which made crimes of "moral turpitude," meaning "anything done contrary to justice, honesty, principle or good morals," a deportable offense.[41] "Along with racism, anxieties about commercial sex are embedded in the histories of immigration controls," Juno Mac and Molly Smith write in *Revolting Prostitutes: The Fight for Sex Workers' Rights*. "These are legislative spaces where race and gender *co-produce* racist categories of exclusion: men of color as traffickers; women of color as helpless, seductive, infectious; both as threats to the body politic of the nation."[42] These anxieties, they argue, are intertwined with white nationalism's anxieties about race: "White women's bodies—threatened by prostitution— come to stand in for the body politic of the nation, threatened by immigration."[43]

Kathleen Belew makes a similar claim: "Ideas about women, sexuality, and birth in this period [the 1980s and 1990s] were deeply intertwined with racial ideology, and not just on the fringe," she writes in *Bring the War Home: The White Power Movement and Paramilitary America*.

> American white supremacy had long depended upon the policing of white women's bodies. In order to propagate a white race, white women had to bear white children. While white men's sexual relationships with nonwhite women mattered less to white supremacists, especially if such activity was secretive, profitable, or part of systematic violence against communities of

color, for a white woman to bear nonwhite children was tantamount to racial annihilation. . . . White power activists claimed that the Zionist Occupational Government (ZOG) wanted to abort white babies, admit immigrants, allow people of color to have unlimited children on the government's welfare dime, allow black men to rape white women, and encourage interracial marriages—all of this, they said, to destroy the white race. In this context, the wombs of white women became battlegrounds.[44]

Thus the powerful, emblematic white nationalist credo: "We must secure the existence of our people and a future for white children."[45] While the "Fourteen Words," as this slogan is known, makes no explicit mention of white women, its fulfillment necessarily demands the maintenance of traditionalist gender relations.

Trump and his allies' obsession with the death of "beautiful Kate Steinle," a young woman who was accidentally shot and killed in San Francisco in July 2015, underscored the white nationalists' instrumentalization of white womanhood.[46] While her accused killer, an undocumented migrant named José Inez García Zárate, would ultimately be acquitted of all murder and manslaughter charges—and would win an appeal overturning his conviction for being a felon in possession of a firearm—Trump did not wait for a jury to deliver a verdict.[47] After all, this was a man who, in 1989, had taken out a full-page advertisement in four New York City newspapers calling for the Central Park Five to be put to death. Thirty years later, after their public exoneration, he still refused to apologize.[48] Trump declared Steinle's death a "senseless and totally preventable act of violence" and "yet another example of why we must secure our border," making her, as Daniel Denvir puts it, "an icon of innocent white womanhood under threat from immigrant criminality."[49] At the Republican National Convention in 2016, as he accepted the party's nomination, he invoked her name: "My opponent wants sanctuary cities," he said. "But where was the sanctuary for Kate Steinle?"[50] Shortly after Steinle's death the year before, a Texan woman named Maria Espinoza organized a meeting between Trump and the families of people who'd been killed by undocumented immigrants. Espinoza's group, the Remembrance Project, had received funding from John Tanton's umbrella organization, US Inc.[51] "Every state," Espinoza once declared, "is a border state."[52]

As the border is more than just a politically defined boundary separating the sovereign states of the United States and Mexico, border fascism is more than just fascistic ideology and practice enacted in the borderlands, or in defense of the US-Mexico border. Border fascism is also about all the other borders that run through our social world, dividing citizen from noncitizen, the Global North from the Global South, white from nonwhite, rich from poor, men from women. This is the root of what historian Alexandra Minna Stern describes as the "near pathological uneasiness with gender nonbinaries" found on the far right, which "wants nothing more than containment and order."[53] While homosexuality among political allies may be tolerated under certain circumstances, Stern argues, "what most unsettles the alt-right and the alt-light are gender nonbinariness, gender fluidity, and transgender bodies."[54] The far right's ubiquitous antifeminism, then, is expressed most acutely and violently in its transphobia—which has the added strategic benefit of aligning with the bigotry of more conventional social conservatives.[55]

Far right hostility toward those who cannot or will not subject themselves to the traditional gender binary draws on the same underlying fear that motivated John Tanton and Cordelia Scaife May, the fear that white people are losing their grip on the machinery of profit and power. It does not need to be the case that this is actually happening, only that it is perceived to be happening. The anxiety over declining white birth rates and subsequent demographic changes—which necessarily erases a class analysis-focused on the many sources of disparity, from health to income—is augmented by a long-standing narrative about the sexuality and fertility of women of color in general, and Latina women in particular, who are figured as hypersexual and hyperfertile.

This is articulated in a number of ways. Consider the depictions in right-wing political cartoons of Representative Alexandria Ocasio-Cortez, which inevitably present her as both sexually and politically ravenous. This anxiety is also seen in the idea of the "anchor baby," the notion that undocumented immigrants are coming to the United States in order to have children here, so that their children may be US citizens. "They come here, they have their babies, and after that they become citizens and all those children use social services," Bette Hammond, one of the organizers behind California's notoriously anti-immigrant Proposition 187, said.[56] The term "anchor baby" was popularized by propagandists like Michelle Malkin, a Fox News regular who would later be embraced by "alt-right" factions seeking to influence establishment Republicans.[57] "Clearly, the custom of granting automatic citizenship at birth to children of tourists, and temporary workers . . . and to countless 'anchor babies' delivered by illegal aliens on American soil, undermines the integrity of citizenship—not to mention national security," she wrote in 2003, drawing paranoia about immigration and terrorism into the same dark fantasy. "The citizenship clause has evolved into a magnet for alien law breakers and a shield for terrorist infiltrators and enemy combatants."[58]

Emerging as they did from the population control panic of the 1960s and 1970s, Tanton, May, and their allies long supported Planned Parenthood and expanding abortion access—a fact that probably kept them on the periphery of mainstream conservatism in the coming decades. However, their support for abortion did not stem from any real commitment to principles of reproductive justice, but the anxious desire to regulate and control the demographic makeup of the country, starting at the site of sexual reproduction: child-bearing bodies. It was not just abortion providers that the Tanton network supported, after all, but controversial sterilization practices, tested on women workers in the Global South.[59]

In recent years, the nativist and antichoice movements have begun to converge. As former House majority leader Tom DeLay put it in 2007, "If we had those 40 million children that were killed over the last thirty years, we wouldn't need illegal immigrants to fill the jobs that they are doing today."[60] Likewise, for all the cues that Iowa representative Steve King takes from the Tanton network and white nationalists, he is also vehemently anti-abortion. "What if we went back through all the family trees and just pulled those people out that were products of rape and incest? Would there be any population of the world left if we did that?" he asked constituents in August 2019, by way of explaining his opposition to exceptions for rape and incest in anti-abortion legislation. "Considering all the wars and all the rapes and pillages taken place and whatever happened to culture after society? I know I can't certify that I'm not a part of a product of that."[61]

In every Congress since 2011, King has introduced legislation that would end birthright citizenship for the children of undocumented immigrants. Long a dream of white nationalists and the nativist right, ending birthright citizenship for the children of undocumented migrants in the United States would inscribe into law what is nominally disavowed: the presence of a hyper-exploitable working underclass with no legal rights or protections, excluded from any kind of political representation or participation. Such a policy would expand the condition of deportability—already more capacious than it once was, as more and more immigrants of varying legal statuses have been criminalized—to include not only adult undocumented migrants but the children to whom they give birth in the United States.

"It is our job here as Congress to decide who will be citizens, not someone in a foreign country that can sneak into the United States and have a baby and then go home with a birth certificate," King said during a 2015 subcommittee hearing on the birthright citizenship question. "Evidence suggests that automatic birthright citizenship incentivizes illegal immigration and abuse of U.S. immigration law and policy," Representative Bob Goodlatte, then chairman of the judiciary committee, said. "And extremely troubling is the rise of the birth tourism phenomenon in which pregnant women from foreign countries briefly come to the U.S. specifically to give birth here so that their children become U.S. citizens."[62]

In other words, the idea that King and his allies were pushing was that migrant women were traveling to the United States in order to have a child here—a so-called anchor baby—who would then entitle them to "access to our huge welfare benefits," as the Claremont Institute's John Eastman, one of the expert witnesses, put it.[63] This had become a deeply embedded narrative in the conservative imagination. "People come here to have babies. They come here to drop a child. It's called drop and leave," Senator Lindsey Graham said on Fox News in 2010. "To have a child in America, they cross the border, they go to the emergency room, they have a child, and that child's automatically an American citizen. That shouldn't be the case. That attracts people for all the wrong reasons."[64] Another witness, Jon Feere of the CIS, who would go on to join the Trump campaign and then the Trump administration, warned in the 2011 hearing that this practice in turn contributed to a phenomenon that the nativist right calls "chain migration."[65]

"A child born to illegal aliens in the United States can initiate a chain of immigration when he reaches the age of eighteen and can sponsor an overseas spouse and unmarried children of his own. When he turns twenty-one, he can also sponsor his parents and any brothers or sisters," Feere testified. "Approximately two-thirds of our annual immigration flow is family-based. . . . And this number continues to rise every year because of the [ever] expanding migration chains that operate independently of any economic downturn or labor need." Asked about his research into the cost of "anchor babies" on the American taxpayer, Feere pointed to the fact that children born to undocumented parents are provided with public education. "Somewhere around $13 billion goes toward the education of illegal immigrants in public schools," he said. "I don't think any Americans would say that we shouldn't try and educate those who are here in our country, but the reality is it does come with actual costs that don't really get addressed."[66]

While the bill had never made it out of committee, it also had not enjoyed a president's support—until Trump. In October 2018, a few months after one of his former national security officials published an op-ed in the *Washington Post* on ending birthright citizenship, Trump said he was considering enacting the policy through executive order.[67] "It was always told to me that you need-ed a constitutional amendment. Guess what? You don't," Trump said in an interview with *Axios*. "You can definitely do it with an act of Congress. But now they're saying I can do it just with an executive order."[68] It wasn't clear who exactly had told Trump this, but, as *BuzzFeed News* pointed out, King, who wrote an op-ed in 2015 titled "Ending Birthright Citizenship Does Not Require a Constitutional Amendment," had recently met with Trump.[69] Meanwhile, Feere, who had written several opinion pieces on the issue, was still ensconced as a policy adviser at ICE.

King reintroduced his bill in January 2019, applauded by the nativist right. "The Birthright Citizenship Act is one of Numbers-USA's 5 Great Solutions to reforming the nation's immigration system," the lobby group said in a press release.[70] In August 2019 Trump reiterated that the administration was looking into end-ing the practice. "We're looking at that very seriously, birthright citizenship, where you have a baby on our land, you walk over the border, have a baby—congratulations, the baby is now a U.S. cit-izen," he told reporters. "It's frankly ridiculous."[71] The bill stalled, but in January 2020 the State Department announced that it was adopting new rules making it more difficult for pregnant women abroad to visit the United States on tourist visas, for fear of some-thing they called "birth tourism."[72]

("Ohhhhh, yes. I'm very familiar with birth tourism," Jon Feere, the former CIS policy analyst working as a senior adviser at ICE, wrote in response to a partially redacted email from Novem-ber 2017, released to me under the Freedom of Information Act. "Here's a piece I wrote a while back," he continued, linking to a blog post published on CIS's website.)

In *The Latino Threat*, Leo Chavez points to the language that both conservatives and liberals use to describe mass immigration: people are "pouring" over the border, the "flow" of migrants needs to be stanched, a "flood" of immigrants threatens to overwhelm the nation's border towns and cities. This "convergence of meta-phors," as Chavez puts it—the "leaky national border," the "porous bodies" giving birth to brown babies—shows us something about the "permeable category of citizenship."[73] Arizona state senator Russell Pearce, who sponsored the anti-immigrant legislation SB 1070, was very explicit in linking his fixation on birthrates with his perception of an invasion: "The birth rate among illegal immigrants is substantially higher than the population at large," he wrote in emails obtained by the press. "Battles commence as Mexican nationalists struggle to infuse their men into American government and strengthen control over their strongholds."[74]

In an investigative series for *Rewire.News*, reporter Tina Vasquez showed that the Trump administration's immigration enforcement policies have had an outsized impact on pregnant women taken into federal custody, including an increased number of patients experiencing heavy or irregular bleeding and pelvic pain, as well as patients receiving treatment while in shackles.[75] "Women are frequently giving birth in [US] Marshals custody," one advocate told Vasquez. "And there have been a lot of atrocities."[76] In Texas, some migrant mothers have even been forced to give their newborn babies up to the state's Department of Family and Protective Services immediately after giving birth.[77]

Even if they are never detained, the experience of immigration itself is a site of violence for undocumented women. Between 2009 and 2015, nearly a third of migrants making the journey to the United States through Mexico were subjected to some form of physical, psychological, or sexual violence. These were disproportionately women and transgender migrants.[78] In some cases, the smugglers that migrants pay to help them across the border will rape and assault the women they are transporting, though such incidents are far from limited to nonstate actors.[79] Between 2013 and 2017, ICE reported 1,310 claims of sexual assault made by detainees.[80] "I didn't know how to refuse because he told me that I was going to be deported," one nineteen-year-old asylum seeker who was held at a family detention center in Pennsylvania with her three-year-old son told the *New York Times*. "I was at a jail and he was a migration officer. It's like they order you to do something and you have to do it." Between October 2014 and July 2018, the Office of Refugee Resettlement received a total of 4,556 allegations of sexual abuse or sexual harassment against minors in its care who had either entered the country alone or been separated from their parents.[81] After the Trump administration enacted its family separation policy in spring 2018, the number of complaints increased.[82] And for migrants fleeing sexual or domestic violence in their countries of origin, the process of applying for asylum can mean reliving their experience over and over again. In 2018, then attorney general Jeff Sessions instructed asylum officers in 2018 that claims to be fleeing domestic or gang violence did not constitute credible fear.[83]

The Lessons of 9/11

Undocumented people bring the border with them wherever they go. So do all migrants. And for nativists, any transgression of a political boundary constitutes a threat to the entire system that must be policed. It is no accident that the primary agencies tasked with enforcing the immigration regime were created, consolidated, and empowered as part of the response to the attacks of September 11, 2001. As the 9/11 Commission report put it: "The American homeland is the planet."[84] Foundations controlled by Richard Mellon Scaife in life and funded generously by him in death have contributed millions not only to FAIR and CIS, but also to sites of anti-Muslim bigotry such as the Center for Security Policy. As a candidate, Trump cited the center, which he described as having members who are "very highly respected people, who I know, actually," when proposing to ban Muslims from entering the United States.[85] Fred Fleitz, senior vice president at the center, was appointed chief of staff of Trump's National Security Council.[86] The global war on terror and the war on migrants intersect and overlap.

"Blocking the enemy's ability to enter our country must be a central objective of homeland security," Mark Krikorian, executive director of CIS, once put it.[87] "Immigration control is to asymmetric warfare what missile defense is to strategic warfare," he has argued, advocating that immigration enforcement in the age of the global war on terror requires "layers overseas, at the borders, and inside the country."[88] Likewise, former Colorado governor Richard Lamm, who hosted the first WITAN meetings and sits on FAIR's board of advisers, wrote in a policy paper for the neoconservative Foundation for the Defense of Democracies, where he is also an adviser, that "if we wish to respond to this new time of warfare" unleashed by the 9/11 terror attacks, "we must confront the relationship between immigration and terrorism."[89]

After 9/11, nativist groups were able to use the global war on terror to make inroads with parts of the conservative movement that had previously been more open to immigration. "Anti-immigrant movements are, of course, nothing new in the United States. Campaigns against new immigrants have generally coincided with the business cycle, rising in intensity with economy slowdowns, declining in times of prosperity," border scholar Tom Barry has observed.

> But now, the restrictionist forces come to the public debate armed with a righteousness that goes beyond perceived economic threats from foreign workers. Immigration restrictionism is increasingly framed as key to homeland and cultural protection. Most of the allied anti-immigrant forces argue that the War on Terror cannot be successfully fought without gaining total control of U.S. borders, downsizing the resident immigrant population and severely restricting new immigration.[90]

The rearticulation of the war on terror on domestic grounds had begun long before Trump launched his presidential campaign, by which point ten state legislatures, driven by right-wing conspiracy theorizing, had passed bills banning "Sharia law."[91] In 2010, hedge fund billionaire Robert Mercer, who would go on to become one of Trump's most generous backers, dropped $1 million on an advertising campaign stirring up a nationwide controversy about plans to build an Islamic center near the site of the September 11, 2001, terror attacks: the so-called Ground Zero mosque, which, as Moustafa Bayoumi pointed out, was neither at Ground Zero nor a mosque.[92] Even within the universe of far right mega-donors, Mercer and his daughter Rebekah, who maintained an ownership stake in *Breitbart News*, distinguished themselves for how much money they gave to some of the most loathsome people on the far right—and how much influence that money would ultimately buy them.[93]

Soon after taking office, Trump issued an executive order banning immigration to the United States from Iran, Iraq, Libya, Somalia, Sudan, Syria, and Yemen. To justify the order, Trump spokeswoman Kellyanne Conway invoked Muslim-inspired terror attacks in Atlanta and Bowling Green, but these attacks were completely fabricated.[94] Massive demonstrations at airports around the country impeded the implementation of this order, known as the "Muslim ban," while federal judges issued injunctions.[95] In June 2018, the Supreme Court upheld a revised version of the ban, which the administration expanded in February 2020, adding Eritrea, Kyrgyzstan, Nigeria, and Myanmar to the list.[96]

In linking the two imagined threats of immigration and terrorism, border fascism reinscribes the discourses surrounding each, gaining strength through the stories they tell—stories that are powerful and contradictory—and draw power precisely from their contradictions. What appears from the outside as hypocrisy instead functions as flexibility, as adaptability; friction generates heat. So it is in the classic fascist story: the nation is under threat, not only from external enemies but internal ones. The people of the nation, once strong, have been laid low by internal enemies, who hide in plain sight and must be identified and purged. The groups are not interchangeable, but the stories that are told about them work in similar ways. Border fascism fixates on each of these figures—the Mexican or Central American migrant, the sex worker, the Muslim, the trans person, the leftist—as a threat to the hierarchies that fascism fetishizes. "The real threats we face today," Tucker Carlson once warned his viewers, "may be from within."[97]

This is not just something that happens at the level of rhetoric. With the passage of the Patriot Act in 2001 and the creation of DHS and ICE in 2002, immigration was further securitized

and criminalized, paving the way for an explosion in border policing technology that has further aligned the state with the defense
and security industry. This is in no small part due to the way that
Islamophobia and nativism have replaced anticommunism as the
animating logics of the security state.

Between 2006 and 2018, ICE, CBP, and the Coast Guard issued more than $80.5 billion in contracts for border and immigra-
tion enforcement services.[98] The Office for Refugee Resettlement, by
comparison, issued $14.9 million to nonprofit agencies to help peo-
ple resettle.[99] In the coming decades, as more people are displaced
by climate catastrophe and economic crises, the industry dedicated
to policing the vulnerable stands to profit enormously. The "homeland security and emergency management market," driven by "increasing terrorist threats and biohazard attacks and occurrence of
unpredictable natural disasters," is projected to grow to more than
$742 billion by 2023, up from $557 billion in 2018, one financial
analysis found.[100] By 2013, the United States was already spending
more on federal immigration enforcement than all other federal law
enforcement agencies combined, including the FBI and DEA.[101]
ICE's budget has doubled since its inception in 2003, while CBP's
has nearly tripled.[102] Between 1993 and 2018, the number of US
Border Patrol agents grew from 4,139 to 19,555.[103] And year after
year, Democrats and Republicans alike have been happy to fuel an
ever more high-tech deportation machine.

Under the Trump administration, DHS officials reportedly considered holding migrant children at Guantánamo Bay, Cuba, where
a new $23 million "contingency mass migration complex" was being
built.[104] The complex, located at the very same navy base where the
Reagan, George H. W. Bush, and Clinton administrations held Haitian migrants and gave birth to the modern immigration detention
system, was projected to have a capacity of thirteen thousand.[105] In
2018, the Department of Justice and US Citizenship and Immigration Services, an agency within DHS, launched a joint operation,
"Operation Janus," targeting thousands of people for denaturaliza-
tion on the grounds that the current immigration system "under-

mine[s] national security and public safety."[106] Meanwhile, Trump ominously warned of "prayer rugs" being found at the US-Mexico border—the implication being that Muslim terrorists were invading the country—a baseless story that he'd picked up from a right-wing reporter who used to work as a spokesperson at FAIR.[107]

When some migrants sought the safety of collective action in the form of the caravans—as sociologist Cecilia Menjívar put it, "There is a huge difference between women traveling alone or even in small groups and traveling with 1,000 others"—the US media and immigration enforcement agencies took the opportunity to justify further militarization of the border.[108] Speculation that ISIS or al-Qaeda or al-Shabbab militants were traveling with the caravans spread quickly, encouraged by far right advocacy groups, including CIS and Judicial Watch.[109] "The caravan thing is an obvious political stunt, but what better way to get terrorists into the country than imbed them in the flood?" Donald Trump Jr. wrote in a tweet, adding a hyperlink to a story published by the dark money–funded Judicial Watch that connected the migrant caravan to the president of Guatemala's dubious claim that security forces there had captured and deported a hundred people with links to the Islamic State of Iraq and the Levant (ISIL). "Leftist policies just endanger our kids."[110]

"Cancer Wants Only to Spread"

The election of Donald Trump—and, before that, the June 2016 British referendum vote to leave the European Union, known as "Brexit"—posed a shock to the liberal Anglo-American media. Not only had mainstream pundits and analysts failed to predict these events, but they had appeared utterly incapable of imagining that either was even possible. Bourgeois politicians and their media, still warm from the glow of the Obama administration, did not recognize the global rise of the far right in the aftermath of the Great Recession for what it was: the product of a deep crisis of legitimacy, and evidence of a fundamental shift in the stakes of political struggle. Seemingly out of nowhere, liberals began sounding the alarm about the rising fascist tide. Cautiously, and more than a little resentfully, radical antifascists welcomed them to the fight. Still, when Madeleine Albright, who served as Bill Clinton's secretary of state, and masked anticapitalists find themselves aligned, if only rhetorically, it is worth pausing to examine what exactly is going on.

The rise of the far right saw the development of a community of journalists and writers who focused their efforts on covering the movement and those resisting it, while pundits and academics debated whether Donald Trump was a fascist. Responses to this question were varied. He had certainly sounded like one on the 2016 campaign trail, in his inauguration speech, and as he campaigned for reelection in 2019 and 2020. The first weeks of his presidency, with its flurry of executive orders, appeared to indicate that he was embracing the role. But the administration's fascistic agenda was consistently undermined by the president and his lackeys' ineptitude: if they were fascists, they weren't very effective ones.

In *The New Faces of Fascism: Populism and the Far Right*, Enzo Traverso expresses an ambivalence about the concept of "fascism" and its utility for describing the present moment, describing this period as one of "postfascism."[111] "This concept emphasizes its chronological distinctiveness and locates it in a historical sequence implying both continuity and transformation; it certainly does not answer all the questions that have been opened up, but it does emphasize the reality of change," Traverso writes.[112] The crucial revelation of the 2016 election, he suggests, is not so much that the United States had gone through or was going through a "fascistization," but that masses of people were rejecting the political and economic establishment, either declining to vote or lending their votes to a demagogic populist.[113]

In itself, such a rejection does not constitute fascism, but it is a precondition. "The conjuncture of fascism corresponds to a *crisis in the dominant ideology*," Nicos Poulantzas argues in *Fascism and Dictatorship*.[114] Looking to examples from fascism's classical period, he writes:

This ideological crisis, in the forms it took within the dominant class itself, could be said to be at the roots of a factor which contributed further to the political crisis: *the break between the political representatives of the bourgeoisie (the parties and politicians) and its ideological representatives (the "watchdogs" and "ideological spokesmen").* The latter seemed to adopt and advocate fascism more radically, directly and openly than the former, and often, because of their attacks on "parties" and "politicians," came into sharp conflict with them. And it was not accidental that the bourgeoisie's ties with its "ideological spokesmen" proved the stronger.[115]

It is hard not to see Tucker Carlson as such a spokesman, but so is Donald Trump himself. As many observers have pointed out, he is more a creature of the media than anything else. For all the conflict between him and the Republican Party establishment during the primary elections, once he claimed the candidacy, the party fell in behind him, as much of its base had already done.

Democrats, Republicans, and bourgeois parties throughout the Global North responded to the 2008 financial crisis with austerity. "The new authoritarianism of the 2016–17 period emerged as an alternative to the previous left-right consensus in favor of cuts," David Renton suggests. "All good things in politics could be achieved: the rich could be protected from taxation, the poor from welfare cuts. All that was needed was the raising of the border of the world's richest countries and the exclusion of anyone outside them who was going to share in their wealth."[116] Or, as Greg Grandin put it, "Donald Trump figured out that to talk about the border—and to promise a wall—was a way to acknowledge capitalism's limits, its pain, without having to challenge capitalism's terms."[117] Of course, the reality was that Trump, who'd campaigned on denunciations of the "globalists" at Goldman Sachs and promises to expand health care, appointed the wealthiest cabinet in US history on his way to repeatedly attempting to overturn the Affordable Care Act and passing massive tax cuts for the wealthy.

This was the beginning of the kind of "sham revolutionary program," that Clara Zetkin, in her June 23, 1923, report on fascism to the Communist International, described as one of fascism's two essential features, "which links up in extremely clever fashion with the moods, interests, and demands of broad social masses." The second essential feature, she said, was "the use of brutal and violent terror."[118] While every fascist movement shares these essential features, fascism takes distinct forms. Fascism's syncretic nature is part of what makes it so dangerous: it uses the rhetoric and rituals that are available to it wherever it arises. "Fascism was not concerned with the originality of the materials it used in the construction of its own symbolic world; only with their adaptability in terms of the presentation of myths," the Italian historian Emilio Gentile has written. "They took on the rituals and symbols of other movements without embarrassment and integrated them into their own."[119] Not just any ritual or symbol will do, however. According to the historian Robert Paxton, "Fascisms seek out in each national culture those themes that are best capable of mobilizing a mass movement of regeneration, unification, and purity, directed against liberal individualism and constitutionalism and against Leftist class struggle."[120]

Just as elements of the wartime radicalization of German fascism—Nazism—in the form of the Holocaust was prefigured in nineteenth-century German and European colonialism in Africa, the rise of fascism in the United States today was prefigured by the near-total extermination of Indigenous people from the continent. "Every colonial nation carries the seeds of fascist temptation in its bosom," the Tunisian writer Albert Memmi warned in 1957. "What is fascism, if not the regime of oppression for the benefit of a few? The entire administrative and political machinery of a colony has no other goal. The human relationships have arisen from the severest exploitation, founded on inequality and contempt, guaranteed by police authoritarianism. There is no doubt in the minds of those who have lived through it that colonialism is one variety of fascism."[121] What is more, colonial fascism, as he calls it, is never isolated in the colony: "Cancer wants only to spread."[122]

All European colonialism, Roxanne Dunbar-Ortiz argues, contained the possibility of genocide, and often resulted in it. What makes the conquests carried out by the United States exceptional is not the violence it perpetrated but the narratives and politics used to justify it. "From the first settlement, appropriating land from its stewards became a racialized war, 'civilization' against 'savagery,' and thereby was inherently genocidal," Dunbar-Ortiz writes.[123] The genocide of Indians was the necessary prerequisite for what David Roediger calls the "*herrenvolk* republicanism" of the nineteenth-century United States.[124] "Never before in history could so many white men consider themselves so free," Greg Grandin writes of the so-called Age of Jackson, beginning with the rise of Andrew Jackson to the presidency and during which time suffrage was extended to most adult white men. "Jacksonian settlers moved across the frontier, continuing to win a greater liberty by putting down people of color, and then continuing to define their liberty in opposition to the people of color they put down."[125]

Time and again, frontier violence against the racialized Other has been used to restore, rejuvenate, and even heal divides among white Americans. According to Grandin, US soldiers committing atrocities in the highly decentralized war of conquest against Mexico "experienced the violence they committed . . . as a form of liberty."[126] After the Civil War, this dynamic manifested again in the unifying project of the US's imperialist adventures at the end of the nineteenth century, especially the campaigns against Spain in the Caribbean and the Philippines, wherein atrocities committed against colonial subjects served to make white soldiers from Union and Confederate states brothers-in-arms once again. Today, the freedom to be violent—a freedom still enjoyed almost exclusively by white men—is upheld by none more aggressively than the National Rifle Association (NRA). The contemporary NRA became what it is following a "coup" in the mid-1970s, led by Harlon Carter, a former US Border Patrol chief who killed a Mexican teenager as a young man and would go on to head the "Operation Wetback" deportation program.[127]

Even after the genocide of Native Americans, the border has remained powerful as both a setting for and source of US mythology about itself, sustained in part by the fact that the border is constantly moving and being reimagined, expanding and contracting according to the needs of capitalists and the state. Even as the United States pushed its frontier ever outward—until hitting its limit, as Grandin has it, in Vietnam—the racial order it delineated was maintained, reabsorbing the violence and lessons of conquest. When, in August 1965, Black Americans rose up in the Watts neighborhood of Los Angeles, and thirty-four people were killed (mostly by police) and 3,952 were arrested, police chief William Parker compared the unrest to "fighting the Viet Cong."[128]

Incarceration and Deportability

Just as we cannot talk about fascism today without talking about neoliberalism, we also cannot talk about fascism without talking about mass incarceration.

As the early civil rights movement began to coalesce after World War II, massive labor strikes, led by both Black and white radicals, shook the United States. This upheaval was driven in part by what historians have come to refer to as the Second Great Migration, when more than five million Black Americans left the South for the cities of the Northeast, Midwest, and West between 1940 and 1970. The shifting economic and political conditions of the Cold War presented the US working class with an ideological choice: were inequality and suffering to be blamed on capitalism or Black migrants? "Striking workers who chose the former narrative faced intense repression," sociologist Mark Jay argues, while "workers who chose the latter racist narrative faced no such resistance."[129] Amid capital and white flight, young Black workers were excluded from the workforce in hugely disproportionate numbers and subsequently criminalized. The number of people imprisoned for drug offenses nearly doubled between 1950 and 1965. "The 'drug war' gave police sanction to harass poor blacks, and the police came to be seen as an 'occupation army' in impoverished black communities," Jay writes.[130] Even as Lyndon B. Johnson built his

Great Society—marked by the introduction of Medicare and Medicaid, as well as the passage of the Civil Rights and Voting Rights Acts—Black-led uprisings and civil disobedience were met with brutal force and further repression.

In this way did the "war on poverty" become a war on the poor, as police response to Black rebellions reshaped Great Society programs, "resulting ultimately in a merger of antipoverty programs with anticrime programs that laid the groundwork for contemporary mass incarceration," historian Elizabeth Hinton argues.

> This entanglement of Great Society policies allowed law enforcement officials to use methods of surveillance that overlapped with social programs—for instance, antidelinquency measures framed as equal opportunity initiatives—to effectively suffuse crime-control strategies into the everyday lives of Americans in segregated and impoverished communities. In time, the entire spectrum of domestic social programs actively participated in national law enforcement, thereby pushing the boundaries of the carceral state beyond penal institutions.[131]

In the late 1960s and early 1970s, people were being incarcerated faster than at any time since the Great Depression, Jay argues, for the simple reason that it proved cheaper to lock people up than to continue expanding the welfare state. "Many scholars have written about how penal spending crowded out social spending at this time, but this misses the larger point that liberal social programs were failing to secure 'bourgeois order,' and the punitive turn proved to be a much more cost-effective option," he writes. By the decade's end, "the War on Poverty, which proved unable to secure bourgeois order, had lost legitimacy, leaving political elites with a choice: either dramatically expand social spending, or shift to a more repressive approach."[132] As Hinton puts it, surveillance and confinement became "the nation's primary social programs."[133]

The criminalization of Black Americans has coincided with the criminalization of immigration, to the point that now immigration offenders regularly equal or slightly outnumber drug offenders in the federal prison system.[134] "Together," historian Torrie Hester wrote in 2015, "immigration and drug offenders were the majority of all prisoners in the federal penal system, making both immigration control and the war on drugs cornerstones of the carceral state."[135] Over the course of the century prior, nearly every adjustment or amendment to US immigration law ended up expanding the condition of deportability—most obviously in the "national origins system" of the 1920s, and in the 1964 reforms that did away with deportability on the explicit basis of race. Although these reforms (and the contemporaneous termination of the violently exploitative Bracero Program) were pursued with an eye toward formal equality, they ended up criminalizing whole new swathes of migrants—at the time, primarily those from Mexico.[136] "These changes in U.S. law did not alter the causes of migration, and millions of workers continued to migrate to fill millions of jobs in the United States," Hester notes.[137] Many of those workers came with the right papers and the proper authorization, but many others could not, and were thus caught up in the burgeoning system of mass incarceration. In 1980, immigrants made up 3.6 percent of the federal inmate population, but by 2011, they made up 34.9 percent. "Most of the imprisoned immigrant men and women in federal prisons serve time not for smuggling or violent crimes; instead, three-quarters of all people in federal prisons for immigration-related crimes are sentenced for entering the United States without inspection or overstaying an immigrant visa," Hester writes. "The federal prisons are filled with immigrants confined simply because they are deportable."[138]

This did not happen by coincidence. Resistance to Black movement into previously white neighborhoods, schools, and jobs, through the 1950s and 1960s, journalist Daniel Denvir argues, "laid the groundwork for mass incarceration, a system emerging in the 1970s to take a people on the move and fix them in place." In creating a model for resisting migration, he adds, it created "a template of white identity politics organized for territorial defense against the fiscal, criminal, and demographic threats posed by racial others."[139] Detention and deportation are functions of the same system of mass incarceration that developed in response to militancy and unrest among Black and brown workers in the 1960s and 1970s. These policies were mutually reinforcing. Like prison expansion, border policing is "a way for a government that failed to ensure social and economic welfare to use repression as a means to present itself as an energetic protector of the public good," Denvir writes. "The state didn't shrink but rather changed, deploying its repressive powers to safeguard the law-abiding, tax-paying citizen from those who broke the citizenship contract through criminality or through receiving stigmatized forms of state aid."[140]

When criminalized immigrants and felons are imprisoned together, historian Kelly Lytle Hernández argues, the meaning of mass incarceration and immigration control is made clear. For the primarily Mexican and Central American undocumented people imprisoned in the course of what is ostensibly an administrative proceeding, Hernández writes, "the arrival in US jails and prisons confirms that the US immigration control system is busy not only removing people from the United States but also in delivering them to peculiar institutions where far-reaching and racialized social, political, and economic inequities are now defined within the United States." Meanwhile, for black Americans, "the arrival of undocumented immigrants in the prison system strengthens the prison's function as a special reserve for those without full citizenship rights in the United States."[141]

The denial of "the right to have rights" was the necessary precondition, the German philosopher Hannah Arendt argued, for the atrocities perpetrated by the Nazi Reich: "A condition of complete rightlessness was created before the right to live was challenged."[142] Today, following the logic of radicalized neoliberalism and the capitalist state, it is undocumented immigrants, the poor of the Global South, and the criminalized and racialized who are thrown into a condition of nearly complete rightlessness. As Lisa Marie Cacho argues, "Criminalization makes sense of the contradictions that ensue when according unequal access to legal universality."[143]

The Monster of Liberalism

In the second decade of the twenty-first century, the United States reached a turning point in the decades-long deprivation of rights, exemplified by the dual practices of mass incarceration and mass expulsion, which have been pursued by "color-blind" liberals and conservative racists alike, creating the machinery that Trump inherited but did not himself set into motion. Understood as necessary for the maintenance of white supremacy and its racialized labor regime, mass incarceration and mass expulsion can be thought of as two sides of the same coin: incarceration means the warehousing of surplus, racialized workers, while deportation means the expulsion of that layer of the working class that does not enjoy even the limited protections of citizenship.

It is in this context that white nationalists fixate on immigration and demographic change. There is nothing particularly subtle about their reasoning: major demographic shifts threaten the existing arrangement of social relations and racial stratification of the working class. It is notable that liberal politicians are given to speaking of immigration as a "problem," as well, if for superficially different reasons. But understanding that the processes of mass incarceration and mass expulsion predated Trump did not necessarily mean that the Trump administration was just more of the same. His 2016 election campaign revealed the dissatisfaction of a national populist voting bloc within the wider conservative movement. Trump's ascent to being the Republican Party's nominee showed the relatively autonomous strength of this bloc against more traditional conservatives, although collaboration with the Koch network and the establishment GOP infrastructure would be necessary in order to win the general election, overcoming Hillary Clinton's popular vote victory. (Clinton and her running mate, Senator Tim Kaine, won nearly three million more votes nationally than Trump and Governor Mike Pence, though the latter would win 304 electoral college votes over the Democrats' 227.) The movement that cohered around Trump's election campaign, then, was ultimately recuperated by the party apparatus, but instability remained.

Over the past few decades, Democrats and Republicans alike have accommodated themselves to right-wing insurgencies, shifting the entire framework in which mainstream politics is conducted. But something else has changed, too: the conditions in which this is all happening. It is not so much that we are in a pre- or proto-fascist moment—realistically, that is something that can only be judged in the future—as that we are in a period of *crisis*. The crisis takes many forms. Inaugurated by the financial collapse of 2007–2008, it is a crisis of politics, finance, and ideology—and of capitalism itself. Many scholars have fixated on the particulars of classical fascism: its party form, its shifting political content, its worldview and theories of history. But for activists in the street, in the unions, in social movements, a fascist is as fascist does. Moreover, it seems to me that what makes the fascist is not simply the content of his beliefs but the circumstances of his actions.

Marx wrote of the potential for the "common ruin" of the contending classes under capitalism. Gramsci of the "time of monsters." Luxemburg, following Frederick Engels, of the choice between socialism and "barbarism."[144] Ruin, monsters, and barbarity were all already present, of course, when each was writing. But what Marx, Gramsci, Luxemburg, and others have foreseen is that the crises of capitalism do not *necessarily* mean the victory of socialism, and that something more monstrous even than capitalism stalks our potential futures.

There is at least one external factor, too, that shapes our present crisis in a way that is without precedent: climate change. It is already upon us. Flooding from Louisiana to the Pacific islands, devastating storms in the Caribbean, droughts from Central America to the Middle East. Considering what outsized reactions we have already seen to the arrival of displaced people in Europe and the United States, it is easy to imagine how the arrival of many more might be perceived as catastrophic. It is not just a matter of popular nativism that will shape the coming political shifts on the right. For the military-industrial complex, the defense industries, the national security apparatus, the future is already present. The militarization of the border and the borderlands—the securitization of society—has already begun.

"Perception of the migrant threat now goes much deeper than the usual nativist intolerance; driven by escalating climate crises, it is now perceived by corporate America as a threat to a much broader socioeconomic political system and the military financed to protect and perpetuate it," Todd Miller writes in *Storming the Wall: Climate Change, Migration, and Homeland Security*.[145] The militarization of borders and the police, he argues, is a response to an emerging threat, which is not climate change itself, but the social dislocation that it will unleash. "It's not about the disaster happening now, but the disaster that could happen in the future. It is not the people panicking now, it is the anticipated mass panic in the future as the fires, floods, dust storms, and water shortages impact larger numbers of people over longer amounts of time. Homeland Security is reacting to this perception of the future, preparing the world for the human panic in the face of turmoil and upheaval before it actually happens," Miller writes.

> It is preemptive pacification. The government anticipates that the coming crises will unleash movements that expose chronic inequalities and undermine the state's capacity to enforce a system that benefits the few and, although they might not admit it, disadvantages the many. The perceived danger is not what imperils the whole of humanity, it is what endangers the power brokers of the very system that continues to poison the atmosphere and environment despite the assertions of a consensus of scientists that we must stop, or at least curb, human pollution.[146]

A 2003 report commissioned by the Pentagon on the national security implications of "severe and rapid climate change" predicted that, in such a scenario, the Department of Defense would be ordered to manage the US borders and refugee flows by 2020.[147] The report predicted that the United States was likely to become akin to a fortress, protecting its technology, wealth, and other resources from "unwanted starving immigrants from the Caribbean islands (an especially severe problem), Mexico, and South America."[148] In April 2019, the annual interagency exercise of US Southern Command, which oversees US military operations in the Caribbean and Central and South America, known as "Integrated Advance," focused "on preparing for a maritime mass migration in the Caribbean."[149]

While the interagency exercise, as a press release noted, was "unrelated to any specific real-world event," about a year and a half before, more than three thousand people were killed when Hurricane Maria's devastating rains swept across Puerto Rico and neighboring islands.[150] According to the US Census Bureau, about 130,000 people were forced to leave the island, which was already drowning in debt before the hurricane hit.[151] On the US Virgin Islands, hit with two Category 5 hurricanes in September 2017, researchers found shocking levels of depression and post-traumatic stress disorder (PTSD) among both adults and children. About six in ten adults displayed symptoms of depression or PTSD in the wake of the storms, while more than 40 percent of children had symptoms of PTSD. A psychologist at a hospital on St. Thomas reported a spike in suicide attempts in the months after the storms. "People lost their jobs," she said. "A lot of them lost their housing, their support network. The stressors in their lives magnified to such an extent that they just felt they couldn't cope anymore."[152]

Just months after the Trump White House blocked a State Department official from testifying before Congress that human-caused climate change is "possibly catastrophic," Bahamians displaced by Hurricane Dorian were denied temporary protected status, which would have allowed them to live and work in the United States.[153] "I don't want to allow people that weren't supposed to be in the Bahamas to come into the United States," President Trump said days before the decision was announced, "including some very bad people and very bad gang members."[154] As it happens, many of the Bahamas' poorest residents are from Haiti or are the children of parents who fled Haiti. The shantytowns on Great Abaco, home to many Haitian day laborers and service workers, bore the brunt of Hurricane Dorian's force.[155] "Why are we having all these people from shithole countries come here?" Trump reportedly asked in a January 2018 meeting about Temporary Protected Status, a federal program whereby nationals of certain countries that have experienced military conflict or natural disaster are eligible to live and work in the United States. "Why do we need more Haitians?" he said. "Take them out."[156]

Meanwhile, a long-term drought, which began in 2014, has led to food shortages across Central America, even as a pathogen known as "coffee rust" has devastated the plantations were farm laborers find work.[157] While the drought and the outbreak of coffee rust are not solely attributable to global warming, climate change has made their effects worse, and already about half of the people detained at the U.S.-Mexico border work in agriculture.[158] "There is no money," Tránsito Gutiérrez, a Guatemalan farmer, told NBC News. "Today, if people don't go far to earn money, they starve."[159] Her sixteen-year-old son, Juan de León Gutiérrez, left home in spring 2019 to look for work in the United States, only to end up at Casa Padre, a converted Walmart in Texas being operated as a migrant detention facility.[160] Shortly thereafter, he contracted an infection and died. "They say he died of an illness," his mother said. "He didn't die of an illness—he died of need. Because there is nothing."[161] And he died in the grips of a global border apparatus enforcing ever more brutally the divide between the Global North and the Global South, the rich and the poor, the hungry and the fed.

An Escape from Politics

Bragging about border enforcement at a campaign rally in October 2019, Trump claimed that the government was building a border wall in Colorado, which is not a border state: "We're building a beautiful wall. A big one that really works."[162] Such a misstatement hardly rated in the grand repertoire of Trump's copious lies, fabrications, and delusions, except that it revealed an important slippage in the nativist project more broadly. The "border" doesn't only exist at the political boundary between the United States and Mexico or Canada. "The people in Texas, the people in South Dakota, the people in the middle of this country, we are going to be armed and ready," Fox News host Tomi Lahren had said a month earlier. "Who knows who's coming in? That's the thing—we don't know, and we have to be able to protect ourselves."[163]

A week after the president's Colorado comment, Mark Morgan, the acting commissioner of Customs and Border Protection, thanked Trump for his administration's immigration policies. "Every town, every city, every state, is a border town, a border city, and a border state," Morgan said at a conference hosted by the International Association of Chiefs of Police. "With every mile of wall that's being built, we are all safer because of it."[164] A few months later, ICE agents helped police in Guatemala detain some three hundred migrants who were forming a caravan headed toward the United States, returning them to the border with Honduras.[165]

To justify the border regime's expansion, its ideological spokespeople insisted that it was simultaneously nonexistent and ever-present—that it only existed to the extent that it was enforced, and that it must be enforced everywhere. By the time Trump was elected, CBP claimed effectively limitless authority anywhere within a hundred miles of an international land border or coastline, a jurisdiction that included some two hundred million people.[166]

The ongoing reconceptualization of the border was not only driven by legal doctrine, however, but by even wider historical forces. At the end of the twentieth century, as capital began to break free of the constraints of the nation-state—or, more specifically, the constraints imposed upon it by the working classes of particular nations—it found itself confronted, once again, with what William I. Robinson and Mario Barrera describe as "the chronic problem of over-accumulation," which manifested as ever-escalating political crises.[167] Increasingly, rather than trying to incorporate surplus labor around the world into capitalism, neoliberal states turned toward exclusion: mass incarceration and surveillance, detention and deportation, and "manipulation of space . . . and ideological campaigns aimed at seduction and passivity."[168] Three sectors in particular contributed to (and stood to gain from) this: speculative financial capital, extractive energy industries, and, perhaps most significantly, the military-industrial-security complex, increasingly tied to the tech sector and its growing monopolies.[169]

Few firms demonstrate this emerging dynamic better than Amazon and Palantir, each of which plays a crucial role in the immigration enforcement apparatus. Founded in 2004 by PayPal and Facebook investor Peter Thiel, with backing from In-Q-Tel, the venture capital branch of the Central Intelligence Agency, Palantir synthesizes vast amounts of data from disparate sources into colorful graphs and graphics for a variety of clients, from banks and hedge funds to city police departments and federal law enforcement agencies.[170] Some of the company's earliest "deployments," as it refers to contracts, were, appropriately enough, with the Pentagon and the CIA in Afghanistan and Iraq, tracking insurgents, predicting the locations of roadside bombs, and even reportedly assisting in the hunt for Osama bin Laden. Such adventures were breathlessly discussed in the tech and business press, although its domestic activities foreshadowed controversies to come. In 2010, the company pitched a secret campaign against progressive and leftist activists to the US Chamber of Commerce.[171] After the proposal was revealed in leaked emails, the company formed an advisory panel on privacy and civil liberties, which was led by a former attorney for the CIA.

Given the views of its founder, such a proposal was hardly surprising. "I no longer believe that freedom and democracy are compatible," Thiel wrote in a now-infamous 2009 essay for a journal published by the Cato Institute, in which he argued that women's suffrage and the New Deal had rendered democracy under capitalism untenable. "In our time, the great task for libertarians is to find an escape from politics in all its forms."[172] Such an escape, he suggested, could be found in three "technological frontiers": cyberspace, outer space, and seasteading—that is, the creation of new societies settled upon the open ocean, an endeavor led at the time by Patri Friedman, grandson of the late Milton Friedman.[173] By 2011, however, Thiel had become disillusioned with seasteading, and in fact would increasingly involve himself in politics in its most conventional form, aligning himself with elected politicians and candidates like Ted Cruz, Kris Kobach, and Donald Trump, and giving heavily to right-wing organizations such as the Club for Growth.

Thiel's interest in nativism had been a matter of public record as early as 2008, when the adversarial tech gossip blog *Valleywag*, whose writers he would later compare to members of al-Qaeda, reported that he'd made a million-dollar contribution to NumbersUSA.[174] VDARE's Peter Brimelow described the report as "yet another left-wing witch hunt."[175] (Years later, VDARE would describe Thiel as an "immigration patriot.")[176] Coauthor of *The Diversity Myth*, Thiel reportedly described apartheid South Africa, where he'd spent time as a child due to his father's work for a uranium mining company, as "a sound economic system" to a Stanford classmate.[177] Ann Coulter dedicated her 2011 book *Demonic: How the Liberal Mob Is Endangering America* to Thiel, and also included him in the list of acknowledgments in her 2015 book *¡Adios, America! The Left's Plan to Turn America into a Third World Hellhole*.[178] Coulter, who was deeply influenced by Brimelow, would later claim that Donald Trump got "all that spicy stuff about Mexican rape culture" from *¡Adios, America!*[179] Somewhat more substantially, Trump got $1.25 million from Thiel during the 2016 election, including $1 million through a contribution to a super PAC run by the mega-donor Mercer family, plus another quarter million in 2018.[180] Also, a Palantir employee helped Cambridge Analytica, the controversial political consulting firm owned by billionaire Trump donor Robert Mercer and once led by Steve Bannon, to refine its targeting of Facebook users in support of the Trump campaign.[181] After Trump was elected, Thiel attended a "Heroes and Villains" costume party hosted by the Mercers. He was dressed as Hulk Hogan.[182]

Thiel's contributions to the Trump campaign bought him a seat on the presidential transition team, while at least three of his acolytes were placed in the administration: Justin Mikolay, a lobbyist ("evangelist") for Palantir, was hired as a special assistant to the defense secretary; Kevin Harrington, managing director of Thiel's personal investment firm, was hired to the senior staff of the National Security Council; and Michael Kratsios, chief of staff at Thiel Capital, was named White House deputy chief technology officer.[183] Other Thiel associates were placed on the transition teams at the Pentagon and the Department of Commerce, both of which subsequently awarded contracts to Palantir.[184] By the end of 2019, Mikolay had left the administration, while Harrington and Kratsios both received promotions. Meanwhile, Thiel was secretly dining with Trump and Facebook CEO Mark Zuckerberg. Thiel, an early Facebook investor, held a seat on Facebook's board. Thiel also funded the rise of one of the Republican Party's brightest young stars, Missouri senator Josh Hawley.[185] "The state of Missouri does not share a border with Mexico," Hawley said during a July 2019 visit to McAllen, Texas, "but in this present crisis we are a border state."[186]

Meanwhile, Palantir was more successful than ever. According to the migrant justice organization Mijente, which led relentless campaigns against tech and financial companies collaborating with the Department of Homeland Security and its agencies, Palantir held at least twenty-nine active contracts with the federal government as of July 2019, worth over $1.5 billion.[187] In August 2019, the *Washington Post* reported that revenue from Palantir's federal contracts in the first two and a half years of the Trump administration exceeded its total during Barack Obama's entire second term.[188] ICE used Palantir's FALCON system, which included a tip line, as well as a mobile application, in a series of devastating workplace raids around the country, from 7-Elevens in New York City to chicken processing plants in Mississippi.[189] Under Trump, ICE was able to bring another "mission critical" Palantir product to full operating capacity, its Investigative Case Management (ICM) system. According to the *Intercept*, this allowed agents to draw upon a vast "ecosystem" of data: intelligence records maintained by the Drug Enforcement Agency and the Bureau of Alcohol, Tobacco, Firearms, and Explosives, for example, and also records of schools attended, relationships with family members and friends, and employment history. If a digital record exists, it can be absorbed into the ICM system.[190] As later reporting from the *Intercept* showed, ICE agents used ICM to investigate the parents and family members of migrant children detained at the US-Mexico border, specifically with an eye toward detaining anyone not authorized to be in the United States as they came forward to claim custody of unaccompanied minors.[191]

Thanks in large part to Mijente organizers' agitation, Palantir employees began raising questions at company town halls about their complicity in the Trump administration's immigration regime. In August 2019, more than two hundred Palantir workers signed a letter addressed to Alex Karp, the company's CEO, expressing their concerns. Unswayed, Karp renewed a $42 million contract with ICE shortly thereafter.[192] In a subsequent petition, more than sixty workers asked management to redirect the profits to a charity, only for Karp to renew another contract with ICE. In a period of growing labor militancy in the tech sector, workers at Google were able to force the company to withdraw from a Defense Department program known as Project Maven, arguing that Google "should not be in the business of war."[193] Workers at Palantir were not so successful, arguably because the surveillance company is too deeply embedded in the federal security apparatus to concede to their demands in the absence of a strike. Likewise, Thiel-backed artificial intelligence and surveillance company Anduril later won a contract on Project Maven.[194] For his part, Karp deflected responsibility, arguing in a *Washington Post* op-ed that workers demanding more control over the ends to which their labor was put actually threatened democracy: "Immigration policy is not a software challenge; it's a political one. The solution lies with our political and judiciary system, not with Silicon Valley's C-suite."[195]

Although Trump's resentment of Jeff Bezos's immense wealth (and his ownership of the *Washington Post*, which reported critically on his administration) may have led to Amazon missing out on a $10 billion Pentagon contract, and Bezos may actually have believed that Trump's behavior "erodes our democracy," the more salient truth is that the detention and deportation apparatus that Trump inherited from Obama was built on Amazon—specifically, Amazon's cloud computing service, Amazon Web Services, or AWS.[196] Palantir, for example, runs on the AWS cloud.[197] According to Mijente, Amazon, which holds more federal authorizations to maintain government data than any other tech company, was the "key contractor" in moving DHS's $6.8 billion information technology portfolio to the cloud—a project launched by Mark Schwartz, who served as US Citizenship and Immigration Services chief information officer from 2010 to 2017 before leaving to work as an "enterprise strategist" at Amazon.[198] That same year, Republican congressman Darrell Issa, who in 2015 had introduced the legislation that would expand the power of CIOs like Schwartz to modernize the federal government's information technology and expand the power of the surveillance state, appeared at FAIR's Hold Their Feet to the Fire conference.[199] Altogether, as of July 2019, more than two-thirds of the cloud services used by federal law enforcement agencies were provided by AWS.[200]

The expansion of the contemporary surveillance state, facilitated by the advent of big tech, has fundamentally reshaped the border and the borderlands, changing the way that immigration enforcement agencies think about their work and how they relate to the communities subject to their authority. "Technology that is used in war is frequently then brought to the border, normalized there, and then brought into the interior for the rest of immigration enforcement," Jacinta Gonzalez, a senior campaign organizer with Mijente, told me. "There's not that much emphasis on actually protecting human life at the border," she continued. "There's a reason border patrol agents go with a gun and a drone and not a gallon of water and a first aid kit—their tools are dependent on what they see as their function. As all of this rhetoric around security has increased, so has the impetus to give them more weapons and more tools and gadgets."

"Once people have access to these technologies, once people have access to this amount of information, once people can rationalize the level of use of force and violation of people's human rights, then that becomes the standard and the norm," Gonzalez said. "They're able to justify why they need more arms, why they need more technology, why it's okay to violate people's human rights when you're trying to detain them."

"It's no longer a question of what actually keeps us safe, it's actually a question about how to build up more force, and show that," she added. "The issue isn't just the technology itself. It's the technology paired with a culture of violence, lack of respect for human rights and complete and utter lack of accountability."

Or, as Thiel himself once put it, "It's the people behind the red-eyed robots that you need to be scared of."[201]

Chapter Six

SAME STRUGGLE, SAME FIGHT

The desire of the immigrant is a world with no borders, a world with no detention, a world in which humans move freely and welcome every stranger. It is the recognition that it is possible to think, speak, and live otherwise.

—Asad Haider

To defeat today's border fascism will require the forging of Clara Zetkin's "iron-like community of struggle," inclusive of all the exploited and oppressed under capitalism.[1] Today, that community must include the migrant and displaced workers that Alain Badiou refers to as the "nomadic proletariat" (a term echoing Marx and Engels, who recognized more than 150 years ago that "working men have no country").[2] While capitalism has organized the world, Badiou argues in his essay "On the Supposed 'Refugee Crisis,'" it has done so for the benefit of a small handful of people, creating a new world of segregation, barriers, bans, and expulsions:

> The crushing majority of men and women in this so-called "world"—the world of commodities and money—have no ac-

cess to it. They are harshly confined to an exterior terrain where there is no money, and very few commodities for them either. And this confinement is something very concrete. Everywhere walls are being built, and camps to imprison migrants and refugees. You have the wall meant to separate Palestinians and Israelis; the border wall between Mexico and the United States; the electrified wall between Africa and Spain. The mayor of one Italian town even suggested building a wall between the center and the suburbs. Always more walls, so that the poor remain imprisoned in their own homes.[3]

The unification of the world by capital necessitates a global contradiction, between North and South, rich and poor, citizen and noncitizen. The nomadic proletariat—those displaced by this division—threaten this separation. While capitalist states are happy to take their money, Badiou writes, they must always also be rendered as alien: criminals, terrorists, rapists, violent, dirty, sick. "We claim that in their very persons, in their provenance, in their way of existing, these men and women are not from our world. A specialized police will impose controls on them and forbid them from staying. The media will anxiously ask: how many of these people from another world do we have here? This is a horrible question, when we think about it; a question that necessarily prepares the way for mass persecution, prohibition, expulsion; a question that feeds the criminal part of politics."[4]

The line of inquiry that Badiou describes will sound familiar to anyone who listens closely to what liberals and centrists say when they talk about immigration—not their condemnations of Trump's asylum policies or child separations, but their argument that immigration is a "problem" to be solved. While Trump's rhetoric, his administration's immigration policies, and the enforcement agencies' practices have made the "border crisis" more visible than ever before, most Democrats and liberals fundamentally agree with the premise that immigration must be controlled and policed, and that the border must be enforced. "While it would be destabilizing and impractical to remove all the people who have been living peaceably in this country for many years, it does not follow that any nonfelon who sets foot in the U.S. has a right to stay here," the neoconservative David Frum wrote in a cover story for the liberal *Atlantic* magazine. "Hundreds of millions of people will want to become Americans. Only a relatively small number realistically can. Who should choose which ones do? According to what rules? How will those rules be enforced?" he asked, looking to the decades to come. "If Americans want to shape their own national destiny, rather than have it shaped by others, they have decisions to make now."[5]

In the establishment paper of record, *New York Times* columnist Thomas Friedman explained that his major complaint with Trump's immigration politics is that he is "wasting" the crisis at the border—an allusion to neoliberal enforcer Rahm Emanuel's now-clichéd remark that "you never want a serious crisis to go to waste."[6] Friedman reported finding the solution after going on a CBP-led tour of the San Ysidro port of entry in San Diego, which left him "more certain than ever regarding the border, the right place for Democrats to be is for a high wall with a big gate."[7] A tour led by CBP agents of the San Ysidro port of entry in San Diego left Friedman "more certain than ever that we have a real immigration crisis and that the solution is a *high wall with a big gate—but a smart gate.*"[8]

But the horror of this logic reveals itself when we ask who might pass through the big, smart gate in the high, high wall: "those who deserve asylum," Friedman says, and "a steady flow of legal, high-energy, and high-I.Q. immigrants."[9] Friedman reveals who he and other liberals consider to be acceptable subjects of deportation and deprivation: the poor, the lazy, and those they consider unintelligent. This is corporate-sponsored, state-sanctioned eugenics: the nativism of technocrats.

High-ranking Democrats—leaders in the second party of capital—and Republicans from the border region have championed this compromise. During the 2018–19 government shutdown, House Homeland Security committee chairman Bennie Thompson told reporters that Democrats would appropriate $5.7 billion for "border security," so long as that did not include a wall of Trump's particular design.[10] "Walls are primitive. What we need to do is have border security," House Majority Whip James Clyburn said in January. He later expanded to CNN: "I've said that we ought to have a smart wall. I defined that as a wall using drones to make it too high to get over, using X-ray equipment to make it too wide to get around, and using scanners to go deep enough not to be able to tunnel under it. To me, that would be a smart thing to do."[11]

Going on the Offensive

One of the functions of fascism, when capitalism is in crisis, is the destruction of workers' movements that might genuinely challenge the system. Behind their cartoonish performance of hypermasculinity, fascists' primary concern is the violent defense of capitalism and the racial order that maintains it. The real question, then, should not be how to make antifascism more palatable to liberals, but how to make antifascism—and the defense of the nomadic proletariat—a core principle of a mass, working-class movement. Without a mass working-class movement, antifascist organizing is doomed to failure, but without antifascist organizing, so, too, is a mass working-class movement.

Since the 2016 election, many have responded to some of Trump's most draconian policies with popular mobilizations to impede their implementation and, in some cases, derail them entirely. Leftist groups of various tendencies have organized mass demonstrations against white supremacists, white nationalists, and the so-called alt-right, in many instances building broad coalitions. Organized labor has played a relatively small but important role in all of this. In New York City, drivers with the Taxi Workers Alliance went on strike in protest of the Muslim ban.[12] Dockworkers with International Longshore and Warehouse Union Local 10 shut down Patriot Prayer rallies in San Francisco immediately following Heather Heyer's murder in Charlottesville.[13] Transit workers in Washington, DC, attempted to disrupt an "alt-right" demonstration a year later and rallied alongside thousands of others when their organizing efforts failed. Following the deportation of one of its members, Teamsters Joint Council 16 declared itself a "sanctuary union," joining the Chicago Teachers Union, the American Federation of Teachers, and the National Union of Healthcare Workers.[14] An iconic image emerged from Occupy ICE Portland, in which a white, bearded International Brotherhood of Electrical Workers (IBEW) Local 48 member in his hard hat stared down a line of Homeland Security cops in riot gear.[15] Elsewhere, a union carpenter tried to convince ICE agents to quit their jobs by offering them a spot in the union.[16] At another antifascist demonstration, I listened as Portland ironworkers invoked women's rights, Black rights, and trans rights, chanting, "Same struggle, same fight, workers of the world unite," even as police ordered protesters, who had mobilized against the Proud Boys, to disperse.

But both the antifascist and labor movements in the United States find themselves reacting to the far right's agenda rather than being able to set their own. Understandably, frustration and disappointment abound. "When fascists have a parade, even if there are a dozen or twenty folks out there, they're on the offensive in regards to the battle of ideas," labor leader Kooper Caraway told me. Now the president of the statewide South Dakota Federation of Labor, at the time he was president of the Sioux Falls AFL-CIO. The labor council represents mostly immigrants, refugees, and workers of color in an overwhelmingly white state that is historically hostile to unions. "They're on the offensive because they're out promoting a vision that they have for how things should be, how the world and this country should work. At antifascist demonstrations, we're out in defensive postures. We're saying 'No, we don't want this to be here and we don't even want you out parading like this.'" The fascists decide they're going to march; antifascists organize a response, sometimes there's a clash and police intervene to keep the sides separate—usually by cracking down on the antifascists—and the process repeats itself.

"We get caught up in the same thing in the labor movement. We're steadily on the defensive," he said. Fighting the same fight over and over again is not a sustainable proposition, however. "Folks get burned out and they get frustrated," he continued.

> I think what both movements need a little bit more of is going on the offensive, as much as possible working together, going out and instead of always combating folks—and fascists need to be combated—but instead of always doing that, or waiting around to do that, share our own vision for how the world should work and how this country should work; share our own vision for what a regular worker's life should be like, what kind of rights, what guarantees, all these things.

Caraway is part of a generation of young labor activists who came of age in the era of Occupy Wall Street, Black Lives Matter, and immigration raids. Only twenty-seven years old when he was elected president of the Sioux Falls AFL-CIO—on a slate with candidates who were mostly immigrants and people of color—he was the youngest person to hold such an office in the labor federation's history. Ahead of the first anniversary of Heyer's killing, Caraway wrote a blog post for the Sioux Falls AFL-CIO's website. Just months before, the council had passed an amendment to its constitution banning fascists and white supremacists from holding elected office. "It is our duty to let our fellow workers know that Fascism, White Supremacy, and its organizations have only ever existed to divide us as workers and do the dirty work of the Boss Class," he wrote. "The White Nationalists have always been bought and paid for by those in power, they exist not to fight for any ideal, but to destroy the progress made by us as working class people."[17]

Three days after the blog post was published, the Loyal White Knights of the Ku Klux Klan dropped propaganda all around the city, proclaiming that "White Lives Do Matter" and demanding that residents "Save Our Land; Join the Klan."[18] "But after that," Caraway told me, "a lot of what people were talking about was that the KKK's out here trying to divide the working class. We see that as a win. We're trying to shift and adjust the messaging as much as we can so that when folks think of the working class, it's not Trump supporters, it's not these far-right reactionary folks. It's regular folks who believe in solidarity over racism." The labor movement that Caraway and others like him envision is radically different than that of the last few decades: beholden to the Democratic Party, more concerned with filing grievances than disrupting the flow of production, and obsessed with preserving what past generations achieved to the exclusion of making new demands. Instead, they seek to build a labor movement that is not only militantly anticapitalist, but also engaged in struggles against all forms of oppression. "There's a lot of folks my age—they've seen what capitalism has to offer, and they're not impressed," Caraway said. "We've lived through capitalism. We don't think it's for us."

Antifascist and antiracist organizers in today's labor movement share stories of the militancy of old: how the Wobblies ran the KKK out of Greenville, Maine, in 1924, telling the *Portland Press Herald*, "We are going to stick . . . and if the Klan starts anything, the I.W.W. will finish it."[19] How the Klan murdered union organizers and workers across the American South and how Black sharecroppers in Depression-era Alabama, organizing with the Communist Party USA—which identified lynching as a weapon of not only racial but also class warfare—fought back.[20] And how communist labor organizers and workers gave their lives standing up to neo-Nazis in Greensboro, North Carolina, in 1979.[21] "All the evidence I have of how the labor movement used to deal with fascist and semi-fascist elements are from things I've read, stories I've heard," Caraway said. "I've been in the labor movement since I was a teenager, but I've never seen really the things I've mentioned. But I've always heard that's how things should be."

The history of the US labor movement is not one of unalloyed commitment to universal liberation. In the late 1800s, the nativist labor leader Samuel Gompers's criticism of US imperialism abroad was motivated more by fear that it would lead to an influx of immigrants, the same kind of anti-migrant politics that endure today.[22] Nearly a century later, the Teamsters broke United Farm

Workers' strikes on behalf of farm owners, while the UFW in turn treated undocumented workers as strikebreakers for many years.[23]

Over the course of the early twentieth century, US capitalists learned patience. Instead of smashing working-class institutions the way the Pinkertons, Klan, or Blackshirts had, they have hollowed them out. Red scare tactics and McCarthyism eroded militant unionism generally and antiracist work specifically, burying the history of organized labor's struggle against white supremacy beneath chauvinistic nationalism and a more accommodating attitude toward bosses and management. So-called right-to-work legislation of the sort legitimated in 2018 by the Supreme Court in *Janus v. American Federation of State, County and Municipal Employees* has its roots in a white supremacist, anti-Semitic conspiracy theory, popularized in the 1930s and 1940s by a lobbyist named Vance Muse, about "Jewish Marxists" threatening to undermine American liberty—and dismantle Jim Crow laws.[24] Southern planters and Northern industrialists alike were happy to support such ideas, just as today they use the threat of "cultural Marxism" and George Soros to attack progressive and socialist causes.

Having won the *Janus* decision, the forces of capital are opening new fronts in their judicial assault on labor.[25] As Caraway sees it, it is not simply the right to bargain collectively that is at stake. "Fascism spreads more easily in places where there are no unions— or when all the union does is negotiate a contract every three to four years," he said. "Folks pay their dues out of their check, maybe some people attend meetings, maybe they don't, but mostly they just do their contract and go home."

"What makes people vulnerable to being influenced by fascism and white supremacy is if they lack a clear identity, or if they feel like they lack a clear identity. Fascists show up and are willing to give them an identity," Caraway continued. "But if you have consistent and active and militant labor organizing on the shop floor, then people don't lack identities. They have an identity: they're a worker. They're part of a class that has been the vanguard of every major movement for social change in the history of the world."

Labor organizers like Caraway have undertaken an enormous task: educating *white* workers in the United States on the history, structure, and mechanics of racism. "We have a more bold and militant stance when it comes to fascists and white supremacists that are organized outside the labor movement," Caraway told me. "But when it comes to our members who maybe have some bad ideas or heard the wrong thing, it's not as bold. It's not as militant. We're not knocking out our own members if they say something dumb, or if they say Donald Trump has a point about something."

The Central Labor Council in Sioux Falls now has an International Solidarity Committee, composed primarily of African and South American immigrants and refugees. "Their goal is twofold: number one, to educate incoming immigrants and refugees on their rights as workers and organize them into unions, and, two, to educate the American-born union members on labor issues going on around the world," Caraway said. Members are invited to participate in political and cultural education sessions on the history of racism, how to recognize right-wing, anti-worker talking points, and the like. "We've had a couple times when some folks get too uncomfortable, get up, and walk out," he said. "But they always come back."

An Organization of Terror

Early in August 2019, after three years of death threats, Luis Marquez wrote his will. "A normal death threat starts off with 'You're the *real* racist,' or 'You're the *real* fascist. Fuck you, you piece of shit.' Something like that," he explained to me. And then there are the scary ones, like the man who sent him a message on Facebook threatening to torture and kill him, and to film the murder and broadcast it for all to see. "Those I take very seriously," he said. "Would I have believed that threat three years ago? No. Do I believe it now? Absolutely. And for what, wanting people to be equal? Wanting health care for everybody? Education for everybody?"

Marquez identifies as a democratic socialist ("in the Rooseveltian model") and a skinhead ("not a bonehead; a skinhead"). Since 2016, he has been showing up to organize, protest, and sometimes fight alongside other Portland antifascists. At first, he wore a mask, but that didn't last long. "I've got a big mouth. It's large and sometimes it has a mind of its own," he joked, acknowledging that his propensity for trash talk made him a more easily identifiable target for retribution. Soon enough, the fascists and other far-right activists who intermittently descended on the city from its suburbs and rural surroundings were calling him out by name. He changed tactics and started protesting openly, which had its benefits: "In a city like Portland, there aren't that many Latino antifascists. For me, I think that white nationalists, nativists, need to see brown faces standing up to them, not cowering like they want them to." But it also means that he's been targeted directly: memes promoting a far-right "End Domestic Terrorism" event in Portland in August 2019 featured Marquez and his partner with a bull's-eye over their faces.

Reflecting on three years of antifascist organizing in Portland, Marquez emphasized how much he had been transformed by the struggles convulsing his city. "Some of my best friends and closest comrades are trans. I've learned so much from them. I still misgender people, but I catch myself. Before, I would never have caught it—I wouldn't have understood why people were mad." Antifascist organizing, he continued, has "made me see misogyny. . . . Once you know the truth, you can ignore it, but you'll know you're a piece of shit for ignoring it."

"I'm not so concerned with myself anymore," he said. "I hear my comrades in distress, and I want to help them."

Uncomfortable with the idea that serious political commitments might require confronting one's political enemies, liberals argue that fascists and the far right ought to be ignored, that paying attention to them somehow imbues them with power—as if fascism derives its power from "attention" rather than a particular set of material conditions arrived at in a particular political conjuncture. Leftist skeptics of direct antifascist action, meanwhile, offer a similar critique, if for different reasons: while fascists and the far right do pose a threat, so long as they remain few in number and disorganized the threat can be dismissed. The left is also small, this line of thinking goes, and it needs to build power and grow stronger, winning victories for the working class and spreading its own political vision. "Put simply, antifascist politics is, in this view, easy," labor journalist Maximillian Alvarez summarized. "It's purely reactive, not painstakingly organized. It's emotional, not well thought out. It's narrowly focused on combating immediate threats with little concern for the optics or long-term effects, limited to directly confronting individuals or small extremist groups without attending to the broader historical conditions of their emergence."[26] Of course it is the duty of the anticapitalist left to confront fascists, someone sympathetic to this perspective might argue, but *these* people are clowns, LARPers, goons. Consider their DIY MAGA flags, their terrible memes, their unhinged conspiracy theorizing: they are so removed from reality as to be irrelevant. They are not *really* fascists, not in the proper, historical sense. Fascists are dangerous; these people are ridiculous.

"But as true dialecticians will concede," Chacón and Davis write in *No One Is Illegal*, "what begins as farce sometimes grows into something much uglier and more dangerous."[27] The men who rallied in support of Joey Gibson's senate bid or Enrique Tarrio's condemnation of "domestic terrorism" were the very same who showed up to harass and intimidate left-wing activists who occupied space around an ICE facility in Portland. The inability or unwillingness to recognize how these phenomena are interrelated impedes our ability to fully grapple with them: US imperialism produces the disaffected veterans who become white nationalists and border vigilantes; the militarized police state fuels Blue Lives Matter.

The president, his allies in Congress, and the right-wing media apparatus that supports him have repeatedly invoked "antifa" to discredit political dissidents. Twice over the summer of 2019, including on the morning of a Proud Boys rally in Portland, the president tweeted that "consideration is being given" to naming "ANTIFA

an 'ORGANIZATION OF TERROR,'" a clear reference to a resolution introduced in the Senate by Bill Cassidy and Ted Cruz.[28]
The far right's gleeful deployment of the "domestic terrorist" epi-
thet against antifascists—even as one fascist murderer after another
enacts (or attempts to enact) their own beliefs, explicitly—reaffirms
that the vocabulary of the security state is of no use in confronting
the real problem, which is not really "domestic terrorism" as such,
but white supremacy, misogyny, and fascism.[29]

Efforts to expand police power in response to fascist violence
will inevitably blow back onto those historically targeted by law
enforcement. As journalist Sam Adler-Bell wrote for the *New
Republic*, "White supremacist police cannot be expected to police
white supremacy."[30] The Antiterrorism and Effective Death Penalty Act (AEDPA) passed in the wake of the 1995 Oklahoma City
bombing, the single most violent act of white supremacist violence on US soil in recent memory, is an instructive example: not
only has the law gutted habeas corpus and been leveraged to fill
migrant detention centers (in combination with the Illegal Immigration Reform and Immigrant Responsibility Act), but it has also
been used to restrict Muslim immigration to the United States.[31]

The fact that the Cruz-Cassidy resolution spent as much time
describing left-wing organizing against ICE as it did the kind of
street-based antifascism that invocations of "ANTIFA" usually
conjure is significant. The groundwork being laid was not necessarily for the official designation of Antifa as a terror organization—
there is no "Antifa" organization, and even if there were, there is no
domestic terrorism law by which it could be officially designated as
such—but for the criminalization of radical left-wing politics more
broadly. Still, that's a long-term project. The short-term effect is to
signal to both nonstate actors and the police that antifascist activists can be brutalized with impunity, or at least with the approval
of the president and his allies.

Less than a year later, during protests against police brutality
unidentifiable federal agents were deployed to the streets of Portland to snatch black-clad activists off the streets, detaining them in

unmarked vans.[32] They were CBP agents, mobilized under the new Protecting American Communities Task Force, created in response to the weeks of unrest that followed the murder of George Floyd.[33] Ostensibly, the task force was formed to defend federal monuments from demonstrators who would topple them. Police around the country felt that their hands were tied, acting DHS deputy secretary Ken Cuccinelli, a CIS and FAIR ally, said on Fox News. "We are seeing the violent results. And, Donald Trump, the president of the United States, is determined to do what he can to push that down," Cuccinelli concluded. "We can't do it everywhere. But, he is determined to bring more peace across some of these violent cities."[34]

No One Is Illegal on Stolen Land

John Tanton died on July 16, 2019, after a sixteen-year battle with Parkinson's disease. Friends, family, and colleagues, an obituary posted to the website of a Michigan funeral home read, "will remember him for his love of nature" and "his intimate familiarity with botany." Naturalist friends "will recall backpacking and camping" and former patients "will remember him for the excellent eye care he provided."[35] Aside from a glancing reference to FAIR, there is no mention of his political legacy. The migrants he spent so many years working to exclude from the United States are also written out of his obituary.

In the medical metaphor that shaped Tanton's worldview, immigrants are represented as poison to which his ideas are the antidote. Trump and his supporters' fetishization of "the wall" is simply an articulation of their commitment to this vision. The wall is white supremacy, the rule of the wealthy few over the impoverished many: a quarantine. It separates the United States from Mexico, Europe from Africa, and Israel from Palestine. But it is politics that made borders—and all the separations of this world—and politics can unmake them. There is no immigration crisis. There is only a political crisis, as the capitalist class scrambles to maintain its barbaric dominance over the world however it can.

The racialized violence of the militarized border and the fascists who express its logic are the "hardening joints of a sclerotic system," Chacón writes.[36] So long as borders remain open for capital and closed for labor—as they must, under capitalism—conditions for all workers, wherever they live, will continue to decline. The workers of the world will not be free until they are able to choose where to live without fear or coercion. "Immigrants migrate to find sanctuary, colonizers come to steal and profit off of the exploitable," Hope-Siihasin, an organizer with the Red Nation, proclaimed on Indigenous Peoples' Day 2019. "No one is illegal on stolen land—except for colonizers."[37]

Today, the struggle against fascism and a world without capitalism demands that we imagine a world without borders. We must imagine a world through which people can freely move, organize, and build a viable future together, liberated not only from wage labor but also from racism, nationalism, and gender-based oppression as well—every wall smashed and every border it marks withering away.

FURTHER RESOURCES

Ana, Otto Santa. *Brown Tide Rising: Metaphors of Latinos in Contemporary American Public Discourse.* Austin: University of Texas Press, 2002.

Badiou, Alain. *Greece and the Reinvention of Politics.* New York: Verso Books, 2018.

———. *The Communist Hypothesis.* New York: Verso Books, 2010.

Beirich, Heidi. *The Nativist Lobby: Three Faces of Intolerance.* Montgomery, AL: Southern Poverty Law Center, 2009. www.splcenter.org/sites/default/files/d6_legacy_files/downloads/splc_nativistlobby.pdf.

Belew, Kathleen. *Bring the War Home: The White Power Movement and Paramilitary America.* Cambridge, MA: Harvard University Press, 2018.

Brown, Wendy. *In the Ruins of Neoliberalism: the Rise of Antidemocratic Politics in the West.* New York: Columbia University Press, 2019.

———. *Walled States, Waning Sovereignty.* Cambridge, MA: MIT Press, 2014.

Cacho, Lisa Marie. *Social Death: Racialized Rightlessness and the*

Criminalization of the Unprotected. New York and London: New York University Press, 2012.

Cammelli, Maddalena Gretel. "Fascism as a Style of Life: Community Life and Violence in a Neofascist Movement in Italy." *Focaal—Journal of Global and Historical Anthropology*, 79 (2017): 89–101. doi:10.3167/fcl.2017.790108.

———. "The Legacy of Fascism in the Present: 'Third Millennium Fascists' in Italy." *Journal of Modern Italian Studies* 23, no. 2 (2018): 199–214. https://doi.org/10.1080/135457 1X.2018.1427952.

Césaire, Aimé. *Discourse on Colonialism.* Trans. Joan Pinkham. New York: Monthly Review Press, 1972.

Chacón, Justin Akers, and Mike Davis. *No One Is Illegal: Fighting Racism and State Violence on the U.S.-Mexico Border.* Chicago: Haymarket Books, 2018.

Chavez, Leo. *The Latino Threat: Constructing Immigrants, Citizens, and the Nation.* Stanford, CA: Stanford University Press, 2008.

Davis, Angela, and Gina Dent. "Prison as a Border: A Conversation on Gender, Globalization, and Punishment." *Signs* 26, no. 4, Globalization and Gender (Summer, 2001), 1235–41. www.jstor.org/stable/3175363.

De León, Jason. *The Land of Open Graves: Living and Dying on the Migrant Trail.* Oakland: University of California Press, 2015.

Denvir, Daniel. *All-American Nativism: How the Bipartisan War on Immigrants Explains Politics as We Know It.* New York: Verso, 2020.

Dunbar-Ortiz, Roxanne. *Loaded: A Disarming History of the Second Amendment.* San Francisco: City Lights Books, 2018.

Estes, Nick. *Our History Is the Future: Standing Rock versus the Dakota Access Pipeline, and the Long Tradition of Indigenous Resistance.* London: Verso Books, 2019.

García Hernández, César Cuauhtémoc. *Migrating to Prison: America's Obsession with Locking Up Immigrants*. New York: New Press, 2019.

Grandin, Greg. *The End of the Myth: From the Frontier to the Border Wall in the Mind of America*. New York: Metropolitan Books, 2019.

Haider, Asad. *Mistaken Identity: Race and Class in the Age of Trump*. New York: Verso Books, 2018.

Hartmann, Betsy. *Reproductive Rights and Wrongs: The Global Politics of Population Control*. Chicago: Haymarket Books, 2016.

Hernández, Kelly Lytle. "Amnesty or Abolition? Felons, Illegals, and the Case for a New Abolition Movement." *Boom: A Journal of California* 1, no. 4 (Winter 2011): 54–68. https://urbanresearchnetwork.org/wp-content/uploads/2014/07/Amnesty-or-Abolition_Dec-2011_BOOM.pdf.

———. *Migra! A History of the U.S. Border Patrol*. Berkeley, CA: University of California Press, 2010.

Hertel-Fernandez, Alexander, and Theda Skocpol. "Billionaires against Big Business: Growing Tensions in the Republican Party Coalition." Prepared for delivery at the 2016 Midwest Political Science Association Conference, April 8, 2016. https://terrain.gov.harvard.edu/files/terrain/files/billionaires_against_big_business-_growing_tensions_in_the_republican_party_coalition.pdf?m=1463891611.

Hester, Torrie. "Deportability and the Carceral State." *Journal of American History* 102, no. 1 (June 2015): 141–51. https://academic.oup.com/jah/article/102/1/141/686644.

Lewis, Rebecca. "Alternative Influence: Broadcasting the Reactionary Right on YouTube." *Data & Society*, September 18, 2018. https://datasociety.net/library/alternative-influence/.

Lindskoog, Carl. *Detain and Punish: Haitian Refugees and the Rise of the World's Largest Immigration Detention System*. Gainsville: University of Florida Press, 2018.

Lowe, Lisa. *Immigrant Acts: On Asian American Cultural Politics*. Durham, NC: Duke University Press, 1996.

Loyd, Jenna M., Matt Mitchelson, and Andrew Burridge, eds. *Beyond Walls and Cages: Prisons, Borders, and Global Crisis*. Athens: University of Georgia Press, 2012.

Lyons, Matthew N. *Insurgent Supremacists: The U.S. Far Right's Challenge to State and Empire*. Oakland: PM Press, 2018.

MacLean, Nancy. *Behind the Mask of Chivalry: The Making of the Second Ku Klux Klan*. New York: Oxford University Press, 1994.

Mayer, Jane. *Dark Money: the Hidden History of the Billionaires behind the Rise of the Radical Right*. New York: Penguin Random House, 2016.

Merlan, Anna. *Republic of Lies: American Conspiracy Theorists and Their Surprising Rise to Power*. New York: Random House, 2019.

Miller, Todd. *Empire of Borders: The Expansion of the US Border around the World*. London: Verso, 2019.

———. "More Than a Wall: Corporate Profiteering and the Militarization of US Borders," TNI, September 16, 2019, www.tni.org/en/morethanawall.

———. *Storming the Wall: Climate Change, Migration, and Homeland Security*. San Francisco: City Lights Books, 2017.

Ngai, Mae M. *Impossible Subjects: Illegal Aliens and the Making of Modern America*. Updated edition. Princeton, NJ: Princeton University Press, 2014.

No More Deaths, No Más Muertes. *A Culture of Cruelty: Abuse and Impunity in Short-Term U.S. Border Patrol Custody*. No More Deaths, No Más Muertes, 2011. https://nomoredeaths.org/abuse-documentation/a-culture-of-cruelty/.

No More Deaths, No Más Muertes, and La Coalicion de Derechos Humans. *Disappeared: How the US Border Enforcement Agencies Are Fueling a Missing Persons Crisis.* No More Deaths, No Más Muertes, 2016. www.thedisappearedreport.org/.

Paxton, Robert O. *The Anatomy of Fascism.* New York: Alfred A. Knopf, 2004.

Poulantzas, Nicos. *Fascism and Dictatorship: The Third International and the Problem of Fascism.* London: Verso, 2018.

Walia, Harsha. *Undoing Border Imperialism.* Oakland: AK Press, 2013.

Zetkin, Clara. *Fighting Fascism: How to Struggle and How to Win.* Chicago: Haymarket Books, 2017.

ACKNOWLEDGMENTS

This book was researched, reported, and written on stolen land—primarily, on that of the Canarsee and Lenape peoples. While I am its author, this text would not exist without the labor of many others. First among those are my parents, Sally-Anne French and Jim O'Connor, and my grandparents, Bob and Rita French, to whom it is dedicated.

Thank you to Kristina Moore for telling me that it was time to write a book proposal and to Katie Cacouris for getting it over the line. Thank you to Anthony Arnove, Dao Tran, and Duncan Thomas for believing that the proposal could actually be a book and for helping to make it happen. Thank you to Anna Merlan, Carly Goodman, and Gaby Del Valle for providing feedback on the manuscript. Thank you to Elaina Katz for research assistance. Thanks to Hassan Ahmad, Humza Kazmi, Stephen Piggott, and Ethan Fauré for their work on Tanton's archives.

I would not be any kind of writer at all were it not for teachers like Marla Kohlman, George McCarthy, and Leigh Wood, or editors like Jess Bergman, Tim Marchman, Tom Scocca, and Kelly Stout, who worked with me on pieces that form part of the core of this book. Thank you also to Choire Sicha for answering my emails. Thank you to Jamie Lauren Keiles for all of the coffee.

Very few of the thoughts that I have are particularly original. Mostly, they are appropriated from friends and comrades—too many to name here—who shared their experiences and their insights. I can only hope this book proves as useful to others as those conversations were for me.

NOTES

Preface

1. Chip Roy, Michael Cloud, Andy Biggs, Jody Hice, Brian Babin, Scott Perry, Louie Gohmert, Randy Weber, Pete Olson, Gregory F. Murphy, and Paul A. Gosar, letter to Alex Azar, Mark T. Esper, and Chad F. Wolf, February 28, 2020, https://roy.house.gov/sites/roy.house.gov/files/wysiwyg_uploaded/Rep.%20Roy%20letter%20to%20HHS.DHS_.DOD%2002.28.20.pdf.

2. Gaby Del Valle and Jack Herrera, "Deportations Are Making the Coronavirus Crisis Worse," *Nation*, March 23, 2020, www.thenation.com/article/politics/deportation-coronavirus-immigration; Jeff Abbott, "U.S. Deportation Policies Are Spreading COVID-19," elfaro.net, April 18, 2020, https://elfaro.net/en/202004/internacionales/24303/US-Deportation-Policies-Are-Spreading-COVID-19.htm.

3. Julia Love and Mica Rosenberg, "Sprawling Mexican Border Camp Ill-Prepared for Coronavirus," Reuters, March 23, 2020, www.reuters.com/article/us-health-coronavirus-mexico-matamoros/sprawling-mexican-border-camp-ill-prepared-for-coronavirus-idUSKBN2190ZD.

4. Hilary Beaumont, "Fears over Coronavirus Grip Migrant Camps on US–Mexico Border," Al Jazeera, March 12, 2020, www.aljazeera.com/news/2020/03/fears-coronavirus-grip-migrant-camps-mexico-border-200312160805524.html.

5. Ashton Pittman, "'They See Us as Disposable': ICE Detainees Plead for Release from COVID-19 'Breeding Grounds,'" *Mississippi Free Press*, April 6, 2020, www.mississippifreepress.com/ice-detainees-plead-release-covid-19.html.

6. Miriam Jordan, "'We're Petrified': Immigrants Afraid to Seek Medical Care

for Coronavirus," *New York Times*, March 18, 2020, www.nytimes.com
/2020/03/18/us/coronavirus-immigrants.html.

7. Miriam Jordan, "Farmworkers, Mostly Undocumented, Become 'Essential'
during Pandemic," *New York Times*, April 2, 2020, www.nytimes.com
/2020/04/02/us/coronavirus-undocumented-immigrant-farmworkers
-agriculture.html; David Bacon, "America's Farmworkers Await the Virus,"
Capital & Main, April 1, 2020, https://capitalandmain.com
/americas-farmworkers-await-the-virus-0401.

8. Andrea Castillo, "Farmworkers Face Coronavirus Risk: 'You Can't Pick
Strawberries over Zoom,'" *Los Angeles Times*, April 1, 2020, www.latimes.com
/california/story/2020-04-01/california-farmworkers-coronavirus.

9. Bacon, "America's Farmworkers."

10. Kate Linthicum, Wendy Fry, and Gabriela Minjares, "U.S. Factories in
Mexico Are Still Open. As the Coronavirus Spreads, Workers Are Dying,"
Los Angeles Times, April 18, 2020, www.latimes.com/world-nation/story
/2020-04-18/u-s-factories-in-mexico-are-still-open-as-the-coronavirus
-spreads-workers-are-dying.

11. Caitlin Dickerson, Zolan Kanno-Youngs, and Annie Correal, "'Flood the
Streets': ICE Targets Sanctuary Cities with Increased Surveillance," *New
York Times*, March 5, 2020, www.nytimes.com/2020/03/05/us/ICE
-BORTAC-sanctuary-cities.html; Caitlin Dickerson and Zolan Kanno-
Youngs, "Border Patrol Will Deploy Elite Tactical Agents to Sanctuary
Cities," *New York Times*, February 14, 2020, www.nytimes.com
/2020/02/14/us/Border-Patrol-ICE-Sanctuary-Cities.html.

12. Ryan Devereaux, "How ICE Operations in New York Set the Stage for a
Coronavirus Nightmare in Local Jails," *Intercept*, March 27, 2020, https://
theintercept.com/2020/03/27/immigrants-coronavirus-ice-detention
-new-york.

13. Hamed Aleaziz, "Immigrants Afraid of the Coronavirus Outbreak Are
Protesting inside ICE Facilities," *BuzzFeed News*, March 26, 2020, www
.buzzfeednews.com/article/hamedaleaziz/immigrants-coronavirus
-outbreak-ice-protests.

14. Dara Lind, "ICE Detainee Says Migrants Are Going on a Hunger Strike
for Soap," ProPublica, March 23, 2020, www.propublica.org/article/ice
-detainee-says-migrants-are-going-on-a-hunger-strike-for-soap.

15. Rupert Neate and Jo Tuckman, "Donald Trump: Mexican Migrants Bring
'Tremendous Infectious Disease' to US," *Guardian*, July 6, 2015, www
.theguardian.com/us-news/2015/jul/06/donald-trump-mexican
-immigrants-tremendous-infectious-disease.

16. Tanya Basu and Tracy Connor, "Fox News Commentator Says Migrants
Are Carrying Smallpox, a Disease Eradicated in 1980," *Daily Beast*,

October 29, 2019, www.thedailybeast.com/fox-news-commentator-says
-migrants-are-carrying-smallpox-a-disease-eradicated-in-1980?ref=scroll.

17. Matt Shuham, "Tomi Lahren Becomes Latest to Fear Monger about
'Caravan of Diseases,'" *Talking Points Memo*, December 4, 2018, https://
talkingpointsmemo.com/news/tomi-lahren-becomes-latest-to-fear
-monger-about-caravan-of-diseases.

18. Zoë Schlanger and Justin Rohrlich, "This Framed Photo of Tomi Lahren
Hangs in US Border Patrol Headquarters," *Quartz*, July 12, 2019, https://
qz.com/1663596/framed-photo-of-tomi-lahren-hangs-in-us-border
-patrol-headquarters/.

19. Ken Klippenstein, "The U.S. Military Is Monitoring Interfaith Group
Opposed to Child Separation, Leaked Document Reveals," *Intercept*,
November 11, 2019, https://theintercept.com/2019/11/11/border
-protest-groups-surveillance/.

20. Suzy Lee, "The Case for Open Borders," *Catalyst* 2, no. 4 (Winter 2019),
https://catalyst-journal.com/vol2/no4/the-case-for-open-borders.

21. "The Border Crossing Us," *Viewpoint Magazine*, November 7, 2018, www
.viewpointmag.com/2018/11/07/from-what-shore-does-socialism-arrive.

22. Simon Carswell, "Trump Will Run for Presidency Again If He Loses,
Says Former Chief of Staff," *Irish Times*, November 5, 2020, https://
www.irishtimes.com/news/world/us/trump-will-run-for-presidency-
again-if-he-loses-says-former-chief-of-staff-1.4401451; Juliet Chung,
Corrie Driebusch, Rebecca Ballhaus, "Trump Allies Explore Buyout of
Conservative Channel Seeking to Compete With Fox News," *Wall Street
Journal*, January 10, 2020, https://www.wsj.com/articles/trump-allies
-explore-buyout-of-conservative-news-channel-one-america-news
-network-11578696767.

23. Richard Henderson, Eric Platt, Colby Smith, Naomi Rovnick, and Tommy
Stubbington, "US Stocks Build on Rally as Election Shakes up Market
Calculus," *Financial Times*, November 4, 2020, https://www.ft.com
/content/dd354faa-5fca-4e0a-8fa2-4386462bc0c7.

24. Jennifer Epstein, "Biden Tells Elite Donors He Doesn't Want to
'Demonize' the Rich," Bloomberg, June 18, 2019, https://www.bloomberg.
com/news/articles/2019-06-19/biden-tells-elite-donors-he-doesn-t-want
-to-demonize-the-rich?sref=LgTOxReD.

Chapter One: The Fear Is Always There

Aimé Césaire, *Discourse on Colonialism*, trans. Joan Pinkham (New York:
Monthly Review Press, 1972), 48–49.

1. Samantha Raphelson, "Border Patrol Crackdown Shines Light on Rising

Number of Migrant Deaths," NPR, January 26, 2020, www.npr.org /2018/01/26/580802374/border-patrol-crack-down-shines-light-on -rising-number-of-migrant-deaths.

2. Jill Castellano, Daniel González, and Rob O'Dell, "The Border's Deaths, and How Many Are Never Known," *USA Today* and *Arizona Republic*, September 20, 2017, www.usatoday.com/border-wall/story/border-patrol -undercounts-deaths-border-crossing-migrants/1009752001/.

3. Jason De León, *The Land of Open Graves: Living and Dying on the Migrant Trail* (Oakland: University of California Press, 2015), 75.

4. De León, *Land of Open Graves*, 81.

5. Reece Jones, *Violent Borders: Refugees and the Right to Move* (London: Verso, 2017), 46.

6. Maru Mora-Villalpando, in discussion with the author, March 2019.

7. "Attendance Drops at Maryland High School, as Deportation Fears Rise," NPR, January 17, 2016, www.npr.org/2016/01/17/463405722/attendance -drops-at-maryland-high-school-as-deportation-fears-rise; Nicole Acevedo, "Immigration Policies, Deportation Threats Keep Kids Out of School, Report States," NBC News, November 20, 2018, www.nbcnews .com/news/latino/immigration-policies-deportation-threats-keep-kids-out -school-report-states-n938566.

8. Heidi Glenn, "Fear of Deportation Spurs 4 Women to Drop Domestic Abuse Cases in Denver," NPR, March 21, 2017, www.npr.org/2017/03 /21/520841332/fear-of-deportation-spurs-4-women-to-drop-domestic -abuse-cases-in-denver; James Queally, "Latinos Are Reporting Fewer Sexual Assaults amid a Climate of Fear in Immigrant Communities, LAPD Says," *Los Angeles Times*, March 21, 2017, www.latimes.com /local/lanow/la-me-ln-immigrant-crime-reporting-drops-20170321-story .html; Carolina Moreno, "Houston Police Announce Decrease in Latinos Reporting Rape, Violent Crimes," *HuffPost*, October 4, 2017, www .huffpost.com/entry/houston-police-announces-decrease-in-latinos -reporting-rape-violent-crimes_n_58ebd5fae4b0df7e204455f4.

9. Sam Levin, "Immigration Crackdown Enables Worker Exploitation, Labor Department Staff Say," *Guardian*, March 30, 2017, www .theguardian.com/us-news/2017/mar/30/undocumented-workers -deportation-fears-trump-administration-department-labor; Monica Campbell, "For Undocumented Workers, Demanding Better Work Conditions Could Mean Deportation," *World*, August 26, 2019, www.pri. org/stories/2019-08-26/undocumented-workers-demanding-better-work -conditions-could-mean-deportation.

10. Gaby Del Valle, "ICE Keeps Arresting Prominent Immigration Activists. They Think They're Being Targeted," *VICE News*, August 24, 2019, www

.vice.com/en_us/article/ywady5/ice-keeps-arresting-prominent
-immigration-activists-they-think-theyre-being-targeted.

11. Claudia Rueda, in discussion with the author, September 2019.

12. Leslie Berestein Rojas, "LA Mother-Daughter Case Highlights Rise of Non-Criminal Immigrant Arrests," Southern California Public Radio, May 20, 2017, www.scpr.org/news/2017/05/20/72026/la-mother -daughter-case-highlights-rise-of-non-cri/.

13. James Queally, "Immigration Activist Who Says She Was Victim of Retaliation by Border Patrol Applies for 'Dreamer' Protections," *Los Angeles Times*, June 19, 2017, www.latimes.com/local/lanow/la-me-ln-claudia-rueda -20170619-story.html.

14. James Queally, "L.A. Immigration Activist Files Suit Claiming DACA Application Was Rejected as 'Political Retaliation,'" *Los Angeles Times*, October 30, 2018, www.latimes.com/local/lanow/la-me-ln-claudia -rueda-lawsuit-dreamer-20181029-story.html.

15. While overall deportations decreased year over year under the Obama administration, formal *removals* of noncitizens as the result of a judge's order, often from the interior (as opposed to the *return* of noncitizens from the border), came to make up a far greater proportion of deportations during his presidency. See: Muzaffar Chishti, Sarah Pierce, and Jessica Bolter, "The Obama Record on Deportations: Deporter in Chief or Not?" Migration Policy Institute, January 26, 2017, www.migrationpolicy.org/article/obama-record-deportations-deporter-chief-or-not; Alicia A. Caldwell and Louise Radnofsky, "Why Trump Has Deported Fewer Immigrants Than Obama," *Wall Street Journal*, August 3, 2019, www.wsj.com/articles/why-trump-has-deported-fewer-immigrants-than-obama-11564824601.

16. No More Deaths, "A Culture of Cruelty: Abuse and Impunity in Short-Term U.S. Border Patrol Custody," 2011, https://nomoredeaths.org/abuse -documentation/a-culture-of-cruelty/.

17. Daniel Gonzalez, "The Remains of 127 Dead Migrants Were Recovered in Southern Arizona in 2018," *AZ Central*, December 15, 2019, www.azcentral.com/story/news/politics/border-issues/2019/01/16/remains -127-dead-migrants-recovered-southern-arizona-2018/2575080002/; Greg Grandin, "The Militarization of the Southern Border Is a Long-Standing American Tradition," *Nation*, January 14, 2019, www.thenation.com /article/the-militarization-of-the-southern-border-is-a-long-standing -american-tradition/; Ryan Devereaux, "The Bloody History of Border Militias Runs Deep—and Law Enforcement Is Part of It," *Intercept*, April 23, 2019, https://theintercept.com/2019/04/23/border-militia-migrants/.

18. James Q. Whitman, *Hitler's American Model: The United States and the Making of Nazi Race Law* (Princeton, NJ: Princeton University Press, 2017), 12.

19. Whitman, *Hitler's American Model*, 46–47.

20. Alexander Cockburn, "Zyklon B on the US Border," *Nation*, June 21, 2007, www.thenation.com/article/archive/zyklon-b-us-border/.

21. The National Origins Formula was a system of immigration quotas introduced by the Emergency Quota Act of 1921 and reinforced by the Immigration Act of 1924, a.k.a. the Johnson-Reed Act. In an effort to limit the number of immigrants from eastern and southern Europe, the formula pegged national quotas to the 1890 census—taken years before the influx of immigrants from countries like Italy, Poland, and Russia in the early twentieth century. See: Susan F. Martin, *A Nation of Immigrants* (New York: Cambridge University Press, 2011), 150-51.

22. Adam Serwer, "Jeff Sessions's Unqualified Praise for a 1924 Immigration Law," *Atlantic*, January 10, 2017, www.theatlantic.com/politics/archive /2017/01/jeff-sessions-1924-immigration/512591/.

23. "Transcript of Donald Trump's Immigration Speech," *New York Times*, September 1, 2016, www.nytimes.com/2016/09/02/us/politics/transcript -trump-immigration-speech.html.

24. Lisa Lowe, *Immigrant Acts: On Asian American Cultural Politics* (Durham, NC: Duke University Press, 1996), 27–28.

25. Lowe, *Immigrant Acts*, 13.

26. Mae M. Ngai, *Impossible Subjects: Illegal Aliens and the Making of Modern America*, updated ed. (Princeton, NJ: Princeton University Press, 2014), 18.

27. Allison O'Connor, Jeanne Batalova, and Jessica Bolter, "Central American Immigrants in the United States," Migration Policy Institute, August 15, 2019, www.migrationpolicy.org/article/central-american-immigrants -united-states.

28. "Southwest Border Migration FY 2019," US Customs and Border Protection, last modified November 14, 2019, www.cbp.gov/newsroom/ stats/sw-border-migration/fy-2019.

29. "ERO FY 2019 Achievements," Department of Homeland Security, last modified February 24, 2020, www.ice.gov/features/ERO-2019.

30. "New ILO Figures Show 164 Million People Are Migrant Workers." International Labour Organization, December 5, 2018, www.ilo.org/global /about-the-ilo/newsroom/news/WCMS_652106/lang--en/index.htm.

31. "Global Report on Internal Displacement," Internal Displacement Monitoring Centre, 2017, www.internal-displacement.org/global-report /grid2017/.

32. Matthew Taylor, "Climate Change 'Will Create World's Biggest Refugee Crisis,'" *Guardian*, November 2, 2017, www.theguardian.com/environment /2017/nov/02/climate-change-will-create-worlds-biggest-refugee-crisis.

33. John Vidal, "'Boats Pass Over Where Our Land Was': Climate Refugees in

Bangladesh," *Guardian*, January 4, 2018, www.theguardian.com/global
-development/2018/jan/04/bangladesh-climate-refugees-john-vidal
-photo-essay; "How Climate Change Can Fuel Wars," *Economist*, May 23,
2019, www.economist.com/international/2019/05/23/how-climate-change
-can-fuel-wars.

34. Izzie Ramirez, "Climate Change Will Create 1.5 Billion Migrants by
2050," *Vice*, September 12, 2019, www.vice.com/en_us/article/59n9qa
/climate-change-will-create-15-billion-migrants-by-2050-and-we-have
-no-idea-where-theyll-go.

35. Kanta Kumari Rigaud et al., "Groundswell: Preparing for Internal Climate
Migration," Open Knowledge Repository, Washington, DC, March 19,
2018, https://openknowledge.worldbank.org/handle/10986/29461.

36. Anouch Missirian and Wolfram Schlenker, "Asylum Applications Respond
to Temperature Fluctuations," *Science* 358, no. 6370 (2017): 1610–14,
https://doi.org/10.1126/science.aao0432.

37. Camilo Montoya-Galvez, "2019: The Year Trump 'Effectively' Shut Off
Asylum at the Border and Restricted Immigration," CBS News, January 5,
2020, www.cbsnews.com/news/immigration-2019-the-year-trump-restricted
-legal-immigration-and-effectively-shut-off-asylum-at-the-border/.

38. Norman L. Zucker and Naomi Flint Zucker, *Desperate Crossings: Seeking
Refuge in America* (London and New York: Routledge, 1996), 119–22.

39. "Examining the Human Rights and Legal Implications of DHS' 'Remain
in Mexico' Policy, Statement of Michael A. Knowles," US House of
Representatives Committee on Homeland Security, Subcommittee on
Border Security, Facilitation and Operations, November 19, 2019, https://
homeland.house.gov/imo/media/doc/Testimony-Knowles.pdf.

40. Julia Ainsley and Jacob Soboroff, "Agents Feared Riots, Armed Themselves
Because of Dire Conditions at Migrant Facility, DHS Report Says," NBC
News, July 1, 2019, www.nbcnews.com/politics/immigration/dhs-warned
-may-border-station-conditions-so-bad-agents-feared-n1025136.

41. Hamed Aleaziz, "Investigators Found Immigrant Kids and Families
Locked in Disgusting Conditions in Border Camps," *BuzzFeed News*, June
26, 2019, www.buzzfeednews.com/article/hamedaleaziz/inspector
-disgusting-conditions-border-migrants-children.

42. Spencer Woodman, Maryam Saleh, Hannah Rappleye, and Karrie Kehoe,
"Solitary Voices: Thousands of Immigrants Suffer in Solitary Confinement
in ICE Detention," *Intercept*, May 21, 2019, https://theintercept.com
/2019/05/21/ice-solitary-confinement-immigration-detention/.

43. Camilo Montoya-Galvez, "Death of British Immigrant Marks Third
Apparent Suicide in ICE Custody in 4 Months," CBS News, January 27,
2020, www.cbsnews.com/news/death-of-british-immigrant-marks-third

-apparent-suicide-in-ice-custody-in-4-months/.

44. Jonathan Blitzer, "A New Report on Family Separations Shows the Depths of Trump's Negligence," *New Yorker*, December 6, 2019, www.newyorker.com /news/news-desk/a-new-report-on-family-separations-shows-the-depths -of-trumps-negligence.

45. Grace Segers and Graham Kates, "Watchdog Details Psychological Trauma among Migrant Children Separated from Families," CBS News, September 4, 2019, www.cbsnews.com/news/hhs-inspector-general-report -details-psychological-trauma-among-separated-migrant-children/.

46. Ginger Thompson, "Listen to Children Who've Just Been Separated from Their Parents at the Border," ProPublica, June 18, 2018, www.propublica. org/article/children-separated-from-parents-border-patrol-cbp-trump -immigration-policy.

47. Cedar Attanasio, Garance Burke, and Martha Mendoza, "Attorneys: Texas Border Facility Is Neglecting Migrant Kids," AP News, June 21, 2019, https://apnews.com/46da2dbe04f54adbb875cfbc06bbc615.

48. Isaac Chotiner, "Inside a Texas Building Where the Government Is Holding Immigrant Children," *New Yorker*, June 22, 2019, www.newyorker.com/news/q-and-a/inside-a-texas-building-where -the-government-is-holding-immigrant-children.

49. Scott A. Allen and Pamela McPherson, "We Warned DHS That a Migrant Child Could Die in U.S. Custody. Now One Has," *Washington Post*, December 19, 2018, www.washingtonpost.com/outlook/2018/12/19/ we-warned-dhs-that-migrant-child-could-die-us-custody-now-one-has/.

50. A. C. Thompson, "Over 200 Allegations of Abuse of Migrant Children; 1 Case of Homeland Security Disciplining Someone," ProPublica, May 31, 2019, www.propublica.org/article/over-200-allegations-of-abuse-of- migrant-children-1-case-of-homeland-security-disciplining-someone.

51. Jacob Bacharach, "There Are Concentration Camps in America," *Outline*, July 1, 2019, https://theoutline.com/post/7645/there-are-concentration- camps-in-america?zd=2&zi=bhwnv2dm.

52. Noah Kulwin, "Whose Concentration Camps?" *Jewish Currents*, June 19, 2019, https://jewishcurrents.org/whose-concentration-camps.

53. John Nichols, "ICE Is Everywhere, So Is Never Again Action," *Nation*, December 13, 2019, www.thenation.com/article/archive/ice-activism- never-again-action.

54. Kelly Weill, "The Jewish Group Taking on ICE—and the 'Concentration Camp' Taboo," *Daily Beast*, July 13, 2019, www.thedailybeast.com /neveragain-action-takes-on-ice-and-the-concentration-camp-taboo.

55. Adam Gabbatt, "The Growing Occupy ICE Movement: 'We're Here for the Long Haul,'" *Guardian*, July 6, 2018, www.theguardian.com/us-

news/2018/jul/06/occupy-ice-movement-new-york-louisville-portland.

56. Mairav Zonszein, "Why Jews Are Getting Themselves Arrested at ICE Centers around the Country," *Vice*, www.vice.com/en_us/article/7xgyw4/why-jews-are-getting-themselves-arrested-at-ice-centers-around-the-country.

57. Weill, "Jewish Group Taking on ICE."

58. Andrea Pitzer, *One Long Night: A Global History of Concentration Camps* (New York: Little, Brown, 2018), 5.

59. Pitzer, *One Long Night*, 14.

60. Patrick Wolfe, "Settler Colonialism and the Elimination of the Native," *Journal of Genocide Research* 8, no. 4 (December 2006): 387–409.

61. Roxanne Dunbar-Ortiz, *Loaded: A Disarming History of the Second Amendment* (San Francisco: City Lights Books, 2018), 111.

62. Wolfe, "Settler Colonialism," 388.

63. Wolfe, "Settler Colonialism," 395–96.

64. Nick Estes, *Our History Is the Future: Standing Rock versus the Dakota Access Pipeline, and the Long Tradition of Indigenous Resistance* (New York: Verso Books, 2019), 210.

65. Estes, *Our History Is the Future*, 108.

66. "Profile of the Unauthorized Population: United States," Migration Policy Institute, accessed April 14, 2020, www.migrationpolicy.org/data/unauthorized-immigrant-population/state/US.

67. "Mexican Aliens Seek to Retake 'Stolen' Land," *Washington Times*, April 16, 2006, www.washingtontimes.com/news/2006/apr/16/20060416-122222-1672r/.

68. "Reconquista: The Movement," *Patriot Post*, accessed April 14, 2020, https://patriotpost.us/pages/172-reconquista-the-movement.

69. "Full Text: Donald Trump Announces a Presidential Bid," *Washington Post*, June 16, 2015, www.washingtonpost.com/news/post-politics/wp/2015/06/16/full-text-donald-trump-announces-a-presidential-bid/.

70. Harsha Walia, *Undoing Border Imperialism* (Oakland: AK Press, 2013), 70.

71. Walia, *Undoing Border Imperialism*, 73.

72. Fred Imbert, "Donald Trump: Mexico Going to Pay for Wall," CNBC, October 28, 2015, www.cnbc.com/2015/10/28/donald-trump-mexico-going-to-pay-for-wall.html.

73. Annie Gowen and David Nakamura, "Rallying Farmers, Trump Pushes Border Wall but Opens Door to More Immigrants in Agriculture Jobs," *Washington Post*, January 14, 2019, www.washingtonpost.com/politics/rallying-farmers-trump-pushes-border-wall-but-opens-door-to-more-immigrants-in-agriculture-jobs/2019/01/14/0c8062a6-1835-11e9-8813-cb9dec761e73_story.html.

74. Mike Dorning, "Trump Administration Proposes New Agriculture

Immigration Rules," *Bloomberg*, July 15, 2019, www.bloomberg.com/news/articles/2019-07-15/trump-administration-proposes-new-agriculture-immigration-rules; Suzanne Monyak, "DHS Eases Migrant Farmworker Rules to Avoid Food Deficit," Law360, April 15, 2020, www.law360.com/articles/1264093/dhs-eases-migrant-farmworker-rules-to-avoid-food-deficit.

75. Daniel Denvir, *All-American Nativism: How the Bipartisan War on Immigrants Explains Politics as We Know It* (New York: Verso, 2020), 269.

76. Carmen Reinicke, "US Income Inequality Continues to Grow," CNBC, July 19, 2018, www.cnbc.com/2018/07/19/income-inequality-continues-to-grow-in-the-united-states.html.

77. Estelle Sommeiller and Mark Price, "The New Gilded Age: Income Inequality in the U.S. by State, Metropolitan Area, and County," Economic Policy Institute, July 19, 2018, www.epi.org/publication/the-new-gilded-age-income-inequality-in-the-u-s-by-state-metropolitan-area-and-county/.

78. Elise Gould, "State of Working America Wages 2018: Wage Inequality Marches On—and Is Even Threatening Data Reliability," Economic Policy Institute, February 19, 2019, www.epi.org/publication/state-of-american-wages-2018/.

79. Lawrence Mishel and Julia Wolfe, "CEO Compensation Has Grown 940% since 1978: Typical Worker Compensation Has Risen Only 12% during That Time," Economic Policy Institute, August 14, 2018, www.epi.org/publication/ceo-compensation-2018/.

80. Jen Deaderick, "The Housing Market Crash and Wealth Inequality in the U.S.," National Bureau of Economic Research, *Digest*, January 2018, www.nber.org/digest/jan18/w24085.shtml.

81. Todd Miller, *Empire of Borders: The Expansion of the US Border around the World* (London: Verso, 2019), 157–58.

82. Robert O. Paxton, *The Anatomy of Fascism* (London: Penguin Books, 2004), 117.

83. Paxton, *Anatomy of Fascism*, 117.

84. Clara Zetkin, *Fighting Fascism: How to Struggle and How to Win* (Chicago: Haymarket Books, 2017), 27.

85. Emilio Gentile, "Fascism as Political Religion," in *Fascism*, ed. Michael S. Neiberg (London and New York: Routledge, 2018), 234.

86. Zetkin, *Fighting Fascism*, 23–24.

87. Zetkin, *Fighting Fascism*, 51.

88. Zetkin, *Fighting Fascism*, 104.

Chapter Two: Only Strong Measures Will Suffice

Eduardo Galeano, "Through the Looking Glass: Q & A with Eduardo Galeano," *Publishers Weekly*, April 27, 2009, www.publishersweekly.com/

pw/by-topic/authors/interviews/article/11635-through-the-looking-glass-q-a-with-eduardo-galeano.html.

1. Walter Francis White and Thurgood Marshall, *What Caused the Detroit Riot? An Analysis* (New York: National Association for the Advancement of Colored People, 1943), 11, https://archive.org/details/whatcauseddetroi00whit/page/10/mode/2up; Dominic J. Capeci Jr. and Martha Wilkerson, "The Detroit Rioters of 1943: A Reinterpretation," *Michigan Historical Review* 16, no. 1 (Spring 1990): 49–72.

2. Michael Jackman, "Forgotten History: Detroit's 1943 Race Riot Broke Out 75 Years Ago Today," *Detroit Metro Times*, June 20, 2018, www.metrotimes.com/news-hits/archives/2018/06/20/forgotten-history-detroits-1943-race-riot-broke-out-75-years-ago-today.

3. John H. Tanton interviewed by Otis L. Graham Jr., "A Skirmish in a Wider War: An Oral History of John H. Tanton, Founder of FAIR, the Federation for American Immigration Reform," April 20–21, 1989. This text is available at the University of Michigan's Bentley Historical Library, as are the rest of Tanton's papers. Digital copies of the publicly reviewable files were provided to me by immigration attorney Hassan Ahmad, who filed a Freedom of Information Act lawsuit against the university to unseal portions of the Tanton archives that are closed until the year 2035. See: Niraj Warikoo, "University of Michigan Fights to Keep Files of Anti-Immigrant Leader Sealed," *Detroit Free Press*, August 29, 2019, www.freep.com/story/news/local/michigan/2019/08/29/university-michigan-immigrant-leader-john-tanton/1994499001/.

4. Tanton and Graham, "Skirmish in a Wider War."

5. John F. Rohe, *Mary Lou and John Tanton: A Journey into American Conservation* (Washington, DC: Fair Horizon Press, 2002), 39.

6. Rohe, *Mary Lou and John Tanton*, 39.

7. Rohe, *Mary Lou and John Tanton*, 40.

8. Rohe, *Mary Lou and John Tanton*, 117.

9. Rohe, *Mary Lou and John Tanton*, 122.

10. Rohe, *Mary Lou and John Tanton*, 123.

11. Rohe, *Mary Lou and John Tanton*, 124.

12. Charles C. Mann, "The Book That Incited a Worldwide Fear of Overpopulation," *Smithsonian Magazine*, January 2018, www.smithsonianmag.com/innovation/book-incited-worldwide-fear-overpopulation-180967499/.

13. Judy Klemesrud, "To Them, Two Children Are Fine, but Three Crowd the World," *New York Times*, January 12, 1971, www.nytimes.com/1971/01/12/archives/to-them-two-children-are-fine-but-three-crowd-the-world.html.

14. William Trombley, "Prop. 63 Roots Traced to Small Michigan City," *Los*

Angeles Times, October 20, 1986. Quoted in Daniel Denvir, *All-American Nativism: How the Bipartisan War on Immigrants Explains Politics as We Know It* (London: Verso Books, 2020), 33.

15. Tanton and Graham, "Skirmish in a Wider War."
16. Kathy Bricker, memorandum, March 6, 1983, "To: JT Biography File"
17. John H. Tanton to Linda Platt, memorandum, July 26, 1985.
18. Nicholas Kulish and Mike McIntire, "Why an Heiress Spent Her Fortune Trying to Keep Immigrants Out," *New York Times*, August 14, 2019, www.nytimes.com/2019/08/14/us/anti-immigration-cordelia-scaife-may.html.
19. John H. Tanton to Cordelia Scaife May, personal letter, March 21, 1995.
20. John H. Tanton to Leon Kolankiewicz, Mark Krikorian, Don Mann, Maria Sepulveda, and Dan Stein, memorandum, September 4, 1997.
21. Kulish and McIntire, "Why an Heiress Spent Her Fortune."
22. See Form 990s for the Colcom Foundation, from 2005 to 2008, available at www.influencewatch.org/non-profit/colcom-foundation/; "Mellon Heiress Bequeaths Most of Estate to Foundations, Conservation Groups," *Philanthropy News Digest*, March 2, 2005, https://philanthropynewsdigest.org/news/mellon-heiress-bequeaths-most-of-estate-to-foundations-conservation-groups.
23. See Forms 990-PF for the Colcom Foundation (EIN: 31-1479839) filed with the Internal Revenue Service between fiscal years 2006 and 2017, www.citizenaudit.org/organization/311479839/. I have defined the "network" as including the following organizations, all of which received grants from the Colcom Foundation: American Immigration Control Foundation, Californians for Population Stabilization, the Center for Immigration Studies, Federation for American Immigration Reform, International Services Assistance Fund, NumbersUSA, Progressives for Immigration Reform, and US Inc.
24. Kulish and McIntire, "Why an Heiress Spent Her Fortune."
25. Maria Santana, "Hard-Line Anti-illegal Immigration Advocates Hired at 2 Federal Agencies," CNN, April 12, 2017, www.cnn.com/2017/04/11/politics/trump-administration-immigration-advisers/index.html; Thomas Burr, "After Being Nominated to a Top State Department Job, Controversial Utahn Ron Mortensen Appears to Be Going Nowhere," *Salt Lake Tribune*, July 12, 2019, www.sltrib.com/news/politics/2019/07/12/controversial-nomination/; Laura Thompson, "Meet the Extreme Nativists Guiding Our Immigration Policy," *Mother Jones*, August 5, 2019, www.motherjones.com/politics/2019/08/meet-the-extreme-nativists-guiding-our-immigration-policy/; Camilo Montoya-Galvez, "Hardliners Gain Key Posts at Trump's Citizenship and Immigration Services Agency," CBS News, November 21, 2019, www.cbsnews.com/news/trump-immigration-policy-posts-

hardliners-including-officials-who-worked-for-a-hate-group-gain-key-positions/; Hamed Aleaziz, "The Ex-Leader of an Anti-immigration Group Is Creating the Office in Charge of Fielding Civil Rights Complaints from Detainees," *BuzzFeed News*, January 30, 2020, www.buzzfeednews.com/article/hamedaleaziz/immigration-hardliner-detention-ombudsman.

26. Tanton and Graham, "Skirmish in a Wider War."

27. "Annual Border Tour," Center for Immigration Studies, accessed April 27, 2020, https://cis.org/Annual-Border-Tour.

28. John Wahala, "A Growing Border Crisis," Center for Immigration Studies, May 24, 2019, https://cis.org/Wahala/Growing-Border-Crisis.

29. Harvey O'Connor, *How Mellon Got Rich* (New York: International Pamphlets, 1933).

30. Paul E. Erdman, "Family Fortune," *New York Times*, June 11, 1978, www.nytimes.com/1978/06/11/archives/family-fortune-mellons.html

31. Quoted in O'Connor, *Mellon*.

32. Mayer, *Dark Money*, 63.

33. Robert G. Kaiser and Ira Chinoy, "Scaife: Funding Father of the Right," *Washington Post*, www.washingtonpost.com/wp-srv/politics/special/clinton/stories/scaifemain050299.htm.

34. Michael Joseph Gross, "A Vast Right-Wing Conspiracy," *Vanity Fair*, January 2, 2008, www.vanityfair.com/news/2008/02/scaife200802; Eric Heyl, "Dick Scaife Found Peace in the Beauty of His Childhood Home, Penguin Court," *Pittsburgh Tribune-Review*, July 5, 2014, https://archive.triblive.com/news/dick-scaife-found-peace-in-the-beauty-of-his-childhood-home-penguin-court/.

35. Kaiser and Chinoy, "Scaife."

36. Jane Mayer, *Dark Money: The Hidden History of the Billionaires behind the Rise of the Radical Right* (New York: Penguin Random House, 2016), 67–68.

37. Kaiser and Chinoy, "Scaife."

38. "Citizen Sciafe," *Columbia Journalism Review*, July/August 1981, https://web.archive.org/web/20080509073630/http://backissues.cjrarchives.org/year/81/4/scaife_sidebars.asp.

39. Kaiser and Chinoy, "Scaife."

40. Michael King, "The Arkansas Project Unmasked," *Texas Observer*, July 21, 2000, www.texasobserver.org/777-the-arkansas-project-unmasked/.

41. Kaiser and Chinoy, "Scaife."

42. Derek Hawkins, "Christopher Ruddy, the Trump Whisperer: 'I'm Honest with Him,'" *Washington Post*, June 15, 2017, www.washingtonpost.com/news/morning-mix/wp/2017/06/15/christopher-ruddy-the-trump-whisperer-im-honest-with-him-he-says/; Philip Weiss, "Clinton Crazy," *New York Times Magazine*, February 23, 1997, www.nytimes.

com/1997/02/23/magazine/clinton-crazy.html.
43. Kaiser and Chinoy, "Scaife."
44. Kaiser and Chinoy, "Scaife."
45. "Mrs. Cordelia S. May Is Wed to Pittsburgh District Attorney," *New York Times*, November 11, 1973, www.nytimes.com/1973/11/07/archives/mrs-cordelia-s-may-is-wed-to-pittsburgh-district-attorney.html.
46. "Mrs. Marjorie Merriweather Post Is Dead at 86," *New York Times*, September 13, 1973, www.nytimes.com/1973/09/13/archives/mrs-marjorie-merriweather-post-is-dead-at-86-a-rich-working-woman.html.
47. Johnna A. Pro and Marylynne Pitz, "Obituary: Cordelia Scaife May / Reclusive Mellon Heiress Known for Her Generosity," *Pittsburgh Post-Gazette*, January 27, 2005, http://old.post-gazette.com/pg/05027/448744.stm.
48. Quoted in Jane Mayer, *Dark Money*, 63.
49. Stella Gibbons, "Excerpt: 'Cold Comfort Farm,'" NPR, January 21, 2008, www.npr.org/templates/story/story.php?storyId=18028876.
50. See Form 990s for the Sidney A. Swensrud Foundation, from 1979 to 1997, which can be requested from the Ruth Lilly Special Collections and Archives at the Indiana University–Purdue University Indianapolis Library, www.ulib.iupui.edu/special/collections/ask_990PF.
51. "Reminiscences of Sidney A. Swensrud," interview with Sidney A. Swensrud by David Fowler, December 19 and 20, 1988, January 27, 28, and 30, 1989, and October 17, 1989, transcript, Rare Book & Manuscript Library, Butler Library, Columbia University, New York, NY.
52. "Reminiscences of Sidney A. Swensrud."
53. "Reminiscences of Sidney A. Swensrud."
54. Ian R. Dowbiggin, "Reproductive Imperialism: Sterilization and Foreign Aid in the Cold War," *Globalization, Empire, and Imperialism in Historical Perspective*, June 1, 2006, www.webcitation.org/5HqPafY8M?url=www.bu.edu/historic/06conf_papers/Dowbiggin.pdf.
55. "Reminiscences of Sidney A. Swensrud."
56. Richard Lamm, foreword to Rohe, *Mary Lou and John Tanton*, viii–ix.
57. "Reminiscences of Sidney A. Swensrud."
58. United States Congress, House of Representatives Select Committee on Small Businesses, *Effects of Foreign Oil Imports on Independent Domestic Producers* (Washington, DC: US Government Printing Office, 1949–50).
59. "Reminiscences of Sidney A. Swensrud."
60. "Reminiscences of Sidney A. Swensrud."
61. Tanton to Linda Platt, memorandum, July 26, 1985.
62. Richard Lamm to Hon. Alan Simpson, memorandum, December 4, 1981, "Legislative Strategy for Immigration Reform."
63. Rohe, *Mary Lou and John Tanton*, 47.

64. Sean McElwee, "Anti-Immigrant Sentiment Is Most Extreme in States without Immigrants," Data for Progress, April 5, 2018, www.dataforprogress.org/blog/2018/4/5/anti-immigrant-sentiment-is-most-extreme-in-states-without-immigrants.

65. John H. Tanton, memorandum, July 28, 1988, "Does the Population/Immigration/Assimilation Movement Need a Journal?"

66. Kathy Bricker, memorandum, October 7, 1985, "To: Tanton Biography File." Recently, CIS officials have tried to push back against media coverage that emphasizes its connections to Tanton and FAIR. While this is likely motivated in part by perception management, it is probably also true that interpersonal disagreements between the organizations' respective leaderships have played a part. In any case, as Tanton's records show, arguments that he had nothing to do with the founding of CIS are simply wrong; moreover, Roger Conner, the first director of FAIR, was a founding member of the CIS board of directors, and Otis Graham was a founding member of both.

67. Brad Plummer, "Congress Tried to Fix Immigration Back in 1986. Why Did It Fail?" *Washington Post*, January 30, 2013, www.washingtonpost.com/news/wonk/wp/2013/01/30/in-1986-congress-tried-to-solve-immigration-why-didnt-it-work/.

68. "Reminiscences of Sidney A. Swensrud."

69. "Reminiscences of Sidney A. Swensrud."

70. "Reminiscences of Sidney A. Swensrud."

71. John H. Tanton, "Press Release: John Tanton Challenges Southern Poverty Law Center (SPLC) to Debate over 'Lies,'" JohnTanton.org, February 3, 2009, www.johntanton.org/answering_my_critics/press_release_2009feb03.html.

72. Scott Bixby, "Anti-Immigration Group Files RICO Suit against Southern Poverty Law Center over 'Hate Group' Label," *Daily Beast*, January 16, 2019, www.thedailybeast.com/anti-immigration-group-files-rico-suit-against-southern-poverty-law-center-over-hate-group-label.

73. "Center for Immigration Studies Files a Civil RICO Lawsuit against the President of Southern Poverty Law Center," Center for Immigration Studies, January 16, 2019, https://cis.org/Litigation/CIS-RICO-Lawsuit-SPLC.

74. Tanton and Graham, "A Skirmish in a Wider War."

75. John H. Tanton to Cordelia Scaife May, personal letter, March 21, 1995.

76. John H. Tanton to Dr. William Hollingsworth, personal letter, February 17, 1995.

77. John H. Tanton to Albert P. Blaustein, personal letter, May 1, 1975, www.documentcloud.org/documents/4523831-1975-05-01-LETTER-Albert-P-Blaustein-Bothered-by.html.

78. John H. Tanton to FAIR Board of Directors, memorandum, December 28, 1998, documentcloud.org/documents/4523833-1998-12-28-MEMO-FAIR-Board-Opposition-Research.html; John H. Tanton to Cordy May, personal letter, December 10, 1998, www.documentcloud.org/documents/4523834-1998-12-10-LETTER-C-S-May-Kevin-MacDonald.html; Dusty Sklar, "The Alt-Right's Antisemitism," *Jewish Currents*, January 9, 2017, https://jewishcurrents.org/the-alt-rights-antisemitism/.

79. John H. Tanton to Dr. Katharine Betts, personal letter, March 14, 1995.

80. John H. Tanton to Coredlia Scaife May, personal letter, November 15, 1996.

81. Konrad Lorenz joined the Nazi party in 1938, almost as soon as it was possible for Austrian citizens to do so. In the early 1940s, he wrote of the need for a "deliberate, scientifically underpinned race policy" and the "elimination of elements afflicted with defects" that would lead to "the improvement of Volk and race." After the war, Lorenz disavowed his Nazi past, and in 1973 he was awarded the Nobel Prize. "I have very different notions now concerning the Nazis," he said. See: Ute Deichmann, *Biologists under Hitler* (Cambridge, MA: Harvard University Press: 1996), p. 193; Peter Klopfer, "Konrad Lorenz and the National Socialists: On the Politics of Ethology," *International Journal of Comparative Psychology* 4, no. 7 (1994) https://escholarship.org/uc/item/50b5r4d6; Walter Sullivan, "Questions Raised on Lorenz's Prize," *New York Times*, December 15, 1973, www.nytimes.com/1973/12/15/archives/questions-raised-on-lorenzs-prize-scientific-journal-here-cites.html.

82. John H. Tanton to Peter Brimelow, personal letter, December 15, 1995.

83. See Form 990s for the Colcom Foundation 990s, from 2006 to 2009, available at www.influencewatch.org/non-profit/colcom-foundation/. VDARE is a project of the Lexington Research Institute, originally established by the Center for American Unity.

84. John H. Tanton to Peter Brimelow, personal letter, October 19, 1995, www.documentcloud.org/documents/4523838-Tanton-Letter-Peter-Brimelow-19951019.html.

85. John H. Tanton to Peter Brimelow, personal letter, June 25, 1997, www.documentcloud.org/documents/4523840-Tanton-Brimelow-41.html.

86. Christopher Mathias, "Police Guard White Nationalist Conference from Protesters at Tennessee State Park," *HuffPost*, April 29, 2018, www.huffpost.com/entry/american-renaissance-white-supremacist-conference-tennessee-state-park_n_5ae5d552e4b02baed1bb2050.

87. Department of Treasury Internal Revenue Service, "Return of Organization Exempt from Income Tax, New Century Foundation," https://projects.propublica.org/nonprofits/display_990/616212159/2002_04_

EO%2F61-6212159_990_200112; "About Wayne Lutton," Southern Poverty Law Center, accessed April 27, 2020, www.splcenter.org/fighting-hate/extremist-files/individual/wayne-lutton.

88. Samuel Francis, "Prospects for Racial and Cultural Survival," *American Renaissance* 6, no. 3 (March 1995), www.amren.com/archives/back-issues/march-1995/.

89. Samuel Francis, "Winning the Culture War," *Chronicles*, December 1, 1993, www.chroniclesmagazine.org/1993/December/17/12/magazine/article/10843305/.

90. Hannah Gais, "Leaked Emails Show How White Nationalists Have Infiltrated Conservative Media," *Splinter*, August 29, 2019, https://splinternews.com/leaked-emails-show-how-white-nationalists-have-infiltra-1837681245.

91. Samuel Francis, "Statement of Principles," Council of Conservative Citizens, 2005, https://web.archive.org/web/20100331205630/http://cofcc.org/introduction/statement-of-principles/.

92. Francis, "Prospects for Racial and Cultural Survival."

93. Joseph Tanfani, "Late Heiress' Anti-immigration Efforts Live On," *Los Angeles Times*, July 25, 2013, http://articles.latimes.com/2013/jul/25/nation/la-na-immigration-birdlady-20130725.

94. Matthew Connelly and Paul Kennedy, "Must It Be the Rest against the West?" *Atlantic*, December 1994, www.theatlantic.com/past/docs/politics/immigrat/kennf.htm.

95. Enzo Traverso, *The New Faces of Fascism: Populism and the Far Right* (London: Verso Books, 2019), 71.

96. Traverso, *New Faces of Fascism*, 71.

97. John H. Tanton to Cordelia Scaife May, personal letter, October 6, 1997.

98. Sarah Jones, "The Notorious Book That Ties the Right to the Far Right," *New Republic*, February 2, 2018, https://newrepublic.com/article/146925/notorious-book-ties-right-far-right.

99. Jones, "Notorious Book That Ties."

100. Julia Hahn, "'Camp of the Saints' Seen Mirrored in Pope's Message," *Breitbart*, September 24, 2015, www.breitbart.com/politics/2015/09/24/camp-saints-seen-mirrored-popes-message/.

101. Andrew Marantz, "Becoming Steve Bannon's Bannon: How Julia Hahn Got from the University of Chicago to Breitbart to the White House," *New Yorker*, February 6, 2017, www.newyorker.com/magazine/2017/02/13/becoming-steve-bannons-bannon; Clio Chang, "As White House Communications Staff Falls Apart, Steve Bannon Protege Julia Hahn Rises," *Splinter*, June 18, 2018, https://splinternews.com/as-white-house-communications-staff-falls-apart-steve-1826916721.

102. Chelsea Stieber, "Camp of the Saints," *Africa Is a Country*, March 17, 2019, https://africasacountry.com/2019/03/camp-of-the-saints.

103. Rod Dreher, "Good Lessons from a Bad Book," *American Conservative*, September 14, 2015, www.theamericanconservative.com/dreher/good-lessons-from-a-bad-book-raspail-camp-of-the-saints/.

104. Peter Maass, "Birth of a Radical," *Intercept*, May 7, 2017, https://theintercept.com/2017/05/07/white-fear-in-the-white-house-young-bannon-disciple-julia-hahn-is-a-case-study-in-extremism/.

105. See Form 990 for the Laurel Foundation, 1983, which can be requested from the Ruth Lilly Special Collections and Archives at the Indiana University–Purdue University Indianapolis Library, www.ulib.iupui.edu/special/collections/ask_990PF.

106. "Drive for U.S. Language Is Accused of Ethnic Bias," *Pittsburg Post-Gazette*, November 5, 1988, https://archives.post-gazette.com/image/89960255/.

107. Paul Blumenthal and J. M. Rieger, "This Stunningly Racist French Novel Is How Steve Bannon Explains the World," *HuffPost*, June 3, 2017, www.huffpost.com/entry/steve-bannon-camp-of-the-saints-immigration_n_58 b75206e4b0284854b3dc03.

108. John H. Tanton to William McNeill, personal letter, March 31, 1995.

109. John H. Tanton to Donna Panazzi, personal letter, January 29, 1999.

110. John H. Tanton, "The Case for Passive Eugenics," April 24, 1975.

111. Heidi Beirich, *The Nativist Lobby: Three Faces of Intolerance* (Montgomery, AL: Southern Poverty Law Center, 2009), www.splcenter.org/sites/default/files/d6_legacy_files/downloads/splc_nativistlobby.pdf.

112. William H. Tucker, *The Funding of Scientific Racism: Wickliffe Draper and the Pioneer Fund* (Chicago: University of Illinois Press, 2007), 44.

113. Tucker, *Funding of Scientific Racism*, 23.

114. "Founders and Former Directors," The Pioneer Fund, November 30, 2012, https://web.archive.org/web/20121130130929/www.pioneerfund.org/Founders.html.

115. John H. Tanton to John B. Trevor Jr., personal letter, June 18, 1984.

116. John H. Tanton to John B. Trevor Jr., personal letter, December 22, 1995.

117. Mae M. Ngai, "The Architecture of Race in American Immigration Law: A Reexamination of the Immigration Act of 1924," *Journal of American History* 86, no. 1 (June 1999): 67–92, www.jstor.org/stable/2567407?seq=1#metadata_info_tab_contents.

118. Beirich, *Nativist Lobby*.

119. Alex Amend, "First as Tragedy, Then as Fascism," *Baffler*, September 26, 2019, https://thebaffler.com/latest/first-as-tragedy-then-as-fascism-amend; John H. Tanton to Garrett Hardin, personal letter.

120. The first woman to win the Nobel Prize in Economics, Elinor Ostrom, earned the award for research that showed, in part, how flawed Hardin's premises were. Still, Hardin's "tragedy" remains an ideologically useful tool for those defending liberal individualism.

121. Garrett Hardin, "Lifeboat Ethics: the Case against Helping the Poor," *Psychology Today* (September 1974), www.garretthardinsociety.org/articles/art_lifeboat_ethics_case_against_helping_poor.html.

122. John H. Tanton to Otis Graham, memorandum, February 6, 1986; Jedediah Purdy, "Environmentalism's Racist History," *New Yorker*, August 13, 2015, www.newyorker.com/news/news-desk/environmentalisms-racist-history.

123. David Dorado Romo, "To Understand the El Paso Massacre, Look to the Long Legacy of Anti-Mexican Violence at the Border," *Texas Observer*, August 9, 2019, www.texasobserver.org/to-understand-the-el-paso-massacre-look-to-the-long-legacy-of-anti-mexican-violence-at-the-border/.

124. F. Roger Devlin, "Book Review: Madison Grant and the Preservation of Buffaloes, Redwoods, and America's European Heritage," *Social Contract* 19, no. 3 (2009), www.thesocialcontract.com/artman2/publish/tsc_19_3/tsc_19_3_devlin.shtml.

125. John H. Tanton to PEB Board of Directors, PEB Governing Board, Greg Curtis, and Robert Gray, memorandum, April 14, 1988.

126. John H. Tanton to Robert K. Graham, personal letter, July 8, 1995.

127. David Plotz, "Darwin's Engineer," *Los Angeles Times*, June 5, 2005, www.latimes.com/la-tm-spermbank23jun05-story.html#page=1.

128. John H. Tanton, "To: Robert Graham File," memorandum, June 20, 1995.

129. John H. Tanton to Richard Lynn, personal letter, January 28, 1998.

130. John H. Tanton to Gregory D. Curtis, personal letter, May 16, 1985.

131. Tanton to Curtis, May 16, 1985.

132. Jonathan Weisman, "Immigration Bill Dies in Senate," *Washington Post*, June 29, 2007, www.washingtonpost.com/wp-dyn/content/article/2007/06/28/AR2007062800963.html; Robert Pear, "Little-Known Group Claims a Win on Immigration," *New York Times*, July 15, 2007, www.nytimes.com/2007/07/15/us/politics/15immig.html.

133. See Form 990s for the Colcom Foundation.

134. Jason DeParle, "The Anti-Immigration Crusader," *New York Times*, April 17, 2011, www.nytimes.com/2011/04/17/us/17immig.html?pagewanted=all&_r=0.

135. Marguerite Telford, "Support of Amnesty Leads to Republican Leader's Defeat," Center for Immigration Studies, June 11, 2014, https://cis.org/Telford/Support-Amnesty-Leads-Republican-Leaders-Defeat.

136. Luciana Lopez, "Two Hawkish Anti-immigration Groups Say Consulted by Trump," Reuters, October 7, 2016, www.reuters.com/article/us-usa-

BLOOD RED LINES

election-trump-immigration-idUSKCN1270Z3; "Transcript: Donald Trump's Full Immigration Speech, Annotated," *Los Angeles Times*, August 31, 2016, www.latimes.com/politics/la-na-pol-donald-trump-immigration-speech-transcript-20160831-snap-htmlstory.html; "Donald Trump's New Election Ad – Two Americas: Immigration," YouTube video, 0:30, "A World of Truth," August 19, 2016, www.youtube.com/watch?v=odYHGAicJ7k; "Donald J. Trump's Vision," donaldjtrump.com, December 27, 2016, web.archive.org/web/20161227164455/www.donaldjtrump.com/policies/immigration/?/positions/immigration-reform.

137. Fernando Peinado, "Man of the Moment: Mark Krikorian, the Influential Immigration Hawk of the Trump Era," Univision, August 5, 2017, www.univision.com/univision-news/immigration/man-of-the-moment-mark-krikorian-the-influential-immigration-hawk-of-the-trump-era.

138. Michael Edison Hayden, "Emails Detail Miller's Ties to Group That Touted White Nationalist Writers," Southern Poverty Law Center, November 14, 2019, www.splcenter.org/hatewatch/2019/11/14/emails-detail-millers-ties-group-touted-white-nationalist-writers.

139. Résumé obtained by author's FOIA request.

140. Jon Feere, @JonFeere, Twitter, January 20, 2017, https://twitter.com/JonFeere/status/822436021593866240.

141. Jon Feere to Stephen Miller, "Breitbart Heads Up," email, July 10, 2017, www.documentcloud.org/documents/6551940-ICE-Email-Communications-With-or-About-White.html#document/p355/a540180.

142. Jon Feere to Stephen Miller, "Progress Updates (ICE-HHS Memo; Fees; Other Items)," email, December 22, 2017, www.documentcloud.org/documents/6551940-ICE-Email-Communications-With-or-About-White.html#document/p355/a540180.

143. US House of Representatives Committee on the Judiciary, Subcommittee on Immigration and Border Security "Birthright Citizenship: Is It the Right Policy for America," April 29, 2015, www.govinfo.gov/content/pkg/CHRG-114hhrg94409/html/CHRG-114hhrg94409.htm.

144. Denvir, *All-American Nativism*, 158; Hans A. von Spakovsky, "Birthright Citizenship: A Fundamental Misunderstanding of the 14th Amendment," *Heritage Foundation*, October 30, 2018, www.heritage.org/immigration/commentary/birthright-citizenship-fundamental-misunderstanding-the-14th-amendment.

145. Subcommittee on Immigration and Border Security "Birthright Citizenship."

146. Patrick J. Lyons, "Trump Wants to Abolish Birthright Citizenship. Can He Do That?" *New York Times*, August 22, 2019, www.nytimes.com/2019/08/22/us/birthright-citizenship-14th-amendment-trump.html.

147. Hamed Aleaziz, "The Ex-Leader of an Anti-Immigration Group Is Creating the Office in Charge of Fielding Civil Rights Complaints from Detainees," *BuzzFeed News*, January 30, 2020, www.buzzfeednews.com/article/hamedaleaziz/immigration-hardliner-detention-ombudsman.

148. John Burnett, "Republican Lawmakers Propose New Law to Reduce Legal Immigration," NPR, February 7, 2017, www.npr.org/2017/02/07/513957928/republican-lawmakers-propose-new-law-to-reduce-legal-immigration.

149. "Read the Full Transcript of Wednesday's Press Briefing," *Boston Globe*, August 2, 2017, www.bostonglobe.com/news/politics/2017/08/02/read-full-transcript-wednesday-press-briefing/jP2IHQrMiF1RA6UE1zOhGJ/story.html.

150. Ashley Parker and Josh Dawsey, "Stephen Miller: Immigration Agitator and White House Survivor," *Washington Post*, January 21, 2018, www.washingtonpost.com/politics/stephen-miller-immigration-agitator-and-white-house-survivor/2018/01/21/7a1f7778-fcae-11e7-b832-8c26844b74fb_story.html; Mark Krikorian, "What to Do about Haiti?" *National Review*, January 21, 2010, https://web.archive.org/web/20100611194345/http://corner.nationalreview.com/t/?q=MTU0MjIyMGVjNjU1ZjIyOTgyZmVhMzdiMmRhM2MwYmI=.

151. Robert T. Law to R. J. Hauman, "RE: DACA Replacement Chart," October 24, 2017, www.americanoversight.org/document/dhs-records-regarding-communications-with-outside-anti-immigrant-groups..

152. Robert T. Law to Bob Dane and Dale Wilcox, "CIS Ombudsman Seventh Annual Conference," email, November 28, 2017, www.americanoversight.org/document/dhs-records-regarding-communications-with-outside-anti-immigrant-groups.

153. Matt O'Brien, Spencer Raley, Robert Law, and Sarah Rehberg, "Immigration Priorities for the 2017 Presidential Transition: A Special Report from the Federation for American Immigration Reform," November 2016, FAIR Horizon Press, https://www.fairus.org/sites/default/files/2017-08/FAIR_2017TransitionDocument.pdf.

154. Robert T. Law to Kathy Nuebel Kovarik, "Re: Haiti draft TPS memo," October 22, 2017, https://www.nationaltpsalliance.org/wp-content/uploads/2018/10/2018-08-23-Doc-96-003-Exhibit-3-235274173_1.pdf.

155. Tina Vasquez, "Lines Blurring between Immigration Priorities of Trump Administration and Hate Groups," *Rewire News*, January 29, 2018, https://rewire.news/article/2018/01/29/lines-blurring-immigration-priorities-trump-administration-hate-groups/.

156. Betsy Swan, "Trump Making 'Nativist' Group's Wish List a Reality," *Daily Beast*, April 10, 2017, www.thedailybeast.com/trump-making-nativist-

groups-wish-list-a-reality; "A Pen and a Phone: 79 Immigration Actions the Next President Can Take," Center for Immigration Studies, April 2016, www.cis.org/sites/cis.org/files/79-actions_1.pdf.

157. Donald J. Trump, "Executive Order: Border Security and Immigration Enforcement Improvements," whitehouse.gov, January 25, 2017, www.whitehouse.gov/presidential-actions/executive-order-border-security-immigration-enforcement-improvements/.

158. Swan, "Trump Making 'Nativist' Group's Wish List."

159. John Kelly, US Department for Homeland Security, "Implementing the President's Border Security and Immigration Enforcement Improvements Policies," memorandum, February 20, 2017, www.dhs.gov/sites/default/files/publications/17_0220_S1_Implementing-the-Presidents-Border-Security-Immigration-Enforcement-Improvement-Policies.pdf.

160. Brendan O'Connor and Daniel Rivero, "This Is What It Looks Like When the President Asks People to Snitch on Their Neighbors," Splinter, October 3, 2017, https://splinternews.com/this-is-what-it-looks-like-when-the-president-asks-peop-1819077393#_ga=2.91247263.40308677.1530641193-1687030522.1528907081.

161. Dan Cadman, "Asylum Law Is Not Intended for Domestic Violence," Center for Immigration Studies, April 20, 2018, https://cis.org/Cadman/Asylum-Law-Not-Intended-Domestic-Violence.

162. Evan Halper, "Trump Administration Moves to Block Victims of Gang Violence and Domestic Abuse from Claiming Asylum," Chicago Tribune, June 11, 2018, www.chicagotribune.com/la-na-pol-sessions-asylum-20180611-story.html; Brian Lonergan, "Sessions Safeguards the Asylum Program," Immigration Law Reform Institute, June 12, 2018, www.irli.org/single-post/2018/06/12/Sessions-Safeguards-the-Asylum-Program; US Department of Justice, Office of the Attorney General, "27 I&N Dec. 227 (A.G. 2018)," March 7, 2018, www.justice.gov/eoir/page/file/1041481/download.

163. Ron Nixon, "About 2,500 Nicaraguans to Lose Special Permission to Live in U.S.," New York Times, November 6, 2017, www.nytimes.com/2017/11/06/us/politics/immigrants-temporary-protected-status-central-americans-haitians.html; Miriam Jordan, "Trump Administration Ends Temporary Protection for Haitians," New York Times, November 20, 2017, www.nytimes.com/2017/11/20/us/haitians-temporary-status.html; Nick Miroff and David Nakamura, "200,000 Salvadorans May Be Forced to Leave the U.S. as Trump Ends Immigration Protection," New York Times, January 9, 2018, www.washingtonpost.com/world/national-security/trump-administration-to-end-provisional-residency-for-200000-salvadorans/2018/01/08/badfde90-f481-11e7-beb6-c8d48830c54d_

story.html; Nick Miroff, "9,000 Nepalis Face Deportation as Trump Administration Prepares to Cancel Residency Permits," *Washington Post*, August 25, 2018, www.washingtonpost.com/world/national-security/9000-nepalis-face-deportation-as-trump-administration-prepares-to-cancel-residency-permits/2018/04/24/e6cd7594-4800-11e8-9072-f6d4bc32f223_story.html; Nick Miroff, "Trump Administration Ends Protections for 50,000 Hondurans living in U.S. since 1999," *Washington Post*, May 4, 2018, www.washingtonpost.com/world/national-security/trump-administration-will-end-protections-for-50000-hondurans-living-in-us-since-1999/2018/05/04/c05c7676-4fc1-11e8-b966-bfb0da2dad62_story.html.

164. "Secretary of Homeland Security Kirstjen M. Nielsen Announcement on Temporary Protected Status for Honduras," Department of Homeland Security, May 4, 2018, www.dhs.gov/news/2018/05/04/secretary-homeland-security-kirstjen-m-nielsen-announcement-temporary-protected.

165. Nick Miroff, Seung Min Kim, and Joshua Partlow, "U.S. Embassy Cables Warned against Expelling 300,000 Immigrants. Trump Officials Did It Anyway," *Washington Post*, May 8, 2018, www.washingtonpost.com/world/national-security/us-embassy-cables-warned-against-expelling-300000-immigrants-trump-officials-did-it-anyway/2018/05/08/065e5702-4fe5-11e8-b966-bfb0da2dad62_story.html.

166. Parija Kavilanz, "Immigration Crackdown: ICE Officials Pledge 400% Increase in I-9 Work Site Audits," CNN, January 15, 2018, https://money.cnn.com/2018/01/15/news/economy/ice-immigration-work-site-crackdown/index.html.

167. Elise Foley, "ICE Director To All Undocumented Immigrants: 'You Need to Be Worried,'" *HuffPost*, June 13, 2017, www.huffpost.com/entry/ice-arrests-undocumented_n_594027c0e4b0e84514eebfbe.

168. Julie Bosman, "Kris Kobach, Face of Trump's Voter Fraud Panel, Is Held in Contempt by Judge," *New York Times*, April 15, 2018, www.nytimes.com/2018/04/18/us/kris-kobach-voter-fraud.html.

169. "IRLI Files Brief Calling for End to Stealth Executive Amnesty," Immigration Reform Law Institute, February 16, 2018, www.irli.org/single-post/2018/02/16/IRLI-Files-Brief-Calling-for-End-to-Stealth-Executive-Amnesty; Aaron Reichlin-Melnick, "Sessions Ends Administrative Closure at the Expense of Due Process in Immigration Court," Immigration Impact, May 18, 2018, https://immigrationimpact.com/2018/05/18/sessions-administrative-closure-immigration-court/.

170. Maggie Haberman and Annie Karni, "A Would-Be Trump Aide's Demands: A Jet on Call, a Future Cabinet Post and More," *New York Times*, May 20, 2019, www.nytimes.com/2019/05/20/us/politics/kris-

kobach-trump.html.

171. Eric Schmitt, "Administration Split on Local Role in Terror Fight," *New York Times*, April 29, 2002, www.nytimes.com/2002/04/29/us/administration-split-on-local-role-in-terror-fight.html.

172. J. David Goodman and Ron Nixon, "Obama to Dismantle Visitor Registry before Trump Can Revive It," December 22, 2016, www.nytimes.com/2016/12/22/nyregion/obama-to-dismantle-visitor-registry-before-trump-can-revive-it.html.

173. Suzy Khimm, "Kris Kobach, Nativist Son: The Legal Mastermind behind the Wave of Anti-immigration Laws Sweeping the Country," *Mother Jones*, March/April 2020, www.motherjones.com/politics/2012/03/kris-kobach-anti-immigration-laws-sb-1070/.

174. Julia Preston, "Lawyer Leads an Immigration Fight," *New York Times*, July 20, 2009, www.nytimes.com/2009/07/21/us/21lawyer.html.

175. Randal C. Archibold, "Arizona's Effort to Bolster Local Immigration Authority Divides Law Enforcement," *New York Times*, April 21, 2010, www.nytimes.com/2010/04/22/us/22immig.html.

176. Alia Beard Rau, "Arizona Immigration Law Was Crafted by Activist," *Arizona Republic*, April 27, 2020, http://archive.azcentral.com/arizonarepublic/news/articles/2010/05/31/20100531arizona-immigration-law-kris-kobach.html.

177. Jessica M. Vaughan, "Attrition through Enforcement: A Cost-Effective Strategy to Shrink the Illegal Population," Center for Immigration Studies, https://cis.org/Report/Attrition-Through-Enforcement.

178. Vaughan, "Attrition through Enforcement."

179. Ed Pilkington, "Mitt Romney in Talks over Nationwide Version of Tough State Immigration Laws," *Guardian*, February 24, 2012, www.theguardian.com/world/2012/feb/24/kris-kobach-immigration-law-mastermind.

180. S.B. 1070, Second Regular Session of 2010 (Ariz. 2010), https://www.azleg.gov/legtext/49leg/2r/bills/sb1070s.pdf

181. Laura Sullivan, "Prison Economics Help Drive Ariz. Immigration Law," NPR, October 28, 2010, www.npr.org/2010/10/28/130833741/prison-economics-help-drive-ariz-immigration-law.

182. Beau Hodai, "Corporate Con Game: How the Private Prison Industry Helped Shape Arizona's Anti-immigrant Law," *In These Times*, June 21, 2010, http://inthesetimes.com/article/6084/corporate_con_game/.

183. Hodai, "Corporate Con Game."

184. Brendan Fischer, "ALEC Disbands Task Force Responsible for Stand Your Ground, Voter ID, Prison Privatization, AZ's SB 1070," *PR Watch*, April 17, 2012, www.prwatch.org/news/2012/04/11454/alec-disbands-task-force-responsible-stand-your-ground-voter-id-prison-privatizat;

John Nichols, "ALEC Exposed: Rigging Elections," *Nation*, July 12, 2011, www.thenation.com/article/alec-exposed-rigging-elections/.

185. Sullivan, "Prison Economics Help Drive."

186. Sullivan, "Prison Economics Help Drive."

187. Nigel Duara, "Arizona's Once-Feared Immigration Law, SB 1070, Loses Most of Its Power in Settlement," *Los Angeles Times*, September 15, 2016, www.latimes.com/nation/la-na-arizona-law-20160915-snap-story.html.

188. Jonathan Blitzer, "Trump's Ideas Man for Hard-Line Immigration Policy," *New Yorker*, November 22, 2016, www.newyorker.com/news/news-desk/trumps-ideas-man-for-hard-line-immigration-policy.

189. Julia Preston, "City's Immigration Restrictions Go on Trial," *New York Times*, March 13, 2007, www.nytimes.com/2007/03/13/us/13hazleton.html?module=inline.

190. Associated Press, "Murder Case Fails against Immigrants in Pennsylvania City," *New York Times*, July 8, 2007, www.nytimes.com/2007/07/08/us/08hazleton.html.

191. Preston, "City's Immigration Restrictions."

192. Eliza Collins, "Rep. Lou Barletta Endorses Trump, Hopes Others Will Too," *Politico*, March 22, 2016, www.politico.com/blogs/2016-gop-primary-live-updates-and-results/2016/03/lou-barletta-endorses-donald-trump-221099.

193. "Who's Who in the New Trump Transition Team Line-up," *Fox News*, November 11, 2016, www.foxnews.com/politics/whos-who-in-the-new-trump-transition-team-line-up; John L. Micek, "Analysis: Trump Stumps for Lou Barletta in Pa., Attacking Media," *Penn Live*, August 3, 2018, www.pennlive.com/news/2018/08/in_a_speech_riddled_with_false.html.

194. See the National Association of Former Border Patrol Officers website at https://nafbpo.org/index.html.

195. Beirich, *Nativist Lobby*.

196. "Paul Nachman," VDARE, https://vdare.com/writers/paul-nachman, accessed September 14, 2020.

197. "Activists with Extremist Ties behind Oregon Immigration Referendum," *ADL*, October 30, 2014, www.adl.org/news/article/activists-with-extremist-ties-behind-oregon-immigration-referendum.

198. Paul Nachman, "Immigrants Bring Poverty, Disease," *Billings Gazette*, August 17, 2018, https://billingsgazette.com/opinion/letters/immigrants-bring-poverty-disease/article_a9c4dba5-d4fc-59a1-aa47-0ebd1e435ab6.html.

199. "Donald A. Collins," VDare, accessed April 28, 2020, https://vdare.com/writers/donald-a-collins-0.

200. "International Services Assistance Fund, Grant History," Weeden Foundation, accessed April 28, 2020, www.weedenfdn.org/Weeden-

Foundation-Grantee-Information.php?id=122.

201. "About Us, Independent Directors," NumbersUSA, accessed April 28, 2020, www.numbersusa.org/about/directors.

202. Emily B. Ndulue et al., "The Language of Immigration Reporting: Normalizing vs. Watchdogging in a Nativist Age," MIT Center for Civic Media and Define American, 2019, https://defineamerican.com/journalismReport/.

203. Rosie Gray, "'Get Out While You Can,'" *BuzzFeed News*, May 1, 2019, www.buzzfeednews.com/article/rosiegray/katie-mchugh.

204. Dylan Matthews, "Heritage Study Co-author Opposes Letting in Immigrants with Low IQs," *Washington Post,* May 8, 2013, www.washingtonpost.com/news/wonk/wp/2013/05/08/heritage-study-co-author-opposed-letting-in-immigrants-with-low-iqs/.

205. Hayden, "Emails Detail Miller's Ties."

206. Joshua Woods, Jason Manning, and Jacob Matz, "The Impression Management Tactics of an Immigration Think Tank," *Sociological Focus* 48, no. 4 (April 2015): 354–72, https://doi.org/10.1080/00380237.2015.1064852.

207. David Nakamura, "'It Had Nothing to Do with Us': Restrictionist Groups Distance Themselves from Accused El Paso Shooter, Who Shared Similar Views on Immigration," *Washington Post*, August 10, 2019, www.washingtonpost.com/politics/it-had-nothing-to-do-with-us-restrictionist-groups-distance-themselves-from-el-paso-shooter-who-shared-similar-views-on-immigrants/2019/08/08/c44dd7f8-b955-11e9-a091-6a96e67d9cce_story.html.

208. Jerry Kammer, "Immigration and the SPLC," Center for Immigration Studies, March 11, 2010, https://cis.org/Immigration-and-SPLC.

209. Kim Bellware, "Leaked Stephen Miller Emails Show Trump's Main Point Man on Immigration Promoted White Nationalism, SPLC Reports," *Washington Post*, November 13, 2019, www.washingtonpost.com/politics/2019/11/12/leaked-stephen-miller-emails-suggest-trumps-point-man-immigration-promoted-white-nationalism/.

210. Zach Basu, @zacharybasu, Twitter, November 12, 2019, https://twitter.com/zacharybasu/status/1194383429879705601; Even the most hardcore anti-Semitic white nationalists appeared willing to look the other way when it came to Miller's religion. "The thing here is: Stephen Miller . . . actually is pushing for white nationalist policies. That doesn't mean he is a 'white nationalist.' But all of the policies he is advocating are the ones that white nationalists would be advocating in his position. Again: everything that he does is intended to stop brown people coming in while getting as many as possible out," the influential neo-Nazi Andrew Anglin wrote on his website, the *Daily Stormer*, in June 2018. "It is simply a fact that there is nothing I

have seen this Jew do that I disagree with. I don't know what that means, or really feel a strong need to make a determination about what that means. I'm happy with him continuing doing what he is doing, as he appears to be doing it very well." See Hayden, "Emails Detail Miller's Ties."

211. Kammer, "Immigration and the SPLC."

212. David Frum, "If Liberals Won't Enforce Borders, Fascists Will," *Atlantic*, April 2010, www.theatlantic.com/magazine/archive/2019/04/david-frum-how-much-immigration-is-too-much/583252/; Robert D. Kaplan, "The Coming Anarchy," *Atlantic*, February 1994, www.theatlantic.com/magazine/archive/1994/02/the-coming-anarchy/304670/.

213. Quoted in Todd Miller, *Storming the Wall: Climate Change, Migration, and Homeland Security* (San Francisco: City Lights Books, 2017), 53.

214. John Tanton, "A New Volkerwanderung?" *Social Contract*, Volume 5, Number 1 (Fall 1994) https://www.thesocialcontract.com/artman2/publish/tsc0501/article_380.shtml.

215. John H. Tanton, "The WITAN Meetings," memorandum, September 16, 1985.

216. See the Laurel Foundation website at http://laurelfdn.org/.

217. Tanton, "WITAN Meetings."

218. Christopher Hayes, "Keeping America Empty," *In These Times*, April 24, 2006, http://inthesetimes.com/article/2608/keeping_america_empty.

219. John H. Tanton to Witan IV Attendees, "Witan MEMO III," October 10, 1986, www.splcenter.org/fighting-hate/intelligence-report/2015/witan-memo-iii.

220. Mayer, *Dark Money*, 70–71.

221. Mayer, *Dark Money*, 69.

222. Mayer, *Dark Money*, 68–69.

223. John Tanton to WITAN IV Attendees, "Commentary on the WITAN IV Memo Dated October 10, 1986," November 16, 1988.

224. Associated Press, "Cronkite Quits English-Only Campaign Body," *Los Angeles Times*, October 14, 1988, www.latimes.com/archives/la-xpm-1988-10-14-mn-4168-story.html.

225. Jason DeParle, "The Anti-Immigration Crusader," *New York Times*, April 17, 2011, www.nytimes.com/2011/04/17/us/17immig.html.

226. Thomas Ricento, "A Brief History of Language Restrictionism in the United States," 1995, retrieved from ERIC database: ED426599, p. 13, https://files.eric.ed.gov/fulltext/ED426599.pdf.

227. Brian Kuang, "John Tanton, the Nativist Next Door," *Michigan Daily*, September 18, 2018, www.michigandaily.com/section/statement/john-tanton-nativist-next-door.

228. John Tanton to the WITAN Defense Committee, memorandum, January 16, 1989, "Fundamentals."

229. Samuel P. Huntington, "The Hispanic Challenge," *Foreign Policy*, October 28, 2009, https://foreignpolicy.com/2009/10/28/the-hispanic-challenge/.

230. Jim Gilchrist and Jerome R. Corsi, *Minutemen: The Battle to Secure America's Borders* (Los Angeles: World Ahead, 2006).

231. Rosalind Helderman and Manuel Roig-Franzia, "Witness in Special Counsel Probe, Former Stone Associate, Collected Payments from Infowars through Job Stone Arranged," *Washington Post*, January 24, 2019, www.washingtonpost.com/politics/witness-in-special-counsel-probe-former-stone-associate-collected-payments-from-infowars-through-job-stone-arranged/2019/01/24/4dfa4300-1e57-11e9-9145-3f74070bbdb9_story.html.

232. Leo Chavez, *The Latino Threat: Constructing Immigrants, Citizens, and the Nation* (Stanford, CA: Stanford University Press, 2008).

233. John H. Tanton to Samuel P. Huntington, personal letter, August 8, 1997.

234. John H. Tanton to William H. McNeill, personal letter, March 31, 1995.

235. Rohe, *Mary Lou and John Tanton*, 143.

236. Nicholas Kulish and Mike McIntire, "In Her Own Words: The Woman Who Bankrolled the Anti-Immigration Movement," *New York Times*, August 14, 2019, www.nytimes.com/2019/08/14/us/cordelia-scaife-may-anti-immigration.html?module=inline.

237. Justin Akers Chacón and Mike Davis, *No One Is Illegal: Fighting Racism and State Violence on the U.S.-Mexico Border* (Chicago: Haymarket Books, 2018), 194.

238. John Tanton to the WITAN Defense Committee, memorandum, January 16, 1989, "Fundamentals."

239. John H. Tanton, introduction to *The Ethics of Immigration Policy: A Collection of Essays*, ed. Tanton (Petoskey, MI: Social Contract Press), www.johntanton.org/docs/ethics_of_immigration_policy_final.pdf.

240. John H. Tanton to WITAN Defense Committee, "Fundamentals," January 16, 1989.

241. John H. Tanton to William H. McNeill, personal letter, September 1, 1995.

242. John H. Tanton to William H. McNeill, personal letter, September 5, 1995.

243. Senate Committee on the Judiciary, Subcommittee on Immigration and Refugee Policy, *Final Report of the Subcommittee on Immigration and Refugee Policy*, Serial No. J-97-38, 1981, available at https://archive.org/details/finalreportofsel1981unit.

244. John H. Tanton to Dr. Leon F. Bouvier, personal letter, May 2, 1988.

245. John H. Tanton to Otis Graham, "Prospectus for LEADERs: League for European-American Defense, Education, and Research," March 3, 1993.

Chapter Three: Think Boots, Not Books

1. Dvora Meyers, "Michigan State's Nassar Settlement Could Set a

Troubling First Amendment Precedent," *Deadspin*, May 18, 2018, https://deadspin.com/michigan-states-nassar-settlement-could-set-a-troubling-1826139831.

2. Vegas Tenold, *Everything You Love Will Burn: Inside the Rebirth of White Nationalism in America* (New York: Nation Books, 2018), 242.

3. Quoted in David Neiwert, *And Hell Followed with Her: Crossing the Dark Side of the American Border* (New York: Nation Books, 2013) , 250.

4. Clio Chang, "The Unlikely Rise of an Alt-Right Hero," *New Republic*, March 31, 2017, https://newrepublic.com/article/141766/unlikely-rise-alt-right-hero; Katie Shepherd, "A Leading Figure at Portland's Alt-Right Protests Defects, Says Dressing as a Spartan Warrior to Fight Antifa Was 'a Horrible Mistake,'" *Willamette Week*, July 30, 2017, www.wweek.com/2017/07/30/a-leading-figure-at-portlands-alt-right-protests-defects-says-dressing-as-a-spartan-warrior-to-fight-antifa-was-a-horrible-mistake-/; Jonah Engel Bromwich and Alan Blinder, "What We Know about James Alex Fields, Driver Charged in Charlottesville Killing," *New York Times*, August 13, 2017, www.nytimes.com/2017/08/13/us/james-alex-fields-charlottesville-driver-.html.

5. Neiwert, *Hell Followed with Her*, 372.

6. Matt Pearce, "Chanting 'Blood and Soil!' White Nationalists with Torches March on University of Virginia," *Los Angeles Times*, August 11, 2017, www.latimes.com/nation/la-na-white-virginia-rally-20170811-story.html.

7. Andy Campbell and Christopher Mathias, "White Supremacist Rally Triggers Violence In Charlottesville," *HuffPost*, August 12, 2017, www.huffpost.com/entry/white-nationalist-charlottesville-virginia_n_598e3fa8e4b0909642972007.

8. P. E. Moskowtiz, "It Was Never Going to Be a Normal Protest. They Came Ready to Fight," *Splinter*, August 14, 2017, https://splinternews.com/it-was-never-going-to-be-a-normal-protest-they-came-re-1797824445.

9. Paul Duggan and Justin Jouvenal, "Neo-Nazi Sympathizer Pleads Guilty to Federal Hate Crimes for Plowing Car into Protesters at Charlottesville Rally," *Washington Post*, April 1, 2019, www.washingtonpost.com/local/public-safety/neo-nazi-sympathizer-pleads-guilty-to-federal-hate-crimes-for-plowing-car-into-crowd-of-protesters-at-unite-the-right-rally-in-charlottesville/20-19/03/27/2b947c32-50ab-11e9-8d28-f5149e5a2fda_story.html; Justin Wm. Moyer and Lindsey Bever, "Vanguard America, a White Supremacist Group, Denies Charlottesville Ramming Suspect Was a Member," *Washington Post*, August 15, 2017, www.washingtonpost.com/local/vanguard-america-a-white-supremacist-group-denies-charlottesville-attacker-was-a-member/2017/08/15/2ec897c6-810e-11e7-8072-73e1718c524d_story.html.

10. Tenold, *Everything You Love*, 128.
11. Matthew Heimbach, interview with author, November 2017.
12. "David Lane," Southern Poverty Law Center, www.splcenter.org/fighting-hate/extremist-files/individual/david-lane.
13. Ahab, "A Picture of Unity," AltRight.com, March 8, 2018, https://altright.com/2018/03/08/a-picture-of-unity/.
14. Joanna Walters, "Prominent US Neo-Nazi Arrested on Domestic Violence Charge," *Guardian*, March 14, 2018, www.theguardian.com/world/2018/mar/14/matthew-heimbach-neo-nazi-white-nationalism-arrest-domestic-violence.
15. Brett Barrouquere and Rachel Janik, "TWP Chief Matthew Heimbach Arrested for Battery after Affair with Top Spokesman's Wife," March 13, 2018, www.splcenter.org/hatewatch/2018/03/13/twp-chief-matthew-heimbach-arrested-battery-after-affair-top-spokesmans-wife.
16. Sam Adler-Bell, "Michigan State University Sent Nine 'Undercover' Cops to Richard Spencer Protest—but It Says That's Not Surveillance," *Intercept*, March 30, 2018, https://theintercept.com/2018/03/30/msu-richard-spencer-antifa/.
17. "College Tour Course Correction," YouTube, AltRight.com, 2018, www.youtube.com/watch?v=SFT9UHytoxI&feature=youtu.be&bpctr=1586551534.
18. Matthew N. Lyons, *Insurgent Supremacists: The U.S. Far Right's Challenge to State and Empire* (Oakland, CA: PM Press, 2018), ii.
19. Kathleen Belew, *Bring the War Home: The White Power Movement and Paramilitary America* (Cambridge, MA: Harvard University Press, 2018), 3.
20. Belew, *Bring the War Home*, 127.
21. Belew, *Bring the War Home*, 60.
22. Greg Grandin, *The End of the Myth: From the Frontier to the Border Wall in the Mind of America* (New York: Metropolitan Books, 2019), 223–24.
23. Grandin, *End of the Myth*, 228–29.
24. Lyons, *Insurgent Supremacists*, 44–45.
25. Lyons, *Insurgent Supremacists*, 55.
26. Belew, *Bring the War Home*, 106.
27. Chacón and Davis, *No One Is Illegal*, 5–6; Randal C. Archibold, "Immigrants Take to U.S. Streets in Show of Strength," *New York Times*, May 2, 2006, www.nytimes.com/2006/05/02/us/02immig.html.
28. Meredith Hoffman, "Whatever Happened to Arizona's Minutemen?" *Vice*, March 22, 2016, www.vice.com/en_us/article/xd7jmn/what-happened-to-arizonas-minutemen.
29. Chavez, *Latino Threat*, 140.
30. Chavez, *Latino Threat*, 136–37.

31. Neiwert, *Hell Followed with Her.*

32. Chacón and Davis, *No One Is Illegal,* 12.

33. Neiwert, *Hell Followed with Her,* 139.

34. Grandin, *The End of the Myth,* 264.

35. Luke Barnes, "Leaked Chatroom Transcripts Reveal Far-Right Group's Violent Ideology," *ThinkProgress,* April 6, 2018, https://thinkprogress.org/chatroom-transcripts-reveal-far-right-violent-ideology-91836c8990cf/.

36. Thomas Chatterton Williams, "The French Origins of 'You Will Not Replace US,'" *New Yorker,* November 27, 2017, www.newyorker.com/magazine/2017/12/04/the-french-origins-of-you-will-not-replace-us.

37. Janet Reitman, "How Did a Convicted Neo-Nazi Release Propaganda from Prison?" *Rolling Stone,* May 25, 2018, www.rollingstone.com/politics/politics-news/how-did-a-convicted-neo-nazi-release-propaganda-from-prison-628437/.

38. Daniel Voshart, "Gavin Trilogy PT 3 – White Noise," *NotVice,* February 17, 2018, https://notvice.com/wrong-link-trilogy-gavin-mcinnes-white-supremacy-709eb38e3f43; Not Vice, @f__kvice, "1/ Can someone have a white power tattoo and not be a white supremacist?" Twitter, February 18, 2019, https://twitter.com/f__kvice/status/965353282809016322.

39. John Liam Policastro, "A Skinhead from Guatemala Tells It Like It Is," *Vice,* September 9, 2012, www.vice.com/en_us/article/yv5x3g/i-interviewed-a-skinhead-from-guatemala.

40. Max Jaeger and Tina Moore, "Vice Co-founder Shames Victims of Alleged Neo-Nazi Beatdown," *New York Post,* February 27, 2017, https://nypost.com/2017/02/27/vice-co-founder-shames-victims-of-alleged-neo-nazi-beatdown/.

41. As in, "We must secure the existence of our people and a future for Western children." See: Hannah Gais, "Leaked Emails Show How White Nationalists Have Infiltrated Conservative Media," *Splinter,* August 29, 2019, https://splinternews.com/leaked-emails-show-how-white-nationalists-have-infiltra-1837681245.

42. Jake Offenhartz, "Manhattan Republican Club Vandalized ahead of Visit from Proud Boys Founder," *Gothamist,* October 12, 2018, https://gothamist.com/news/manhattan-republican-club-vandalized-ahead-of-visit-from-proud-boys-founder#photo-1.

43. Hatewatch staff, "Why Are the Proud Boys So Violent? Ask Gavin McInnes," Southern Poverty Law Center, October 18, 2018, www.splcenter.org/hatewatch/2018/10/18/why-are-proud-boys-so-violent-ask-gavin-mcinnes.

44. Carol Schaeffer, "Inside the Proud Boy Event That Sparked Violence outside of Uptown GOP Club," *Bedford Bowery,* October 13, 2018, https://

bedfordandbowery.com/2018/10/inside-the-proud-boy-event-that-sparked-violence-outside-of-uptown-gop-club/.

45. Sandi Bachom, "Proud Boys Violent Assault after Gavin McInnes Republican Club Event 10/12/18," YouTube video, 1:30, October 12, 2018, www.youtube.com/watch?v=2d3MRZC5FQI&has_verified=1.

46. Jake Offenhartz, @jangeloof, "Three people were arrested last night," Twitter, October 13, 2018, 5:05pm, https://twitter.com/jangelooff/status/1051170094208954369?s=21.

47. Christopher Mathias, "Pro-Trump Gang Seen in Footage Assaulting Anti-fascist Protesters in Manhattan," *HuffPost*, Octboer 13, 2018, www.huffpost.com/entry/proud-boys-new-york-assault-gavin-mcinnes_n_5bc20d60e4b0bd9ed55a96ee.

48. Rebecca Kavanagh, @DrRJKavanagh, "The three anti-racist protesters were just arraigned," Twitter, October 13, 2018, 10:56pm, https://twitter.com/DrRJKavanagh/status/1051230191983501312.

49. "Proud Boys Founder Gavin McInnes: 'I Have a Lot of Support in the NYPD and I Very Much Appreciate That,'" Media Matters, October 15, 2018, www.mediamatters.org/gavin-mcinnes/proud-boys-founder-gavin-mcinnes-i-have-lot-support-nypd-and-i-very-much-appreciate.

50. Pervaiz Shallwani and Kelly Weill, "NYPD Looks to Charge 9 Proud Boys with Assault for Manhattan Fight," *Daily Beast*, October 16, 2018, www.thedailybeast.com/nypd-looks-to-charge-9-proud-boys-with-assault-for-manhattan-fight.

51. Nidhi Prakash and Tanya Chen, "Manhattan Republicans Are Defending Their Invitation to a Violent Far-Right Group," *BuzzFeed News*, October 14, 2018, www.buzzfeednews.com/article/nidhiprakash/ew-york-gop-defends-proud-boys.

52. "Kavanaugh: 'I Liked Beer. I Still Like Beer,'" *Daily Beast*, September 27, 2018, www.thedailybeast.com/kavanaugh-i-liked-beer-i-still-like-beer.

53. Katie Shepherd, "Police Crackdown Sends a Woman to the Hospital, but Portland Avoids Unhinged Violence in Protester Showdown," *Willamette Week*, August 4, 2018, www.wweek.com/news/2018/08/04/police-crackdown-sends-a-woman-to-the-hospital-but-portland-avoids-unhinged-violence-in-protester-showdown/.

54. "Patriot Prayer Rally Organizer Says He's Not Religious or White Supremacist: 'I'm Japanese,'" Fox2, August 23, 2017, www.ktvu.com/news/patriot-prayer-rally-organizer-says-hes-not-religious-not-white-supremacist-im-japanese.

55. Tim Gordon, "'I'm a Proud Western Chauvinist': Proud Boys Member Tusitala 'Tiny' Toese Speaks Out in Court," KGW8, October 7, 2019,

www.kgw.com/article/news/crime/proud-boy-member-tusitala-tiny-toese-appears-in-court/283-c7593f37-8e00-4ff1-a8ee-d89b1c388c66.

56. "Patriot Prayer's Anti-Immigrant Hate Rally Brings Out the Fascists in Droves," Rose City Antifa, December 11, 2017, https://rosecityantifa.org/articles/12-09-17-report-back/; "The Pacific Northwest Proud Boys–White Nationalist Social Club," Rose City Antifa, June 6, 2018, https://rosecityantifa.org/articles/pb-intro/.

57. Daniel Martinez Hosang and Jospeh E. Lowndes, *Producers, Parasites, Patriots: Race and the New Right-Wing Politics of Precarity* (Minneapolis and London: University of Minnesota Press, 2019), 5.

58. Brendan O'Connor, "An Afternoon with Portland's 'Multiracial' Far Right," *Nation*, August 10, 2018, www.thenation.com/article/archive/afternoon-portlands-multi-racial-far-right/.

59. Katie Shepherd, "ICE Contractor Posted Bail for Proud Boy Jailed in Portland for Assault," *Willamette Week*, May 15, 2019, www.wweek.com/news/2019/05/15/ice-contractor-posted-bail-for-proud-boy-jailed-in-portland-for-assault/.

60. "Chile Recognises 9,800 More Victims of Pinochet's Rule," BBC News, August 18, 2011, www.bbc.com/news/world-latin-america-14584095.

61. "Pinochet Did Nothing Wrong! Limited T-Shirt RWDS," 1776.shop, accessed April 10, 2020, https://web.archive.org/web/20190508013805/https://1776.shop/product/pinochet-did-nothing-wrong-limited-t-shirt/; April Glaser, "It Just Got a Lot Harder for the Proud Boys to Sell Their Merch Online," *Slate*, February 7, 2019, https://slate.com/technology/2019/02/proud-boys-1776-shop-paypal-square-chase-removed.html.

62. Trip Gabriel, @tripgabriel, "From a disillusioned GOP operative," Twitter, June 29, 2019, https://twitter.com/tripgabriel/status/1141158817817927681?ref_src=twsrc%5Etfw.

63. Jason Wilson, "Portland Man Says He Was Attacked by Man Linked to Far-Right Senate Candidate," *Guardian*, June 16, 2018, www.theguardian.com/world/2018/jun/16/portland-proud-boys-alleged-attack-man-patriot-prayer-joey-gibson; Lisa Balick, "Despite Notice, Protesters Still Occupying ICE," KOIN, June 27, 2018, www.koin.com/local/multnomah-county/despite-notice-protesters-still-occupying-ice/.

64. Alexandra Minna Stern, *Proud Boys and the White Ethnostate: How the Alt-Right Is Warping the American Imagination* (Boston: Beacon Press, 2019), 77.

65. Stern, *Proud Boys and the White Ethnostate*, 75.

66. HoSang and Lowndes, *Producers, Parasites, Patriots*, 125.

67. HoSang and Lowndes, *Producers, Parasites, Patriots*, 125.

68. Stern, *Proud Boys and the White Ethnostate*, 124.

264 | BLOOD RED LINES

69. Stern, *Proud Boys and the White Ethnostate*, 75
70. Wayne King, "Computer Network Links Rightist Groups and Offers 'Enemy' List," *New York Times*, February 15, 1985, https://www.nytimes .com/1985/02/15/us/computer-network-links-rihtist-groups-and-offers -enemy-list.html.
71. Belew, *Bring the War Home*, 237–38.
72. Manoel Horta Ribeiro et al., "Auditing Radicalization Pathways on YouTube," Proceedings of the 2020 Conference on Fairness, Accountability, and Transparency, January 2020, 131–41, https://doi.org/ 10.1145/3351095.3372879.
73. Rebecca Lewis, "Alternative Influence: Broadcasting the Reactionary Right on YouTube," Data & Society Research Institute, September 18, 2018, https://datasociety.net/library/alternative-influence/.
74. Fred Turner, "Trump on Twitter: How a Medium Designed for Democracy Became an Authoritarian's Mouthpiece," in *Trump and the Media*, ed. Pablo J. Boczkowski and Zizi Papacharissi (Cambridge, MA: MIT Press, 2018), 143–50.
75. Rebecca Lewis, "'This Is What the News Won't Show You': YouTube Creators and the Reactionary Politics of Micro-celebrity," *Television and New Media* 21, no. 20 (2020): 201–17.
76. Lewis, "Alternative Influence," 8.
77. Lewis, "Alternative Influence," 13.
78. Lewis, "Alternative Influence," 20.
79. Lewis, "Alternative Influence," 22.
80. David Neiwert, *Alt-America: The Rise of the Radical Right in the Age of Trump* (London: Verso Books, 2017), 217–18.
81. Kyle Wagner, "The Future of the Culture Wars Is Here, and It's Gamergate," *Deadspin*, October 14, 2014, https://deadspin.com/the- future-of-the-culture-wars-is-here-and-its-gamerga-1646145844; Caitlin Dewey, "Inside the 'Manosphere' That Inspired Santa Barbara Shooter Elliot Rodger," *Washington Post*, May 27, 2014, www.washingtonpost.com/ news/the-intersect/wp/2014/05/27/inside-the-manosphere-that-inspired- santa-barbara-shooter-elliot-rodger/.
82. Wendy Brown, *In the Ruins of Neoliberalism* (New York: Columbia University Press, 2019), 171.
83. Alex Kotch and Jared Holt, "Koch Network Alums Are Going Full- On White Nationalist," *Sludge*, May 30, 2019, https://readsludge. com/2019/05/30/koch-network-alums-are-going-full-on-white- nationalist/.
84. Freddy Martinez and Chris Schiano, "Marketing Hate: Inside Identity Evropa's Neo-Nazi Messaging," Unicorn Riot, March 14, 2019, https://

unicornriot.ninja/2019/marketing-hate-inside-identity-evropas-neo-nazi-messaging/.

85. Jared Holt, "Young Americans for Liberty 'Officer' Identified as Member of Identity Evropa," *Right Wing Watch*, June 11, 2019, www.rightwingwatch.org/post/young-americans-for-liberty-officer-identified-as-member-of-identity-evropa/.

86. To view this database, see https://discordleaks.unicornriot.ninja/discord/.

87. Discord Leaks, "Message from Sam Southern - TN in Nationalist Review #tpusa-general," Unicorn Riot, December 22, 2018, https://discordleaks.unicornriot.ninja/discord/view/1126616?q=#msg.

88. Elizabeth Llorente, "As New US-Bound Caravan Grows to More Than 2,000, Mexicans Lash Out," Fox News, January 15, 2019, www.foxnews.com/world/as-new-u-s-bound-caravan-grows-to-more-than-2000-mexicans-lash-out-at-the-migrants.

89. Discord Leaks, "Message from Dusty Morgan in Subverse #general," Unicorn Riot, January 1, 2019, https://discordleaks.unicornriot.ninja/discord/view/9465133?q=american+immigration+reform.

90. Discord Leaks, "Message from Jacob in Nice Respectable People Group #general," Unicorn Riot, October 24, 2018, https://discordleaks.unicornriot.ninja/discord/view/1717654?q=american+immigration+reform.

91. Discord Leaks, "Message from Wood-Ape - OK/MN in Nice Respectable People Group #general," Unicorn Riot, October 24, 2018, https://discordleaks.unicornriot.ninja/discord/view/1721128?q=numbersusa.

92. Erin Corbett, "The Leaked Chats That Show How a Far-Right Group Is Trying to Infiltrate the GOP," Unicorn Riot, March 6, 2019, https://splinternews.com/the-leaked-chats-that-show-how-a-far-right-group-is-try-1833068732.

93. Discord Leaks, "Message from Logan in Nice Respectable People Group #general," Unicorn Riot, October 24, 2018, https://discordleaks.unicornriot.ninja/discord/view/1720992?q=numbersusa.

94. Discord Leaks, "Message from Alex Kolchak - NY in Nice Respectable People Group #general," Unicorn Riot, December 13, 2018, https://discordleaks.unicornriot.ninja/discord/view/1552464#msg.

95. New York City Antifa, "Christopher Hodgman: University of Rochester Student, US Army Reserve Signal Support Systems Specialist, and US Army ROTC Cadet," Identify Evropa, March 7, 2019, https://identifyevropa.org/christopher-hodgman-student-army-reserve-and-rotc/.

96. RighteousIndignation, "I'm Not Sure If Everyone Is Aware of a Great Site," Iron March Exposed, July 28, 2016, 00:52 a.m., https://ironmarch.exposed/post/37569.

97. Jason Wilson, "Leak from Neo-Nazi Site Could Identify Hundreds of

Extremists Worldwide," *Guardian*, November 7, 2019, www.theguardian. com/us-news/2019/nov/07/neo-nazi-site-iron-march-materials-leak.

98. Wilson, "Leak from Neo-Nazi Site."

99. Discord Leaks, "Message from Trumpster1899 in Nick Fuentes Server #realpolitik," Unicorn Riot, June 14, 2018, https://discordleaks.unicornriot. ninja/discord/view/1852347?q=numbersusa.

100. Discord Leaks, "Message from Deleted User in MacGuyver - Skills & Academics #general," Unicorn Riot, September 25, 2017, https:// discordleaks.unicornriot.ninja/discord/view/1891362?q=numbersusa.

101. Discord Leaks, "Message from Isabella Locke-MT in Nice Respectable People Group #general," Unicorn Riot, April 12, 2018, https:// discordleaks.unicornriot.ninja/discord/view/1578297?q=#msg.

102. Discord Leaks, "Message from MPI - VA in Nice Respectable People Group #general," Unicorn Riot, April 12, 2018, https://discordleaks. unicornriot.ninja/discord/view/1578136?q=#msg.

103. Angela Nagle, "The Left Case against Open Borders," *American Affairs* 11, 4 (Winter 2018), https://americanaffairsjournal.org/2018/11/the-left-case-against-open-borders/.

104. Matthew Yglesias, "The Bell Curve Is about Policy. And It's Wrong," *Vox*, April 10, 2018, www.vox.com/2018/4/10/17182692/bell-curve-charles-murray-policy-wrong; Nathan J. Robinson, "Why Is Charles Murray Odious?" *Current Affairs*, July 17, 2017, www.currentaffairs.org/2017/07/why-is-charles-murray-odious.

105. Discord Leaks, "Message from MPI - VA."

106. Stern, *Proud Boys and the White Ethnostate*, 90.

107. Rosie Gray, "'Get Out While You Can': Once Notorious for Her Racist and Bigoted Tweets, Katie McHugh Saw the Dark Insides of the White Nationalist Movement," *BuzzFeed News*, May 1, 2019, www.buzzfeednews.com/article/rosiegray/katie-mchugh.

108. Gais, "Leaked Emails Show."

109. Callum Borchers, "Blog Known for Spreading Hoaxes Says It Will Have a Correspondent in Trump White House," *Washington Post*, January 20, 2017, www.washingtonpost.com/news/the-fix/wp/2017/01/20/blog-known-for-spreading-hoaxes-says-it-will-have-a-correspondent-in-trump-white-house/?utm_term=.5e08a5270780.

110. "Border Security and Immigration," *Eagle Forum*, https://eagleforum.org/topics/border-security-immigration.html.

111. "US Immigration Reform PAC," Open Secrets, www.opensecrets.org/pacs/lookup2.php?strID=C00253906&cycle=2020.

112. "Who We Are," USIRPAC, March 15, 2017, https://web.archive.org/web/20170315112349/http://usimmigrationreformpac.org/who-we-

are/; Nick Miroff, "Homeland Security Staffer with White Nationalist Ties Attended White House Policy Meetings," *Washington Post*, August 30, 2018, www.washingtonpost.com/world/national-security/homeland-security-staffer-with-white-nationalist-ties-attended-white-house-policy-meetings/2018/08/30/7fcb0212-abab-11e8-8a0c-70b618c98d3c_story.html.

113. Christopher Mathias and Nick Robins-Early, "Rep. Steve King Goes Full White Nationalist in Interview with Austrian Site," *HuffPost*, October 19, 2018, www.huffpost.com/entry/iowa-rep-steve-king-austria-white-nationalist_n_5bca4851e4b0a8f17eec6001.

114. Philip Bump, "Rep. Steve King Warns That 'Our Civilization' Can't Be Restored with 'Someone Else's Babies," *Washington Post*, March 12, 2017, www.washingtonpost.com/news/politics/wp/2017/03/12/rep-steve-king-warns-that-our-civilization-cant-be-restored-with-somebody-elses-babies/?utm_term=.b667bcdc3be9.

115. David Freedlander, "The Creepily Influential Trumpist Foreign-Policy Think Tank You've Never Heard Of," *Daily Beast*, October 17, 2017, www.thedailybeast.com/the-creepily-influential-trumpist-foreign-policy-think-tank-youve-never-heard-of.

116. Liz Fekete, *Europe's Fault Lines: Racism and the Rise of the Right* (London: Verso Books, 2017), 108.

117. Katrin Bennhold, "Chemnitz Protests Show New Strength of Germany's Far Right," *New York Times*, August 30, 2018, www.nytimes.com/2018/08/30/world/europe/germany-neo-nazi-protests-chemnitz.html; "Jewish Restaurant Attacked during Chemnitz Protests," DW.com, September 8, 2018, www.dw.com/en/jewish-restaurant-attacked-during-chemnitz-protests/a-45406856.

118. Liz Fekete, *Europe's Fault Lines: Racism and the Rise of the Right* (London: Verso Books, 2017), 108.

119. Kai Arzheimer, "Update: How the AfD Ditched Euroscepticism and Embraced Immigration, in One Picture," Kai Arzheimer, May 14, 2018, www.kai-arzheimer.com/how-the-afd-ditched-euroscepticism-and-embraced-immigration-in-one-picture/.

120. "Germany's AfD Calls for a 'Fortress Europe' at Party Conference," DW.com, June 30, 2018, www.dw.com/en/germanys-afd-calls-for-a-fortress-europe-at-party-conference/a-44474739; Franz Neuman, Herbert Marcuse, and Otto Kirchheimer, *Secret Reports on Nazi Germany: The Frankfurt School Contribution to the War Effort* (Princeton, NJ: Princeton University Press, 2013); Katrin Bennhold, "Germany's Far Right Rebrands: Friendlier Face, Same Doctrine," *New York Times*, December 27, 2018, www.nytimes.com/2018/12/27/world/europe/germany-far-right-generation-identity.html.

Chapter Four: It's the Birthrates

1. David Adler, "Centrists Are the Most Hostile to Democracy, Not Extremists," *New York Times*, May 23, 2018, www.nytimes.com/interactive/2018/05/23/opinion/international-world/centrists-democracy.html.

2. Fekete, *Europe's Fault Lines*, 54.

3. Douglas R Holmes, "Fascism at Eye Level," *Focaal* 2019, no. 84, accessed Jul 17, 2020, https://doi.org/10.3167/fcl.2019.840105, p. 83.

4. Zetkin, *Fighting Fascism*.

5. "TDS247: Prison Rapes for the Cause," *Right Stuff*, January 18, 2018. https://archive.is/nIc86#selection-187.0-187.34.

6. "Global Warming of 1.5°C. An IPCC Special Report on the Impacts of Global Warming of 1.5°C above Pre-Industrial Levels and Related Global Greenhouse Gas Emission Pathways, in the Context of Strengthening the Global Response to the Threat of Climate Change, Sustainable Development, and Efforts to Eradicate Poverty," Intergovernmental Panel on Climate Change, 2019, www.ipcc.ch/sr15/.

7. IPCC, "Global Warming of 1.5°C."

8. "2014 Quadrennial Defense Review," Department of Defense, March 4, 2014. https://archive.defense.gov/pubs/2014_Quadrennial_Defense_Review.pdf.

9. William I. Robinson, "'Aqui Estamos y No Nos Vamos!' Global Capital and Immigrant Rights," *Race & Class* 48, no. 2 (2006): 77–91, https://doi.org/10.1177/0306396806069525.

10. Abby Ohlheiser and Ian Shapira, "Gab, the White Supremacist Sanctuary Linked to the PIttsburgh Suspect, Goes Offline (for Now)," *Washington Post*, October 28, 2018, www.washingtonpost.com/technology/2018/10/28/how-gab-became-white-supremacist-sanctuary-before-it-was-linked-pittsburgh-suspect/?utm_term=.a6d98c58af99.

11. Alex Amend, "Analyzing a Terrorist's Social Media Manifesto: The Pittsburgh Synagogue Shooter's Posts on Gab," Southern Poverty Law Center, October 28, 2018, www.splcenter.org/hatewatch/2018/10/28/analyzing-terrorists-social-media-manifesto-pittsburgh-synagogue-shooters-posts-gab.

12. Paula Reed Ward, "Authorities: Mass Shooting Suspect Said He Wanted 'All Jews to Die,'" *Pittsburgh Post-Gazette*, October 28, 2018, www.post-gazette.com/news/crime-courts/2018/10/28/Affidavit-Suspect-robert-bowers-pittsburgh-squirrel-hill-mass-shooting-tree-of-life-synagogue/stories/201810280173.

13. Megan Guza, "Court Filings Show Prosecutors Rejected Robert Bowers' Plea Offer for Life in Prison," *Trib Live*, October 15, 2019, https://triblive.

com/local/pittsburgh-allegheny/court-filings-reveal-federal-prosecutors-rejected-bowers-life-in-prison-plea-offer/.

14. "'Hello, Brother': Muslim Worshipper's 'Last Words' to Gunman," Al Jazeera, March 16, 2019, www.aljazeera.com/news/2019/03/brother-muslim-worshipper-words-gunman-190315152715528.html.

15. Scott Neuman, "Man Accused in New Zealand Mosque Shootings That Killed 51 Pleads Not Guilty," NPR, June 14, 2019, www.npr.org/2019/06/14/732615781/man-accused-in-new-zealand-mosque-shootings-that-killed-51-pleads-not-guilty.

16. Copies of Tarrant's manifesto circulated on social media in the immediate wake of the massacre, along with clips of the livestream he had hosted. Major sites like Twitter and Facebook moved quickly to remove the document and the videos, but they can still be found in certain Telegram channels. See: Brenton Tarrant, "The Great Replacement," March 15, 2019; Marc Fisher and Joel Achenbach, "Boundless Racism, Zero Remorse: A Manifesto of Hate and 49 Dead in New Zealand," *Washington Post*, March 15, 2019, www.washingtonpost.com/national/boundless-racism-zero-remorse-a-manifesto-of-hate-and-49-dead-in-new-zealand/2019/03/15/3d407c64-4738-11e9-90f0-0ccfeec87a61_story.html.

17. Dave Phillips, "Christopher Hasson, Coast Guard Officer, Plotted Attacks at His Desk, Filings Say," *New York Times*, February 21, 2019, www.nytimes.com/2019/02/21/us/coast-guard-christopher-hasson-terrorist-attack.html.

18. Sindre Bangstad, *Anders Breivik and the Rise of Islamophobia* (London: Zed Books, 2014), 31.

19. Bangstad, *Anders Breivik*, 78.

20. Bangstad, *Anders Breivik*, 96–97.

21. "Factbox: Excerpts from 1,500-Page Norway Killer Manifesto," Reuters, July 24, 2011, www.reuters.com/article/us-norway-manifesto-factbox/factbox-excerpts-from-1500-page-norway-killer-manifesto-idUSTRE76N14J20110724.

22. Jason Wilson, "'Cultural Marxism': A Uniting Theory for Rightwingers Who Love to Play the Victim," *Guardian*, January 19, 2015, www.theguardian.com/commentisfree/2015/jan/19/cultural-marxism-a-uniting-theory-for-rightwingers-who-love-to-play-the-victim.

23. Ellen Engelstad and Mímir Kristjánsson, "The Return of 'Judeo-Bolshevism,'" *Jacobin*, February 16, 2019, https://jacobinmag.com/2019/02/antisemitism-judaism-bolsheviks-socialists-conspiracy-theories.

24. Jana Winter and Elias Groll, "Here's the Memo That Blew Up the NSC," *Foreign Policy*, August 10, 2017, https://foreignpolicy.com/2017/08/10/heres-the-memo-that-blew-up-the-nsc/.

25. Tarrant, "The Great Replacement."

26. Arthur Bright, "Why Does Norway's Breivik Invoke the Knights Templar?" *Christian Science Monitor*, April 18, 2018, www.csmonitor.com/ World/Global-News/2012/0418/Why-does-Norway-s-Breivik-invoke-the-Knights-Templar.

27. Jason Wilson, "Christchurch Shooter's Links to Austrian Far Right 'More Extensive Than Thought,'" *Guardian*, May 16, 2019, www.theguardian. com/world/2019/may/16/christchurch-shooters-links-to-austrian-far-right-more-extensive-than-thought.

28. James Kleinfeld, "NZ Suspect Donated Money to French Branch of Far-Right Group," Al Jazeera, April 5, 2019, www.aljazeera. com/news/2019/04/nz-suspect-donated-money-french-branch-group-190405090848567.html.

29. Rick Noak, "Christchurch Endures As Extremist Touchstone, as Investigators Probe Suspected El Paso Manifesto," *Washington Post*, August 6, 2019, www.washingtonpost.com/world/2019/08/06/christchurch-endures-extremist-touchstone-investigators-probe-suspected-el-paso-manifesto/.

30. Stephanie Liechtenstein, "Austria's Big Political Crisis—What Just Happened?" *Washington Post*, May 26, 2019, www.washingtonpost.com/ politics/2019/05/26/austrias-big-political-crisis-what-just-happened/.

31. Manès Weisskircher, "Austria's New Government Includes the Pro-Environment Greens. That's a First," *Washington Post*, January 7, 2020, www.washingtonpost.com/politics/2020/01/07/austrias-new-government-includes-pro-environment-greens-thats-first/.

32. Joe Heim and James McAuley, "New Zealand Attacks Offer the Latest Evidence of a Web of Supremacist Extremism," *Washington Post*, March 16, 2019, www.washingtonpost.com/world/europe/new-zealand-suspect-inspired-by-far-right-french-intellectual-who-feared-nonwhite-immigration/2019/03/15/8c39fba4-6201-4a8d-99c6-aa42db53d6d3_story.html.

33. John Eligon, "The El Paso Screed, and the Racist Doctrine Behind It," *New York Times*, August 7, 2019, www.nytimes.com/2019/08/07/us/el-paso-shooting-racism.html.

34. Sarah Wildman, "'You Will Not Replace Us': A French Philosopher Explains the Charlottesville Chant," *Vox*, August 15, 2017, www.vox.com/ world/2017/8/15/16141456/renaud-camus-the-great-replacement-you-will-not-replace-us-charlottesville-white.

35. Dave Renton, *The New Authoritarians: Convergence on the Right* (Chicago: Haymarket Books, 2019), 148.

36. Renton, *New Authoritarians*, 148.

37. J. Lester Feder and Pierre Buet, "They Wanted to Be a Better Class of White Nationalists. They Claimed This Man as Their Father," *BuzzFeed News*, December 26, 2017, www.buzzfeednews.com/article/lesterfeder/the-man-who-gave-white-nationalism-a-new-life.

38. Bangstad, *Anders Breivik*, 91.

39. Keegan Hankes, Rachel Janik, and Michael Edison Hayden, "Shooting at Poway Synagogue Underscores Link between Internet Radicalization and Violence," Southern Poverty Law Center, April 28, 2019, www.splcenter.org/hatewatch/2019/04/28/shooting-poway-synagogue-underscores-link-between-internet-radicalization-and-violence.

40. Robert Evans, "Ignore the Poway Synagogue Shooter's Manifesto: Pay Attention to 8chan's /pol/ Board," *Bellingcat*, April 28, 2019, www.bellingcat.com/news/americas/2019/04/28/ignore-the-poway-synagogue-shooters-manifesto-pay-attention-to-8chans-pol-board/.

41. Robert Evans, "The El Paso Shooting and the Gamification of Terror," *Bellingcat*, August 4, 2019, www.bellingcat.com/news/americas/2019/08/04/the-el-paso-shooting-and-the-gamification-of-terror/.

42. Evans, "Ignore Poway Synagogue."

43. Hankes, Janik, and Hayden, "Shooting at Poway Synagogue."

44. Nicholas Bogel-Burroughs, "Gilroy Gunman Fatally Shot Himself after Killing 3 at Garlic Festival," *New York Times*, August 2, 2019, www.nytimes.com/2019/08/02/us/gilroy-garlic-shooting.html.

45. Mark Berman, "FBI Opens Terror Probe into Calif. Attack, Says Shooter Explored 'Violent Ideologies,'" *Washington Post*, August 6, 2019, www.washingtonpost.com/national/fbi-opens-domestic-terror-probe-into-gilroy-festival-attack-says-shooter-explored-violent-ideologies/2019/08/06/1d618bee-b877-11e9-a091-6a96e67d9cce_story.html.

46. Alexandria Sage, "Gunman Scorned California Garlic Festival on Social Media before Mass Shooting," Reuters, July 31, 2019, www.reuters.com/article/us-california-shooting/gunman-scorned-california-garlic-festival-on-social-media-before-mass-shooting-idUSKCN1UO11W.

47. Anthony Hilton, "Book Review: Might Is Right or the Survival of the Fittest, by Ragnar Redbeard," *Occidental Observer*, September 29, 2009, https://archive.is/ROLUE.

48. Amanda Jackson, Emanuella Grinberg, and Nicole Chavez, "Police Believe the El Paso Shooter Targeted Latinos. These Are the Victims' Stories," CNN, August 7, 2019, www.cnn.com/2019/08/04/us/el-paso-shooting-victims/index.html.

49. Nicholas Bogel-Burroughs, "'I'm the Shooter': El Paso Suspect Confessed to Targeting Mexicans, Police Say," *New York Times*, August 9, 2019, www.nytimes.com/2019/08/09/us/el-paso-suspect-confession.html.

50. "The Inconvenient Truth."

51. "The Inconvenient Truth."

52. "The Inconvenient Truth," August 4, 2019.

53. "The Inconvenient Truth."

54. "The Inconvenient Truth."

55. Aaron Montes, "El Paso Native Tried to Stop Walmart Shooter, Saw He Targeted Hispanic Shoppers," *El Paso Times*, December 13, 2019, www. elpasotimes.com/story/news/2019/08/05/el-paso-shooting-man-tried-stop-walmart-shooter/1928443001/.

56. "The Inconvenient Truth."

57. Michael Edison Hayden, "White Nationalists Praise El Paso Attack and Mock the Dead," Southern Poverty Law Center, August 4, 2019, www. splcenter.org/hatewatch/2019/08/04/white-nationalists-praise-el-paso-attack-and-mock-dead.

58. Hayden, "White Nationalists Praise El Paso Attack and Mock the Dead."

59. "The Great Replacement," March 15, 2019.

60. "The Great Replacement."

61. "The Great Replacement."

62. Matthew Phelan, "The Menace of Eco-Fascism," New York Review of Books, October 22, 2018, www.nybooks.com/daily/2018/10/22/themenace-of-eco-fascism/; Jedediah Purdy, "Environmentalism's Racist History," *New Yorker*, August 13, 2015, www.newyorker.com/news/news-desk/environmentalisms-racist-history; Gaby Del Valle, "When Environmentalism Meets Xenophobia," *Nation*, November 8, 2018, www.thenation.com/article/archive/environment-climate-eugenics-immigration/.

63. Phelan, "Menace of Eco-Fascism."

64. Richard Spencer, "What It Means to Be Alt-Right," AltRight.com, August 11, 2017, archive.today/vuZGm.

65. "The Great Replacement."

66. Simon Romero, Caitlin Dickerson, Miriam Jordan, and Patricia Mazzei, "'It Feels Like Being Hunted': Latinos across U.S. in Fear after El Paso Massacre," *New York Times*, August 6, 2019, www.nytimes. com/2019/08/06/us/el-paso-shooting-latino-anxiety.html.

67. Bobby Allyn, "California Is 1st State to Offer Health Benefits to Adult Undocumented Immigrants," NPR, July 10, 2019, www.npr. org/2019/07/10/740147546/california-first-state-to-offer-health-benefits-to-adult-undocumented-immigrants.

68. Mark Joyella, "Fox News Dominates Q2 Ratings, Hitting 70 Consecutive Quarters at No. 1," *Forbes*, July 2, 2019, www.forbes.com/sites/markjoyella/2019/07/02/fox-news-dominates-2q-ratings-hitting-70-

consecutive-quarters-at-1/.

69. Joseph Neese, "Fox News Host Jeanine Pirro Embraces Racist 'Replacement' Theory Shared by El Paso Shooter," *Salon*, August 30, 2019, www.salon.com/2019/08/30/fox-news-host-jeanine-pirro-traffics-white-supremacist-replacement-theory-shared-by-el-paso-shooter/.

70. "Transcript of January 9, 2019 Episode of the Ingraham Angle," FOX News Network, January 10, 2019, www.foxnews.com/transcript/house-minority-whip-steve-scalise-on-whether-president-trump-is-facing-republican-defections-on-border-security.

71. "Transcript of May 16, 2019 Episode of the Ingraham Angle," FOX News Network, May 17, 2019, www.foxnews.com/transcript/papadopoulos-intel-agents-tried-to-get-my-wife-to-wear-a-wire.

72. Signal Staff, "Abbott Sends Out Anti-immigrant Fundraising Letter a Day before El Paso Attack," *Signal*, August 22, 2019, https://texassignal.com/exclusive-abbott-sends-out-anti-immigrant-fundraising-letter-a-day-before-el-paso-attack/.

73. Alex Press, "Doubling Down after Pittsburgh," *Jacobin*, October, 29, 2018, www.jacobinmag.com/2018/10/squirrel-hill-synagogue-shooting-antisemitism-pittsburgh.

74. "Laura Ingraham: Vote Republican or You Will Be Replaced by Immigrants," Media Matters, October 16, 2018, www.mediamatters.org/laura-ingraham/laura-ingraham-vote-republican-or-you-will-be-replaced-immigrants.

75. "Laura Ingraham Warns That Undocumented Immigrants Are Coming to 'Replace Kind of the Old America with a New America,'" Media Matters, March 7, 2019, www.mediamatters.org/laura-ingraham/laura-ingraham-warns-undocumented-immigrants-are-coming-replace-kind-old-america-new.

76. "Ingraham and Buchanan Warn Immigration Will Change 'the Whole Character and Composition of the Nation,'" Media Matters, March 18, 2019, www.mediamatters.org/laura-ingraham/laura-ingraham-and-pat-buchanan-warn-immigration-will-change-whole-character-and.

77. "Laura Ingraham: Congress Wants to Change America 'Demographically' and 'in Ways That Nobody Voted For,'" Media Matters, June 11, 2019, www.mediamatters.org/laura-ingraham/laura-ingraham-congress-wants-change-america-demographically-and-ways-nobody-voted.

78. "Laura Ingraham: Democrats Support 'Replacing the Current American Population' with 'New Immigrants,'" Media Matters, June 18, 2019, www.mediamatters.org/laura-ingraham/laura-ingraham-democrats-support-replacing-current-american-population-new.

79. Neese, "Fox News Host."

80. Shira Tarlo, "Nation's Largest Hispanic Journalist Group Cuts Ties with

Fox News over Migrant 'Invasion' Rhetoric," *Salon*, August 23, 2019, www.salon.com/2019/08/23/nations-largest-hispanic-journalist-group-cuts-ties-with-fox-news-over-migrant-invasion-rhetoric/.

81. Audrey McNamara, "Fox News Analyst on New Zealand Suspect: 'Very Understandable' What Shooter 'Was Trying to Do on a Political Level,'" *Daily Beast*, March 15, 2019, www.thedailybeast.com/fox-news-analyst-on-new-zealand-shooting-its-very-understandable-what-the-shooter-was-trying-to-do-on-a-political-level.

82. "Fox's Tucker Carlson Rants about the 'Invasion' of Refugees That Are Changing Europe's Demographics," Media Matters, April 17, 2017, www.mediamatters.org/tucker-carlson/foxs-tucker-carlson-rants-about-invasion-refugees-are-changing-europes-demographics.

83. "Tucker Carlson: Democrats Want 'Demographic Replacement,' with a 'Flood of Illegals' to Create 'a Flood of Voters for Them,'" Media Matters, December 20, 2017, www.mediamatters.org/tucker-carlson/tucker-carlson-democrats-want-demographic-replacement-flood-illegals-create-flood.

84. Lee Moran, "Fox News' Tucker Carlson Goes on Lengthy Rant about Immigrants Replacing Americans," *HuffPost*, December 5, 2018, www.huffpost.com/entry/fox-news-tucker-carlson-immigrants-replacing-ameri cans_n_5c077cd9e4b0fc2361113ebe.

85. Tom Scocca, "Tucker Carlson, Unbowed," *New Republic*, April 15, 2019, https://newrepublic.com/article/153501/tucker-carlson-unbowed.

86. "Fox's Tucker Carlson: Clinton Pointing Out Implicit Racial Bias in the US Was 'Absurd,'" Media Matters, September 27, 2016, www.mediamatters.org/tucker-carlson/foxs-tucker-carlson-clinton-pointing-out-implicit-racial-bias-us-was-absurd.

87. "Fox's Tucker Carlson: 'The American Nazi Party and the KKK Don't Really Exist in a Meaningful [Way],'" Media Matters, November 17, 2016, www.mediamatters.org/tucker-carlson/foxs-tucker-carlson-american-nazi-party-and-kkk-dont-really-exist-meaningful-way.

88. "Fox's Tucker Carlson Attacks the NAACP during Defense of Jeff Sessions' Racist Past," Media Matters, November 18, 2016, www.mediamatters.org/tucker-carlson/foxs-tucker-carlson-attacks-naacp-during-defense-jeff-sessions-racist-past.

89. Brian Stelter, "Tucker Carlson Wrongly Tells His Viewers the Country's White Supremacy Problem 'Is a Hoax,'" CNN, August 7, 2019, www.cnn.com/2019/08/07/media/tucker-carlson-white-supremacy-reliable-sources/index.html.

90. Christina López, "Leaked Chat Messages Show Members of White Supremacist Group Identity Evropa Are Obsessed with Tucker Carlson," Media Matters, March 8, 2019, www.mediamatters.org/tucker-carlson/

leaked-chat-messages-show-members-white-supremacist-group-identity-evropa-are.

91. Emily Steel and Michael S. Schmidt, "Bill O'Reilly Thrives at Fox News, Even as Harassment Settlements Add Up," *New York Times*, April 1, 2017, www.nytimes.com/2017/04/01/business/media/bill-oreilly-sexual-harassment-fox-news.html.

92. Matt Gertz, "Why Neo-Nazis Are Kvelling over Tucker Carlson," Media Matters, April 27, 2017, www.mediamatters.org/tucker-carlson/why-neo-nazis-are-kvelling-over-tucker-carlson?redirect_source=/blog/2017/04/27/why-neo-nazis-are-kvelling-over-tucker-carlson/216182.

93. Tamar Auber, "Son of Stormfront Founder Tells CNN His Family Watches Tucker Carlson for Tips on 'White Nationalist Talking Points," *Mediaite*, March 30, 2019, www.mediaite.com/tv/son-of-stormfront-founder-reveals-his-family-watches-tucker-carlson-for-tips-on-white-nationalist-talking-points/.

94. Erik Wemple, "Tucker Carlson Said Immigration Makes America 'Dirtier.' So an Advertiser Took Action," *Washington Post*, December 15, 2018, www.washingtonpost.com/opinions/2018/12/15/tucker-carlson-said-immigration-makes-america-dirtier-so-an-advertiser-took-action/.

95. "Tucker Carlson: 'My Country Actually Is Being Invaded by Other Countries from the South,'" Media Matters, September 30, 2019, www.mediamatters.org/tucker-carlson/tucker-carlson-my-country-actually-being-invaded-other-countries-south.

96. "Tucker Carlson Says Immigrants Have 'Plundered' American Wealth and Warns That 'They Are Coming' for More," Media Matters, May 21, 2019, www.mediamatters.org/tucker-carlson/tucker-carlson-says-immigrants-have-plundered-american-wealth-and-warns-they-are.

97. Jarod Holt, "White Nationalist Podcast Hosts: Tucker Carlson Does What We Do 'For an Audience of Millions,'" Right Wing Watch, January 4, 2019, www.rightwingwatch.org/post/white-nationalist-podcast-hosts-tucker-carlson-does-what-we-do-for-an-audience-of-millions/.

98. German Lopez and Jane Coaston, "Tucker Carlson Suggested Immigration Makes America 'Dirtier.' It's Costing Him," *Vox*, December 18, 2018, www.vox.com/policy-and-politics/2018/12/17/18144620/tucker-carlson-immigration-dirtier-advertiser-pacific-life.

99. Jonathan Mahler and Jim Rutenburg, "How Rupert Murdoch's Empire of Influence Remade the World: Part 3," *New York Times Magazine*, April 3, 2019, www.nytimes.com/interactive/2019/04/03/magazine/new-fox-corporation-disney-deal.html.

100. Brian Stelter, "Tucker Carlson Blasts Rep. Ilhan Omar, and She Calls Him a 'Racist Fool'," CNN, July 11, 2019, www.cnn.com/2019/07/10/media/

tucker-carlson-ilhan-omar-fox-news/index.html.

101. Alex Pareene, "The Long, Lucrative Right-wing Grift Is Blowing Up in the World's Face," *Splinter*, April 5, 2017, https://splinternews.com/the-long-lucrative-right-wing-grift-is-blowing-up-in-t-1793944216.

102. "Clear Difference," YouTube video, Donald J. Trump for President, 2016, https://youtu.be/gq-i8fTlExs.

103. Thomas Kaplan, "How the Trump Campaign Used Facebook Ads to Amplify His 'Invasion' Claim," *New York Times*, August 5, 2019, www.nytimes.com/2019/08/05/us/politics/trump-campaign-facebook-ads-invasion.html.

104. Tommy Tuberville, 2019, "Let's Call This What It Is—an Invasion of Our Country," Facebook, May 2, 2019, www.facebook.com/ads/library/?active_status=all&ad_type=political_and_issue_ads&country=US&impression_search_field=has_impressions_lifetime&page_ids%5B0%5D=2225580284361712&q=invasion.

105. Michael Folk for West Virginia Governor, "I Am Running for Governor of West Virginia," Facebook, April 24, 2019, www.facebook.com/ads/library/?active_status=all&ad_type=political_and_issue_ads&country=US&impression_search_field=has_impressions_lifetime&page_ids[0]=387887044562107&q=invasion.

106. Sandy Smith, "Sign the Petition to Stop the Invasion," Facebook, July 19, 2019, www.facebook.com/ads/library/?active_status=all&ad_type=political_and_issue_ads&country=US&impression_search_field=has_impressions_lifetime&page_ids[0]=620619085055774&q=invasion.

107. Joel Rose, Carrie Kahn, and Kelsey Snell, "Trump's Tweets on 'Caravans' Crossing the Border, Annotated," NPR, April 2, 2018, www.npr.org/2018/04/02/598781060/trumps-tweets-on-caravans-crossing-the-border-annotated.

108. Adolfo Flores, "A Huge Caravan of Central Americans Is Headed for the US, and No One in Mexico Dares to Stop Them," *BuzzFeed News*, March 31, 2018, www.buzzfeednews.com/article/adolfoflores/a-huge-caravan-of-central-americans-is-headed-for-the-us.

109. Katherine Lam, "Trump Declares 'NO MORE' DACA Deal after Report of Caravan with Central Americans Heading to US," Fox News, April 1, 2018, www.foxnews.com/politics/trump-declares-no-more-daca-deal-after-report-of-caravan-with-central-americans-heading-to-us.

110. Alexandra Villarreal, "Rapes, Murders . . . and Coronavirus: The Dangers US Asylum Seekers in Mexico Must Face," *Guardian*, March 23, 2020, www.theguardian.com/us-news/2020/mar/23/us-mexico-immigration-coronavirus-asylum.

111. Sarah Stillman, "When Deportation Is a Death Sentence," *New Yorker*,

January 15, 2018, www.newyorker.com/magazine/2018/01/15/when-deportation-is-a-death-sentence; Kevin Sieff, "When Death Awaits Deported Asylum Seekers," *Washington Post*, December 26, 2018, www.washingtonpost.com/graphics/2018/world/when-death-awaits-deported-asylum-seekers/; Alison Parker, "The U.S. Deported Them, Ignoring Their Pleas. Then They Were Killed," *Washington Post*, February 10, 2020, www.washingtonpost.com/opinions/2020/02/10/us-deported-them-ignoring-their-pleas-then-they-were-killed/.

112. "Border Patrol Reaction to Caravan of Immigrants Headed to US," Fox News, April 1, 2018, https://video.foxnews.com/v/5761781386001#sp=show-clips.

113. Flores, "Huge Caravan of Central Americans."

114. Michael D. Shear and Thomas Gibbons-Neff, "Trump Sending 5,200 Troops to the Border in an Election-Season Response to Migrants," *New York Times*, October 29, 2018, www.nytimes.com/2018/10/29/us/politics/border-security-troops-trump.html.

115. Tucker Higgins, "Trump Declares without Evidence That 'Criminals and Unknown Middle Easterners Are Mixed In' with Migrant Caravan Making Its Way from Honduras," CNBC, October 22, 2018, www.cnbc.com/2018/10/22/trump-says-unknown-middle-easterners-are-mixed-in-migrant-caravan.html.

116. Donald J. Trump, @realDonaldTrump, "Many gang members and some very bad people are mixed into the caravan heading to our southern border," Twitter, October 29, 2018, https://twitter.com/realDonaldTrump/status/1056919064906469376.

117. United States House of Representatives Committee on Oversight and Government Reform, Subcommittee on National Security, Testimony of Andrew R. Arthur, "A Caravan of Illegal Immigrants: A Test of U.S. Borders," April 12, 2018, https://docs.house.gov/meetings/GO/GO06/20180412/108118/HHRG-115-GO06-Wstate-ArthurA-20180412.pdf.

118. "Jessica Vaughan Discusses Updates on the Migrant Caravan," Fox News video clip, Center for Immigration Studies, November 12, 2018, https://cis.org/Jessica-Vaughan-Discusses-Updates-Migrant-Caravan-0.

119. Jonathan Albright, "Rumores Sin Fronteras," Medium, October 25, 2018, https://medium.com/@d1gi/rumores-sin-fronteras-e181aadf7743.

120. Aaron Blake, "How the Trumps and Conservative Media Helped Mainstream a Conspiracy Theory Now Tied to Tragedy," *Washington Post*, October 29, 2018, www.washingtonpost.com/politics/2018/10/29/how-trumps-conservative-media-helped-mainstream-conspiracy-theory-now-tied-tragedy/.

121. Rep. Matt Gaetz, @RepMattGaetz, "BREAKING: Footage in Honduras giving cash 2 women & children," Twitter, October 17, 2018, https://twitter.com/RepMattGaetz/status/1052629557826736129.
122. Blake, "How the Trumps."
123. Jeremy W. Peters, "How Trump-Fed Conspiracy Theories about Migrant Caravan Intersect with Deadly Hatred," *New York Times*, October 29, 2018, www.nytimes.com/2018/10/29/us/politics/caravan-trump-shooting-elections.html.
124. Anna Merlan, *Republic of Lies: American Conspiracy Theorists and Their Surprising Rise to Power* (Random House, 2019), 243.
125. Merlan, *Republic of Lies*, 244.
126. Theodor W. Adorno, *Critical Models: Interventions and Catchwords* (New York: Columbia University Press, 2005).
127. Victoria Bekiempis, "Cesar Sayoc, Who Sent Pipe Bombs to Trump Critics, Gets 20 Years in Prison," *Guardian*, August 5, 2019, www.theguardian.com/us-news/2019/aug/05/cesar-sayoc-sentencing-pipe-bombs-targets-trump-critics; William K. Rashbaum, "At George Soros's Home, Pipe Bomb Was Likely Hand-Delivered, Officials Say," *New York Times*, October 23, 2018, www.nytimes.com/2018/10/23/nyregion/soros-caravan-explosive-bomb-home.html; Aaron Rupar, @atrupar, "REPORTER: do you think somebody is funding the caravan?" Twitter, October 31, 2018, https://twitter.com/atrupar/status/1057742231937912833.
128. Peters, "How Trump-Fed Conspiracy."
129. Federal Defenders of New York, "Case 1:18-cr-00820-JSR, Document 38, United States v. Cesar Altieri Sayoc," July 22, 2019, https://drive.google.com/file/d/1082hJDDDBWO7dOXn8bZguLiqStzvYX4U9/view.
130. Jon Swaine and Juweek Adolphe, "Violence in the Name of Trump," *Guardian*, August 28, 2019, www.theguardian.com/us-news/ng-interactive/2019/aug/28/in-the-name-of-trump-supporters-attacks-database.
131. Christopher Mathias, "A Fascist Trump Rally in Greenville," *HuffPost*, July 18, 2019, www.huffpost.com/entry/fascist-trump-rally-greenville-ilhan-omar-send-her-back_n_5d30529fe4b0419fd328b270.
132. Christopher Mathias, "Go Back to Your Country, They Said," *HuffPost*, November 4, 2019, www.huffpost.com/feature/go-back-to-your-country.
133. Joseph Gerth, "Trump Ignites Emotions in KY Visit," *Courier Journal*, March 1, 2016, www.courier-journal.com/story/news/politics/elections/kentucky/2016/03/01/donald-trump-rally-louisville/81023044/; Kenneth Vogel, "White Nationalist Claims Trump Directed Rally Violence," Politico, April 17, 2017, https://www.politico.com/story/2017/04/donald-trump-rally-violence-237302.

134. Steve Benen, "Despite Reality, Trump Insists Mexico Is 'Paying for the Wall,'" MSNBC, March 3, 2020, www.msnbc.com/rachel-maddow-show/despite-reality-trump-insists-mexico-paying-wall-n1147941.

135. Rachel Morris, "Trump Got His Wall, After All," *HuffPost: Highline*, November 24, 2019, www.huffpost.com/highline/article/invisible-wall/.

136. Julie Hirschfeld Davis and Michael D. Shear, *Border Wars: Inside Trump's Assault on Immigration* (New York: Simon & Schuster, 2019), 24–25.

137. Julia Edwards Ainsley, "Exclusive – Trump Border 'Wall' to Cost $21.6 Billion, Take 3.5 Years to Build: Internal Report," Reuters, February 9, 2017, www.reuters.com/article/us-usa-trump-immigration-wall-exclusive-idUSKBN15O2ZN.

138. Ron Nixon, "Border Wall Could Cost 3 Times Estimates, Senate Democrats' Report Says," *New York Times*, April 18, 2017, www.nytimes.com/2017/04/18/us/politics/senate-democrats-border-wall-cost-trump.html.

139. Peter Baker and Jennifer Steinhauer, "Wall 'Will Get Built,' Trump Insists, as He Drops Funding Demand," *New York Times*, April 25, 2017, www.nytimes.com/2017/04/25/us/politics/mexico-wall-spending-trump.html.

140. Kelsey Snell, "Senate Democrats Prepare for Spring Battle over Trump's Border Wall," *Washington Post*, March 13, 2017, www.washingtonpost.com/news/powerpost/wp/2017/03/13/senate-democrats-prepare-for-spring-battle-over-trumps-border-wall/.

141. Burgess Everett, "Trump Loses Temper over Border Wall Funding," *Politico*, June 19, 2018, www.politico.com/story/2018/06/19/trump-border-wall-funding-immigration-653530.

142. Glenn Kessler, "Does President Trump's Border Wall Pay for Itself?" *Washington Post*, March 16, 2018, www.washingtonpost.com/news/fact-checker/wp/2018/03/16/does-president-trumps-border-wall-pay-for-itself/.

143. Julián Aguilar, "How Donald Trump's Border Wall Fared in the $1.3 Trillion Spending Bill He Just Signed," *Texas Tribune*, www.texastribune.org/2018/03/23/donald-trump-border-wall-16-million-funding-restrictions-attached.

144. Jacob Pramuk, "Trump Signs Bill to Temporarily Reopen Government after Longest Shutdown in History," CNBC, January 25, 2019, www.cnbc.com/2019/01/25/senate-votes-to-reopen-government-and-end-shutdown-without-border-wall.html.

145. Davis and Shear, *Border Wars*, 375.

146. Mary Ann Ahern, "Trump Campaigns with Indiana Gov. Mike Pence amid VP Speculation," NBC Chicago, July 12, 2016, www.nbcchicago.com/news/national-international/trump-could-select-indiana-gov-mike-pence-for-vp/2009013/.

147. Beau Hodai, "What Are Steve Bannon, Kris Kobach and Co. Up To at

the Arizona-Mexico Border?" *Phoenix New Times*, March 30, 2019, www.
phoenixnewtimes.com/news/webuildthewall-protecting-border-raising-
campaign-funds-donald-trump-11255960.

148. Brianna Sacks and Claudia Koerner, "The Veteran Who Has Raised over
$12 Million to Fund Trump's Wall Made Money Off Peddling Conspiracy
Theories and Fake News," *BuzzFeed News*, December 21, 2018, www.
buzzfeednews.com/article/briannasacks/veteran-gofundme-border-wall-
fake-news.

149. Hodai, "What Are Bannon, Kobach and Co. Up To?"

150. Hodai, "What Are Bannon, Kobach and Co. Up To?"

151. Michael Brice-Saddler, "The GoFundMe Border Wall Finally Broke
Ground. Then a Cease-and-Desist Order Arrived," *Washington Post*, May
29, 2019, www.washingtonpost.com/nation/2019/05/29/border-wall-
gofundme-finally-broke-ground-then-cease-and-desist-order-arrived/.

152. "Sunland Park: Construction of Private Border Barrier Not in Compliance
with City Ordinance," KVIA ABC-7, May 29, 2019, https://kvia.com/
news/2019/05/28/sunland-park-construction-of-private-border-barrier-
not-in-compliance-with-city-ordinance/.

153. Gus Bova, "'We Build the Wall' Lands in South Texas, Vilifies Priest and
Butterfly Refuge," *Texas Observer*, November 21, 2019, www.texasobserver.
org/we-build-the-wall-south-texas-vilifies-priest-butterfly-refuge/.

154. Brice-Saddler, "GoFundMe Border Wall."

155. See "We Build the Wall," https://webuildthewall.us/.

156. Mallory Falk and Abigail Clukey, "Privately Funded Border Wall
Near Completion in New Mexico," NPR, May 31, 2019, www.npr.
org/2019/05/31/728332148/privately-funded-border-wall-near-
completion-in-new-mexico.

157. Falk and Clukey, "Privately Funded Border Wall."

158. Julian Resendiz, "DHS Officials Welcome Privately Built Border Wall,"
Border Report, November 21, 2019, www.borderreport.com/news/dhs-
officials-welcome-privately-built-border-wall/.

159. Resendiz, "DHS Officials Welcome."

160. Bova, "'We Build the Wall.'"

161. Sandra Sanchez, "'Walls Work,' Declares DHS Head during Visit to South
Texas Border," *Border Report*, November 22, 2019, www.borderreport.com/
hot-topics/the-border-wall/walls-work-declares-dhs-head-during-visit-
to-south-texas-border/.

162. Emily D'Gyves, "Private Border Wall Construction Continues
amid Federal TRO," *Monitor*, December 9, 2019, www.themonitor.
com/2019/12/09/private-border-wall-construction-continues-despite-
federal-tro/.

163. Julia Reinstein, Rosie Gray, and Salvador Hernandez, "Former Top Trump Aide Steve Bannon and 'Build the Wall' Founder Brian Kolfage Have Been Charged With Fraud," August 20, 2020, https://www.buzzfeednews.com/article/juliareinstein/stephen-bannon-brian-kolfage-wall-charged.

164. Stern, "Private Border Wall"; WeBuildTheWall, "WeBuildTheWall's Primary Contractor Fisher Industries Awarded $270 Million Government Project for Border Wall," Cision PR Newswire, December 4, 2019, www.prnewswire.com/news-releases/webuildthewalls-primary-contractor-fisher-industries-awarded-270-million-government-project-for-border-wall-300969353.html.

Chapter Five: Every State Is a Border State

1. Nicos Poulantzas, *Fascism and Dictatorship: The Third International and the Problem of Fascism* (London: Verso, 2018), 17.

2. Adam Tooze, *Crashed: How a Decade of Financial Crises Changed the World* (London: Allen Lane, 2018), 164–65.

3. Grace Blakeley, *Stolen: How to Save the World from Financialisation* (London: Repeater Books, 2019), 178.

4. Tooze, *Crashed*, 20.

5. Pierre Dardot and Christian Laval, *Never-Ending Nightmare: The Neoliberal Assault on Democracy* (London: Verso Books, 2019), 15 (emphasis in original).

6. Wendy Brown, *Walled States, Waning Sovereignty* (Boston: MIT Press, 2014), 36.

7. Miller, *Empire of Borders*, 33.

8. Leo Chavez, *The Latino Threat: Constructing Immigrants, Citizens, and the Nation* (Stanford, CA: Stanford University Press, 2008), 11.

9. Kelly Lytle Hernández, "Amnesty or Abolition? Felons, Illegals, and the Case for a New Abolition Movement," *Boom: A Journal of California* 1, no. 4 (Winter 2011): 57.

10. William I. Robinson, "'*Aqui estamos y no nos vamos!*' Global Capital and Immigrant Rights," *Race & Class* 48, no. 2 (2006): 77–91.

11. Lowe, *Immigrant Acts*, 20–21.

12. Brown, *Walled States*, 79–80.

13. Lowe, *Immigrant Acts*, 12–13.

14. Dardot and Laval, *Never-Ending Nightmare*, 6.

15. Margaret E. Peters, *Trading Barriers: Immigration and the Remaking of Globalization* (Princeton, NJ: Princeton University Press, 2017), 4.

16. Peters, *Trading Barriers*, 4

17. Alexander Hertel-Fernandez and Theda Skocpol, "Billionaires against Big

Business: Growing Tensions in the Republican Party Coalition," Prepared for delivery at the 2016 Midwest Political Science Association Conference, April 8, 2016.

18. Denvir, *All-American Nativism*, 268–69.

19. Lee Fang, "David Koch's Most Significant Legacy Is the Election of Donald Trump," *Intercept*, August 26, 2019, https://theintercept.com/2019/08/26/david-koch-donald-trump/.

20. Lee Fang, "Koch Brothers' Operatives Fill Top Whitehouse Positions, Ethics Forms Reveal," April 4, 2017, https://theintercept.com/2017/04/04/koch-trump-wh/.

21. Peters, *Trading Barriers*, 88.

22. Wendy Brown, *In the Ruins of Neoliberalism: The Rise of Antidemocratic Politics in the West* (New York: Columbia University Press, 2019), 62.

23. Samuel Brittan, "Thatcher Was Right—There Is No 'Society,'" *Financial Times*, April 18, 2018, www.ft.com/content/d1387b70-a5d5-11e2-9b77-00144feabdc0.

24. Brown, *Ruins of Neoliberalism*, 44–45.

25. Greg Afinogenov, "Society as Checkpoint," *n+1* 32 (Fall 2018), https://nplusonemag.com/issue-32/politics/society-as-checkpoint/.

26. Debbie Nathan, "A Vigilante Militia Defends an Imaginary Border," *Intercept*, May 18, 2019, https://theintercept.com/2019/05/18/border-militia-texas-mexico-guardian-patriots/.

27. Melissa del Bosque, "Border Control Union Endorses Extremist Video Featuring White Nationalists," *Intercept*, October 23, 2018, https://theintercept.com/2018/10/23/border-patrol-union-killing-free-speech-video/.

28. Roxanne Dunbar-Ortiz, *Loaded: A Disarming History of the Second Amendment* (San Francisco: City Lights Books, 2018), 171–72.

29. William I. Robinson and Mario Barrera, "Global Capitalism and Twenty-First Century Fascism: A US Case Study," *Race & Class* 53, no. 3 (2012): 19.

30. Robinson and Barrera, "Global Capitalism," 20.

31. Brendan O'Connor, "Border Profiteers," *Baffler*, July 2, 2019, https://thebaffler.com/outbursts/border-profiteers-oconnor.

32. Robert Moore, "'They Treated Us Like We Are Animals': Holding Pen for Migrant Families in El Paso Shut Down," *Texas Monthly*, March 31, 2019, www.texasmonthly.com/news/holding-pen-migrant-families-shut-down-el-paso/?fbclid=IwAR0o78puiBSqGh1Ay8FyRFpjpJw9qi_3Wr9A2q5xnGiwMiXsf8w_-dEpTOc.

33. Peter Alexander and Adam Edelman, "Trump, in Unexpected Move, Withdraws Nomination to Head ICE," NBC News, April 5, 2019, www.nbcnews.com/politics/immigration/trump-unexpected-move-withdraws-nomination-head-ice-n991286.

34. SAVA Workforce Solutions [DUNS 145725763], USAspending. gov, accessed April 15, 2020, www.usaspending.gov/#/search/ ad85f83c391bccb568f1259a270bbba7.

35. Yaakov Lappin, "Elbit to Build Surveillance Towers on Arizona's Border with Mexico," *Jerusalem Post*, March 2, 2014, www.jpost.com/ International/Elbit-to-build-surveillance-towers-on-Arizonas-border-with-Mexico-344005.

36. Graham Kates, "John Kelly Joins Board of Company Operating Largest Shelter for Unaccompanied Migrant Children," CBS News, May 3, 2019, www.cbsnews.com/news/john-kelly-joins-board-of-caliburn-international-company-operating-largest-unaccompanied-migrant-children-shelter/.

37. United States Securities and Exchange Commission, "Form S-1 Registration Statement, Caliburn International Corporation," October 19, 2018, www.sec.gov/Archives/edgar/data/1750690/000119312518303218/ d632104ds1.htm.

38. Salvador Rodriguez, "Oculus Founder Palmer Luckey Scores $1 Billion-Plus Valuation for His Virtual Border Wall Start-Up," CNBC, September 11, 2019, www.cnbc.com/2019/09/11/anduril-valued-at-1-billion-in-round-including-andreessen-horowitz.html.

39. Richard Cooke, "A Serial Killer at the Border—and the Women Who Stood Up to Him," *Guardian*, May 9, 2019, www.theguardian.com/us-news/2019/may/09/juan-david-ortiz-laredo-serial-killer-border-patrol-agent-women-stood-up-deaths.

40. Torrie Hester, "Deportability and the Carceral State," *Journal of American History* 102, no. 1 (June 2015): 148.

41. Derrick Moore, "Crimes Involving Moral Turpitude: Why the Void-for-Vagueness Argument Is Still Available and Meritorious," *Cornell International Law Journal* 41, no. 3 (2008): 813–43, https://scholarship.law.cornell.edu/cilj/vol41/iss3/6.

42. Juno Mac and Molly Smith, *Revolting Prostitutes: The Fight for Sex Workers' Rights* (London: Verso Books, 2008), 16.

43. Mac and Smith, *Revolting Prostitutes*, 74.

44. Belew, *Bring the War Home*, 158–59.

45. "David Lane," Southern Poverty Law Center, accessed April 15, 2020, www.splcenter.org/fighting-hate/extremist-files/individual/david-lane.

46. Salvador Hernandez, "Man Acquitted in Kate Steinle Killing Faces Federal Gun and Immigration Charges," *BuzzFeed News*, December 6, 2017, www.buzzfeednews.com/article/salvadorhernandez/man-acquitted-in-kate-steinle-killing-faces-federal-gun-and.

47. Evan Sernoffsky, "Kate Steinle Case: Appeals Court Overturns

Gun Conviction of Jose Inez Garcia Zarate," www.sfchronicle.com/crime/article/Kate-Steinle-case-Appeals-court-overturns-gun-14403382.php.

48. Jan Ransom, "Trump Will Not Apologize for Calling for Death Penalty over Central Park Five," *New York Times*, June 18, 2019, www.nytimes.com/2019/06/18/nyregion/central-park-five-trump.html.

49. Denvir, *All-American Nativism*, 244.

50. Chris Nguyen, "Kate Steinle's Family Speaks after Mention by Donald Trump at RNC," ABC7 News, July 23, 2016, https://abc7news.com/1439363/.

51. Denvir, *All-American Nativism*, 236–37.

52. Jonathan Blitzer, "The Hard-Liners Standing behind Trump against Sanctuary Cities," *New Yorker*, January 30, 2017, www.newyorker.com/news/news-desk/the-hard-liners-standing-behind-trump-against-sanctuary-cities.

53. Stern, *Proud Boys and the White Ethnostate*, 87.

54. Stern, *Proud Boys and the White Ethnostate*, 87.

55. Stern, *Proud Boys and the White Ethnostate*, 75–76.

56. Chavez, *Latino Threat*, 75.

57. Will Sommer, "Conservative Group Fires Michelle Malkin over Support for Holocaust Denier," *Daily Beast*, November 18, 2019, www.thedailybeast.com/conservative-group-yaf-fires-michelle-malkin-over-support-for-holocaust-denier.

58. Quoted in Chavez, *Latino Threat*, 194.

59. Alix M. Freedman, "Two American Contraceptive Researchers Export Sterilization Drug to Third World," *Wall Street Journal*, June 18, 1998, www.wsj.com/articles/SB898049641324732000?ns=prod/accounts-wsj; Aaron Flanagan et al., "The Quinacrine Report: Sterilization, Modern Day Eugenics, and the Anti-Immigrant Movement," Center for New Community (2013).

60. Aviva Galpert, "Of Bombs and Wombs: Nativist Myths of Weaponized Fertility," Political Research Associates, July 18, 2014, www.politicalresearch.org/2014/07/18/bombs-and-wombs.

61. Robin Opsahl, "U.S. Rep. Steve King: If Not for Rape and Incest, 'Would There Be Any Population Left?'"*Des Moines Register*, December 26, 2019, www.desmoinesregister.com/story/news/politics/2019/08/14/steve-king-abortion-rape-incest-westside-conservative-iowa-representative-birth-iowa-civilization/2007230001/.

62. Subcommittee on Immigration and Border Security "Birthright Citizenship."

63. Subcommittee on Immigration and Border Security, "Birthright Citizenship."

64. Quoted in Chavez, *Latino Threat*, 195.

65. Subcommittee on Immigration and Border Security, "Birthright Citizenship."

66. Subcommittee on Immigration and Border Security, "Birthright Citizenship."

67. Michael Anton, "Citizenship Shouldn't Be a Birthright," *Washington Post*, July 18, 2018, www.washingtonpost.com/opinions/citizenship-shouldnt-be-a-birthright/2018/07/18/7d0e2998-8912-11e8-85ae-511bc1146b0b_story.html.

68. Jonathan Swan and Stef W. Kight, "Exclusive: Trump Targeting Birthright Citizenship with Executive Order," *Axios*, October 30, 2018, www.axios.com/trump-birthright-citizenship-executive-order-0cf4285a-16c6-48f2-a933-bd71fd72ea82.html.

69. Tasneem Nashrulla, "This Racist Member of Congress Has Been Pushing Trump's Plan to Revoke Birthright Citizenship All Along," *BuzzFeed News*, October 31, 2018, www.buzzfeednews.com/article/tasneemnashrulla/steve-king-racist-birthright-citizenship-trump-legislative.

70. "Rep. Steve King Reintroduces Birthright Citizenship Act," NumbersUSA, January 8, 2019, www.numbersusa.com/news/rep-steve-king-reintroduces-birthright-citizenship-act.

71. Ellie Hall, "Now Trump Is Saying He'll Stop Babies Born in the US from Becoming Citizens, Though He Probably Can't," *BuzzFeed News*, October 30, 2018, www.buzzfeednews.com/article/ellievhall/trump-executive-order-birthright-citizenship-float; Jeff Mason and Makini Brice, "Trump Says He Is Seriously Looking at Ending Birthright Citizenship," Reuters, August 21, 2019, www.reuters.com/article/us-usa-immigration-trump/trump-says-he-is-seriously-looking-at-ending-birthright-citizenship-idUSKCN1VB21B.

72. Michelle Hackman, "State Department to Issue Rules Restricting U.S. Travel for Pregnant Foreigners," *Wall Street Journal*, January 23, 2020, www.wsj.com/articles/state-department-to-issue-rules-restricting-u-s-travel-for-pregnant-foreigners-11579790313.

73. Chavez, *Latino Threat*, 75.

74. Denvir, *All-American Nativism*, 213.

75. Tina Vasquez, "OB-GYN Says U.S. Marshals Service Is Shackling Detained Pregnant Migrants," *Rewire.News*, May 14, 2019, https://rewire.news/article/2019/05/14/ob-gyn-says-u-s-marshals-service-is-shackling-detained-pregnant-migrants/.

76. Tina Vasquez, "Meet the Federal Agency Helping to Criminalize Pregnant Migrants," *Rewire.News*, May 14, 2019, https://rewire.news/article/2019/05/14/meet-the-federal-agency-helping-to-criminalize-

pregnant-migrants/.

77. Tina Vasquez, "Trump Administration Separates Some Migrant Mothers from Their Newborns before Returning Them to Detention," *Rewire. News*, May 28, 2019, https://rewire.news/article/2019/05/28/trump-administration-separates-pregnant-migrants-newborns-before-returning-detention/.

78. PLOS, "Nearly 1/3 of Migrants through Mexico to US Experience Significant Violence during Journey," *Science Daily*, August 21, 2019, www.sciencedaily.com/releases/2019/08/190821142712.htm.

79. Manny Fernandez, "'You Have to Pay with Your Body': The Hidden Nightmare of Sexual Violence on the Border," *New York Times*, March 3, 2019, www.nytimes.com/2019/03/03/us/border-rapes-migrant-women.html.

80. Emily Kassie, "Sexual Assault inside ICE Detention: 2 Survivors Tell Their Stories," *New York Times*, July 17, 2018, www.nytimes.com/2018/07/17/us/sexual-assault-ice-detention-survivor-stories.html.

81. Caitlin Owens, Stef W. Kight, and Harry Stevens, "Thousands of Migrant Youth Allegedly Suffered Sexual Abuse in U.S. Custody," *Axios*, February 26, 2019, www.axios.com/immigration-unaccompanied-minors-sexual-assault-3222e230-29e1-430f-a361-d959c88c5d8c.html.

82. Matthew Haag, "Thousands of Immigrant Children Said They Were Sexually Abused in U.S. Detention Centers, Report Says," *New York Times*, February 27, 2019, www.nytimes.com/2019/02/27/us/immigrant-children-sexual-abuse.html.

83. Daniella Silver, "ACLU Sues Jeff Sessions over Restricting Asylum for Victims of Domestic, Gang Violence," NBC News, August 7, 2018, www.nbcnews.com/news/us-news/aclu-sues-jeff-sessions-over-restricting-asylum-domestic-gang-violence-n898496.

84. National Commission on Terrorist Attacks upon the United States, *The 9/11 Commission Report: Final Report of the National Commission on Terrorist Attacks upon the United States (9/11 Report)*, July 22, 2004, www.9-11commission.gov/report/911Report.pdf.

85. Joel Gunter, "Trump's 'Muslim Lockdown': What Is the Center for Security Policy?" BBC News, December 8, 2015, www.bbc.com/news/world-us-canada-35037943.

86. Brendan O'Connor, "The Man Behind Donald Trump's Latest Policy Platform Is a Crackpot Anti-Muslim Extremist," *Gawker*, December 8, 2015, https://gawker.com/the-man-behind-donald-trumps-latest-policy-platform-is-1746804097; Margaret Talev and Jennifer Epstein, "Bolton Adds Loyalists to National Security Council Staff," *Bloomberg*, May 29, 2018, www.bloomberg.com/news/articles/2018-05-29/bolton-adds-loyalists-to-national-security-council-staff.

87. Quoted in Chavez, *Latino Threat*, 39.

88. Tom Barry, "Anti-Immigrant Backlash on the 'Home Front,'" *NACLA Report on the Americas* 38, no. 6 (2016): 29–30.

89. Barry, "Anti-Immigrant Backlash," 30.

90. Barry, "Anti-Immigrant Backlash," 28–29.

91. Renton, *New Authoritarians*, 126.

92. Chris McGreal, "Ground Zero Mosque Plans 'Fuelling Anti-Muslim Protests across US,'" *Guardian*, August 12, 2010, www.theguardian.com/world/2010/aug/12/ground-zero-mosque-islamophobia; Ben Smith, "Hedge Fund Figure Financed Mosque Campaign," *Politico*, January 18, 2011, www.politico.com/blogs/ben-smith/2011/01/hedge-fund-figure-financed-mosque-campaign-032525; Moustafa Bayoumi, "Peter King's 'Islamic Radicalization' Hearings Fan Paranoid Fantasies," *Nation*, March 10, 2011, www.thenation.com/article/archive/peter-kings-islamic-radicalization-hearings-fan-paranoid-fantasies/.

93. Jane Mayer, "The Reclusive Hedge-Fund Tycoon behind the Trump Presidency," *New Yorker*, March 17, 2017, www.newyorker.com/magazine/2017/03/27/the-reclusive-hedge-fund-tycoon-behind-the-trump-presidency; Derek Siedman, "Jeff Sessions and the Islamophobia Industry," *Jacobin*, February 8, 2017, www.jacobinmag.com/2017/02/jeff-sessions-attorney-general-trump-islamophobia-breitbart-horowitz/.

94. Renton, *New Authoritarians*, 132.

95. Lauren Gambino, Sabrina Siddiqui, Paul Owen, and Edward Helmore, "Thousands Protest against Trump Travel Ban in Cities and Airports Nationwide," *Guardian*, January 30, 2017, www.theguardian.com/us-news/2017/jan/29/protest-trump-travel-ban-muslims-airports.

96. Adam Liptak and Michael D. Shear, "Trump's Travel Ban Is Upheld by Supreme Court," *New York Times*, June 26, 2018, www.nytimes.com/2018/06/26/us/politics/supreme-court-trump-travel-ban.html; Elora Mukherjee, "The Supreme Court Made the African Ban Possible," *Slate*, February 3, 2020, https://slate.com/news-and-politics/2020/02/supreme-court-african-ban-possible.html.

97. "Tucker Carlson Warns about the Threat of American Leaders 'Who Hate the Country They Govern So Much That They Seek to Make American Citizenship Irrelevant,'" Media Matters, September 11, 2018, www.mediamatters.org/tucker-carlson/tucker-carlson-warns-about-threat-american-leaders-who-hate-country-they-govern-so.

98. Todd Miller, "More Than a Wall: Corporate Profiteering and the Militarization of US Borders," TNI, September 16, 2019, www.tni.org/en/morethanawall.

99. Miller, "More Than a Wall."

100. "Homeland Security and Emergency Management Market Worth $846.5 Billion by 2025," MarketsandMarkets, press release, April 9, 2020, www.marketsandmarkets.com/PressReleases/homeland-security-emergency-management.asp.

101. "U.S. Spends More on Immigration Enforcement Than on FBI, DEA, Secret Service & All Other Federal Criminal Law Enforcement Agencies Combined," Migration Policy Institute, press release, January 7, 2013, www.migrationpolicy.org/news/us-spends-more-immigration-enforcement-fbi-dea-secret-service-all-other-federal-criminal-law.

102. "U.S. Spends More on Immigration Enforcement."

103. "The Cost of Immigration Enforcement and Border Security," American Immigration Council, October 14, 2019, www.americanimmigrationcouncil.org/research/the-cost-of-immigration-enforcement-and-border-security.

104. Caitlin Dickerson, "ICE Faces Migrant Detention Crunch as Border Chaos Spills into Interior of the Country," *New York Times*, April 22, 2019, www.nytimes.com/2019/04/22/us/immigration-detention.html.

105. Carl Lindskoog, *Detain and Punish: Haitian Refugees and the Rise of the World's Largest Immigration Detention System* (Gainesville: University of Florida Press, 2018).

106. Tina Vasquez, "Trump Administration Is Conflating Immigration with Terrorism at the Expense of Domestic Threats," *Rewire.News*, February 15, 2018, https://rewire.news/article/2018/02/15/trump-administration-conflating-immigration-terrorism-expense-domestic-threats/; Tina Vasquez, "Justice Department Announces Court Order Revoking Naturalized Citizenship, Citing Fingerprint Issue," *Rewire.News*, January 9, 2018, https://rewire.news/article/2018/01/09/justice-department-revokes-naturalized-citizenship-citing-fingerprint-issue/.

107. David A. Graham, "Trump's Entire Shutdown Approach, Encapsulated in One Tweet," *Atlantic*, January 18, 2019, www.theatlantic.com/politics/archive/2019/01/trump-tweet-prayer-rugs-border-shutdown/580765/; FAIR, "One-Stop Shopping for Credentialed Media Covering Immigration Policy," Cision PR Newswire, April 1, 2015, www.prnewswire.com/news-releases/one-stop-shopping-for-credentialed-media-covering-immigration-policy-300059535.html. Islamophobic rumors that prayer rugs were found at the US-Mexico border have circulated through right-wing media since the early 2000s. See Linda Qiu, "Trump's Baseless Claim about Prayer Rugs Found at the Border," *New York Times*, January 18, 2019, www.nytimes.com/2019/01/18/us/politics/fact-check-trump-prayer-rugs-border.html.

108. Daniel Gonzalez, "Migrant Caravan in Mexico: Are Women Traveling

with the Group Being Raped?" *Arizona Republic*, April 9, 2018, www.azcentral.com/story/news/politics/border-issues/2018/04/08/migrant-caravan-mexico-women-traveling-group-being-raped/497906002/.

109. Todd Bensman, "A Remarkable Unverified Claim by the President of Guatemala: 100 Migrants Linked to Terrorism Arrested in That Country," Center for Immigration Studies, October 16, 2018, https://cis.org/Bensman/Remarkable-Unverified-Claim-President-Guatemala-100-Migrants-Linked-Terrorism-Arrested.

110. Donald Trump Jr., @DonaldJTrumpJr, "The caravan thing is an obvious political stunt," Twitter, October 23, 2018, https://twitter.com/DonaldJTrumpJr/status/1054717268813324288.

111. Traverso, *New Faces of Fascism*, 4.

112. Traverso, *New Faces of Fascism*, 4.

113. Traverso, *New Faces of Fascism*, 20.

114. Poulantzas, *Fascism and Dictatorship*, 76.

115. Poultanzas, *Fascism and Dictatorship*, 78–79.

116. Renton, *New Authoritarians*, 21.

117. Grandin, *End of the Myth*, 8.

118. Zetkin, *Fighting Fascism*, 34.

119. Gentile, "Fascism as Political Religion," 242.

120. Paxton, *The Anatomy of Fascism*, 39–40.

121. Albert Memmi, *The Colonizer and the Colonized* (Lexington, MA: Plunkett Lake Press, 2013), 106–107.

122. Memmi, *Colonizer and the Colonized*, 107.

123. Dunbar-Ortiz, *Loaded*, 42.

124. David Roediger, *The Wages of Whiteness: Race and the Making of the American Working Class* (New York: Verso, 2007), 59.

125. Grandin, *End of the Myth*, 67.

126. Grandin, *End of the Myth*, 98.

127. Dunbar-Ortiz, *Loaded*, 124.

128. Mark Jay, "Cages and Crises: A Marxist Analysis of Mass Incarceration," *Historical Materialism* 21, no. 1 (March 2019): 13.

129. Jay, "Cages and Crises," 10.

130. Jay, "Cages and Crises," 12.

131. Elizabeth Hinton, "'A War within Our Own Boundaries': Lyndon Johnson's Great Society and the Rise of the Carceral State," *Journal of American History* 102, no. 1 (June 2015): 100–102.

132. Jay, "Cages and Crises," 14, 16.

133. Hinton, "'War within Our Own Boundaries,'" 111.

134. Hester, "Deportability and the Carceral State," 141.

135. Hester, "Deportability and the Carceral State," 141.

136. Douglas S. Massey and Karen A. Pren, "Unintended Consequences of US Immigration Policy: Explaining the Post-1965 Surge from Latin America," Population and Development Review, 2012a;38:1–29, https://www.ncbi.nlm.nih.gov/pmc/articles/PMC3407978/.

137. Hester, "Deportability and the Carceral State," 145.

138. Hester, "Deportability and the Carceral State," 147.

139. Denvir, *All-American Nativism*, 148.

140. Denvir, *All-American Nativism*, 96, 98.

141. Kelly Lytle Hernández, "Amnesty or Abolition?" 65.

142. Quoted in Traverso, *New Faces of Fascism*, 159.

143. Lisa Marie Cacho, *Social Death: Racialized Rightlessness and the Criminalization of the Unprotected* (New York and London: New York University Press, 2012), 8.

144. Rosa Luxemburg, "The Junius Pamphlet: The Crisis of German Social Democracy," Marxists Internet Archive, accessed April 15, 2020, www.marxists.org/archive/luxemburg/1915/junius/.

145. Miller, *Storming the Wall*, 40.

146. Miller, *Storming the Wall*, 112–13.

147. Peter Schwartz and Doug Randall, "An Abrupt Climate Change Scenario and Its Implications for United States National Security," United States, Department of Defense, October 2003, p. 19, https://apps.dtic.mil/dtic/tr/fulltext/u2/a469325.pdf.

148. Schwartz and Randall, "An Abrupt Climate Change Scenario," 18.

149. SOUTHCOM Public Affairs, "SOUTHCOM Hosts Interagency Exercise," US Southern Command, April 15, 2019, www.southcom.mil/MEDIA/NEWS-ARTICLES/Article/1814091/southcom-hosts-interagency-exercise/. As it happens, Trump's first DHS secretary, John Kelly, was the former head of SOUTHCOM for years. In that role, he oversaw some of the worst excesses of twenty-first century neo-colonialism. See: Jonah Walter, "Blood on His Hands," *Jacobin*, December 9, 2016, www.jacobinmag.com/2016/12/trump-kelly-homeland-security-southcom-colombia-honduras/.

150. SOUTHCOM Public Affairs, "SOUTHCOM Hosts Interagency Exercise"; Rebecca Hersher, "Climate Change Was the Engine That Powered Hurricane Maria's Devastating Rains," NPR, April 17, 2019, www.npr.org/2019/04/17/714098828/climate-change-was-the-engine-that-powered-hurricane-marias-devastating-rains.

151. John D. Sutter, "130,000 Left Puerto Rico after Hurricane Maria, Census Bureau Says," CNN, December 19, 2018, www.cnn.com/2018/12/19/health/sutter-puerto-rico-census-update/index.html.

152. Greg Allen, "After 2 Hurricanes, a 'Floodgate' of Mental Health

Issues in U.S. Virgin Islands," NPR, April 23, 2019, www.npr. org/2019/04/23/716089187/after-two-hurricanes-a-floodgate-of-mental-health-issues-in-the-virgin-islands.

153. Juliet Eilperin, Josh Dawsey, and Brady Dennis, "White House Blocked Intelligence Agency's Written Testimony Calling Climate Change 'Possibly Catastrophic,'" *Washington Post*, June 8, 2019, www. washingtonpost.com/climate-environment/2019/06/08/white-house-blocked-intelligence-aides-written-testimony-saying-human-caused-climate-change-could-be-possibly-catastrophic/; Julia Ainsley, "Trump Admin Won't Give Temporary Protected Status to Bahamian Victims of Hurricane Dorian," NBC News, September 11, 2019, www.nbcnews. com/politics/immigration/trump-admin-will-deny-temporary-protected-status-bahamians-who-fled-n1052561.

154. Aaron Blake, "Trump Contradicts CBP Head on Bahamian Refugees, Argues They Might Have Been Infiltrated by 'Very Bad People,'" *Washington Post*, September 9, 2019, www.washingtonpost. com/politics/2019/09/09/trump-contradicts-cbp-head-bahamian-refugees-argues-they-might-have-been-infiltrated-by-very-bad-people/?noredirect=on.

155. Brianna Sacks, "The Bahamas Is Using Hurricane Dorian to Push Out Haitian Immigrants, Critics Say," *BuzzFeed News*, October 3, 2019, www.buzzfeednews.com/article/briannasacks/haitian-immigrants-the-bahamas-dorian.

156. Josh Dawsey, "Trump Derides Protections for Immigrants from 'Shithole' Countries," *Washington Post*, January 12, 2011, www.washingtonpost. com/politics/trump-attacks-protections-for-immigrants-from-shithole-countries-in-oval-office-meeting/2018/01/11/bfc0725c-f711-11e7-91af-31ac729add94_story.html.

157. Food and Agriculture Organization of the United Nations and World Food Programme, "FAO and WFP Concerned about the Impact of Drought on the Most Vulnerable in Central America," World Food Programme, August 24, 2018, www.wfp.org/news/fao-and-wfp-concerned-about-impact-drought-most-vulnerable-central-america; Jeff Koehler, "Coffee Rust Threatens Latin American Crop; 150 Years Ago, It Wiped Out an Empire," NPR, October 16, 2018, www.npr.org/sections/thesalt/2018/10/16/649155664/coffee-rust-threatens-latin-american-crop-150-years-ago-it-wiped-out-an-empire.

158. "Food Security and Emigration: Why People Flee and the Impact on Family Members Left behind in El Salvador, Guatemala and Honduras," World Food Programme, 2017, https://docs.wfp.org/api/documents/WFP-0000022124/download/?_ga=2.85460124.46423775.1540402016-

1767178983.1540402016.

159. Georgina Gustin and Mariana Henninger, "Central America's Choice: Pray for Rain or Migrate," NBC News, July 9, 2019, www.nbcnews.com/news/latino/central-america-drying-farmers-face-choice-pray-rain-or-leave-n1027346.

160. Associated Press, "A Week Later, No Answers on Why a Migrant Teen Died in U.S Custody," NBC News, May 9, 2019, www.nbcnews.com/news/latino/week-later-no-answers-why-migrant-teen-became-ill-died-n1003831.

161. Gustin and Henninger, "Central America's Choice."

162. Daniel Dale, @ddale8, "Alert: The President said a couple minutes ago, 'We're building a wall in Colorado,'" Twitter, October 23, 2019, https://twitter.com/ddale8/status/1187104954504433666.

163. "Fox Host Tomi Lahren Suggests That Americans May Need to Shoot Immigrants Who Are Coming to the United States," Media Matters, September 13, 2019, www.mediamatters.org/tomi-lahren/fox-host-tomi-lahren-suggests-americans-may-need-shoot-immigrants-who-are-coming-united.

164. The White House, @White House, quoting @CBPMarkMorgan: "Every town, every city, every state, is a border town, a border city, and a border state," Twitter, October 28, 2019, https://twitter.com/WhiteHouse/status/1188877066231566339.

165. Sonia Pérez, "Guatemala Sweeps Up Migrant Group, Returns Them to Border," Latino Rebels, January 16, 2020, www.latinorebels.com/2020/01/16/guatemalareturnsmigrants/.

166. Max Rivlin-Nadler, "Newly Released Documents Shed Light on Border Patrol's Seemingly Limitless Authority," *Intercept*, January 7, 2019, https://theintercept.com/2019/01/07/cbp-border-patrol-enforcement-law-course/; "The Constitution in the 100-Mile Border Zone," ACLU, www.aclu.org/other/constitution-100-mile-border-zone.

167. Robinson and Barrera, "Global Capitalism," 5–6.

168. Robinson and Barrera, "Global Capitalism," 10.

169. Joshua Brustein, "Tech's Most Controversial Startup Now Makes Drone-Killing Robots," *Bloomberg*, March 10, 2019, www.bloomberg.com/news/features/2019-10-03/tech-s-most-controversial-startup-now-makes-attack-drones.

170. Sam Biddle, "How Peter Thiel's Palantir Helped the NSA Spy on the Whole World," *Intercept*, February 22, 2017, https://theintercept.com/2017/02/22/how-peter-thiels-palantir-helped-the-nsa-spy-on-the-whole-world/.

171. Peter Waldman, Lizette Chapman, and Jordan Robertson, "Palantir Knows

Everything about You," *Bloomberg*, April 19, 2018, www.bloomberg.com/
features/2018-palantir-peter-thiel/.

172. Peter Thiel, "The Education of a Libertarian," *Cato Unbound*, April
13, 2009, www.cato-unbound.org/2009/04/13/peter-thiel/education-
libertarian.

173. Lizette Chapman, "Floating Island Project Pushes On, without Peter
Thiel's Support," *Bloomberg*, July 30, 2018, www.bloomberg.com/news/
articles/2018-07-30/floating-island-project-pushes-on-without-peter-
thiel-s-support.

174. Owen Thomas, "Billionaire Facebook Investor's Anti-Immigrant Heresy,"
Gawker, November 14, 2008, https://gawker.com/5083655/billionaire-
facebook-investors-anti-immigrant-heresy.

175. Peter Brimelow, "NumbersUSA, Peter Thiel, and the Wages of
Moderation," VDARE, November 20, 2008, https://vdare.com/posts/
numbersusa-peter-thiel-and-the-wages-of-moderation.

176. John Reid, "Turnabout Is Fair Play: Immigration Patriot Peter Thiel
Does to GAWKER What Left Did to Hazleton, Farmer's Branch,"
VDARE, June 3, 2016, https://vdare.com/articles/turnabout-is-fair-
play-immigration-patriot-peter-thiel-does-to-gawker-what-left-did-to-
hazleton-farmer-s-branch.

177. George Packer, *The Unwinding: An Inner History of the New America* (New
York: Farrar, Straus and Giroux, 2013), 120–21; Julie Lythcott-Haims,
"My Conversation with Peter Thiel about Apartheid . . . and Its Unfolding
Aftermath," Medium, November 2, 2016, https://medium.com/indian-
thoughts/my-conversation-with-peter-thiel-about-apartheid-and-its-
aftermath-3fdf4249b08d#.xz4kamaam.

178. Ann Coulter, *Demonic: How the Liberal Mob Is Endangering America* (New
York: Crown Publishing Group, 2012); Ann Coulter, *¡Adios, America!: The
Left's Plan to Turn Our Country into a Third World Hellhole* (Washington,
DC: Regnery Publishing, 2015).

179. Denvir, *All-American Nativism*, 243.

180. Federal Election Commission, "Report of Receipts and Disbursements
for Other Than an Authorized Committee, Trump Victory," FEC
Form 3x, February 14, 2017, p. 276, https://docquery.fec.gov/cgi-bin/
fecimg/?201702149049355045; Federal Election Commission, "Report of
Receipts and Disbursements for Other Than an Authorized Committee,
Make America Number 1," FEC Form 3x, May 30, 2017, p. 6, https://
docquery.fec.gov/cgi-bin/fecimg/?201705309055158634; Federal Election
Commission, "Report of Receipts and Disbursements for Other Than an
Authorized Committee, Trump Victory," FEC Form 3x, October 15, 2018,
p. 62, https://docquery.fec.gov/cgi-bin/fecimg/?201810159125212736.

181. "Mercer Sisters Liquidate Beleaguered Cambridge Analytica," Associated Press, May 18, 2018, https://apnews.com/64280ae1f30c44eb8b82049f6875dddd/Mercer-sisters-liquidate-beleaguered-Cambridge-Analytica; Waldman, Chapman, and Robertson, "Palantir Knows Everything."

182. Zachary Mider and Jennifer Epstein, "Trump Takes 'Thank-You Tour' to Wealthy Donor's Costume Ball," *Bloomberg*, December 4, 2016, www.bloomberg.com/news/articles/2016-12-04/trump-takes-his-thank-you-tour-to-wealthy-donor-s-costume.

183. Colin Lecher, "Peter Thiel Is Joining Donald Trump's Transition Team," *Verge*, November 11, 2016, www.theverge.com/2016/11/11/13602026/peter-thiel-trump-transition-team-facebook; William Alden, "Palantir's Man in the Pentagon," *BuzzFeed News*, March 9, 2017, www.buzzfeednews.com/article/williamalden/palantirs-man-in-the-pentagon; Max Chafkin, "Trump Finally Names a U.S. CTO," *Bloomberg*, March 21, 2019, www.bloomberg.com/news/articles/2019-03-21/donald-trump-to-name-michael-kratsios-as-white-house-cto.

184. Douglas MacMillan and Elizabeth Dwoskin, "The War inside Palantir: Data-Mining Firm's Ties to ICE under Attack by Employees," *Washington Post*, August 22, 2019, www.washingtonpost.com/business/2019/08/22/war-inside-palantir-data-mining-firms-ties-ice-under-attack-by-employees/.

185. Bryan Lowry, "Silicon Valley Billionaire Thiel Invests in Kobach, Hawley and Rise of Nationalism," *Kansas City Star*, September 29, 2019, www.kansascity.com/news/politics-government/article235516452.html.

186. "Senator Hawley Addresses the Crisis at the Border from McAllen, Texas," Hawley.senate.gov, July 13, 2019, www.hawley.senate.gov/senator-hawley-addresses-crisis-border-mcallen-texas.

187. "BREAKING: Palantir's Technology Used in Mississippi Raids Where 680 Were Arrested," Mijente, October 4, 2019, https://mijente.net/2019/10/04/palantirpowersraids/.

188. Macmillan and Dwoskin, "War inside Palantir."

189. "BREAKING: Palantir's Technology"; George Joseph, "Data Company Directly Powers Immigration Raids in Workplace," WNYC, July 16, 2019, www.wnyc.org/story/palantir-directly-powers-ice-workplace-raids-emails-show/.

190. Spencer Woodman, "Palantir Provides the Engine for Donald Trump's Deportation Machine," *Intercept*, March 2, 2017, https://theintercept.com/2017/03/02/palantir-provides-the-engine-for-donald-trumps-deportation-machine/.

191. Sam Biddle and Ryan Devereaux, "Peter Thiel's Palantir Was Used to Bust Relatives of Migrant Children, New Documents Show," *Intercept*, May 2,

2019, https://theintercept.com/2019/05/02/peter-thiels-palantir-was-used-to-bust-hundreds-of-relatives-of-migrant-children-new-documents-show/.

192. Macmillan and Dwoskin, "War Inside Palantir."

193. Drew Harwell, "Google to Drop Pentagon AI Contract after Employee Objections to the 'Business of War,'" *Washington Post*, June 1, 2018, www.washingtonpost.com/news/the-switch/wp/2018/06/01/google-to-drop-pentagon-ai-contract-after-employees-called-it-the-business-of-war/?tid=lk_inline_manual_47.

194. Lee Fang, "Defense Tech Startup Founded by Trump's Most Prominent Silicon Valley Supporters Wins Secretive Military AI Contract," *Intercept*, March 9, 2019, https://theintercept.com/2019/03/09/anduril-industries-project-maven-palmer-luckey/.

195. Alex Karp, "I'm a Tech CEO, and I Don't Think Tech CEOs Should Be Making Policy," *Washington Post*, September 5, 2019, www.washingtonpost.com/opinions/policy-decisions-should-be-made-by-elected-representatives-not-silicon-valley/2019/09/05/e02a38dc-cf61-11e9-87fa-8501a456c003_story.html.

196. Alina Selyukh, "Amazon Appeals Pentagon's Choice of Microsoft for $10 Billion Cloud Contract," NPR, November 14, 2019, www.npr.org/2019/11/14/777585675/amazon-appeals-pentagons-choice-of-microsoft-for-10-billion-cloud-contract; Maya Kosoff, "Jeff Bezos: Peter Thiel Is 'a Contrarian,' and Contrarians 'Are Usually Wrong,'" *Vanity Fair*, October 20, 2019, www.vanityfair.com/news/2016/10/jeff-bezos-peter-thiel-trump-contrarian.

197. Rosalie Chan, "Read the Internal Letter Sent by a Group of Amazon Employees Asking the Company to Take a Stand against ICE," *Business Insider*, July 12, 2019, www.businessinsider.com/amazon-employees-letter-protest-palantir-ice-camps-2019-7.

198. "Who's Behind ICE? The Tech and Data Companies Fueling Deportations," Mijente, Immigrant Defense Project, and National Immigration Project, 2018, https://mijente.net/wp-content/uploads/2018/10/WHO%E2%80%99S-BEHIND-ICE_-The-Tech-and-Data-Companies-Fueling-Deportations_v3-.pdf.

199. Addy Baird, "Darrell Issa Called for Hearings on White Supremacists after Appearing at Conference for Hate Group," *ThinkProgress*, August 21, 2017, https://archive.thinkprogress.org/issa-letter-fair-82c935ac46f8/. Frank R. Konkel, "Love Him or Hate Him, Darrell Issa Changed Government Technology," *Nextgov*, January 10, 2018, www.nextgov.com/cio-briefing/2018/01/love-him-or-hate-him-darrell-issa-changed-government-technology/145119/.

200. Ron Knox, "Monopolies, Trump, the Border, and Fascism," *American*

Prospect, July 18, 2019, https://prospect.org/power/monopolies-trump-border-fascism/.

201. Maureen Dowd, "Peter Thiel, Trump's Tech Pal, Explains Himself," January 11, 2017, www.nytimes.com/2017/01/11/fashion/peter-thiel-donald-trump-silicon-valley-technology-gawker.html.

Chapter Six: Same Struggle, Same Fight

1. Zetkin, *Fighting Fascism*, 104.
2. Alain Badiou, *Greece and the Reinvention of Politics* (London: Verso Books, 2018), 63.
3. Badiou, *Greece and the Reinvention of Politics*, 64.
4. Badiou, *Greece and the Reinvention of Politics*, 66.
5. David Frum, "If Liberals Won't Enforce Borders, Fascists Will," *Atlantic*, April 2019, www.theatlantic.com/magazine/archive/2019/04/david-frum-how-much-immigration-is-too-much/583252/.
6. Thomas L. Friedman, "Trump Is Wasting Our Immigration Crisis," *New York Times*, April 23, 2019, www.nytimes.com/2019/04/23/opinion/trump-immigration-border-wall.html. Frequently stripped of context, Emanuel's comment, it is worth noting, was made in the throes of the 2008 financial meltdown, at the *Wall Street Journal*'s CEO Council, shortly after President Obama's election.
7. Thomas L. Friedman, "We Need a High Wall with a Big Gate," *New York Times*, November 27, 2018, www.nytimes.com/2018/11/27/opinion/immigration-republicans-democrats-climate-change.html.
8. Friedman, "Trump Is Wasting."
9. Friedman, "Trump Is Wasting."
10. Leigh Ann Caldwell, Kasie Hunt, and Rebecca Shabad, "Top House Dem Says New Offer Will Focus on Funding 'Smart Wall,'" NBC News, January 23, 2019, www.nbcnews.com/politics/congress/top-house-dem-says-new-offer-will-focus-funding-smart-n961746.
11. CNN transcripts, "Interview with Rep. James Clyburn (D-SC). Aired 7:30–8a ET," CNN, February 6, 2019, http://transcripts.cnn.com/TRANSCRIPTS/1902/06/nday.04.html.
12. "NYTWA Statement on the Muslim Ban," New York Taxi Workers Alliance, www.nytwa.org/solidarity/.
13. Peter Cole, "These Dockworkers Just Showed the Labor Movement How to Shut Down Fascists," *In These Times*, August 29, 2017, http://inthesetimes.com/working/entry/20465/ILWU-Dockworkers-fascists.
14. Adam K. Raymond, "NYC Teamsters Becomes a 'Sanctuary Union' after Member Is Deported," *New York*, September 14, 2017, https://nymag.com/intelligencer/2017/09/nyc-teamsters-becomes-a-sanctuary-union.html;

"Campaign: Sanctuary Schools," Chicago Teachers Union, www.ctulocal1.
org/movement/campaign-sanctuary-schools/; American Federation
of Teachers, "AFT Resolution: In Support of Sanctuary Schools and
Campuses," 2018, www.aft.org/resolution/support-sanctuary-schools-
and-campuses; Porfirio Quintano, "Health Care Workers Bring Sanctuary
Movement into the Union," *Labor Notes*, April 13, 2017, https://labornotes.
org/2017/04/health-care-workers-bring-sanctuary-movement-union.

15. Danny McGlashing, @DannyMcGlashing, "IBEW electrical worker
staring down DHS lines in Portland after Occupy ICE blockaded the
facility," Twitter, June 28, 2018, https://twitter.com/DannyMcGlashing/
status/1012361030297669632.

16. Portland General Defense Committee, @pdxgdc, "A union carpenter is
walking around camp," Twitter, June 30, 2018, https://twitter.com/pdxgdc/
status/1013136544251576320.

17. "'No Union for Fascists': Why the Sioux Falls AFL-CIO Banned White
Supremacists," Sioux Falls AFL-CIO, August 10, 2018, https://sd.aflcio.
org/sftrades/news/no-union-fascists-why-sioux-falls-afl-cio-banned-
white-supremacists.

18. Erika Leigh, "Sioux Falls Homeowners Finding KKK Recruitment
Materials," *Dakota News Now*, August 14, 2018, www.ksfy.com/
content/news/Sioux-Falls-homeowners-finding-KKK-recruitment-
materials-490884381.html.

19. Southern Maine IWW, "The IWW versus the KKK in Maine," *Portland
Press Herald*, February 5, 1924, https://southernmaineiww.org/library/the-
iww-versus-the-kkk-in-maine/.

20. Lyn Wells, "The Cedartown Story: The Ku Klux Klan & Labor in 'The
New South,'" *Labor Research Review* 1, no. 8 (1986): 69–79; Robin D. G.
Kelley, "The Black Belt Communists," *Jacobin*, August 20, 2015, www.
jacobinmag.com/2015/08/alabama-hammer-and-hoe-robin-kelley-
communist-party/; Erin Gray, Harry Haywood, and Milton Howard,
"Lynching: A Weapon of National Oppression (1932)," *Viewpoint
Magazine*, January 9, 2017, www.viewpointmag.com/2017/01/09/
lynching-a-weapon-of-national-oppression-1932/.

21. "Remembering the 1979 Greensboro Massacre: 25 Years Later Survivors
Form Country's First Truth and Reconciliation Commission," *Democracy
Now!*, November 18, 2004, www.democracynow.org/2004/11/18/
remembering_the_1979_greensboro_massacre_25.

22. William George Whittaker, "Samuel Gompers, Anti-Imperialist," *Pacific
Historical Review* 38, no. 4 (1969): 429–45, doi:10.2307/3637623. Jennifer
Jung Lee Choi, "The Rhetoric of Inclusion: The I.W.W. and Asian
Workers," *Ex Post Facto* 8 (May 2001), https://history.sfsu.edu/sites/

default/files/EPF/1999_Jennifer Jung Hee Choi.pdf.

23. Ray Stern, "Cesar Chavez's Rabid Opposition to Illegal Immigration Not Covered in New Movie," *Phoenix New Times*, March 28, 2014, www. phoenixnewtimes.com/news/cesar-chavezs-rabid-opposition-to-illegal-immigration-not-covered-in-new-movie-6643666.

24. Michael Pierce, "The Origins of Right-to-Work: Vance Muse, Anti-Semitism, and the Maintenance of Jim Crow Labor Relations," LAWCHA, January 12, 2017, www.lawcha.org/2017/01/12/origins-right-work-vance-muse-anti-semitism-maintenance-jim-crow-labor-relations/.

25. C. M. Lewis, "Welcome to the Jungle: Uradnik v. Inter Faculty Organization," *Strike Wave*, January 4, 2019, www.thestrikewave.com/original-content/2019/1/4/welcome-to-the-jungle-uradnik-v-inter-faculty-organization.

26. Maximillian Alvarez, "Antifascism and the Left's Fear of Power," *Baffler*, May 16, 2018, https://thebaffler.com/latest/antifascism-power-alvarez.

27. Chacón and Davis, *No One Is Illegal*, 5–6.

28. Donald J. Trump, @realDonaldTrump, "Consideration is being given to declaring ANTIFA . . . a major Organization of Terror," Twitter, July 27, 2019, https://twitter.com/realDonaldTrump/status/1155205025121132545; Donald J. Trump, @realDonaldTrump, "Major consideration is being given to naming ANTIFA an 'ORGANIZATION OF TERROR,'" Twitter, August 17, 2019, https://twitter.com/realDonaldTrump/status/1162726857231544320; Marisa Iati, "Two Senators Want Antifa Activists to Be Labeled 'Domestic Terrorists.' Here's What That Means," *Washington Post*, July 20, 2019, www.washingtonpost.com/politics/2019/07/20/senators-want-antifa-activists-be-labeled-domestic-terrorists-heres-what-that-means/.

29. Sam Levin, "Police Thwarted at Least Seven Mass Shootings and White Supremacist Attacks since El Paso," *Guardian*, August 23, 2019, www.theguardian.com/world/2019/aug/20/el-paso-shooting-plot-white-supremacist-attacks.

30. Sam Adler-Bell, "More Government Power Is the Wrong Way to Fight White Supremacy," *New Republic*, August 7, 2019, https://newrepublic.com/article/154700/fbi-domestic-white-terrorism-el-paso-expansion-security-state.

31. Liliana Segura, "Gutting Habeus Corpus: The Inside Story of How Bill Clinton Sacrificed Prisoners' Rights for Political Gain," *Intercept*, May 4, 2016, https://theintercept.com/2016/05/04/the-untold-story-of-bill-clintons-other-crime-bill/; "Analysis of Immigration Detention Policy," ACLU, www.aclu.org/other/analysis-immigration-detention-policies; Raquel Aldana, "The September 11 Immigration Detentions and

Unconstitutional Executive Legislation," *Southern Illinois University Law Journal* 29 (Fall 2004): 5–42, https://scholarlycommons.pacific.edu/cgi/viewcontent.cgi?article=1106&context=facultyarticles.

32. Jonathan Levinson and Conrad Wilson, "Federal Law Enforcement Use Unmarked Vehicles to Grab Protesters Off Portland Streets," *OPB*, July 16, 2020, www.opb.org/news/article/federal-law-enforcement-unmarked-vehicles-portland-protesters/.

33. Ken Klippenstein, "The Border Patrol Was Responsible for an Arrest in Portland," *Nation*, July 17, 2020, www.thenation.com/article/society/border-patrol-portland-arrest/; "DHS Announces New Task Force to Protect American Monuments, Memorials, and Statues," Department of Homeland Security, July 1, 2020, www.dhs.gov/news/2020/07/01/dhs-announces-new-task-force-protect-american-monuments-memorials-and-statues.

34. Julia Musto, "Portland Protestors Are 'Seeking Opportunities to Destroy,' DHS' Cuccinelli Says," Fox News, July 17, 2020, www.foxnews.com/media/portland-clashes-not-peaceful-protests-dhs.

35. Obituary of John Hamilton Tanton, Stone Funeral Home, www.stonefuneralhomeinc.com/notices/John-Tanton.

36. Justin Akers Chacón, "Opening the Border through Class Struggle and Solidarity," *Puntorojo*, January 13, 2020, www.puntorojomag.org/2020/01/13/opening-the-border-through-class-struggle-and-solidarity/.

37. Hope-Siihasin, "'Let Everyone In!' Indigenous Peoples Day Has No Borders," Red Nation, October 17, 2019, https://therednation.org/2019/10/17/let-everyone-in-indigenous-peoples-day-has-no-borders/.

INDEX

ABOUT HAYMARKET BOOKS

Haymarket Books is a radical, independent, nonprofit book publisher based in Chicago. Our mission is to publish books that contribute to struggles for social and economic justice. We strive to make our books a vibrant and organic part of social movements and the education and development of a critical, engaged, international left.

We take inspiration and courage from our namesakes, the Haymarket martyrs, who gave their lives fighting for a better world. Their 1886 struggle for the eight-hour day—which gave us May Day, the international workers' holiday—reminds workers around the world that ordinary people can organize and struggle for their own liberation. These struggles continue today across the globe—struggles against oppression, exploitation, poverty, and war.

Since our founding in 2001, Haymarket Books has published more than five hundred titles. Radically independent, we seek to drive a wedge into the risk-averse world of corporate book publishing. Our authors include Noam Chomsky, Arundhati Roy, Rebecca Solnit, Angela Y. Davis, Howard Zinn, Amy Goodman, Wallace Shawn, Mike Davis, Winona LaDuke, Ilan Pappé, Richard Wolff, Dave Zirin, Keeanga-Yamahtta Taylor, Nick Turse, Dahr Jamail, David Barsamian, Elizabeth Laird, Amira Hass, Mark Steel, Avi Lewis, Naomi Klein, and Neil Davidson. We are also the trade publishers of the acclaimed Historical Materialism Book Series and of Dispatch Books.

ALSO AVAILABLE
FROM HAYMARKET BOOKS

Blood in the Face
White Nationalism from the Birth of a Nation to the Era of Trump
James Ridgeway

Marxists in the Face of Fascism
Writings by Marxists on Fascism From the Inter-war Period
Edited by David Beetham

The Nazis, Capitalism and the Working Class
Donny Gluckstein

The New Authoritarians: Convergence on the Right
David Renton

No One is Illegal (Updated Edition)
Fighting Racism and State Violence on the U.S.-Mexico Border
Justin Akers Chacón and Mike Davis

The Precipice
Neoliberalism, the Pandemic, and the Urgent Need for Radical Change
Noam Chomsky and C. J. Polychroniou

Reproductive Rights and Wrongs
The Global Politics of Population Control
Betsy Hartmann

White Bred
Hillbillies, White Trash, and Rednecks Against White Supremacy
Eric Kerl

ABOUT THE AUTHOR

Tayarisha Poe

Brendan O'Connor is a freelance writer and journalist covering inequality, political violence, and white supremacy. He was formerly an investigative reporter at Gizmodo Media's Special Projects Desk, reporting on dark money, the "alt-right" and militia movements, and immigration. He began his journalism career at the *Awl*, *Gawker*, and *Jezebel*. He is based in New York.